Critical Management Studies

"Edited by a highly competent team of academics, this book fills a wholly neglected area of discourse relating to Critical Management Studies in providing a set of original contributions from a wide range of countries rather than just from the Anglo-American tradition. Given globalisation in postmodern culture and economy, this is long overdue".
—*David Knights, Lancaster University, UK*

Critical Management Studies (CMS) is often dated from the publication of an edited volume bearing that name (Alvesson and Willmott, 1992). In the two decades that have followed, CMS has been remarkably successful in establishing itself not just as a 'term' but also as a recognizable tradition or approach. The emerging status of CMS as an overall approach has been both encouraged and marked by a growing range of handbooks, readers and textbooks. Yet the literature is dominated by writings from the UK and Scandinavia in particular, and the tendency is to treat this literature as constituting CMS. However, the meaning, practice, constraints and context of CMS vary considerably between different countries, cultures and language communities. This volume surveys 14 various countries and regions where CMS has acquired some following and seeks to explore the different ways in which CMS is understood and the different contexts within which it operates, as well as its possible future development.

Christopher Grey is Professor of Organization Studies at Royal Holloway, University of London, UK, and Professeur-invité at Université Paris-Dauphine, France.

Isabelle Huault is Professor of Organization Studies at Université Paris-Dauphine, France.

Véronique Perret is Professor of Management at Université Paris-Dauphine, France.

Laurent Taskin is Professor of Human Resource and Organization Studies at Louvain School of Management, Université catholique de Louvain, Belgium.

Routledge Studies in Management, Organizations and Society

For a full list of titles in this series, please visit www.routledge.com

This series presents innovative work grounded in new realities, addressing issues crucial to an understanding of the contemporary world. This is the world of organized societies, where boundaries between formal and informal, public and private, local and global organizations have been displaced or have vanished, along with other nineteenth-century dichotomies and oppositions. Management, apart from becoming a specialized profession for a growing number of people, is an everyday activity for most members of modern societies.

Similarly, at the level of enquiry, culture and technology and literature and economics can no longer be conceived as isolated intellectual fields; conventional canons and established mainstreams are contested. **Management, Organizations and Society** addresses these contemporary dynamics of transformation in a manner that transcends disciplinary boundaries, with books that will appeal to researchers, students and practitioners alike.

21 **Leadership as Emotional Labour**
Management and the 'managed heart'
Edited by Marian Iszatt-White

22 **On Being At Work**
The social construction of the employee
Nancy Harding

23 **Storytelling in Management Practice**
Dynamics and implications
Stefanie Reissner and Victoria Pagan

24 **Hierarchy and Organisation**
Toward a general theory of hierarchical social systems
Thomas Diefenbach

25 **Organizing Through Empathy**
Edited by Kathryn Pavlovich and Keiko Krahnke

26 **Managerial Cultures**
A comparative historical analysis
David Hanson

27 **Management and Organization of Temporary Agency Work**
Edited by Bas Koene, Christina Garsten, and Nathalie Galais

28 **Liquid Organization**
Zygmunt Bauman and organization theory
Edited by Jerzy Kociatkiewicz and Monika Kostera

29 Management and Neoliberalism
Connecting policies and practices
Alexander Styhre

30 Organizations and the Media
Organizing in a mediatized world
*Edited by Josef Pallas, Lars
Strannegård and Stefan Jonsson*

31 Sexual Orientation at Work
Contemporary Issues and
Perspectives
*Edited by Fiona Colgan and
Nick Rumens*

32 Gender Equality in Public Services
Chasing the dream
Hazel Conley and Margaret Page

33 Untold Stories in Organisations
*Edited by Michal Izak, Linda
Hitchin, and David Anderson*

**34 Pierre Bourdieu, Organisation
and Management**
*Edited by Ahu Tatli, Mustafa
Özbilgin and Mine Karatas-Özkan*

**35 The Dark Side of Emotional
Labour**
*Jenna Ward and Robert
McMurray*

36 For Robert Cooper
Collected Work
*Edited by Gibson Burrell and
Martin Parker*

37 Critical Management Studies
Global Voices, Local Accents
*Edited by Christopher Grey,
Isabelle Huault, Véronique Perret
and Laurent Taskin*

Other titles in this series:

Contrasting Involvements
A study of management accounting
practices in Britain and Germany
Thomas Ahrens

Turning Words, Spinning Worlds
Chapters in organizational ethnography
Michael Rosen

Breaking Through the Glass Ceiling
Women, power and leadership in
agricultural organizations
Margaret Alston

The Poetic Logic of Administration
Styles and changes of style in the art
of organizing
Kaj Sköldberg

Casting the Other
Maintaining gender inequalities in the
workplace
*Edited by Barbara Czarniawska and
Heather Höpfl*

**Gender, Identity and the Culture
of Organizations**
*Edited by Iiris Aaltio and Albert J.
Mills*

Text/Work
Representing organization and
organizing representation
Edited by Stephen Linstead

**The Social Construction of
Management**
Texts and identities
Nancy Harding

Management Theory
A critical and reflexive reading
Nanette Monin

Critical Management Studies
Global Voices, Local Accents

Edited by
Christopher Grey, Isabelle Huault,
Véronique Perret and Laurent Taskin

LONDON AND NEW YORK

First published 2016
by Routledge

2 Park Square, Milton Park, Abingdon, Oxfordshire OX14 4RN
711 Third Avenue, New York, NY 10017

Routledge is an imprint of the Taylor & Francis Group, an informa business

First issued in paperback 2018

Copyright © 2016 Christopher Grey, Isabelle Huault, Véronique Perret
and Laurent Taskin

The right of the editors to be identified as the authors of the editorial
material, and of the authors for their individual chapters, has been asserted
in accordance with sections 77 and 78 of the Copyright, Designs and
Patents Act 1988.

All rights reserved. No part of this book may be reprinted or reproduced or
utilised in any form or by any electronic, mechanical, or other means, now
known or hereafter invented, including photocopying and recording, or in
any information storage or retrieval system, without permission in writing
from the publishers.

Notice:
Product or corporate names may be trademarks or registered trademarks,
and are used only for identification and explanation without intent to infringe.

Library of Congress Cataloging-in-Publication Data
Names: Grey, Christopher, 1964– editor.
Title: Critical management studies : global voices, local accents / edited by
    Christopher Grey, Isabelle Huault, Vâeronique Perret and Laurent Taskin.
Other titles: Critical management studies (Routledge)
Description: New York : Routledge, 2016. | Series: Routledge studies in
    management, organizations and society ; 37 | Includes bibliographical
    references and index.
Identifiers: LCCN 2015039726 | ISBN 9780415749497 (hardback : alk.
    paper) | ISBN 9781315796086 (ebook)
Subjects: LCSH: Management. | Critical theory.
Classification: LCC HD31 .C7445 2016 | DDC 658—dc23
LC record available at http://lccn.loc.gov/2015039726

ISBN: 978-0-415-74949-7 (hbk)
ISBN: 978-1-138-61696-7 (pbk)

Typeset in Sabon
by Apex CoVantage, LLC

Contents

List of Figures and Table	ix
Acknowledgements	xi
List of Contributors	xiii
Introduction: Beginning a Conversation	xvii

CHRISTOPHER GREY, ISABELLE HUAULT, VÉRONIQUE PERRET
AND LAURENT TASKIN

1 Australia and New Zealand: Drawn Together
   Yet Worlds Apart?   1
   DEBORAH JONES, CRAIG PRICHARD AND GRAHAM SEWELL

2 Non-Managerial Management Scholarship in Belgium,
   the Netherlands and Luxemburg   21
   PATRIZIA ZANONI AND LAURENT TASKIN

3 "CMS, Canada & the Network": An Actor-Network
   Analysis   36
   CATERINA BETTIN, ALBERT J. MILLS AND JEAN HELMS MILLS

4 CMS with a Local Accent: Is Critical Management
   Education Possible in China?   54
   SHIH-WEI HSU

5 The Awakening of Critical Management Studies in
   France: Mimicry or a Process of Coming Out?   68
   ISABELLE HUAULT AND VÉRONIQUE PERRET

6 Critical Scholarship in Management and Organization
   Studies in German-Speaking Countries: An Overview
   and Historical Reconstruction   85
   RONALD HARTZ

viii *Contents*

7 From Anti-Managerialism to Over-Managerialism: How Critical Management Studies in Israel Were Exiled from Local Business Schools and Emerged Elsewhere 100
MICHAL FRENKEL

8 Italian Voices from the Outside: The Context for CMS in Italy 116
MARIA LAURA TORALDO, GIANLUIGI MANGIA, PAOLO CANONICO, STEFANO CONSIGLIO AND RICCARDO MERCURIO

9 Self-Problematization and Relational Problematization: A Critical-Constructive Approach in the Japanese Context 126
TORU KIYOMIYA

10 CMS in Scandinavia: A Hitchhiker's Guide to the Realm of the Scandocrits 144
RASMUS KOSS HARTMANN, DAN KÄRREMAN AND MATS ALVESSON

11 CMS in the Periphery: A Look at South America 159
ERNESTO R. GANTMAN

12 The Ghost in the System: Critical Management Studies in Turkey 175
BEYZA OBA AND MEHMET GENÇER

13 CMS in the United Kingdom 191
MARTIN PARKER

14 Galumphing and Critical Management Studies: Perspective and Paradox from the United States 206
GORDON E. DEHLER AND M. ANN WELSH

Conclusion: Diverse Accents, Common Voice? 227
LAURENT TASKIN, VÉRONIQUE PERRET, ISABELLE HUAULT AND CHRISTOPHER GREY

Index 237

Figures and Table

FIGURES

6.1	The Construct 'Organization'	92
8.1	List of Institutions Taking Part in the Survey and Their Perception of CMS	118
8.2	Topics That Participants Perceive as Needing to Be Critically Approached	120
9.1	Basic Idea of Confucianism Self-Cultivation	134
9.2	Basic Framework of Confucianism *Toku*	134
14.1	A Mapping of Exemplar Critical Scholars onto the Alvesson and Deetz (2000) Framework	212

TABLE

9.1	Seven Types of *Toku* (徳)	135

Acknowledgements

We are grateful to the following:

Martin Parker (Leicester University, UK) and Pierre-Yves Gomez (EM Lyon, France) for their inspiring participation in the initial conversation in Paris in 2013 that led to this book

The *DRM Research Center (Dauphine Recherches en Management)* for funding a workshop in Paris in 2014 which enabled the contributors to meet and discuss early draft chapters and ideas, and Mahaut Fanchini and Margot Leclair of Université Paris-Dauphine for organizing that workshop.

David Varley at Routledge/Taylor & Francis for commissioning this book and showing such enthusiasm for it, the six anonymous reviewers who to varying degrees supported the proposal, Brianna Ascher for gently managing us, and the team at Routledge who brought the book through production.

Contributors

Mats Alvesson is Professor of Business Administration at Lund University, Sweden, honorary professor at the University of Queensland, Australia, and visiting professor at Stockholm University, Sweden.

Caterina Bettin is a PhD (Management) student at Saint Mary's University, Halifax, Canada.

Paolo Canonico is Associate Professor of Organization Studies at the University of Napoli Federico II, Italy.

Stefano Consiglio is Full Professor of Organization Theory at the University of Naples Federico II, Italy.

Gordon E. Dehler is an Adjunct Faculty Member at the University of Cincinnati, USA.

Michal Frenkel is Senior Lecturer of Sociology, Anthropology and Organizations Studies at the Hebrew University of Jerusalem, Israel.

Ernesto R. Gantman is Professor at the Facultad de Ciencias Económicas, Universidad De Buenos Aires and the Escuela de Posgrado en Negocios, Universidad de Belgrano, Argentina.

Mehmet Gençer is Associate Professor of Organization Studies at Istanbul Bilgi University, Turkey.

Christopher Grey is Professor of Organization Studies at Royal Holloway, University of London, UK, and Professeur-invité at Université Paris-Dauphine PSL, France.

Rasmus Koss Hartmann is a Postdoctoral Fellow in Behavioral and Policy Sciences at MIT Sloan School of Management, USA, and in process innovation at Copenhagen Business School, Denmark.

xiv *Contributors*

Ronald Hartz is Junior Professor of European Management at the Faculty of Economics and Business Administration, Chemnitz University of Technology, Germany.

Jean Helms Mills is Professor of Management at Saint Mary's University, Halifax, Canada.

Isabelle Huault is Professor of Organization Studies at Université Paris-Dauphine PSL, France.

Shih-wei Hsu is Assistant Professor in Organisational Behaviour at University of Nottingham, Ningbo, China.

Deborah Jones is Associate Professor in the School of Management, Te Kura Whakahaere, Victoria University of Wellington, New Zealand.

Dan Kärreman is Professor in Organization and Management Studies at Copenhagen Business School, Denmark, and Professor in Management at Royal Holloway, University of London, UK.

Toru Kiyomiya is Professor of Organizational Communication at Seinan Gakuin University, Japan.

Gianluigi Mangia is Associate Professor of Organization Studies at the University of Naples Federico II, Italy.

Riccardo Mercurio is Full Professor of Organization Studies at the Department of Economics, Management and Institutions, University of Naples Federico II, Italy.

Albert J. Mills is Professor of Management at Saint Mary's University, Halifax, Canada.

Beyza Oba is Professor of Organization Studies at İstanbul Bilgi University, Turkey.

Martin Parker is Professor of Culture and Organization at the University of Leicester, UK.

Véronique Perret is Professor of Management at Université Paris-Dauphine PSL, France.

Craig Prichard is Associate Professor of Management in Te Kahui Kahurangi/ School of Management, Massey University (Turitea), New Zealand.

Contributors xv

Graham Sewell is Professor of Organization Studies in the Department of Management & Marketing, University of Melbourne, Australia.

Laurent Taskin is Professor of Human Resource and Organization Studies at Louvain School of Management, Université catholique de Louvain, Belgium.

Maria Laura Toraldo is a Postdoctoral Researcher at Grenoble Ecole de Management, France.

M. Ann Welsh is Professor Emerita of Management at the University of Cincinnati, USA.

Patrizia Zanoni is Professor of Organization Studies at Hasselt University, Belgium.

Introduction
Beginning a Conversation

Christopher Grey, Isabelle Huault,
Véronique Perret and Laurent Taskin

> The future of CMS must be imagined as a set of multiple dialogues and conversations between scholars and people of different regions and cultures to learn from each other . . .
>
> (Ibarra-Colado, 2008, p. 935)

The origins of this book lie in a conversation between us and some other colleagues who ran the 2013 Critical Management Studies Workshop at Université Paris-Dauphine. After the workshop, we began to reflect on the difficulties of engaging in a research community whose dominant language is English when not being a native English speaker. For three of us, that is a common experience; for the fourth, the fact that this conversation took place in French had a particular resonance, since it provided a ready illustration of how immediately disabling and disempowering it is to participate in a discussion without the fluency that is taken for granted in one's own tongue. But language was not the only issue in this conversation: we also reflected upon the ways that the knowledge base, theoretical resources, dialectical style and political context of Critical Management Studies (CMS) seemed to have inflected it in particular ways. Somehow, what constitutes CMS seems to have a particular hue which is both Anglophone and perhaps especially Anglo-Scandinavian in character.

Of course the Anglophone dominance of management studies is well known and, again, this has been associated with the presentation of research from particular contexts and countries, as if it represented universal experience (e.g. Boyacigiller and Adler, 1991; Westwood et al., 2014). Within management studies in general—that is, mainstream management studies—this linguistic dominance and universalization is primarily associated with the US, and from this perspective, European work in general and Anglo-Scandinavian CMS work in particular, would be seen as quite marginal (Grey, 2010; Meyer and Boxenbaum, 2010). This contrast is significant in two ways. One is that centres and margins, or cores and peripheries, in management studies (as in other domains) are not immutable or self-evident: what is peripheral in one context may be central in another and vice versa.

xviii *Grey et al.*

The other, though, is that although CMS might be expected to be critical of, or at least sensitive to, issues of include, exclusion and marginalization, it can in many ways be seen to enact these issues quite as much as, even if sometimes in different ways from, mainstream management studies.

CMS is often dated from the publication of an edited volume bearing that name (Alvesson and Willmott, 1992). Of course, this does not mean that there was no 'critical' research on management prior to 1992, but that it is from this time that CMS emerged as an umbrella term to describe such work. In the two decades that have followed, CMS has been fairly successful in establishing itself not just as a 'term' but as a recognizable tradition or approach. It has been able to institutionalize itself through, for example, a biennial conference that has run since 1999 and which attracts hundreds of delegates from around the world. There is also a CMS division at the Academy of Management (AoM) which has over 700 members and is the most internationalized of the AoM divisions.

The emerging status of CMS as an overall approach has also been both encouraged and marked by a growing range of handbooks (e.g. Alvesson et al., 2009; Prasad et al., 2014), readers (e.g. Grey and Willmott, 2005), textbooks (e.g. Wolfram-Cox et al., 2009; Tadajewski et al., 2011); and even a collection of 'classic' writings (Alvesson, 2011). At the same time, CMS has engaged in a reflexive commentary upon itself in terms of explaining its existence (e.g. Fournier and Grey, 2000) and, increasingly, criticizing and problematizing its practices (e.g. Perriton and Reynolds, 2004; Spicer et al., 2009; Rowlinson and Hassard, 2011; Fournier and Smith, 2012; Malin et al., 2013; Prasad et al., 2014) while also developing in non-English-speaking areas (Golsorkhi et al., 2009; Palpacuer et al., 2010; Taskin and de Nanteuil, 2011).

In this way, CMS has, to a degree, achieved a global presence, yet that globality is not straightforward and has been little analysed: two decades on, it is time to stock. It is not straightforward because it remains dominated by Anglophone writings, and especially writings emanating from the UK and Scandinavia. For example, of the 28 CMS 'classics' in Alvesson (2011), just one was written by an author not based in the UK, USA or Sweden (he was based in Germany).[1] Other countries, and other language communities, have both utilised and contributed to this literature, but this take up has itself been quite varied so that in some countries CMS barely figures at all (in terms of, say, participation in the CMS Conference of AoM Division), whilst in others it is, to varying degrees, an established part of the management research field.

This presents issues which CMS, as a critical and reflexive approach, should be attentive to. It involves a potentially double translation. The first translation is to different national contexts: how do ideas developed primarily in Northern Europe translate into, say, an Australian context? The second, additional, translation is into other language communities: how does CMS translate into, say, a Brazilian context? Nor is the issue simply one of the travel of ideas (Battilana et al., 2010). The institutional contexts and systems within which management researchers' work may vary considerably between different countries, and the possibilities and constraints of undertaking critical work may similarly vary.

Underneath these questions lurk some important political issues. For it is not just a matter of 'different countries', it is a matter of the politics of difference (Frenkel et al., 2014). To the extent that CMS is dominated by Northern European writings, there must be some tendency for the terms of critique to be inflected through the political priorities and intellectual traditions of those countries. In postcolonial understandings, in particular, if CMS is predicated on a Eurocentric critique of management and, ultimately, modernity, the question arises as to "what else can there be beyond Euro-American CMS"? (Faria, 2013, p. 282). When the 'classic' writings of CMS emanating from those countries are treated as trans-cultural and transnational, then at least implicit hegemony is being enacted, just as it is with mainstream management studies. That possibility becomes all the more pronounced when the literature is dominated by Anglophone writings, which both politically and in basic, literal ways skew the global conversation. Those who work in other languages, traditions and polities may find it both harder to contribute and harder to be heard.

CENTRES, MARGINS AND BEYOND

The earlier section is a more formalized version of the discussion we had in 2013, and it is within this terrain that the present volume is located. We wanted to ask and answer a deceptively simple question: what does CMS mean within different cultural and linguistic contexts? By phrasing the question this way, we also angle it in some particular ways. First, we do not position this book in terms of marginal or peripheral voices speaking of or to a supposed centre. That is to say, we are also interested in understanding what CMS currently means within what might be taken to be its heartlands meaning, certainly, the UK and Sweden and, possibly, the US, Denmark, Australia and New Zealand. Whilst there is a sense in this volume of giving attention to a wider range of voices than are sometimes heard within the CMS literature, this is not the only motivation. We want also to hear the more dominant voices, not least because as we indicated earlier these are relative terms and CMS, even where it is relatively strong, is by definition in other respects marginal to the mainstream. While in some ways CMS mimics the mainstream in the ways indicated earlier, it would perhaps be rather premature to lump the CMS centre in with that mainstream. If that is not so, then the possibility of conceiving of CMS as a meaningful term at all ceases to exist, since it would just be another part of 'management studies'.

On the other hand, we want to avoid some idea that 'proper' CMS is that which exists within its Anglophone Northern European heartlands and that existing in other places and languages is to be compared with it as in some way less developed. This would seem to fall into precisely the trap of

xx Grey et al.

hegemonizing the centre. Instead, we want to emphasize the different contexts of CMS as existing side by side, having their own specificities which are equally interesting and important whether they arise in the centre or periphery. We want to capture the plurality and multiplicity of what CMS can be. Moreover, we want to emphasize what might be seen as issues of migration and interrelation, because although we have talked so far in terms of centre/core and periphery/margin (and this does have some traction), we actually want to suggest a far more complex, nuanced and fluctuating set of relationships between these.

To put this in more concrete terms, one might consider a number of issues, all of which arise within the various contributions to this volume. First, whereas the position of CMS in the UK might seem from the outside relatively assured (and, indeed, might be so) and in that sense central, from the inside it might seem more schismatic, as Martin Parker's contribution suggests, and also more fragile than might be imagined. For example, it has had as one of its conditions of possibility the high value placed upon 'top journal publication' within the UK university system. With that system now shifting towards placing more value upon winning research grants and demonstrating managerial 'impact', it is easy to envisage CMS becoming considerably weakened in the future in which case the position of the UK as a 'centre' for CMS may change. Or, to take a different aspect, consider how in a number of the contributions the existence of centres of CMS (with its books, journals, conference, etc.) is a vital legitimating factor for critical scholarship within contexts where it is more marginal—this is evident in, for example, the chapters on Turkey, Italy and the Benelux region.

The point here is that there is an interdependence of the centre and periphery of CMS in the face of the far more hegemonic centre of the mainstream. Even, in the case of Israel, Michal Frenkel's chapter shows how the legitimation derived from the US training of two of CMS's leading Israeli scholars (Gideon Kunda and Yehouda Shenhav) has substantially structured the development of CMS in that country. But now, let us take a third aspect of these relations. Yes, it may be that the existence of a CMS centre serves to legitimate CMS work outside the centre, but it does not follow that we should lionize that centre as the holder of the true flame of 'real' CMS. On the contrary, we can see in, for example, the chapter on France how attempts may be made to recuperate 'French theory' from its many appropriations by Anglophone CMS; or, in the chapter on Japan, how Buddhist and Confucian traditions may be deployed to rewrite one of CMS's core concepts, that of emancipation. There are thus multiple migrations—of people, of ideas—within, between and across the boundaries implied by centre and periphery (see Frenkel et al., 2014 for a much more sophisticated discussion of centres and peripheries in management research).

In short, given the relative marginality of CMS (compared with mainstream management studies), it makes little sense to treat the CMS centre as a powerful, hegemonic, colonial ogre to be excoriated. Yet, equally, it is

Introduction xxi

important to recognize that it is in some respects powerful and hegemonic with respect to CMS margins. It is *both* powerful and weak, central and marginal, attackable and defendable, good and bad. This is not a cartoon with black hats and white hats but a more complex arena in which there are many shades of grey. So our approach has been to provide a space for CMS in different contexts to set out its stall, or stalls, attentive to the problematic nature of centres and margins and how the CMS centre does serve to dominate and marginalize other voices but not locked into a binary view which either castigates the centre as irredeemably Eurocentric or privileges it as trans-cultural truth.

WHICH CONTEXTS?

We have said that the core question we are concerned with is: what does CMS mean within different cultural and linguistic contexts? And it will be clear from our references so far to some of the chapters that the way we have approached 'contexts' is in terms of particular countries or, in some cases, regions. This is not self-evident or unproblematic and requires some explanation. It is clearly not the case that nation-states are contiguous with either cultural or linguistic contexts. So far as language is concerned, there are obviously many countries which share languages. Equally, some of the regions we look at (Benelux, Scandinavia, South America) do not share languages, and for that matter, some countries have a range of official languages. On the other hand, one of the regions (Germanic: Germany, Austria, German-speaking Switzerland) is unified only by language. Things become even more difficult if we approach things in terms of culture, a notoriously slippery concept. Do nation-states have a shared culture? In many ways this is manifestly not the case. Do different nations share aspects of culture? In many ways this manifestly is the case.

Some of our choices here are pragmatic. For example, if we had organized by language, then this would have meant a potentially huge section on Anglophone countries, despite their many differences. But beyond pragmatics, there are some defensible reasons for taking the nation-state as a unit of analysis. CMS, after all, takes place largely within universities and these are embedded within political and institutional systems, which are to some large extent an artefact of the nation-state. For sure the nation-state is a political and historical construct rather than being 'natural', yet it is a construct which powerfully shapes the way in which, if at all, CMS operates. Regions are rather more difficult to justify as units, and where we use them, the chapters concerned invariably show that there is quite a bit of variation in the constituent elements; still, they do enable a breadth of coverage that might otherwise be difficult to achieve. For example, in the Scandinavian chapter, it is clear that there is much more CMS activity in Sweden and Denmark than in Finland or Norway so that we would hardly have been justified in

xxii *Grey et al.*

having separate chapters on the latter, yet by including them in a region, we achieve some coverage.

What is clearly more problematic is the fact that great swathes of the globe, including the whole of Africa, the Indian subcontinent and Russia and most of Eastern Europe are not represented here. Issues of exclusion and inclusion are not innocent or accidental matters, and in a volume such as this they have a particular resonance. In many cases, the reason is that the countries and regions not present do not have much, or any, CMS activity; in some cases, this is because there is little management research of any description or even very little in the way of university systems. That absence is deeply rooted in global inequalities and global politics which impact upon the existence and extent of CMS as much as they do upon everything else. However, to approach these issues in terms of the absence of CMS would seem bizarre: they clearly require a much wider analysis which is not the focus of this volume. Equally, a long catalogue of chapters discussing the ways and reasons for the absence of CMS would be repetitive and perhaps unilluminating, even if authors could be found who were willing to write them, and given the limitations of length, it would probably not the best use of the space we have (even as it is, each chapter is relatively short). It is, after all, relatively difficult to write about what is not present.

However, in other cases, there are countries and regions where there is some CMS activity and yet these are not all covered here by any means. The problem is that in many cases, the CMS presence is tied to one or two individuals; and where these could not be persuaded to contribute, we were not able to include them. It seemed like a bad alternative to commission an author from outside of such countries to prepare a chapter, even assuming anyone with the requisite knowledge could be found. So the best strategy that we could come up with was to include as many places as we could find authors for and hope that as CMS continues to develop, it might be possible in the future to develop a new edition which would be more comprehensive in coverage. In that sense, this volume is very much a first attempt at something that has not as yet been attempted at all. But the problem will never go away: if we added country X, well then, what about country Y?

In making, or having to make, decisions about inclusion and exclusion, we were also mindful of ourselves as an editorial team, all of whom are based in North-West Europe. This too was a choice. Whilst the book arose from a particular conversation, we could, after all, have invited in additional editors and considered doing so. The trade-off was greater representativeness versus easier coordination. In opting for the latter, our thinking was that we do not claim to be a 'representative committee' for CMS globally, and there seemed to be something rather bogus about inviting in additional editors in order to imply otherwise. And again, as with the issue of chapter inclusion, adding a new editor would not really make the problem go away.

In any case, to be quite clear, we do not aspire to be spokespeople for CMS: we are a group of editors with no more, but no less, right and ability

Introduction xxiii

to make editorial decisions than anyone else. In this regard, our earlier discussion of the complexities of centrality and marginality in CMS becomes particularly important. From one perspective, because we are all from North-West Europe, we might be considered part of 'the centre' of CMS; from another, because of our linguistic and gender diversity, we are not. For example, whilst for some purposes we can talk of 'Euro-American CMS', from within Europe, and especially in those countries where English is not routinely spoken (unlike some Scandinavian countries, for example), the lumping together of them into a homogenous Euro, let alone Euro-American, bloc makes very little sense.

We are dwelling on these issues of inclusion, exclusion and representation because they clearly have a particular significance in a volume that is in part devoted to extending the range of voices heard. For that matter, CMS, precisely because of its avowed sensitivities to such issues, is inevitably vulnerable to more or less fair charges that collections of its writings have privileged some voices at the expense of others (e.g. Prasad, 2008; Parker, 2010). But although we have to acknowledge these issues, we should not become hamstrung by them: any selection entails exclusions, any speaking entails silences. Should we then cease to select and cease to speak because of this? Or, rather, be alive to and open about the difficulties, limitations and compromises of selecting and speaking?

Which brings us, finally, to the most troubling feature of the inclusions, exclusions and representations in this volume. What started as a conversation in French about the difficulties of undertaking CMS in English when English is not one's first language has become a book largely written and edited by people for whom English is not their first language—in English! This has been a constant concern for us, and in a way, it encapsulates all of the other dilemmas we have discussed in this section. Just as the absence or near absence of CMS in many parts of the world is inseparable from global power relations, including the legacy of colonialism, so does the global dominance of the English language reflect these things. That is not something that derives from CMS, but it surely affects CMS just as it does many or most other areas—not just of academia but of business, the media, international institutions, etc. The consequence is that, amongst those contributing to this volume, English is the only language which is held in common; and moreover, the only language in which an international publishing company would be likely to publish in. So although we will return to this issue in the conclusion, we simply don't have a solution to it, and CMS, in itself, cannot generate a solution to it.

Thus we have made choices—some of them heavily constrained, all of them unavoidable—and in all cases, other choices could have been made. We are sensitive to the fact that others would make these choices differently and that some may find our choices unsatisfactory. Yet, despite this, we believe that having made them, we at least have the beginnings of the kind of conversations that Eduardo Ibarra Colado, with whose words we began this chapter, urged. We now turn to introducing some of what the participants have to say.

xxiv *Grey et al.*

OVERVIEW OF CONTENTS

The first geographical area presented in this book brought together two close countries: New Zealand and Australia. Deborah Jones, Craig Pritchard and Graham Sewell start with challenging this closeness, reminding us of some historical facts before reviewing 'critters' and research topics that have been especially studied by critters—often in close connection with Britain, where a lot of the authors mentioned originally came from before migrating to Australia and New Zealand. Considering CMS in this part of Oceania inevitably raises the issue of distance and marginalized spaces, identities and knowledges within the institution of CMS.

In order to introduce critical management research in the heterogeneous Benelux (Belgium-The Netherlands-Luxemburg) context, Patrizia Zanoni and Laurent Taskin present an overview of the topics studied by critters. These range from gender and identity issues to methodological and episte-mological considerations, as well as workplace transformations, entrepre-neurship or ethics. Adopting a neo-institutionalist analysis, they observe that critical research on management in Benelux is part of the global CMS debate led by British critters, while adopting a more pragmatic tone, offer-ing, with some exceptions, a soft critique to management practices.

Drawing on Actor Network Theory (ANT), Caterina Bettin, Albert Mills and Jean Helms Mills consider CMS as effects of a global network, in the Canadian context. Their chapter focuses on the enacted role of the Sobey PhD programme in the context of the institutionalization of the Halifax School. Through an ANT analysis drawing on a specific investigation amongst human and non-human actors involved in the PhD programme, they reveal the entrepreneurial setting of CMS emergence and activism in Canada.

Is critical management education possible in China? That is the question raised by Shih-wei Hsu in his chapter. Historically speaking, the Chinese social system privileges a non-critical attitude, critical thinking being pre-sented as negative and management scholars being hardly able to develop an interest in critical theory and pedagogy of management. Yet the author introduces the critical impulse in Chinese world views and illustrates the challenges and opportunities for CMS in China. This leads him to advocate an epistemologically and theoretically pluralized CMS academic discipline as a way to develop a critical engagement with local realities.

The upsurge of interest in CMS in France is documented by Isabelle Huault and Véronique Perret, who explain this in terms of a reaction, in the early part of the twenty-first century, to the mainstream, managerialist way that 'management science' had been institutionalized in that country. Ironically, what had by then emerged as CMS in Anglophone literatures was heavily inspired by French intellectual traditions, and the reappropriation of these enables French CMS scholars not simply to mimic but to make significant new conceptualizations of, for example, workplace suffering and emancipation.

It has been long established that the German Frankfurt School constituted a common background for the many critiques of labour and management.

Introduction xxv

Ronald Hartz decides to introduce the reader to three other contemporary critical traditions (the so-called labour-oriented business administration, a critique of the political economy of organizations and a deconstructionist perspective on gender issues) and to their most emblematic authors (Aoewl, Türk and Krell). By doing so, Hartz contributes to sharing specific German-speaking references through presenting theories that have not been—so far—disseminated to the Anglophone CMS literature.

Michal Frenkel applies a critical approach of 'glocalization' to account for the exclusion of CMS from Israel's management education industry. The juxtaposition of geopolitical pressures (e.g. the US neocolonial project, the Cold War dynamic) and local interests (e.g. the Israeli academy's local struggle for international recognition) has led to the marginalization of any critical theoretical perspective as part of the management education system. Yet the same conditions that led to its marginalization in Israeli business schools explain the development of CMS theoretical and empirical efforts in other academic locations, such as in departments of sociology, anthropology and labour studies.

Maria Laura Toraldo and her colleagues take us through the history of the organization of the Seventh CMS Conference in Naples. This journey invites us to discover the specificities of the institutional context of Italian universities and of management research and teaching. In a context of scarce (financial) resources, the boundaries between disciplines are reinforced within universities, where management education mainly takes place. The authors illustrate how CMS emerges in Italy as a claim for multidisciplinary approaches in the study of management, although this critical project only concerns less than a dozen universities.

Examining the relevance of CMS to the Japanese context, Toru Kiyomiya analyses how capitalism and critical perspectives have been translated from Western concepts into the Japanese context. He highlights then how the cultural context of Japanese discourses with regard to Buddhism and Confucianism may offer an alternative and meets the need for a more constructive approach to CMS. Kiyomiya finally proposes the concepts of 'self-problematization' and 'relational problematization' in order to highlight a Japanese contribution to the CMS field able to face what he calls 'the ontological distortions' brought by commodification.

Hartmann, Kärreman and Alvesson map CMS in Scandinavia, immediately pointing out the problems associated with this term, and indeed they show just how much variety it conceals. They identify a number of different 'schools' of CMS associated with particular institutions, individuals and research groups across the four countries, whilst also suggesting that these should be understood as articulating rather different versions of CMS with similarly varied intellectual and political agendas.

Examining the development of CMS in South America on a country-by-country basis, Ernesto Gantman reviews the main aspects of critical management thought in Argentina, Brazil, Chile, Colombia and Venezuela. He underlines, contrary to what could have been expected because of the

xxvi *Grey et al.*

anti-imperialist political context of some of those countries, that scholarship in this field has not received much attention except in the case of Brazil where an indigenous tradition in CMS existed since the 1970s. The author provides a comparative analysis to explain some of the differences observed and proposes some reflections about the future of CMS in these countries.

In Turkey, CMS is depicted by Oba and Gençer as a very marginal development when compared to a strongly established mainstream which is positivist, managerialist and economistic in nature. This indeed is the situation in many countries, most of which are not covered in this book for reasons given earlier, but what the authors manage to do, using the case of the Soma mine disaster, is to show how and why this marginalization persists. This chapter therefore provides one (local) explanation for the absence of CMS.

Martin Parker wrote his chapter as an ex-sociologist who now works in a business school. He underlines that the story of CMS in the UK could be told from a variety of other perspectives and that CMS in this part of the world is too big for a single chapter. He argues that different understandings of the role of social science provides the deep structure for a tension between CMS on the one hand and industrial relations and the sociology of work and employment on the other. He concludes with some reflections concerning the critical lens of CMS given that it has now institutionalized so effectively in the UK.

In the final chapter, Gordon Dehler and M. Ann Welsh explore CMS in the US, finding it to be largely marginal there and yet having been the site of important contributions to it. The authors enumerate the reasons for this marginality but also point to the possibilities afforded by global collaborations to construct a worldwide CMS community. In this way, what matters for the future is sustaining and enhancing a global conversation.

This brings us full circle to where we began this endeavour. Taken together, these chapters provide a selection of voices from across the globe, inflected in the accents of the locality from which they come, written in a language which is often not their own. Partial and limited as it surely is, it is the beginning of a conversation.

NOTE

1. The full breakdown, counting all authors of the selected classics each time they appear (i.e. in some cases the same author appears on more than one contribution) is: UK–19, US–13, Sweden–4, Germany–1.

REFERENCES

Alvesson, M. (Ed.) (2011). *Classics in Critical Management Studies*. Cheltenham, UK: Edward Elgar.
Alvesson, M., Bridgman, T. and Willmott, H. (Eds.) (2009). *The Oxford Handbook of Critical Management Studies*. Oxford: Oxford University Press.

Introduction xxvii

Alvesson, M. and Willmott, H. (Eds.) (1992). *Critical Management Studies*. London: Sage.

Battilana, J., Anteby, M. and Sengul, M. (2010). The Circulation of Ideas across Academic Communities: When Locals Re-import Exported Ideas. *Organization Studies*, 31(6): 695–713.

Boyacigiller, N. and Adler, N. (1991). The Parochial Dinosaur: Organisational Science in a Global Context. *Academy of Management Review*, 5(4): 262–290.

Faria, A. (2013). Border Thinking in Action: Should Critical Management Studies Get Anything Done? In V. Malin, J. Murphy and M. Siltaoja (Eds.), *Getting Things Done. Dialogues in Critical Management Studies Volume 2*, 277–300. Bingley, UK: Emerald Group Publishing Limited.

Fournier, V. and Grey, C. (2000). At the Critical Moment: Conditions and Prospects for Critical Management Studies. *Human Relations*, 53(1): 7–32.

Fournier, V. and Smith, W. (2012). Making Choice, Taking Risk: On the Coming Out of Critical Management Studies. *Ephemera*, 12(4): 463–474.

Frenkel, M., Jack, G., Westwood, R. and Khan, F.R. (2014). Carrying Across the Line. In R. Westwood, G. Jack, F.R. Khan and M. Frenkel (Eds.), *Core-Periphery Relations and Organization Studies*, 223–248. Basingstoke, UK: Palgrave.

Grey, C. (2010). Organizing Studies: Publications, Politics and Polemic. *Organization Studies*, 31(6): 677–694.

Grey, C. and Willmott, H. (Eds.) (2005). *Critical Management Studies: A Reader*. Oxford: Oxford University Press.

Golsorkhi, D., Huault, I. and Leca, B. (Eds.) (2009). *Les Études Critiques en Management. Une Perspective Française*. Laval, France: Les Presses de l'Université Laval.

Ibarra Colado, E. (2008). Is There Any Future for Critical Management Studies in Latin America? Moving from Epistemic Coloniality to 'trans-discipline'. *Organization*, 15(6): 932–935.

Malin, V., Murphy, J. and Siltaoja, M. (Eds.) (2013). *Getting Things Done. Dialogues in Critical Management Studies Volume 2*. Bingley, UK: Emerald Group Publishing Limited.

Meyer, R. and Boxenbaum, E. (2010). Exploring European-ness in Organization Research. *Organization Studies*, 31(6): 737–755.

Palpacuer, F., Leroy, M. and Naro, G. (Eds.) (2010). *Management, mondialisation, écologie. Regards critiques en sciences de gestion*. Paris, France: Hermès Science Publications.

Parker, M. (2010). The Sclerosis of Criticism: A Handbook of Critical Management Studies? *Critical Policy Studies*, 4(3): 297–302.

Perriton, L. and Reynolds, M. (2004). Critical Management Education: From Pedagogy of Possibility to Pedagogy of Refusal. *Management Learning*, 35(1): 61–77.

Prasad, A. (2008). Review of *Critical Management Studies: A Reader*, Christopher Grey and Hugh Willmott (Eds.), *Academy of Management Review*, 33(1): 278–283.

Prasad, A., Prasad, P., Mills, A. and Helms Mills, J. (Eds.) (2014). *The Routledge Companion to Critical Management Studies*. London: Routledge.

Rowlinson, M. and Hassard, J. (2011). How Come the Critters Came to be Teaching in Business Schools? Contradictions in the Institutionalization of Critical Management Studies. *Organization*, 18(5): 673–689.

Spicer, A., Alvesson, M. and Kärreman, D. (2009). Critical Performativity: The Unfinished Business of Critical Management Studies. *Human Relations*, 62(4): 537–560.

Tadajewski, M., Maclaran, P. Parsons, E and Parker, M. (Eds.) (2011). *Key Concepts in Critical Management Studies*. London: Sage.

Taskin, L. and de Nanteuil, M. (Eds.) (2011). *Perspectives Critiques en Management. Pour une Gestion Citoyenne*. Brussels, Belgium: De Boeck, coll. Recherches & Méthodes.

xxviii *Grey et al.*

Westwood, R., Jack, G., Khan, F.R. and Frenkel, M. (2014). Situating Core-Peripheral Knowledge in Management and Organization Studies. In R. Westwood, G. Jack, F.R. Khan and M. Frenkel (Eds.), *Core-Periphery Relations and Organization Studies*, 1–32. Basingstoke, UK: Palgrave Macmillan.

Wolfram Cox, J., LeTrent-Jones, T. and Voronoy, M. (Eds.) (2009). *Critical Management Studies at Work: Negotiating Tensions between Theory and Practice.* Cheltenham, UK: Edward Elgar.

1 Australia and New Zealand
Drawn Together Yet Worlds Apart?

Deborah Jones, Craig Prichard and Graham Sewell

Some of the differences between Australia and New Zealand as far-flung former colonies of Great Britain are obvious: while settlement of the former was prompted by the crisis of where to send convicts and undesirables following the American War of Independence, the latter was always a destination for free settlers, even before it separated from the Colony of New South Wales in 1841. A less well-known difference is in the way these countries have treated their respective first peoples, where New Zealand's 1840 Treaty of Waitangi establishing Māori land rights and Australia's policy of *Terra Nullius* or "empty land" legitimating the genocide of entire indigenous populations (Tatz, 2003) stand in stark contrast. Indeed, to be true to the spirit of Waitangi we should, more correctly, refer to Aotearoa rather than to New Zealand. Yet today, setting aside the way we fire jokes across the Tasman Sea about each other's alleged primitive ways, both countries are poster children for the modern integrated and globalized economy and both possess vibrant and internationally active academic communities of critical scholars. Indeed, New Zealand and Australia were striding ahead of the pack when Thatcher or Reagan were barely out of their neo-liberal economic policy blocks. In this way, both countries have been fertile incubators for Critical Management Studies, and this chapter shows how, in contrasting ways, each one has contributed to the development of this emerging movement. Graham Sewell begins with his reflections on Australia and then Deborah Jones and Craig Pritchard together offer their perspective from New Zealand.

AUSTRALIA (Graham Sewell)

Southern Theory from a Great Southern Land?

Growing up in Britain, my knowledge of Australia, like most Britons, was acquired through the kind of distorting prism that only the resident of a former colonial power possesses, where my attitudes toward the Great Southern Land were simultaneously romanticized and patronizing. Even as an undergraduate, I remember being disappointed to discover on reading Asa Briggs

2 *Jones et al.*

Victorian Cities that Melbourne was actually a well-established and sophisticated metropolitan conurbation with unpredictable weather rather than a sunburnt outback town surrounded by red desert as far as the eye could see (a view developed exclusively through the voracious consumption of *Smiley* films and *The Sundowners*, all of which were screened by the BBC on high rotation). Worse still—considering I was in my mid-twenties, a PhD student, and an official guest at a major US university—I remember asking my host whether he liked rugby after he told he was from Melbourne (at that time rugby union was played almost exclusively in parts of New South Wales and Queensland, and then it was restricted to a few expensive suburbs and a smattering of elite private schools). Although in hindsight this looks hopelessly ill informed, I don't think it was unusual for the time. For example, in the mid-1990s, when I told a very senior colleague I was giving up an orthodox British academic trajectory to move to Australia, his response was a combination of bemusement and disbelief. "You know it will be the end of your career, don't you?" he finally managed to splutter. Perhaps if I had read for a different degree or been interested in researching a different topic for my PhD then I would have been more aware of Australia's contradictory history of radical working-class politics and its status as a loyal vassal, first of British, then US cultural, political, and economic imperialism. I might even have been aware of its more recent and important contributions to the social sciences, the humanities, and cultural studies through the efforts of the likes of Elizabeth Grosz, Raewyn Connell, and Bryan S. Turner that have become part of what Connell (2007) herself calls "Southern Theory". Perhaps I would have also been aware that a small but significant part of the Australian population were institutionally condemned to be second-class citizens for, in terms of the mistreatment of its first peoples, Australia has always been truly "world-class".

Elsewhere I have been involved in producing something akin to Southern Theory as part of Australia's contribution to Critical Management Studies (see Clegg et al., 1999) but for this chapter, I am adopting a much more traditional approach that combines an orthodox chronological take on the history of ideas with an unashamedly selective list of authors. While Australia may not yet have produced coherent versions of the social sciences or the humanities in the same way that France has produced the Regulation School or Germany the Frankfurt School (Connell's Southern Theory notwithstanding) there have certainly been immigrants and emigrants that have made many distinguished contributions to Critical Management Studies. This is fitting for such a relatively new country (it was first possible to become a citizen of a distinct sovereign nation rather than a subject of the British Empire only as recently as 1948) because what it means to be Australian these days owes so much to our continuously ambivalent stance toward migration, both inward and outward. In light of this, I shall be using the themes of immigration and emigration as the organizing framework for my section of this chapter. I will start in an unlikely place: Harvard University and the Human Relations School of Elton Mayo and his acolytes. Although by any stretch of the

Australia and New Zealand 3

imagination this could never be described as an embryonic form of Critical Management Studies, I shall show that Mayo's formative years in Australia did much to shape the Human Relations School's attitudes towards work organization and, thus, set in train much of what Critical Management Studies actually criticizes. I shall then go on to look at the Australian influence on the Tavistock Institute's take on human relations before bringing matters right up to date by reflecting on the foundation on the Critical Management Studies division of the Academy of Management. I shall then conclude this section's focus on Australia by examining the contribution made by immigrants to the country in the broad area of Critical Management Studies. Prominent amongst these will be Stewart Clegg through his sustained interest in power relations and Cynthia Hardy through her important theoretical and empirical work using discourse analysis.

Everywhere You Go, Always Take the Weather with You:[1] Australia's Critical Management Émigrés

Dorothy Mackellor wrote the best known poem about the Australian bush, not in the "sunburnt country" she so memorably invoked in *My Country*, but while living in London. It was published in 1919 in that bastion of the conservative British Establishment, the *Spectator*. In the same year, another conservative—originally from Adelaide but by then a lecturer in philosophy and ethics at the University of Queensland—published his first substantial work, *Democracy and Freedom*. The author was Elton Mayo, and he had produced a treatise on political theory that contained a trenchant critique of socialism along with a defence of the minimal state (obviously pressing topics at the time so soon after the 1917 October Revolution) that drew on the likes of J. S. Mill and Herbert Spencer. It is very much a book of its time, and I wouldn't recommend it as light holiday reading now but its fourth chapter provides a crucial insight into the development of Mayo's later thinking; much like Mackellor in London, when Mayo was sitting in his office at Harvard, he must have often been thinking back to his formative experiences in Australia and the apparently recondite industrial relations problem of compulsory arbitration. In short, Mayo's abiding dislike of organized labour was clearly expressed through his critique of a uniquely antipodean way of dealing with workplace conflict.

Building on developments in New Zealand and the independent colonies of New South Wales and South Australia, in 1904, the recently federated Australian Commonwealth ". . . made class warfare into a legal process" (Rowse, 2004, p. 17) through an Act of Parliament that, among other things, created a legally binding system for resolving industrial disputes. This infuriated Mayo, who wrote,

> So far as arbitration encourages the mutual discussion of difficulties between masters and men, the effect is excellent . . . But the notion of

4 *Jones et al.*

an Arbitration Court goes far beyond this . . . Its primary assumption is that the interests of masters and men cannot be made identical, that the intervention of an intermediary is necessary in the general interest. This assumption serves in practice to stereotype the breach and to multiply the causes of dispute; arbitration courts have the effect of recognising and legalising social disintegration.

(Mayo, 1919, pp. 47–48)

While Australian scholars (e.g. Gillespie, 1991, Bruce and Nyland, 2011) have long pointed to baleful ideological influence that Mayo exerted over the subsequent development of the Human Relations School (and, thus, over much of mainstream management studies for the best part of a century), nothing quite captures his position in such a succinct form as this quote. Spontaneous rational debate between employers and employees is to be encouraged (to be fair, I am assuming that the terms "masters" and "men" simply reflect the conventions of the time), but the intrusion of third parties such as unions, let alone the state, into such relations are to be abhorred because they only serve to undermine a meeting of minds over what ought to be quite obvious unitary interests. In this respect, it could be argued that much of what Critical Management Studies sets itself against—the belief that cooperation, consent, and harmony somehow are (or should be) the natural state of organizations and, as a consequence, conflict, coercion, and discord are pathological manifestations of irrational thinking and behaviour—at least had some of its origins in the founding of Australia as an independent modern state.

Although its shares part of its name with an intellectual and political movement forever associated with Elton Mayo, the Tavistock Institute of Human Relations represents a subtly different take on social cohesion in organizations. To be sure, it was founded with a grant from that prime instrument of US imperialism, the Rockefeller Foundation, and some of its earliest contributors such as Alfred Bion and Elliott Jacques shared Mayo's interest in psychotherapeutic responses to individual cases of neurosis in organizational settings (see Trist and Murray, 1990). Others such as Eric Trist, however, also started with an interest in psychoanalysis. With Kenneth Bamford, he adopted a much more critical view of the operation of group dynamics in organizations, recognizing an important source of conflict in the workplace was the drive, as part of the quest for productivity in post-war Britain, toward increased mechanization that consequently eroded employees' autonomy (see Trist and Bamforth, 1951). Although they never explicitly adopted a Marxist approach, Trist and Bamforth's critique thus anticipated some of the arguments of labour process theory's "deskilling thesis" (Braverman, 1974), and it was as part of this vibrant intellectual milieu that two Australians made important early contributions to the British variant of the human relations movement. The first of these was the Sydney-born J. A. Barnes who had a considerable career as a sociologist and

Australia and New Zealand 5

social anthropologist at major universities in Australia and Britain. It was while he was at the London School of Economics, however, that he made the contribution in which we are most interested, for it was from here that he published an article in the institute's flagship journal, *Human Relations*, in which he coined the phrase, "social network analysis" (Barnes, 1954). Unlike many of his successors in the burgeoning world of social network analysis in management studies, his two-year study of a tiny Norwegian fishing village included an explicit consideration of the role played by class in creating the social stratification that enabled local elites to hold sway in the control and distribution of resources. I would contend that, if only today's advocates of social network analysis would emulate Barnes's interest in class, it could rightly become an important part of the Critical Management Studies family.

The second Australian I wish to mention in relation to the Tavistock Institute is Fred Emery who made many and varied contributions to the development of management thinking in the second half of the twentieth century (see Heller, 1997). Emery was the son of a Western Australian sheep shearer and was an active member of the Communist party in Australia and later in Britain until he resigned after Soviet invasion of Hungary in 1956. Although he initially saw himself primarily as a psychologist, he also undertook developmental work in remote Aboriginal communities before moving to the Tavistock Institute in 1951 where he embarked on a fruitful and (by all accounts) sometimes tempestuous period of work. Speaking to people who knew him well, some colleagues found him difficult to get on with (probably for the same reasons that others loved him), and Heller (1997) politely alludes to this in Emery's obituary. This genius, for upsetting the "establishment", later came to a head at the Australian National University (ANU) in the mid-'70s when he was denied tenure after publishing a government-commissioned report (with, it has to be said, numerous co-authors) containing a passing references to what can best be described as "unconventional" ideas about the effects of watching television on children's brain plasticity (Emery et al., 1975). By the standards of some of the more outlandish claims made today by social scientists jumping on the neuroscience bandwagon, these ideas may seem innocuous; but according to his friends, he was nothing short of hounded out of Australia's preeminent university at the time by narrow-minded, petty, and envious scientists who felt threatened by this tiny incursion into their bailiwick. Perhaps his famed Australian directness was a little too Australian and a little too direct for the blue bloods of the ANU. It is fair to say, however, that the same friends also acknowledged that Emery's confrontational style with intellectual opponents did not make his predicament any easier. It is sad that his university career suffered such an inglorious end as, by then, he should have been hailed as an august elder statesman of management studies after his seminal contributions on topics such as "open" and "closed" systems, environmental turbulence, and information theory (see Emery and Trist, 1965; Ackoff and Emery, 1972).

6 Jones et al.

Later on he also became a pioneering champion of sustainability but, as far as critical management scholars are concerned, his main legacy is as a tireless advocate of industrial democracy (see Emery and Thorsrud, 1976). This work was itself controversial in that it found the compulsory presence of employee representatives on company boards in many European countries had little real positive effect on the predicament of shop floor workers at the very time that British trades unions were campaigning for this very thing. He went as far as to contend that legislating to put workers on boards was worse than useless, as it diverted attention from making meaningful reforms to work organization on the shop floor (although he did later moderate this view—Heller, 1997). Some trades unionists who were active at the time have told me that this research played a small but not inconsequential role in killing off the industrial democracy movement in Britain in the 1970s, as it was seized on by opponents as evidence that having workers on boards was a distraction for employees and businesses alike. In contrast, I would like to think that it should have been taken as a signal to redouble efforts to bring about meaningful reform of traditional management structures at the point where it would have the most effect: on the shop floor.

From the perspective of current critical management scholars, my focus on Australia's influence on the Tavistock Institute may be seen as diverting attention away from the activities of dedicated researchers who were undertaking much more radical work on organizations in the same period, but I would contend that it made things such as elites, identity, and employee autonomy legitimate topics for debate in polite management scholarship circles. In this sense, it formed something of a bridgehead for the later incursions by the critical scholars we see today, to the extent that the biggest international grouping of management academics—the US-based Academy of Management—has a dedicated Critical Management Studies division. Mention of this brings me to my final Australian émigré, as it is unlikely that this division would exist without the tireless efforts of Paul Adler (at least in its current form). Adler's parents arrived in Melbourne as French refugees from the Holocaust and quickly became politically active members of the city's vibrant Jewish community, but it was the anti-Vietnam War movement that played a key role in the development of his political consciousness (500 Australians were killed and over 3,000 were wounded in the war between 1962–1972). After dropping out of Monash University, Adler was attracted to the intellectual milieu of France—especially work developing around the theories of Louis Althusser—where he studied economics and ended up working for the Ministry of Labour while completing a PhD, which took a labour process perspective on the deskilling effects of computer technology in the banking sector (Adler, 1983).

It was while working as a post-doctorate researcher at Harvard Business School and later as an assistant professor at Stanford University that Adler began to hone his interest in what would later become known as Critical Management Studies. He became increasingly frustrated by the political

Australia and New Zealand   7

sterility of the formal and informal aspects of the annual Academy of Management meeting but was also surprised at how many members privately held progressive views. Now a major intellectual force in the world of organization and management research and with a broad and deep body of work that includes important critical contributions on topics such as technology, teamwork, bureaucracy, and social capital (see Adler and Borys, 1996; Adler and Kwon, 2002; Adler, 2012; Kwon and Adler, 2014; Adler et al., 2014), Adler has been able to balance his position in the academic mainstream as a professor at the University of Southern California's Marshall Business School and as a member of the Academy of Management's executive body (he was president in 2014) with his crucial role as a soi-disant "paleo-Marxist" in the foundation of the academy's Critical Management Studies special interest group (later to become a full division). Paleo-Marxism here was a conscious reference to Eric Hobsbawm's coinage of the term, and Adler too uses it to describe his preference for Marx's original works over their myriad reinterpretations. There was a time when it was de rigueur to read Marx in many disciplines, whether you were sympathetic to his ideas or not, but those times seem to have long passed. Adler is one of the few prominent voices in the social sciences—let alone organization and management studies—who keeps the spirit of Marx's integrated social critique alive.

Standing at the Limit of an Endless Ocean:[2] Australia's Critical Management Immigrants

> The Ladybird, Government schooner, visited the settlement on ordinary occasions twice a year, and such visits were looked forward to with no little eagerness by the settlers. To the convicts the arrival of the Ladybird meant arrival of new faces, intelligence of old comrades, news of how the world, from which they were exiled, was progressing. When the Ladybird arrived, the chained and toil-worn felons felt that they were yet human, that the universe was not bounded by the gloomy forests which surrounded their prison, but that there was a world beyond, where men, like themselves, smoked, and drank, and laughed, and rested, and were Free.
>
> (Clarke 1874/2001: p. 120)

For the Term of His Natural Life, *Marcus Clarke*

The origins of Australia's aforementioned system of legally binding arbitration lie in the social and industrial unrest of the 1890s (Harley, 2004) when the country was in the depths of a severe economic recession. At this time, antagonism towards non-white immigration—a perennial feature of Australian life—was particularly acute and organized labour played a prominent role in first establishing and then perpetuating what became known as the "white Australia" policy (Markey, 1996) that was only formally dismantled

8 *Jones et al.*

by the 1966 Immigration Act. There were even allusions to this policy as recently as 2001 when Prime Minister John Howard addressed an election rally with the now infamous line, "But we will decide who comes to this country and the circumstances in which they come". Today refugees from conflicts that Australia has played a part in fomenting—from Afghanistan and Iraq to Syria—are dismissed as "economic migrants". But, except for Australia's first peoples and transported convicts, aren't we all sons and daughters of economic migrants? It is a fact that modern Australia is a country of migrants, often in search of greater opportunity, that serves as the theme for my final section.

Before I go on, I first need to acknowledge that Australia has a long history of critical scholarship in the area of industrial relations which, due to our unique institutional arrangements, has meant that scholars in this discipline have always played a prominent role in national economic and social policy debates (especially under the auspices of the Workplace Research Centre at the University of Sydney—formerly the Australian Centre for Industrial Relations Research and Training). Through Australia's now defunct automobile assembly industry, the country was also an early adopter of "lean production" and, therefore, the source of early criticism of this development (see Hampson et al., 1994). When it comes to the role played by Australian-based scholars in the recent emergence of Critical Management Studies as a recognizable intellectual community, however, I would like to focus my attention on three migrants—Craig Littler, Stewart Clegg, and Cynthia Hardy.

Craig Littler, who died suddenly in 2010, was the founder of the Australian-based journal *Labour and Industry*, which has served as an important outlet for critical scholarship on the social, organizational, and institutional aspects of work and industrial relations since 1987. He is, however, probably best known in international critical management circles as a major contributor to labour process theory. His earliest foray into this notoriously factionalized part of our community was his important study of Taylorism as a new social mechanism for establishing effort levels in the context of work rationalization (Littler, 1978) and, as such, it was a major influence on my own ideas about workplace surveillance (Sewell and Wilkinson, 1992; Sewell, 1998). Indeed, Craig was not known for being the shy and retiring type, and he would often tell me that I wasn't saying anything he hadn't already said (although he was usually gracious enough to admit that I was, perhaps, saying it in a slightly different way).

The 1980s proved to be a very productive time for Littler, as he turned his London School of Economics PhD thesis into a well-received book on the labour process (Littler, 1982) while striking up a fruitful collaboration with Graeme Salaman that produced, among other things, two very influential works (Littler and Salaman, 1982, 1984). Although he was peripatetic and shuttled between universities in Australia and the UK for much of his career, I would argue that Littler's lasting legacy for Critical Management Studies lies in the work he produced leading up to and immediately after his move to

Griffith University in Queensland, where he became for a time an important advocate for labour process theory on an international scale.

This connection with Griffith University is significant, as it was the first Australian academic home for my second migrant, Stewart Clegg. This name is likely to be very familiar to readers of this volume, for Clegg has been a significant figure in organization and management studies for many years. It was as an undergraduate at Aston University—then one of the most prominent centres for management studies outside the US—that Clegg encountered the classics of organizational sociology under the influence of people such as Colin Fletcher and Mike Hall. After completing his PhD at Bradford Management Centre under the nominal supervision of prominent "Aston Studies" figure David Hickson (but, according to Clegg himself, with help from many others), he published his first major works, *Power, Rule & Domination* (Clegg, 1975) and the co-edited *Critical Issues in Organizations* (Clegg and Dunkerley, 1977). This latter book can legitimately claim to be one of the first books to map out the terrain of Critical Management Studies, but even such a high-profile start wasn't enough to secure an academic career in recession-hit Britain, so Clegg took up the offer of a job at Griffith University in 1976 where he produced *Organization, Class & Control* (Clegg and Dunkerley, 1980) and *State, Class and the Recession* (Clegg et al. 1980). He took up a chair at the University of New England in 1985 and, but for a brief spell in Scotland, he has been based in Australia ever since.

Now at the University of Technology, Sydney, Clegg has continued to publish prodigiously across a wide range of topics while also playing important professional roles in the European Group on Organizations Studies (publishers of *Organization Studies*, which he once edited) and its Asia-Pacific equivalent, APROS. Given the breadth and depth of his work then, it is difficult to single out particular contributions but there is little doubt that his books—*Frameworks of Power* (Clegg, 1989) and *Modern Organizations* (Clegg, 1990)—are certainly the most influential if we go by the crude measure of citations. Arguably, these two books did much to reshape the terrain of Critical Management Studies and draw in people who took positions that were not just restricted to a Marxist treatment that analytically privileges the "base" (i.e. the capitalist mode of production) over the "superstructure" (i.e. everything else). In particular, *Frameworks'* combination of (at the time, relatively esoteric) authors such as Hobbes, Machiavelli, Latour, and Foucault with, what were for management scholars at least, more familiar names such as Parsons, Giddens, and Lukes did much to reformulate the long-standing sociological "problem of order" to recognize, in Foucault's terms, that the exercise of power is not simply repressive but is also productive and allows us to achieve things collectively. In this way ". . . a theory of power must also be a theory of organization" (Clegg, 1990, p. 17). With this in mind, *Modern Organizations* can be seen as an empirical companion piece to *Frameworks* that, among other things, traces the history of modernity as one of organizational diversity rather than one of the triumph

10   *Jones et al.*

of a single hegemonic form of domination (as institutional theorists and Marxists alike might claim). Indeed, I would go as far as to say that Clegg was onto something akin to the "varieties of capitalism" thesis well before Hall and Soskice (2001).

I leave my final comments for a consideration of what has become known as critical discourse analysis or CDA. Some have argued (e.g. Wodak, 2006) that discourse analysis is not intrinsically critical (at least in the same way that labour process theory is, by definition, critical) and thus must be consciously radicalized (e.g. Fairclough, 2005). This is where Cynthia Hardy comes in. She received her PhD from Warwick Business School under the supervision of Andrew Pettigrew and spent several years at McGill University in Montreal, rising to the position of full professor. She was thus already a well-established academic force when she moved to the University of Melbourne in 1998, where she has remained. Hardy is known for developing a wide international research network that has established CDA at the heart of Critical Management Studies. In addition to contributing to highly regarded books and edited collections (Clegg et al., 1996, 2001; Hardy and Phillips, 2002; Grant et al., 2004; Grant et al., 2011), she has also written some landmark articles that have breached the walls of the Academy of Management's citadel (Lawrence et al., 2002; Phillips et al., 2004; Maguire and Hardy, 2009; Hardy and Maguire, 2010). Not only do these articles disrupt the comfortable mainstream consensus in terms of their theoretical approach, they also often empirically deal with marginalized groups and, in this sense, her work is truly critical.

AOTEAROA/NEW ZEALAND (Deborah Jones and Craig Prichard)

Flows to and from "Some Forsaken Land"[3]

One of the challenges posed by this volume is how to best present critical scholarly analysis with an eye on what influences or shapes that analysis in a particular location. One response would be to follow Graham Sewell's lead and identify the "brilliant careers" of expatriate and immigrant scholars who contributed mightily to the centres of critical studies of management and to the spread of such work. But there are other ways of accounting for such a history.

If we look through Sewell's contribution, we can identify how changing colonial and imperialist processes bear on the nature of academic knowledge. Sewell's narrative suggests that in the first half of the twentieth century, the flow of scholarly labour involved those born in colonial Australia being "finished" in elite academic schools in the metropolitan centres of Boston and London, with Elton Mayo and Fred Emery being the illustrative cases in this instance. However, by the latter half of the century, the flow had switched. Clegg, Littler, Hardy, and Sewell himself are the working examples here. Each was born, literally and academically, "there" and arrived "here"

Australia and New Zealand 11

to further develop their contribution to critical studies of management. But what other flows are underway and what of the more recent period since the turn of the century?

While these earlier flows are still with us, we suggest that under the sway of changing flows of labour and goods produced by that labour more generally, and the rise of nationalist postcolonial movements, a third flow has emerged. This third flow does not involve exporting "raw" colonial labour from "home" for final finishing elsewhere, as Aotearoa and Australia did with wool and meat carcasses and large blocks of butter in the initial colonial period. Nor does it involve importing "finished" expert academic labour to supervise local production, which, as Sewell suggests, may have constrained the development of uniquely local responses to the key questions of management and organization studies. Rather this third flow involves "homegrown" academic subjects formed out of, and emboldened by, nationalist and postcolonial movements developing and extending distinctive forms of analysis that are underpinned by changing global flows of commodities that demand distinctive local narratives. There are a number of strands to this third flow, which is the core of our contribution. In this section, our focus is on themes and issues in critical studies of management in Aotearoa/New Zealand. We begin by exploring the strands of the "third flow" of scholarly labour and go on to trace two types of "locale-based" critical studies of management and organizations. We then go on to briefly discuss in more detail two specific, related topics that have been central to the critique of management knowledge here: the question of Māori knowledges, and the non-Māori response to Māori claims, and feminist perspectives on management.

As Fournier and Grey (2000, p. 16) have argued, CMS is theoretically plural and ". . . there is no single way of demarcating the critical from the non-critical". Further, as they point out, the intellectual traditions from which critical scholars in management are located in specific local and historical conditions, and the term itself, originated in British business schools. An initial and generative strand to our "third flow" is work that applies the critical theoretical and analytical framework produced by the academic "chiefs"/"chefs" of the metropolitan centres (the names Giddens, Foucault, Derrida, Lacan, and more recently Ranciere and Badiou are prominent) to the empirical nuances and conditions on the periphery. One of the effects of this work is to problematize colonial history and as such to problematize the very concepts and structures of critique. Such work could be said to turn the academic tools of the metropolis on the colonial master and then back on the metropolitan master.

The Empire Strikes Back: Pākehā and Kaupapa Māori Research

An example of such work with respect to the critical studies of management and organizations from the Easterly side of Te Tai-o-Rehua (Tasman Sea) is the series of genealogical investigations carried out by Keith Hooper and his

12 *Jones et al.*

colleagues (Hooper and Pratt, 1993, 2002; Kearins and Hooper, 2002). This work offers a compelling critical analysis of nineteenth-century accounting processes in the context of colonization. It reveals how Pākehā (originally, white New Zealanders of European descent) application of seemingly technical and objective accounting language was deeply implicated in the theft, forced sale, and alienation of land inhabited by Māori, the indigenous people. This colonizing move not only enriched Aotearoa's early Pākehā capitalists but also initiated a tradition of socializing to the state losses incurred from capital's misadventures.

In brief, critical rereadings of colonial history exposes how, beyond forced confiscation, early capitalists and the state used mundane forms of management knowledge to subordinate the original inhabitants. But such work also raises questions about the universalist assumptions of critical social science (Fay, 1987). In the context of nationalist, postcolonial movements, local scholars have inevitably become suspicious of the effects of theoretical importation as a means of overlooking locally relevant modes of critical analysis or of more directly blocking the emergence of nonmetropolitan critical studies (Prichard, 2006). While not to dismiss the importance of such work, we might, for example, ask to what extent is Keith Hooper's Foucauldian critique of colonial accounting, which obviously takes it's conceptual lead from the conditions that inform the creation of the much vaunted French academic milieu, overlooks traditions or modes of critique that already exist "here", or that emerged from contentious relations and circumstances in response to early state and capitalist domination. In response to such questioning, at least two types of "locale-based" critical studies of management and organizations have emerged in Aotearoa.

The first is a critique based on principles of Kaupapa Māori research (Smith, 2012). This is a decolonizing epistemology moulded by a broad Māori sovereignty movement that has challenged Pākehā dominance in light of the partnership agreed to in the nation's founding document, The Treaty of Waitangi, in (1840). It is also fuelled by significant difference in class position and life chances of Pākehā and Māori that has endured since colonial domination in the late nineteenth century. The problem to which this strand of critique is directed is succinctly expressed by Ruwhiu and Wolfgramm (2006). They argue that "despite mainstream organizational research's best intentions and increasing use of more interpretive methodologies . . . it typically reinforces a view of the world consistent with underlying Western oriented assumptions".

Research guided by Kaupapa Māori principles meanwhile emphasizes Māori cultural norms, value systems, and practices as a basis of critique. Such principles assume the interconnection of natural, spiritual, and social worlds and are expressed through a set of concepts including wairua (a totalizing force that connects all living things), mauri (the life essence), hau (a system of gift relations that govern social relations), tapu (sacred power), and mana (religious power and authority and ancestral connectedness).

Australia and New Zealand 13

Kaupapa Māori research can be regarded as a local form of critical theory (Smith, 2000) based on a naturalist philosophy of connectedness and abiding forces. Meanwhile, critical organizational research informed by such principles has the explicit aim of strengthening the Māori struggle, resistance, and emancipation in the face of contemporary political, economic, and social forces. Such work involves strengthening tribal authorities and business corporations and education and health initiates but also contributing to guiding investment, management, and market strategies (e.g. Panoho and Stablein, 2012).

The concept of "indigeneity", therefore, is a highly salient political term in this country, with global resonances grounded in international claims for the rights of indigenous people in the wake of colonization (Verbos and Humphries, 2015). These resonances imply peoples with continuous relationships over time with specific territories in a historical context of colonization and ongoing marginalization or dispossession. The relationships between indigenous and nonindigenous people are central to critical discourse of all kinds in Aotearoa/New Zealand (Bell, 2006) and therefore to critical studies of management (Henry and Pringle, 1996).

The second strand of work that flows from this questioning of the universalism, adequacy, and relevance of metropolitan theoretical resources (albeit critical sources), which have in part been shaped by export economic flows no longer restricted to a small number of parental trading location, is what we might call critical-locale studies of management and organizations. Such a mode of critique is concerned with identifying the symbolic and political distinctiveness of locality-based organizing and particularly their symbolic and embodied coordinates. In other words, if critical metropolitan explanations of organizational phenomena carry with them universalist, and thus inevitably reductionist assumptions, critical location studies assume multiple indeterminacies (Jack et al., 2012) that contribute to distinctive local institutional forms (e.g. of bureaucracy, professions, market, and family) and thus create distinctive organizing practices and structures that we might say lead to an international "division of subjectivities". From a critical-locale perspective then, one cannot say much about organizations and organizing beyond simple claims to dependency, contingency, and mimesis. But one can explain a lot based on the distinctive characteristics of local conditions and circumstances that confront and shape efforts to organize labour, land, and language (Prichard et al., 2007). In particular, Aotearoa/New Zealand is not the post-industrial landscape addressed by CMS scholars in the north, but rather a small agricultural economy based on primary industries such as dairy, fishing, and forestry and struggling to become a "knowledge-based economy" (Prichard, 2006). An exemplary critical intervention is the work of Simmons and Stringer (2014) on slave-like conditions in the New Zealand fishing industry, where local fishing companies used foreign-chartered fishing vessels staffed by foreign companies. Simmons and Stringer (2014) carried out extremely demanding local research with crew members to help

14   *Jones et al.*

establish the basis for claims of human rights violations, leading, along with other local and global activism, to law changes. This case is instructive as a local critical intervention; the title of one of their articles, "Not in New Zealand's Waters, Surely?", shows that it is hard for New Zealanders to imagine that local companies can be involved in the kinds of power abuses that are the typical targets of Critical Management Studies.

The small size of the New Zealand academic community seems to foster interdisciplinarity, so while there are no major groupings of what might be called Critical Management Studies scholars in any given business school, there are networks of critical engagement with organizational and management studies centred in business schools but including scholars working in a range of other contexts. During the 2000s, the authors of this section facilitated a yearly two-day conference known as "OIL" or Organization, Identity and Locality, hosted in turn at business schools in most of New Zealand's universities. The conference sought to develop, extend, and refine forms of critical study of organizations in Aotearoa. While the two strands of critique identified earlier were featured in work published beyond the OIL events, the conference's annual proceedings (OIL, n.d.a) and a partial bibliography (OIL, n.d.b) provide a snapshot of the form of critical studies of organizations and management informed in part by some distancing from metropolitan theorizing. Since then, various other similar workshops and conferences have continued the OIL format, including workshops on social movements in Aotearoa. The organization was initially subtitled Organization, Identity and Locality (OIL).

Critical Studies of Management and Organizing in Aotearoa/New Zealand and the key objective of OIL was articulated as: "what does it mean to do critical organisation studies here in the Aotearoa/New Zealand locality?" (Boon and Walton, 2008). It is instructive to review proceedings over time to see both the connection with what could be seen as a CMS "franchise" (Prichard et al., 2007) and a converse determination to pay attention to the local and its associated identities. To see CMS as a franchise requires imitation and duplication of theoretical paradigms and topics of study developed elsewhere; as scholars located on the margins, New Zealanders are expected to prove their research "quality" by publishing in "international" journals. The current of privileged management knowledge pulls against the local, except to the extent that it can be framed in terms of the "international" literature. OIL scholars have been concerned not so much with seeking legitimacy from the metropolitan centre, as with bringing critical perspectives to local issues. In the context of calls in the CMS literature for CMS to be more engaged, more activist (Bridgman and Stephens, 2008), achieving "international" legitimacy requires the opposite: it requires either high-concept papers stripped of local content, the sanction of an international comparison, or the hard labour of explaining why "international" readers should be interested in the "New Zealand case". There is no corresponding task for Northern CMS writers to establish the "English" or the "American" case.

Combining Local and Global Voices

We now briefly highlight two specific, related topics that have been central to the critique of management knowledge here: the question of Māori knowledges, the non-Māori response to Māori political and epistemological claims, and feminist perspectives on management. Here we are talking about knowledges articulated with specific kinds of raced and gendered bodies, identities, and power relations within, cutting across and beyond institutionalized CMS. These topics also represent active engagement with key issues of social inequality, which has intensified dramatically in New Zealand over the last decade (Rashbrooke, 2013).

Māori scholars located within business schools are connected with Māori communities, as "Māori intellectuals [who] have begun to question and re-evaluate the tenets of their disciplines, from a distinctively Māori perspective" (Henry and Pene, 2001, p. 234). These scholars are strongly connected in global, interdisciplinary indigenous intellectual, and activist networks. Some are based within specifically Māori teaching or research programmes in business schools (e.g. Mira Szászy, n.d.), others distributed across business programmes. Without necessarily being interested in institutionalized CMS, their often radical ontological, epistemological, and methodological challenges, premised on the political challenge of Tino Rangatiratanga, indigenous self-determination, not only open up different perspectives on management topics such as leadership, organization, and work (Mika and O'Sullivan, 2014) but also demand of the academy a decolonizing role and "the development of counter-hegemonies [which] embrace and celebrate . . . alternative ways of knowing and being" (Henry and Pene, 2001, p. 240). This challenge extends to ethical frameworks based in Māori values, with a strong focus on the possibilities of ethical relationships between Māori and nonindigenous people (Spiller et al.). This possibility is also the basis of non-Māori, Pākehā responses in management studies and across disciplines and organizations to the politics of race/ethnicity and culture in Aotearoa New Zealand. These draw from the history of Pākehā anti-racist activism and are understood in terms of a power-sharing model between indigenous people and later settlers signified by the Treaty of Waitangi, 1840 and embodied in a wide range of new organizing practices across government, NGOs, and business (Jones and Creed, 2011). In their editorial to a special issue of the Journal of Management Education on management education and indigenous knowledge (Fitzgibbons and Humphries (2011) point to the increasingly strong voices of indigenous people globally in the stewardship and management of natural, social, and cultural resources and the specific types of management knowledges that these require.

There is a strong relationship between feminist and Māori critical management scholarship in Aotearoa New Zealand, reflecting a wider history of activist coalitions. For instance, we see Henry and Pringle, as Māori and Pākehā feminists sharing an outsider perspective in exploring Māori and non-Māori women's organizations (Henry and Pringle, 1996). They also explore,

16 *Jones et al.*

with Wolfgramm, the complexities and power relations inherent in collaborative Māori and non-Māori management research, in a context where Māori scholars are still located in the margins of Western management knowledge and its institutions (Pringle et al., 2010). Pringle's feminist contribution also exemplifies our location in the margins as a point of critique within management studies. Pringle and Mallon's (2003) challenge to the theory of "boundaryless careers" drew on gendered career experiences and also the experiences of Māori and Pacific people in New Zealand to expose the universalizing assumptions in career theory. Similarly, Jones, Pringle, and Shepherd challenged the "knowledge transfer" model of "managing diversity" exported from the US and hegemonic in management knowledges as a "globalising vocabulary of difference" (Jones et al., 2000, p. 364). As with indigenous scholars, feminists occupy a marginal space with CMS and operate across and beyond CMS to create new critical spaces. For instance, Vida is a network of women CMS scholars. Vida argues that "we feel that we often occupy a place of 'double Otherness' in terms of our relationship to mainstream management studies as well as to the masculinist Centre of academia". The Vida objective is

> without necessarily attempting to define and clarify our Otherness—or indeed the differences that exist between us as a group of female scholars—we want to challenge in a very real and material way the "automatisms" of academic work that tend to reproduce existing processes, ways of being and even desires.

Vida operates at times as a stream or session within CMS events, such as the CMS division at the Academy of Management, as well as offering alternative "Critical Friendship" events to develop the work of women scholars. Feminist CMS scholars also attend conferences, such as Gender, Work and Organization, where their work is central, not marginal.

Whither Critical Management Studies in Aotearoa?

In discussing Māori and feminist critical scholarship in Aotearoa New Zealand, we are not simply alluding to inevitable "special interests" within the wider framework of CMS. We are referring to marginalized spaces, identities, and knowledges within the institution of CMS. In this country, we are further marginalized by location. In very practical terms, we are less likely to attend the many CMS-inflected events available in Europe, for instance, or to work in large clusters of CMS scholars. While locally based scholars have at times been active in British- or USA-based CMS organizations and projects, this direct connection is still the exception. In our marginality, however, we see clearly the central importance of location to all CMS practices, whether it is taken for granted as in the centre, or centrally problematized, as in the margins. After all, ultimately each of us lives ". . . at the edge/of the universe/like everybody else" (Manhire, 1991).

NOTES

1. This is a line from the chorus of one of Crowded House's most loved songs. The band's experience captures much about the close relationship between Australia and New Zealand, as it was founded in Melbourne by members of Auckland's Split Endz and local musicians.
2. This is the opening line to "Great Southern Land" by Icehouse.
3. "Some forsaken land" is a reference to New Zealand in the lyrics of the Split Endz's song, "Another Great Divide".

REFERENCES

Ackoff, R.L. and Emery, F. (1972). *On Purposeful Systems*. Chicago: Aldine Press.

Adler, P.S. (1983). Trente ans d'automatisation et coûts opératoires dans les banques Françaises. *Revue Économique*, 34: 987–1020.

Adler, P.S. (2012). The Ambivalence of Bureaucracy: From Weber via Gouldner to Marx. *Organization Science*, 23: 244–266.

Adler, P.S. and Borys, B. (1996). Two Types of Bureaucracy: Enabling and Coercive. *Administrative Science Quarterly*, 41: 61–89.

Adler, P.S., du Gay, P., Morgan, G. and Reed, M. (Eds.) (2014). *The Oxford Handbook of Sociology, Social Theory, and Organization Studies: Contemporary Currents*. Oxford: Oxford University Press.

Adler, P.S., Goldoftas, B., and Levine, D. (1997). Ergonomics, Employee Involvement, and the Toyota Production System: A Case Study of NUMMI'S 1993 Model Introduction. *Industrial and Labor Relations Review*, 50: 416–437.

Adler, P.S. and Kwon, S.-W. (2002). Social Capital: Prospects for a New Concept. *Academy of Management Review*, 27: 17–40.

Barnes, J.A. (1954). Class and Committees in a Norwegian Island Parish. *Human Relations*, 7: 39–58.

Bell, A. (2006). Bifurcation or Entanglement? Settler Identity and Biculturalism in Aotearoa New Zealand. *Continuum*, 20: 253–268.

Boon, B. and Walton, S. (Eds.) (2008). Organisation, Identity & Locality (IV): Exploring the Local Within the Aotearoa/New Zealand Locality [Proceedings 2008]. Retrieved from http://www.massey.ac.nz/~cprichar/OIL/OIL_IVPublished Proceedings_revised.pdf

Braverman, H. (1974). *Labor and Monopoly Capital. The Degradation of Work in the Twentieth Century*. New York: Monthly Review Press.

Bridgman, T. and Stephens, M. (2008). Institutionalizing Critique: A Problem of Critical Management Studies. *Ephemera*, 8(3): 258–270.

Bruce, K. and Nyland, C. (2011). Elton Mayo and the Deification of Human Relations. *Organization Studies*, 32: 383–405.

Clarke, M. (2011, original 1874) *For the Term of His Natural Life*. Boston, MA: Adamant Media.

Clegg, S.R. (1975). *Power, Rule and Domination: A Critical and Empirical Understanding of Power in Sociological Theory and Organizational Life*. London: Routledge & Kegan Paul.

Clegg, S.R. (1989). *Frameworks of Power*. London: Sage.

Clegg, S.R. (1990). *Modern Organizations*. London: Sage.

Clegg, S.R., Dow, D. and Boreham, P. (Eds.) (1980). *State, Class, and Recession*. London: Croom Helm.

Clegg, S.R. and Dunkerley, D. (1980). *Organization, Class and Control*. London: Sage.

18 *Jones et al.*

Clegg, S.R. and Dunkerley, D. (Eds.) (1977). *Critical Issues in Organizations.* London: Routledge & Kegan Paul.

Clegg, S.R., Hardy, C., Lawrence, T. and Nord, W. (2001). *Handbook of Organizational Studies* (2nd edition). London: Sage.

Clegg, S.R., Hardy, C. and Nord, W. (1996). *Handbook of Organizational Studies.* London: Sage.

Clegg, S.R., Linstead, S. and Sewell, G. (1999). Only Penguins: A Polemic on Organization Theory from the Edge of the World. *Organization Studies*, 20(7): 103–117.

Connell, R. (2007). *Southern Theory: The Global Dynamics of Knowledge in Social Science.* Sydney: Allen & Unwin.

Emery, M., Emery, F., and Associates (1975). *A Choice of Futures: To Enlighten and Inform.* Canberra, Australia: Center for Continuing Education, Australian National University.

Emery, F. and Thorsrud, E. (1976). *Democracy at Work.* Leiden: Martinus Nijoff.

Emery, F. and Trist, E. (1965). The Causal Texture of Organizational Environments. *Human Relations*, 18: 21–32.

Fairclough, N. (2005). Discourse Analysis in Organization Studied: The Case for Critical Realism. *Organization Studies*, 26: 915–939.

Fitzgibbons, Dale E. and Maria, Humphries (2011). Enhancing the Circle of Life: Management Education and Indigenous Knowledge. *Journal of Management Education*, 35(1): 3–7.

Fournier, V. and Grey, C. (2000). At the Critical Moment: Conditions and Prospects for Critical Management Studies. *Human Relations*, 53(1): 7–32.

Gillespie, R. (1991). *Manufacturing Knowledge: A History of the Hawthorne Experiments.* Cambridge: Cambridge University Press.

Grant, D., Hardy, C., Oswick, C. and Putnam, L. (Eds.) (2004). *The Sage Handbook of Organizational Discourse.* London: Sage.

Grant, D., Hardy, C. and Putnam, L. (Eds.) (2011). *Organizational Discourse Studies (Volumes I–III).* London: Sage.

Hall, P.R. and Soskice, D. (2001). *Varieties of Capitalism: The Institutional Foundations of Comparative Advantage.* Oxford: Oxford University Press.

Hampson, I., Ewer, P. and Smith, M. (1994). Post-Fordism and Workplace Change: Towards a Critical Research Agenda. *Journal of Industrial Relations*, 36: 231–257.

Hardy, C. and Maguire, S. (2010). Discourse, Field-Configuring Events, and Change in Organizations and Institutional Fields: Narratives of DDT and the Stockholm Convention. *Academy of Management Journal*, 53: 1365–1392.

Hardy, C. and Phillips, N. (2002). *Discourse Analysis: Investigating Processes of Social Construction.* London: Sage.

Harley, B. (2004). Managing Industrial Conflict. In J. Isaac and S. Macintyre (Eds.), *The New Province for Law and Order: 100 Years of Australian Industrial Conciliation and Arbitration*, 316–354. Cambridge: Cambridge University Press.

Heller, F. (1997). Sociotechnology and the Environment. *Human Relations*, 50: 605–624.

Henry, E. and Pene, H. (2001). Kaupapa Māori: Locating Indigenous Ontology, Epistemology and Methodology in the Academy. *Organization*, 8(2): 234–242.

Henry, E. and Pringle, J. (1996). Making Voices, Being Heard in Aotearoa/New Zealand. *Organization*, 3(4): 534–540.

Hooper, K. and Pratt, M. (1993). The Growth of Agricultural Capitalism and the Power of Accounting: A New Zealand Study. *Critical Perspectives on Accounting*, 4: 247–274.

Jack, Gavin, Zhu, Yunxia, Barney, Jay, Brannen, Mary Jo, Prichard, Craig, Singh, Kulwant and Whetton, David (2012). Reinforcing and Reimagining Universal and Indigenous Theory Development in International Management. *Journal of Management Inquiry*, 22(2): 148–164.

Australia and New Zealand   19

Jones, D. and Creed, D. (2011). Your Basket and My Basket: Teaching and Learning About Māori-Pākehā Bicultural Organizing. *Journal of Management Education*, 35(1): 84–101.

Jones, D., Pringle, J. and Shepherd, D. (2000). 'Managing Diversity' Meets Aotearoa/ New Zealand. *Personnel Review*, 29(3): 364–380.

Kearins, K. and Hooper, K. (2002). Genealogical Method. *Accounting, Auditing & Accountability Journal*, 15(5): 733–757.

Kwon, S.-W. and Adler, P.S. (2014). Social Capital: Maturation of a Field of Research. *Academy of Management Review*, 39: 412–442.

Lawrence, T., Hardy, C. and Phillips, N. (2002). Institutional Effects of Interorganizational Collaboration: The Emergence of Proto-Institutions. *Academy of Management Journal*, 45: 281–290.

Littler, C.R. (1978). Understanding Taylorism. *British Journal of Sociology*, 29: 185–202.

Littler, C.R. (1982). *The Development of the Labour Process in Capitalist Societies: A Comparative Study of the Transformation of Work Organization in Britain, Japan, and the USA*. London: Heinemann.

Littler, C.R. and Salaman, G. (1982). Bravermania and Beyond: Recent Theories of the Labour Process. *Sociology*, 16: 251–269.

Littler, C.R. and Salaman, G. (1984). *Class at Work: The Design, Allocation & Control of Jobs*. London: Batsford.

Maguire, S. and Hardy, C. (2009). Discourse and Deinstitutionalization: The Decline of DDT. *Academy of Management Journal*, 52: 148–178.

Manhire, B. (1991). Milky Way Bar. In *Milky Way Bar*. Wellington: Victoria University Press. Retrieved from www.wellingtonwriterswalk.co.nz/the-sculptures/bill-manhire/

Markey, R. (1996). Race and Organised Labor in Australia, 1850–1901. *The Historian*, 58: 343–61.

Mayo, E. (1919). *Democracy and Freedom: An Essay in Social Logic*. Melbourne: Macmillan.

Mika, J.P. and O'Sullivan, J.G. (2014). A Māori Approach to Management: Contrasting Traditional and Modern Māori Management Practices in Aotearoa New Zealand. *Journal of Management & Organization*, 20(5): 648–670.

Mira Szászy, F. (n.d.) The Mira Szászy Research Centre for Māori and Pacific Economic Development. University of Auckland. Retrieved from http://www.business. auckland.ac.nz/en/about/our-research/bs-research-institutes-and-centres/mira-szaszy-research-centre-for-māori-and-pacific-economic-development.html

OIL (n.d.a) Organization, Identity and Locality (OIL): Critical Studies of Management and Organizing in Aotearoa/New Zealand. Retrieved from http://www. massey.ac.nz/~cprichar/oil.htm

OIL (n.d.b) OIL Bibliography. Retrieved from http://www.massey.ac.nz/~cprichar/ OIL/Bibliography.htm

Panoho, J. and Stablein, R.E. (2012). A Postcolonial Perspective on Organizational Governance in New Zealand: Reconciling Māori and Pākehā Forms. In A. Prasad (Ed.), *Against the Grain: Advances in Postcolonial Organization Studies*, Vol. 28, 200–217. Copenhagen, Denmark: Copenhagen Business School Press/Liber.

Phillips, N., Lawrence, T. and Hardy, C. (2004). Discourse and Institutions. *Academy of Management Review*, 29: 635–652.

Prichard, C. (2006). A Warm Embrace? New Zealand, Universities and the 'Knowledge-based Economy'. *Social Epistemology*, 20(3–4): 283–297.

Prichard, C., Sayers, J. and Bathurst, R. (2007). Franchise, Margin and Locale; Notes on Constructing a Critical Management Studies Locale in Aotearoa/New Zealand. *New Zealand Sociology*, 22(1): 22–44.

Pringle, J. and Mallon, M. (2003). Challenges for the Boundaryless Career Odyssey. *International Journal of Human Resource Management*, 14(5): 839–853.

20 *Jones et al.*

Pringle, J.K., Wolfgramm, R. and Henry, E. (2010). Extending Cross-ethnic Research Partnerships: Researching with Respect. In S. Katila, S. Meriläinen and J. Tienari (Eds.), *Making Inclusion Work: Experiences from Academia Around the World*, 127–141. Cheltenham, UK: Edward Elgar.

Rashbrooke, M. (Ed.) (2013). *Inequality: A New Zealand Crisis*. Wellington: Bridget Williams Books.

Rowse, T. (2004). Elusive Middle Ground: A Political History. In J. Isaac and S. Macintyre (Eds.), *The New Province for Law and Order: 100 Years of Australian Industrial Conciliation and Arbitration*, 17–34. Cambridge: Cambridge University Press.

Ruwhiu, D., and Wolfgramm, R. (2006). Kaupapa Māori Research, A Contribution to Critical Management Studies in New Zealand. In *Critical Management in Aotearoa*, New Zealand Symposium, 9–10 February 2006. Victoria School of Management, Victoria University of Wellington.

Sewell, G. (1998). The Discipline of Teams: The Control of Team-Based Industrial Work Through Electronic and Peer Surveillance. *Administrative Science Quarterly*, 43: 397–428.

Sewell, G. and Wilkinson, B. (1992). 'Someone to Watch Over Me': Surveillance, Discipline and the Just-in-Time Labour Process. *Sociology*, 26: 271–289.

Simmons, G., and Stringer, C. (2014). New Zealand' s fisheries management system: forced labour an ignored or overlooked dimension? *Marine Policy*, 50: 74–80.

Smith, G. (2012). Interview: Kaupapa Māori—The dangers of domestication. *New Zealand Journal of Educational Studies*, 47(2): 10–20.

Smith, L. (1999). Decolonizing methodologies: research and indigenous peoples. London: Zed Books.

Tatz, C. (2003). *With Intent to Destroy: Reflecting on Genocide*. London: Verso.

Trist, E. and Bamforth, K.W. (1951). Some Social and Psychological Consequences of the Longwall Method of Coal-Getting: An Examination of the Psychological Situation and Defences of a Work Group in Relation to the Social Structure and Technological Content of the Work System. *Human Relations*, 4: 3–38.

Trist, E. and Murray, H. (1990). Historical Overview: The Foundation and Development of the Tavistock Institute to 1989. In E. Trist and H. Murray (Eds.), *The Social Engagement of Social Science: Volume I, The Socio-Psychological Perspective*, 1–37. London: Tavistock Institute.

Verbos, A.K., and Humphries, M. (2015). Amplifying a Relational Ethic: A Contribution to PRME Praxis. *Business and Society Review*, 120: 23–56.

Wodak, R. (2006). Dilemmas of Discourse (Analysis). *Language in Society*, 35: 595–611.

2 Non-Managerial Management Scholarship in Belgium, the Netherlands and Luxemburg

Patrizia Zanoni and Laurent Taskin

In this chapter, we would like to reconstruct the critically oriented scholarship in management studies conducted in the Benelux—the European cross-national region including Belgium, the Netherlands and Luxemburg—over the last two decades. While reflecting national and regional specificities, we will show how this scholarship relates to the ideas at the core of Critical Management Studies (CMS) and, to a large extent, the broader international community, which has come to identify with it since its origins in the early 1990s. Indeed, the CMS community has from its very beginning included scholars from around the globe, as indicated by the 20 countries of origins of the 400 participants to the first CMS Conference held in Manchester in 1999 (Adler et al., 2007) and the fact that the membership of the CMS Interest Group and later CMS Division has historically been one of the most international of the Academy of Management.

While it has been stressed that critiques of capitalism and management have been present in the whole second half of the twentieth century and draw on prior classical sociological traditions, such as Marx, Weber and Durkheim, the historical origins of CMS as a political scholarly project are more recent and geographically more circumscribed. They lie in the UK and the Scandinavian countries, two regions which remain today central in the production of critical work. These roots are grounded in a theoretical debate within the neo-Marxist scholarly community in the UK of the late 1980s and 1990s. Till then, critically oriented research had, in the wake of Braverman's *Labor and Monopoly Capital* (1974), largely studied organizations through a labour-process lens evidencing long-term changes in the material organization of work, entailing deskilling, enabling capital accumulation and eroding the position of labour in its relation to capital (Gomez, 2013). Influenced by the linguistic turn in the social sciences and the increasing popularity of post-structuralist theories, some critically oriented scholars drew attention to the need to adopt new theoretical lenses enabling them to address the role of ideology and language in the operation of power and control in contemporary capitalist workplaces. It called for attending to the operation of power in organizations in novel ways in order to cater to the effects on subjects and subjectivity of fundamental shifts capitalism was undergoing at the time (Knights and Willmott, 1989; Alvesson and Willmott, 1992).

22   Patrizia Zanoni and Laurent Taskin

Against the backdrop of far-reaching structural changes in late capitalism during the Thatcher-Reagan era, CMS scholars initially highlighted the role of language and ideology—often in the form of hegemonic discourses—in shaping, sustaining and legitimizing the new realities of work and organizations and novel forms of subjectivities within them (Knights and Willmott, 1989). At its origin, CMS thus emerged as an alternative, critically oriented scholarly project breaking away from materialism and its underlying positivistic epistemology. While this ongoing epistemological, theoretical and political debate within the critical community in the past often took sharp, polemical and even personal tones (e.g. Thompson and Ackroyd, 2005; cf. the debate published in third issue of volume 7 of *Organization* in 2000), in the last years, it has somewhat tempered. This is illustrated by edited volumes including critical management scholarship resting on a broad variety of theoretical and epistemological traditions under the label CMS (cf. Alvesson et al., 2009) as well as broader theoretical debates in the discipline on the articulation of the symbolic and the material in organization studies (e.g. Putnam, 2015), likely triggered by the indisputably 'material' effects of a long-lasting economic crisis, raising inequality and global environmental degradation.

MAPPING CMS IN BENELUX: A PRAGMATIC PERSPECTIVE

Against the backdrop of this scholarly movement, in the remainder of the text, we attempt to draw a map of the critically oriented management research geographically and thematically most close to us and of which we are ourselves a part. Needless to say, this is in no way an easy task, and the result will inevitably reflect our own specific spatio-temporal position within this region in the historical periphery of CMS. To complicate matters, although we are both in Belgium, Patrizia is in the Dutch-speaking Flemish region, a region whose academic community is more connected—both institutionally and in terms of networks—to the Netherlands, and Laurent is in the French-speaking Walloon region, whose academics have historically been more connected to France and Luxembourg. In the light of the institutional complexity within our own country and, even more, of the Benelux, we would like to stress that we have no pretention to portray 'Benelux CMS' as a coherent body of scholarship. We will more humbly identify critically oriented scholars active in this region, bottom up, and discuss how we understand their work in relation to the main tenets of CMS as an intellectual tradition and a community.

Our overview is organized around select key topics which have been investigated by individuals or small groups. These scholars are embedded in partially different networks and do not even necessarily identify with the CMS community. However, they—we—do share a basic non-functionalistic, non-managerial approach to management research, one that could best

Non-Managerial Scholarship in Belgium 23

be labelled, with Fournier and Grey (2000), as denaturalizing and non-performative. Whereas we all address the dynamics of power and meaning in the world of work and organizations, this occurs through heterogeneous theoretical lenses, more or less stressing the discursive versus the material, and more or less performing critique through the deconstruction of meaning versus a more direct focus on power and inequality in se. Notwithstanding these differences, all the research presented here is in line with the ambitions of CMS as a political project. We deliberately exclude from our discussion scholarship which, despite its critical orientation, is embedded in other disciplines, such as sociology, social policy, political science, education, labour market studies, industrial relations and the humanities and which does not regularly engage in dialogue with management.

While we are aware that disciplinary borders are porous and our decision quite arbitrary, we ground our choice in political and practical reasons. Politically, we would like to focus our analysis on the distinctive contribution of critical scholars in the Benelux to management, a discipline in which the legitimacy of critical thinking is in many contexts permanently interrogated, to the extent that mainstream scholars see 'non-performative' management research as an oxymoron. This puts many of us more often than our colleagues in other disciplines under close intellectual scrutiny. Practically, including scholarship produced outside management would reduce our map to a (much longer) list of people and topics and stand in the way of any attempt to make sense of it, given that many enabling and hampering contextual factors are discipline specific.

In the following section, we present five key research topics which have made the object of critical investigation by scholars based in the Benelux: gender, diversity and identity; workplace transformations; entrepreneurship; management, ethics and sustainability; and qualitative research, epistemology and reflexivity. In the concluding section of the chapter, we reflect on the context factors which in our eyes help explain the existence of these pockets of critical scholarship in an otherwise quite mainstream Benelux management field. Doing so, we attempt to provide explanations that go beyond the interests and preferences of individual scholars, accounting for the institutional conditions of (im)possibility for certain types of scholarship to emerge in our specific context(s).

GENDER, DIVERSITY AND IDENTITY

Undoubtedly, the largest cluster of critically oriented management research in the Benelux deals with gender, diversity and identity. In the Netherlands, critically oriented research on these topics is conducted by Yvonne Benschop and Marieke van den Brink at the Radboud Universiteit Nijmegen, Sierk Ybema and Ida Sabelis at the Free University of Amsterdam and Hans Siebers at the Universiteit van Tilburg. In Belgium, we can think of the work

24 *Patrizia Zanoni and Laurent Taskin*

of Maddy Janssens at KU Leuven, Patrizia Zanoni and Koen Van Laer at Hasselt University. In Luxembourg, Christina Constantinidis, previously at the University of Liège, is currently affiliated with the University of Luxembourg. These scholars draw from a variety of theoretical traditions yet as a whole share attention for the discursive construction of social identities—ranging from gender to ethnicity, nationality, religion, age and disability—and their intersections in work settings. They examine their hegemonic representations, the social and discursive processes through which they are negotiated and come into being, their relation to workplace and professional social practices, their effects on the work experiences of members of historically subordinated groups and, more broadly, on inequality.

Most of these scholars know each other personally, are familiar with each other's work, sometimes publish together, organize joint activities (e.g. streams at international conferences, guest edit special issues, the EqualDiv@ Work network, etc.), have sat in each other's PhD students' committees, etc. With few exceptions, they are also embedded in the CMS community through regular participation in conferences and positions on the editorial boards of European management journals which have historically been hospitable to CMS research, such as Organization, Gender, Work & Organization, Human Relations, Organization Studies, and Journal of Management Studies.

The critically oriented scholarship of the researchers at the Radboud Universiteit Nijmegen became internationally visible with the publication of an article on the gendered subtext of organizations by Yvonne Benschop and Hans Doorewaard in Organisation Studies in the late 1990s (Benschop and Doorewaard, 1998). Benschop's critically oriented work in the last decade, often in collaboration with Marieke van den Brink, has focused on gender inequality in organizations. Taking a micropolitical perspective, paying great attention to social (informal) practices within organizations, their research has contributed to international debates on the micro-processes of power and resistance leading to (im)possibilities of organizational change towards more gender equality. Specific topics include the gendered dynamics of networks leading to women's exclusion (Benschop, 2009; van den Brink and Benschop, 2014), gendered professional ideals and part-time work (Benschop et al., 2013) and gendered selection practices in the Dutch academia (van den Brink and Benschop, 2012a, 2012b; van den Brink et al., 2010).

In the late 1990s, Maddy Janssens initiated a line of critical research on diversity at the Faculty of Business and Economics of KU Leuven, which resulted in the publication, with Chris Steyaert, of a book, *Meerstemmigheid: Organiseren met verschil (Multi-Vocality: Organising with Difference*, 2001), which pioneered a non-positivistic approach to diversity in Dutch-speaking Belgium. In the following years, this research was further developed together with Patrizia, leading to the publication of an article on HR managers' discursive constructions of diversity reflected and reproduced power relations between social groups as well as management and labour (Zanoni and Janssens, 2004). As a whole, this work has contributed to

Non-Managerial Scholarship in Belgium 25

denaturalizing the meaning of social identities and theorizing their role in the reproduction of unequal power relations by highlighting their constitutive relation to specific organizational contexts and work processes (Janssens and Zanoni, 2005), occupations (Zanoni and Janssens, 2015), managerial control and employees' resistance (Zanoni and Janssens, 2007) and class relations (Zanoni, 2011). Maddy Janssens's work with Chris Steyaert, based at the University of Sinkt-Gallen in Switzerland, has rather taken the lens of cosmopolitanism to deconstruct the assumptions behind the dominance of English in the academia and advance alternatives (Steyaert and Janssens, 2013; Janssens and Steyaert, 2014).

In the last decade, some scholarship has emerged in the Benelux about the experiences, careers and identities of ethnic minorities at work from critical perspectives. Based at the Universiteit van Tilburg, Hans Siebers' scholarly work has combined discursive analysis, organizational ethnography and quantitative methods to expose the negative effects of xenophobic, anti-Islam societal discourses on everyday intergroup dynamics in organizations putting ethnic minority employees in a position of constant insecurity and harming their careers in terms of promotions and wages (Siebers, 2009a, 2009b). Taking a more discursive, identity-focused approach, Koen Van Laer at Hasselt University has investigated, in collaboration with Maddy Janssens, Muslim professionals' experiences of discrimination and their struggles to construct viable identities in the workplace (Van Laer and Janssens, 2011, 2014).

Last but not least, some scholars have worked on various aspects in the construction of identity in work settings. Sierk Ybema's work (in collaboration, among others, with Ida Sabelis) at the Vrije Universiteit Amsterdam notably deals with identity construction processes (Ybema et al., 2009), managers' identity construction in interorganizational relationships (Ellis and Ybema, 2010), intercultural settings (Ybema and Byun, 2009) and the temporal and collective nature of identity (Ybema, 2010). Affiliated to the same research group, Ida Sabelis also conducts research on identity and temporality (Sabelis, 2001, 2003, 2004) as well as gender and diversity in organizations (Sabelis et al., 2008; Ghorashi and Sabelis, 2013; Sabelis and Schilling, 2013). Finally, also addressing identity and power in international settings, Maddy Janssens published, with Tineke Cappellen and Patrizia, on identities in multinational contexts characterized by power struggles (Janssens et al., 2006; Cappellen et al., 2012).

WORKPLACE TRANSFORMATIONS

A second, more recent thematic cluster of critically oriented research in the Benelux deals with the organization of work and its transformations. In Belgium, critically oriented research on these topics is commonly associated with Matthieu de Nanteuil, Isabelle Ferreras, Evelyne Léonard, Laurent Taskin and Marc Zune at Université catholique de Louvain, François

26 Patrizia Zanoni and Laurent Taskin

Pichault at the Université de Liège and Claire Dupont at the University of Mons. These scholars draw in various ways from labour sociology, yet as a whole share attention for the discursive construction of new forms of work organization, exploring underlying justifications and rationalities as well as their consequences in terms of work regulation (social dialogue, corporate democracy, control or discipline) and the processes through which this re-regulation of work happens. They all denaturalize these 'new' forms of work organization by deconstructing the rationalities of the discourses used for promoting them as organizational 'innovations' and 'change'.

All affiliated to universities in the French-speaking region of Belgium, these scholars know each other, are familiar with each other's work, publish together, conduct common research projects and serve together as jury members of PhDs. In this cluster, Laurent is structurally tied to the international CMS community through participation in CMS conferences and his attempts, in collaboration with colleagues from Paris-Dauphine, EM Lyon Business school and Montpellier in France, to constitute a French-speaking CMS community, also referred to as the "French-Belgian CMS chapter" (see Palpacuer et al., 2014).

The critically oriented scholarship of the researchers at Louvain gained in visibility with the publication of a book on CMS theoretical, empirical and educational orientations in French-speaking regions, edited by Laurent and Matthieu de Nanteuil (2011). This book positioned the Louvain's tradition of critical thinking[1] under the umbrella of CMS and contributed to the institutionalization of critical management research in Wallonia. Also at the Université catholique de Louvain, Matthieu de Nanteuil has investigated labour flexibilization from a sociological and political philosophical point of view, in its subjective dimension and particularly its embodiment (de Nanteuil, 2009, 2011), and developing a political consideration of flexibilization processes in organizations, namely through theorizing compromise (El Akremi and de Nanteuil, 2005). He actively contributes to study workplace transformations in line with a critique of capitalism and labour relations drawing on justice theories (de Nanteuil, 2014). Isabelle Ferreras developed a critique of capitalism governance (Ferreras, 2012), while Marc Zune investigates the formation of a collective subject for action in free software communities (Demazière et al., 2009). Evelyne Léonard's research develops a non-managerial perspective on management from an institutionalist perspective on workplace transformations emphasizing how HRM-related regulations produce social norms and order (Léonard, 2015).

In the mid-2000s, Laurent initiated a line of critical research on 'new' forms of work organization, studying especially the transformation of control norms in the context of teleworking (Taskin and Edwards, 2007; Heckscher et al., 2012). His research highlighted the raise of more socio-ideological forms of control contributing to the disciplinarization of workers (and their bodies) as well as to work degradation (Taskin and Raone, 2014), far from the promised 'liberating' perspective associated to new forms of organization. His work also contributed to international debates on the role of space and identity in the study of workplace transformations through

Non-Managerial Scholarship in Belgium   27

the conceptualization of the notions of distantiation and de spatialization (Taskin, 2010; Sewell and Taskin, 2015).

Based at the University of Liège, François Pichault's research focuses on the effects ICT-driven changes may have on organizations, management and employees. He developed a multiparadigmatic approach for studying and managing change (Pichault, 2013). While refusing to consider himself as a member of the CMS community, he published a book, with Jean Nizet, summarizing theories, methodologies and other common traits to critical research in management (Nizet and Pichault, 2015).

ENTREPRENEURSHIP

Over the last decade, a few Benelux management scholars have adopted alternative approaches to entrepreneurship. It would be inappropriate here to talk about a community, as these researchers do not collaborate and take quite distinct angles to this topic of study. Amélie Jacquemin and Frank Janssen (2013), based at the Université catholique de Louvain, adopted a Foucauldian approach to deconstruct the taken-for-granted discourses on entrepreneurship, showing how they rest on an ideology of economic dereg-ulation. A similar analysis denaturalizing the neo-liberal dominant discourse on entrepreneurship has been conducted by Janssen and Schmitt (2011), while other essays inviting more critical perspectives to entrepreneurship also gained momentum (Janssen and Taskin, 2012).

The interrogation of dominant representations of entrepreneurship is also central to the work of Christina Constantinidis, Caroline Essers and, more recently, of Patrizia with Annelies Thoelen. Leveraging the 'diversity' lens thesis, scholars examine entrepreneurship from its margins, through the eyes of subordinate social groups: women, self-employed ethnic minority cre-atives and female Muslim entrepreneurs, respectively. Affiliated today to the University of Luxembourg, Christina Constantinidis has examined the challenges encountered by girls in the succession dynamics within family firms (Constantinidis, 2010a; Constantinidis and Nelson, 2009) and decon-structed dominant representations of gender within female entrepreneurial networks (Constantinidis, 2010b). Rather intersecting ethnicity and gender, Caroline Essers has, partially in collaboration with Yvonne Benschop and others, examined the complexity of identity construction by ethnic minority female entrepreneurs in the Netherlands (Essers and Benschop, 2007, 2009; Essers et al., 2010, 2013; Essers and Tedmanson, 2014; Pio and Essers, 2014). Highlighting the discursive performativity required from individuals who make a living through self-employment, Patrizia's recent work with Annelies Thoelen (Thoelen and Zanoni, 2014, forthcoming), deploys dis-course analysis to deconstruct the identities of ethnic minority entrepreneurs in the Belgian creative industries and rhetoric to investigate their claims on symbolic and economic value from their contradictory position as alleged repository of superior creativity and as ethnic 'others'.

28 *Patrizia Zanoni and Laurent Taskin*

MANAGEMENT, ETHICS AND SUSTAINABILITY

In multiple collaborations with other critically oriented scholars based in other countries, René Ten Bos has drawn on post-structuralist theories to examine a broad variety of managerial subjects often highlighting their ethical dimension (Ten Bos, 2003, 2007; Kaulingfreks and Ten Bos, 2005; Campbell et al., 2006). Sustainability is also investigated by Matthieu de Nanteuil (2009), who questions the related issues in terms of justice, proposing to emancipate from a functionalist perspective of corporate social responsibility. Drawing on an ethic of recognition, he sketches the outlines of a social critique promoting a post-distributive solidarity. In Liège, Xhauflair and Pichault (2012, 2014) propose a reflexive approach on sustainable employment relations, drawing on previous action research they conducted on flexicurity. Finally, Maddy Janssens has drawn on the concept of cosmopolitanism to envision a more ethical approach to international HRM (Janssens and Steyaert, 2012).

QUALITATIVE RESEARCH, EPISTEMOLOGY AND REFLEXIVITY

Critically oriented scholars in the Benelux have also published on qualitative methodologies and reflective papers on their own research and educational practice. Perhaps most known in this area of study is the work of Dwora Yanow, who was affiliated to the Vrije Universiteit Amsterdam between 2005 and 2010. She has mainly published on organizational ethnography, regularly in collaboration with Sierk Ybema and Ida Sabelis (Miettinen et al., 2009; Yanow, 2014; Yanow et al., 2012). Other examples of scholarship in this cluster include a volume edited by Sierk Ybema and colleagues (2009) on organizational ethnography, Caroline Essers' (2009) reflective article in *Organization* on her own fieldwork and, more recently, a reflective chapter on doing qualitative research on diversity (Zanoni and Van Laer, 2015). In addition, much of the critical research produced in our region reflects a consolidated expertise in a variety of qualitative research methods (ethnography, narratives, discursive analysis, etc.) and often includes a self-reflective stance and a broader epistemological reflection (Essers, 2009; Taskin and de Nanteuil, 2011; Van Laer and Janssens, 2014).

MAKING SENSE OF LOCAL ACCENTS: BETWEEN GLOBAL AND LOCAL DYNAMICS

Attempting to make sense of the scholarship presented earlier, in this section, we first reflect on three aspects that, in our eyes, have enabled Benelux researchers to conduct management research through critical lenses in line with the broader CMS as a political project and that are thus recognizable to CMS as a scholarly community. We then point to the specificities, 'the local accents', of the critically oriented scholarship in the Benelux and advance what we see as possible explanations for it.

Perhaps first and most important is the observation that critically oriented management scholarship in our region reflects those same broad social, economic and institutional trends which historically triggered the emergence of CMS as an intellectual project within the UK and Scandinavian countries. To the extent that these small, open-economy countries partake in contemporary global capitalism, they similarly see the emergence of critiques to it. Over the two last decades, the role of the market has substantially increased in all areas of society, away from classical 'coordinated market economies' in the sense of Hall and Soskice (2001), although at different paces and in partially specific ways. A second point of convergence across national borders lies in critical theoretical traditions on which CMS rests. To the extent that these traditions are shared across national borders, they provide common analytical languages to conduct critical research which can be understood and diffused internationally. Stressing the advantages of eclecticism, Willmott observes that

> the plurality of approaches and debates collected within the 'big tent' of CMS (. . .) can be a strength when it enables management academics, who might otherwise be isolated and vulnerable, to gain a degree of credibility and respect by gathering under its broad banner.
>
> (2011, p. 13)

Finally, and quite paradoxically, the accelerated internationalization of the social sciences and business research in particular, including the increased dominance of English as the language of international scholarship, the multiplication of international management conferences and the diffusion of officially ranked, international peer-reviewed journals as the main criterion for assessing research quality and making or breaking academic careers have homogenized academics' professional experiences and facilitated critical dialogues across national borders. In this sense, the globalization of management research has paradoxically enabled the emergence of critical management research in multiple locations for consumption by an international CMS audience. The international currency of critically oriented management studies has enabled scholars at the geographical centre of CMS to acquire and retain key positions within the academic field to uphold the legitimacy of CMS within the broader field of management (cf. Fournier and Grey, 2000). This has undoubtedly, in turn, opened up possibilities for critical scholars and critical scholarship at the historical periphery of CMS—including our own—albeit, as some have observed, not without costs in terms of exclusion (Bridgman and Stephens, 2008; Tatli, 2012).

30   *Patrizia Zanoni and Laurent Taskin*

At the same time, we should remark that critically oriented scholarship in the Benelux remains, at least numerically, a quite marginal phenomenon. Perhaps because of this reason, we observe an almost complete absence of most radical and overtly polemical approaches to management critique, which are more common elsewhere in CMS. In other words, Benelux CMS scholarship is not very 'muscular' nor does it f*** management. While we write for an informed public, we often do not write for a partisan one. In general, we work on issues that are recognizable to a wider audience and attempt to 'unpack' them critically, analysing, deconstructing, de-essentializing and sometimes sensitizing. The force of this work lies in the alternative readings of organizational reality advanced in a more or less radical, yet seldom an aggressive, rhetoric, although politeness is sometimes equated with theoretical weakness (cf. Sandberg and Alvesson, 2011).

At the risk of overinterpreting, we are tempted to see these characteristics as reflecting not only individual preferences but also the societal and institutional contexts in which we function. Specifically, we are thinking of the demise of the variety of coordinated capitalism models on which our societies have historically rested, which is today interrogating the functioning of institutions and organizations around us. Despite their own specificities, in the last two decades, our societies have all been struggling with the flexibilization of protective employment regimes, the demise of welfare state provisions, marketization of public services, the limits encountered by women's emancipation in the professional sphere and the persistence of large-scale ethnic inequality against the backdrop of rising ethnic diversity.

These of course are not Benelux-specific issues. What is specific, however, is how we, as scholars embedded within universities which have historically been public and 'democratic', are expected (and even forced) to engage on these issues. In systems in which university students are 'non-paying clients' (although this is somewhat changing in the Netherlands, where marketization is most advanced, as shown by the recent students' protest in Amsterdam) and public funding is limited and even eroding, academics are called to enter multiple dialogues beyond their intellectual community, structurally engaging with other audiences, including policy makers, public administrations, companies, university apparatuses, trade unions, etc. We are, more than others, caught in multiple nets of accountability on which we depend for funding, visibility, legitimacy and overall impact. While this praxis might feed into a sense of alienation of the intellect and certainly make us more vulnerable to co-optation, it does help keep one reflective on one's work as part of society, not outside, not above (cf. Fournier and Smith, 2012). This praxis reflects the specificity and the complexity of our positions at the 'periphery of CMS', which, as is often the case, undoubtedly hampers the emergence of some modalities of critically oriented work, yet enables other that are less likely and common elsewhere.

NOTE

1. It is interesting to note that this critique developed at the periphery of the school of management and, primarily, within the Institute for Labour Studies of the Université catholique de Louvain, where a critique of labour relations has developed over a long time. All the scholars mentioned here are also affiliated to this multidisciplinary school devoted to labour studies.

REFERENCES

Adler, P., Forbes, L. and Willmott, H. (2007). Critical Management Studies. *Annals of the Academy of Management*, 1(1): 1–61.

Alvesson, M., Bridgman, T. and Willmott, H. (Eds.) (2009). *The Oxford Handbook of Critical Management Studies*. Oxford: Oxford University Press.

Alvesson, M. and Willmott, H. (Eds.) (1992). *Critical Management Studies*. London: Sage.

Benschop, Y. (2009). The Micro-Politics of Gendering in Networking. *Gender, Work and Organization*, 16(2): 217–237.

Benschop, Y. and Doorewaard, H. (1998). Covered by Equality, the Gender Subtext of Organizations. *Organization Studies*, 19(5): 787–805.

Benschop, Y., van den Brink, M., Doorewaard, H. and Leenders, J. (2013). Beyond the Usual Suspects: Ambition, Gender and Part-Time Work. *Human Relations*, 66(5): 699–723.

Bridgman, T. and Stephens, M. (2008). Institutionalizing Critique: A Problem of Critical Management Studies. *Ephemera*, 8(3): 258–270.

Campbell, J., Parker, M. and Ten Bos, R. (2006). *For Business Ethics*. London: Routledge.

Cappellen, T., Zanoni, P. and Janssens, M. (2012). Human Resource Management in Contemporary Transnational Companies. In R. Kramar and J. Syed (Eds.), *Human Resource Management in a Global Context: A Critical Approach*, 55–74. London: Palgrave McMillan.

Constantinidis, C. (2010a). Entreprise familiale et genre: Les enjeux de la succession pour les filles. *Revue Française de Gestion*, 36(200): 143–159.

Constantinidis, C. (2010b). Représentations sur le genre et réseaux d'affaires chez les femmes Entrepreneures. *Revue Française de Gestion*, 36(202): 127–143.

Constantinidis, C. and Nelson, T. (2009). Integrating Succession and Gender Issues from the Perspective of the Daughter of Family Enterprise across the U.S. and EU. *Management International*, 14(1): 43–54.

de Nanteuil, M. (2009). *La démocratie insensible. Economie et politique à l'épreuve du corps*. Toulouse: Eres.

de Nanteuil, M. (2011). Un autre monde . . . ou un monde plus juste ? Pour une anthropologie critique du Management. In L. Taskin and M. de Nanteuil (Eds.), *Perspectives critiques en management: Pour une gestion citoyenne*, 239–265. Brussels: de Boeck, coll. Recherches et Méthodes.

de Nanteuil, M. (2014). Travail et sens de la justice en régime libéral: Perspectives critiques pour la réflexion et l'action. In L. Taskin, D. Desmette, E. Léonard, P. Reman, P. Vendramein and M. Zune (Eds.), *Transformations du travail: Regards Multidisciplinaires*, 78–99. Louvain-la-Neuve: Presses universitaires de Louvain.

Demazière, D., Horn, F., Zune, M., 2009. La socialisation dans les "communautés" de développement de logiciels libres. *Sociologie et sociétés*, 40(2): 217–238.

El Akremi, A. and de Nanteuil, M. (Eds.) (2005). *La société flexible. Travail, emploi, organisation en débat*. Toulouse: Eres.

32 Patrizia Zanoni and Laurent Taskin

Ellis, N. and Ybema, S. (2010). Marketing Identities: Shifting Circles of Identification. *Organization Studies*, 31(3): 279–305.

Essers, C. (2009). Reflections on the Narrative Approach: Dilemmas of Power, Emotions and Social Location While Constructing Life-Stories. *Organization*, 16(2): 163–181.

Essers, C. and Benschop, Y. (2007). Enterprising Identities: Female Entrepreneurs of Moroccan and Turkish Origin in the Netherlands. *Organization Studies*, 28(1): 49–69.

Essers, C. and Benschop, Y. (2009). Muslim Businesswomen Doing Boundary Work: The Negotiation of Islam, Gender and Ethnicity Within Entrepreneurial Contexts. *Human Relations*, 62(3): 403–424.

Essers, C., Benschop, Y. and Doorewaard, H. (2010). Female Ethnicity: Understanding Muslim Migrant Businesswomen in the Netherlands. *Gender, Work and Organization*, 17(3): 320–340.

Essers, C., Doorewaard, H. and Benschop, Y. (2013). Family Ties: Migrant Business Women Doing Identity Work on the Public-Private Divide. *Human Relations*, 16(12): 1645–1665.

Essers, C. and Tedmanson, D. (2014). Upsetting 'others' in the Netherlands: Narratives of Muslim Turkish Migrant Business Women at the Crossroads of Ethnicity, Gender and Religion. *Gender, Work and Organization*, 21(4): 353–367.

Ferreras, I. (2012). *Gouverner le capitalisme?* Paris: Presses Universitaires de France.

Fournier, V. and Grey, C. (2000). At the Critical Moment: Conditions and Prospects for Critical Management Studies. *Human Relations*, 53(1): 7–32.

Fournier, V. and Smith, W. (2012). Making Choice, Taking Risk: On the Coming Out of Critical Management Studies. *Ephemera*, 12(4): 463–474.

Ghorashi, H. and Sabelis, I.H.J. (2013). Juggling Difference and Sameness: Rethinking Strategies for Diversity in Organizations. *Scandinavian Journal of Management*, 29(1): 78–86.

Gomez, P.-Y. (2013). *Le travail invisible: Enquête sur une disparition*. Paris: François Bourin Editeur.

Hall, P.A. and Soskice, D. (2001). *Varieties of Capitalism: The Institutional Foundations of Comparative Advantage*. Oxford: Oxford University Press.

Heckscher, C., Sewell, G. and Taskin, L. (2012). New Forms of (Work) Organization: Studying the Transformation of Work in an Amoral and Lawless World. *International Journal of Work Innovation*, 1(1): 5–9.

Jacquemin, A. and Janssen, F. (2013). Deconstructing Research on Regulation and Entrepreneurship: A Foucaldian Discourse Analysis. *8th International Conference on CMS*, Manchester, MA.

Janssen, F. and Schmitt, C. (2011). L'entrepreneur, héros des temps modernes? Pour une analyse critique de l'entrepreneuriat, In L. Taskin and M. de Nanteuil (Eds.), *Perspectives critiques en management. Pour une gestion citoyenne*, 163–184. Brussels: De Boeck, coll. Méthodes et Recherche.

Janssen, F. and Taskin, L. (2012). Quelles spécificités pour l'étude du changement entrepreneurial? *Revue Interdisciplinaire sur le Management et l'Humanisme*, 3: 87–95.

Janssens, M., Cappellen, T. and Zanoni, P. (2006). Successful Female Expatriates as Agents: Positioning Oneself Through Gender, Hierarchy and Culture. *Journal of World Business*, 41(2): 133–148.

Janssens, M. and Steyaert, C. (2012). Towards an Ethical Research Agenda for International HRM: The Possibilities of a Plural Cosmopolitan Framework. *Journal of Business Ethics*, 111(1): 61–72.

Janssens, M. and Steyaert, C. (2014). Re-Considering Language Within a Cosmopolitan Understanding: Towards a Multilingual Franca Approach in International Business Studies. *Journal of International Business Studies*, 45: 623–639.

Non-Managerial Scholarship in Belgium 33

Janssens, M. and Zanoni, P. (2005). Many Diversities for Many Services: Theorizing Diversity (Management) in Service Companies. *Human Relations*, 58(3): 311–340.

Kaulingfreks, R. and Ten Bos, R. (2005). Are Organizations Bicycles? *Culture & Organization*, 11(2): 29–44.

Knights, D. and Willmott, H. (1989). Power and Subjectivity at Work: From Degradation to Subjugation in Social Relations. *Sociology*, 23: 251–273.

Léonard, E. (2015). *Ressources humaines: Gérer les personnes et l'ordre social dans l'entreprise*. Brussels: De Boeck, coll. Manager RH.

Miettinen, R., Samra-Fredericks, D. and Yanow, D. (2009). Re-turn to Practice. *Organization Studies*, 30(12): 1309–1493.

Nizet, J. and Pichault, F. (2015). *Les critiques de la gestion*. Paris: La Découverte, coll. Repères.

Palpacuer, F., Perret, V. and Taskin, L. (2014). *The French-Belgian CMS Chapter*. Retrieved from http://www.criticalmanagement.org/node/3192

Pichault, F. (2013). *Change Management: Towards Polyphony*. Brussels: De Boeck, coll. Manager RH.

Pio, E. and Essers, C. (2014). Professional Migrant Women Decentering Otherness: A Transnational Perspective. *British Journal of Management*, 25(2): 252–265.

Putnam, L.L. (2015). Unpacking the Dialectic: Alternative Views on the Discourse–Materiality Relationship. *Journal of Management Studies*, 52(5): 706–716.

Sabelis, I.H.J. (2001). Time Management. Paradoxes and Patterns. *Time and Society*, 10(2/2): 387–400.

Sabelis, I.H.J. (2003). Tijd: hoe meer beheersing, hoe drukker het wordt. *Maandblad voor accountancy en bedrijfseconomie*, 77(1/2): 60–66.

Sabelis, I.H.J. (2004). Versnelling en verbinding, een timescape-perspectief op organisaties. *Filosofie in Bedrijf*, 16(2–3): 37–44.

Sabelis, I.H.J., Knights, D., Nencel, L.S. and Odih, P. (2008). Questioning the Construction of 'balance': A Time Perspective on Gender and Organization. *Gender, Work and Organization*, 15(5): 423–429.

Sabelis, I.H.J. and Schilling, E. (2013). Frayed Careers: Exploring Rhythms of Working Lives. *Gender, Work and Organization*, 20(2): 127–132.

Sandberg, J. and Alvesson, M. (2011). Ways of Constructing Research Questions: Gap-spotting or Problematization? *Organization*, 18(1): 23–44.

Sewell, G. and Taskin, L. (2015). Out of Sight, Out of Mind in a New World of Work? Autonomy, Control, and Spatiotemporal Scaling in Telework. *Organization Studies*, 36(11): 1507–1529

Siebers, H. (2009a). (Post)Bureaucratic Organizational Practices and the Production of Racioethnic Inequality at Work. *Journal of Management and Organization*, 15(1): 62–81.

Siebers, H. (2009b). Struggles for Recognition: The Politics of Racioethnic Identity Among Dutch National Tax Administrators. *Scandinavian Journal of Management*, 25(1): 73–84.

Steyaert, C. and Janssens, M. (2013). Multilingual Scholarship and the Paradox of Translation and Language in Management and Organization Studies. *Organization*, 20(1): 131–142.

Taskin, L. (2010). Déspatialisation: un enjeu de gestion. *Revue Française de Gestion*, 36(202): 61–76.

Taskin, L. and de Nanteuil, M. (Eds.) (2011). *Perspectives Critiques en Management: Pour une gestion citoyenne*. Brussels: De Boeck, coll. Recherches et Méthodes.

Taskin, L. and Edwards, P.K. (2007). The Possibilities and Limits of Telework in a Bureaucratic Environment: Lessons from the Public Sector. *New Technology, Work and Employment*, 22(3): 195–207.

Taskin, L. and Raone, J. (2014). Flexibilité et disciplinarisation: repenser le contrôle en situation de distanciation. *Economies et Sociétés*, Série KC, 3(1): 35–69.

34 Patrizia Zanoni and Laurent Taskin

Tatli, A. (2012). On the Power and Poverty of Critical (Self) Reflection in Critical Management Studies: A Comment on Ford, Harding and Learmonth. *British Journal of Management*, 23(1): 22–30.

Ten Bos, R. (2003). *Rationele engelen. Moraliteit en management*. Amsterdam: Boom.

Ten Bos, R. (2007). Business ethics. In S. Clegg and J. Bailey (Eds.), *International Encyclopedia of Organization Studies*, Vol. 1, 118–122. London: Sage Publications.

Thoelen, A. and Zanoni, P. (2014). Making Claims on Value: The Rhetoric Construction of Aesthetic Innovation by Ethnic Minority Creative. *Culture and Organization*. doi:10.1080/14759551.2014.921819

Thoelen, A. and Zanoni, P. (forthcoming). Ethnic Minority Entrepreneurs' Construction of Legitimacy: 'Fitting in' and 'standing out' in the Creative Industries. In C. Essers, P. Dey, D. Tedmanson and K. Verduyn (Eds.), *Critical Perspectives on Entrepreneurship: Challenging Dominant Discourses in Entrepreneurship*. London: Routledge.

Thompson, P. and Ackroyd, S. (2005). A Little Knowledge is Still a Dangerous Thing: Some Comments on the Indeterminacy of Graham Sewell. *Organization*, 12(5): 705–710.

van den Brink, M. and Benschop, Y. (2012a). Slaying the Seven-Headed Dragon; The Quest for Gender Change. *Gender, Work & Organization*, 19(1): 71–92.

van den Brink, M. and Benschop, Y. (2012b). Gender Practices in the Construction of Academic Excellence: Sheep with Five Legs. *Organization*, 19(4): 507–524.

van den Brink, M. and Benschop, Y. (2014). Gender in Academic Networking: The Role of Gatekeepers in Professorial Recruitment. *Journal of Management Studies*. doi: 10.1111/joms.12060

van den Brink, M., Benschop, Y. and Jansen, W. (2010). Transparency as a Tool for Gender Equality. *Organization Studies*, 31(11): 1459–1483.

Van Laer, K. and Janssens, M. (2011). Ethnic Minority Professionals' Experiences with Subtle Discrimination in the Workplace. *Human Relations*, 64(9): 1203–1227.

Van Laer, K. and Janssens, M. (2014). Between the Devil and the Deep Blue Sea: Exploring the Hybrid Identity Narratives of Ethnic Minority Professionals. *Scandinavian Journal of Management*, 30(2): 186–196.

Xhauflair, V. and Pichault, F. (2012). Can Flexicurity Make Ethical Sense? The 'terceisation function' as a Moral Lever for Inter-Organisational Employment Schemes. *International Journal of Work Innovation*, 1(1): 65–78.

Xhauflair, V. and Pichault, F. (2014). Towards Sustainable Employment Schemes at the Inter-Organizational Level. In B. Koene, C. Garsten and N. Galais (Eds.), *Management and Organization of Temporary Agency Work*, 87–99. New York: Routledge.

Yanow, D. (2014). Methodological Ways of Seeing and Knowing. In E. Bell, S. Warren and J. Schroeder (Eds.), *The Routledge Companion to Visual Organization*, 167–89. London: Routledge.

Yanow, D., Ybema, S. and van Hulst, M. (2012). Practicing Organizational Ethnography. In C. Cassell and G. Symon (Eds.), *The Practice of Qualitative Organizational Research: Core Methods and Current Challenges*, 331–350. London: Sage.

Ybema, S. (2010). Talk of Change: Temporal Contrasts and Collective Identities. *Organization Studies*, 31(4): 481–503.

Ybema, S. and Byun, H. (2009). Cultivating Cultural Differences in Asymmetric Power Relations. *International Journal of Cross-Cultural Management*, 9(3): 339–358.

Ybema, S., Keenoy, T., Oswick, C., Beverungen, A., Ellis, N. and Sabelis, I. (2009). Articulating Identities. *Human Relations*, 62(3): 299–322.

Ybema, S., Yanow, D., Wels, H. and Kamsteeg, F. (Eds.) (2009). *Organizational Ethnography: Studying the Complexities of Everyday Life*. London: Sage.

Zanoni, P. (2011). Diversity in the Lean Automobile Factory: Doing Class Through Gender, Disability and Age. *Organization*, 18(1): 105–127.

Zanoni, P. and Janssens, M. (2004). Deconstructing Difference: The Rhetoric of Human Resource Managers' Diversity Discourses. *Organization Studies*, 25(1): 55–74.

Zanoni, P. and Janssens, M. (2007). Minority Employees Engaging with (Diversity) Management: An Analysis of Control, Agency, and Micro-Emancipation. *Journal of Management Studies*, 44(8): 1371–1397.

Zanoni, P. and Janssens, M. (2015. The Power of Diversity Discourses at Work: On the Interlocking Nature of Diversities and Occupations. *Organization Studies*, 36 (11): 1463–1483

Zanoni, P. and Van Laer, K. (2015). Collecting Narratives and Writing Stories of Diversity: Reflecting on Power and Identity in Our Professional Practice. In R. Bendl, I. Bleijenbergh, E. Henttonen and A. Mills (Eds.), *Oxford Handbook of Diversity*, 261–283. Oxford: Oxford University Press.

3 "CMS, Canada & the Network"
An Actor-Network Analysis

*Caterina Bettin, Albert J. Mills and
Jean Helms Mills*

INTRODUCTION

Reflections on Politics of Knowledge

When we were first approached to write a chapter for this book, we were both drawn to and repelled by the idea of contributing a chapter on Critical Management Studies in Canada. We were, of course, pleased to reflect on Canadian contributions to the growing networks of communities identified with Critical Management Studies, or CMS. This was particularly true in the face of recent research detailing the marginalization of Canadian contributions to Management and Organization Studies (MOS) per se (Boothman, 2000; Coller et al., 2015; Genoe McLaren and Mills, 2015). On the other hand, we found it daunting to attempt to label the work of colleagues as critical studies of management, let alone CMS (Mills and Helms Mills, 2013), or for that reason fail to include other colleagues under the CMS banner. Not that we personally eschew the label,[1] but rather we recognize its contested character—not so much according to who identifies with the label but with the different meanings that have come to be associated with CMS and, in particular, those whose work is, in the process of labelling, excluded from consideration (Tatli, 2012; A. Prasad et al., 2015).

Our resolve of this (self-imposed) dilemma was to produce an Actor Network Theory (ANT) analysis (Latour, 2005), whereby we can discuss the particular production and performance of a selected group of networked actors and their links to broader networks. Here we are interested not so much in celebrating the work of certain individuals so much as contributing to the knowledge of how some people may come to be enrolled as CMS scholars.

In the 1990s, a particular enactment of management studies emerged (Fournier and Grey, 2000; Mills and Helms Mills, 2013). This "other" performance has been labelled "Critical Management Studies" or CMS (Alvesson and Willmott, 1992),[2] and since then the CMS network has become so widespread that, as suggested by the title of this book, we can now see it as a "global phenomenon".

"CMS, Canada & the Network" 37

In this chapter, we consider CMS as an international heterogeneous network constituted by local CMS enactments that are in relation with each other. Indeed, certain commonalities are shared, such as the critique of the hegemonic economic rational understanding of the social, a certain degree of reflexivity and a particular attention to the voices that are not in positions of wielding power.

We detect as a theme the emergence of critical pockets as outcomes of processes of *othering*. We contend that local pockets assume their specific "critical" boundaries by virtue of being in relation with non-critical enactments. This negotiation for critical identity gives to the local enactment of CMS a particular "flavour", a composition specific to that context.

The following chapter is dedicated to a CMS actor network in Canada. In particular, we attempt to (re)assemble an account of Critical Management Studies in the Sobey PhD programme (management), of Saint Mary's University, Halifax, Nova Scotia, on Canada's Eastern Shore.

We approach CMS as an effect of specific enactments (Law, 1987) rather than an "ostensible entity" (Durepos and Mills, 2012c, p. 99) that exists on its own (Latour, 1999; Law, 1987). To do so, we rest on methodological insights from actor-network scholarship or ANT, paying particular attention to the ontological discussion voiced by the "ANT and after" literature (Law and Hassard, 1999; Mol, 2005). Furthermore, we draw on existentialism to discuss the role that individual intentionality plays in the performance of CMS.

Our commitment is twofold: first, we would like to explore CMS from a non-essentialist perspective. In particular, we consider CMS as *effects* of a global network, and we focus on the particular performance of CMS that emerges from our local context. Second, we take advantage of this opportunity to engage in a self-reflection on the enactments of the specific "flavour" of CMS that characterizes what has become known in some quarters as the "Halifax School".[3] Here we admittedly find ourselves in the ironic position of using a label while arguing that the very act of labelling not only defines reality, it also performs it (Law and Urry, 2004). We are aware of the paradoxical situation that the language game necessarily imposes when we grapple with "amodern" (Latour, 1993, p. 47) and postmodern (Lyotard, 1984) takes on the social, but sometimes escaping this circularity is a hard task. Consequently, before proceeding, we would like to make space for some necessary acknowledgements.

As authors situated in a postpositivist perspective (P. Prasad, 2005), we are mindful that in this work we are in a somewhat overly subjectivist position in pointing out signification (Foucault, 1977). We know that by virtue of being researchers embedded in the specific social context of a school of business in a Canadian university in 2015 we are favouring some themes and at the same time we are necessarily excluding others. We are aware that some voices will be given attention and some others will not. We also acknowledge what Derrida (1978) suggested with his deconstructive techniques: as

38 *Bettin et al.*

authors we do not own the totality of control on our text. Our intentionality, still privileged, is only our interpretation of our narrative among other interpretations; hence something will inevitably be slipping away from our words. Moreover, we are very aware of the representational power that we are bringing to this work, and we do not claim guiltlessness from the "stabilizing" force that we are exercising when we refer to the intellectual space of the "Halifax School". Using ANT language, we know that we are possibly about to create a breeding ground for a "punctuation". There is no self-celebrating motivation here, but only curiosity in exploring a specific enactment of CMS, one that we have access to because we are part of it. We argue that CMS does not exist per se in an essentialist way, but becomes an effect of particular enactments. Here is an account of one particular situation, the one that happens in the Sobey PhD programme. This is our small story (Lyotard, 1984; Calás and Smircich, 1999), not a universal claim of truthfulness.

However, along with the mindfulness of the power/knowledge processes (Foucault, 1979) that as authors we are certainly and unavoidably enacting comes the awareness that punctuations or "fixed points" are not fixed at all (Law, 1999). They are not immutable; they are relational and located in time and space. What might be perceived as a "pinned down" and a "fixed" point is only an unstable and discursive "fact" and, its "definition" or "stability" is to last as long as it is enacted and performed.

This chapter is partly a story of ontologies. More specifically, it is a problematization of the ontology of CMS, and we use the Sobey PhD programme as our stage. First, we will discuss our methodological framework—viz. ANT. We will then build our exploration around two main topics: (1) how the process of "othering" creates a fertile intellectual space for the emerging of "the Halifax School", enabling this particular enactment of criticality and (2) the role of intentionality in the process of "enrolment". Our attempt here is not to fully explore this last topic, but only to ask some questions. We would like to outline how a focus on intentionality can suggest insights on our case and possibly raise questions on how the identity projects of human actors come to be constituted.

Realities Made in Practice: CMS as Effects of Actor-Network Relations

In this chapter, we use ANT as a methodological framework[4] to elaborate on the constitution of CMS in a situated context, the Sobey PhD programme.

ANT was developed by scholars, including Latour (1999, 2005), Law (1986, 1992) and Callon (1986). It is also referred to as "sociology of translation" or "material semiotics". The aim of ANT is to expose that entities linked together in a network, human beings included, are constituted and shaped by their interactions with each other. The question that ANT researchers are committed to answer is how the networks that we refer to as "the social" come to be composed as an effect of performances by their actors (Latour, 1986).

The ontological assumption of ANT is that the social is not a pre-given entity, something that already "is out there". The social world is considered something that is *enacted*. Hence ANT offers a way of assembling stories about "the world out there" that problematizes and denaturalizes the idea of an already existing composition of society. ANT is not interested in testing hypothesis, because the very act of trying to verify a theory necessarily informs the way in which the researcher will see and interpret that phenomenon. In other words, the assumption of a stable reality in itself imposes the researcher's ontology on the object of the study (Calás and Smircich, 1999). For Latour (1986), this is one of the limits of positivist knowledge: its normative narratives not only describe the social, they also enact it. The problem is that if we follow the realist rationale, we end up confusing the "answer" that we are looking for (the explanation of reality) with the "question" itself (our assumptions on reality that we impose on the question) (Durepos and Mills, 2012a). Hence in ANT, the first rule for the researcher is to stay clear from imposition of theories or interpretations in the attempt of avoiding perspectivism (Alcadipani and Hassard, 2010). The role of researchers is to "follow the actors" (Latour, 1987) and map their associations, for the social emerges in heterogeneous networks (Law, 1992), as performative outcomes of relations between actors as they oscillate into networks (Durepos and Mills, 2012a).

Actors have the ability to act upon and influence another (Latour, 1986). It is important to stress that ANT makes no distinction between human and non-human actors, both are included in its analytical outlook. As Law noted, "the stuff of the social is not simply human" (1992, p. 2). This is one of the most controversial aspects of ANT; in fact, one of the criticism that has been moved against it is the lack of adequate problematization of human agency (Lee and Brown, 1994). We will briefly address this topic in the last part of this chapter.

According to ANT, every interaction can be seen as a fight between conditions of possibilities. Actors are seen as continuously engaged in trials; and hidden in these "transactions" there is the opportunity of recruiting other actors. This recruiting process is constituted by dynamics of "translation" and "enrolment" (Callon and Latour, 1981; Callon, 1987; Law, 1999). "Translation" happens when an actor is so strong that it speaks or acts on behalf of another/other actors. When an actor translates, he/she/it becomes a "spokesman" (sic) (Callon, 1986, p. 223) and in doing so silences the voices of the other actors.

Translation is not an innocent practice, and it has to do with power; in fact, as an actor, I become more powerful by having other actors "conforming to my norms", "doing what I want" (Callon and Latour, 1981, p. 279). As Law (1992) noted, given the empirical commitment of ANT, processes of translations are necessarily contingent, local and variable.

40   Bettin et al.

"Enrolments" occur when actors succeed in altering other actors' interests and imposing their own. An actor's power depends on its ability to enrol other actors in its world view and its growth is associated to the extent that "durable" or powerful actors are enrolled. (Callon and Law, 1982). ANT is interested in tracing processes of enrolments and translations, investigating how some actors become more "stable" and why others are just provisional or they do not enrol at all.

In some cases, when actor networks realize a homogeneous alignment among its constituents, it acts as a single block (Law, 1992, p. 5). When enrolled actors act as if they are one, their network disappears and it is replaced by a "precarious and simplifying effect" (Law, 1992, p. 5). This "effect" starts to be viewed as a new actor, and the network behind it is ignored. This process takes the name of "punctuation".

Relationalism and multiplicity (Mol, 2005) are two other key aspects of ANT. "Interaction is all there is" writes Law. "[. . .] society, organizations, agents and machines are all effects generated in patterned networks of diverse (not simply human) materials" (1992, p. 2). Moreover, as the "ANT and After" literature suggests (Law and Hassard, 1999; Mol, 2005), it is more appropriate to discuss multiple enactments of reality, rather that "a" singular reality. For ANT theorists the performances of the social that emerge through associations and/or disassociations among actor networks create "more than one but less than many" (Law, 1999) conditions of possibility in which one phenomenon can be enacted. In Mol's words, multiplicity refers to the idea that "different realities [. . .] co-exist in the present" (2005, p. 79). Moreover, Mol (2005) suggests that looking at the different enactments of the same phenomenon can provide insights on the constitution of that reality. She argues that different performances of the same phenomenon can be in contrast with one another, but the presence of this tension is still very relevant, because it highlights how reactions still contribute to the enactment of a certain reality.

Following this intuition, we start off our ANT analysis of CMS with a question: how does CMS come to be performed in the Sobey PhD programme? What are the relations that have allowed these specific enactments to emerge?

CMS IN THE SOBEY PHD PROGRAMME

Introducing the "Canadian" Actor Network(s)

In this chapter, we look at CMS as a phenomenon that "comes to be" in its multiple enactments (Mol, 2005). Our aim is to avoid playing an essentialist identification game; we are not interested in becoming the Canadian CMS police in charge of deciding the criteria according to which one can become a member of the CMS club. Our social constructionist perspective stands in contrast with realist takes on CMS as a discipline with more or

"CMS, Canada & the Network" 41

less defined boundaries following an established agenda. This is why, rather than engaging in the quest for the ultimate definition of CMS, we prefer to focus on how the CMS phenomenon is produced, in particular by exploring its conditions of possibilities. Nonetheless, we believe that providing some contextual information about the Canadian network of CMS can be relevant. Thus, for example, scholars who self-identify with CMS can be found in several universities across Canada, including, several Nova Scotia business schools (Acadia, Dalhousie, Mount Saint Vincent, Saint Mary's) but also at the Haute Ecole Commerciale and McGill University (Quebec); Brock, Trent, and York (Ontario); Athabasca University and the University of Alberta (both in Alberta); and the University of Victoria and Thompson River University (British Columbia). We have surely missed various colleagues who either identify with CMS and or critical studies of management, and we humbly apologize, as this was not intended as a comprehensive listing, but rather an impression of the (as yet) sustaining environment in which such critical management scholars exist.

We traced the aforementioned enactments of CMS by following performative outcomes. One of the most visible effects of performing criticality, for example, is to participate in the global community that self-identifies as "critical". This includes, but is not limited to, enactments such as being a member of the CMS division of the Academy of Management, having published (or wishing to) in journals that identify as "critical"' including *Organization, Qualitative Research in Organizations and Management, Tamara: Journal for Critical Organization Inquiry, Ephemera: Theory and Politics in Organization, Critical Perspectives on International Business* and *Management & Organizational History*, as well as attending conferences such as the international conference for Critical Management Studies and the CMS Division of the Academy of Management.

Given the multidisciplinary inclination of the grand majority of the enactments of CMS, providing a clear-cut topography of how criticality is performed is a hard task, and it will not be addressed further in this chapter. The point that we are trying to bring forward here is that CMS do not exist per se. Its essence is highly situated and exists in different pockets, emerging as effects of particular enactments. Hence our research question: how does the composition of CMS emerge in the Sobey PhD programme in management?

To do so, we "followed" and "interrogated" four human actors who were chosen in virtue of their self-identification with CMS. We used the interviews to gain a general or overall sense of people's thinking and relationships to CMS and the Sobey PhD. The list of the interviewees includes Terrance Weatherbee and Gabrielle Durepos who graduated, respectively, in 2007 and 2009, Isabella Krysa and Mariana Paludi, currently PhD candidates. Of course, given the self-reflective nature of this paper, we also include ourselves—Caterina Bettin (Sobey PhD student), Albert J. Mills (Sobey PhD Director) and Jean Helms Mills (Sobey PhD faculty member)[5]—in the list of human actors that are participating in assembling this narrative.

42 *Bettin et al.*

We also paid attention to some key non-human actors: the grants from the Social Sciences and Humanities Research Council of Canada (SSHRC) awarded to Albert J. Mills and to Jean Helms Mills, the archives that students have access to in order do their research, the data coming from these archives and the book *Sociological Paradigms and Organizational Analysis* by Gibson Burrell and Gareth Morgan, which serves as a key text for one of the PhD courses. Moreover, we could not ignore the presence of the global CMS network and all the other local enactments of CMS that we relate to.

Introducing the Sobey PhD in Management

The following assembling of the Sobey PhD Programme in management starts off from the institutional material produced by the Sobey School of Business of Saint Mary's University (Halifax).

The description that opens the official website of the PhD programme reports various information, such as the number of students who graduated from the programme, the flexibility in the delivery of the coursework and the positive reviews from the AACSB (Association to Advance Collegiate Schools of Business) accreditation body. The page "Program Overview" features more details: the goals of the programme are discussed in detail and the areas of study covered are listed. Particular attention is dedicated to the structure of the programme, which includes coursework for the first 15 months, with mandatory presence in class during two months of intensive courses. Comprehensive exams have to be completed no later than 28 months after the acceptance into the programme. If successful in their comprehensive exams, candidates are left to work on their theses with a supervisor of their choice. Potentially the programme can be completed in three years; however, in the majority of cases, it takes four to five years to be ready to defend the thesis.

On the entire website, Critical Management Studies is mentioned only twice but never explicitly and always small 'c'. The first time is through the selective reproduction of the words of an external reviewer of the programme,

> The Saint Mary's Ph.D. in Business Administration is . . . highly effective [in] building a strong understanding of a variety of philosophies underlying management theorizing and an appreciation of multiple paradigmatic approaches to management scholarship, such as positivist, critical and feminist approaches.[6]

Later, the idea of "multiparadigmatic approach" appears once again:

> A central part of the programme's focus is to develop professionals with an excellent understanding of both quantitative and qualitative research methods [. . .]. This unique, multiparadigmatic approach exposes students

"CMS, Canada & the Network" 43

to debates across management and organization studies. Alongside issues in (positivist) scientific research, students are asked to consider the impact on management research of other selected (postpositivist) systems of thought (e.g., feminism and Critical Management Studies).[7]

One thing is clear: the PhD programme is *not* a PhD in Critical Management Studies. The programme is portrayed as offering a multiparadigmatic approach, but there is no doubt that the PhD is broadly in the field of management studies rather than being specifically focused on Critical Management Studies.

The programme consists of eight courses—six core courses taught in classroom settings and two independent studies. Only three of the six core courses contain anything approximating material that can be described as relating to CMS themes. Of these the first year "Management Thought and the Management Environment" (MGMT 7701 taught by Albert Mills) devotes one of 12 classes to feminism, one to "radical" organizational theory, one to post-structuralism and part of one class to postcolonial organization theory. The second year "Qualitative Methods" course (MGMT 7703—also taught by Albert Mills) includes segments of classes that examine critical methodological perspectives (including Critical Discourse Analysis and Critical Hermeneutics). Another second year "Doctoral Seminar on Organization Theory" (MGMT 7720, taught by Jean Helms Mills) contains some material (e.g. Marxist theory) that can relate to current CMS thinking but which only constitutes a smattering of items in one or two classes.

So on paper there is nothing inherently critical in the Sobey PhD programme, yet here we are self-reflecting on our critical edge. In the programme, in fact, a number of students and graduates come to self-identify as critical scholars, and to date, almost half of the students have completed (or are in the process of completing) a thesis on a topic that is far from what might be said to be akin to managerialist-positivist ontology. How so?

Tracing the Network

Let us interrogate one of the non-human actors as an (inevitably arbitrary) starting point of our assembling exercise: finance, or more usually referred to as research grants. Grants are key actors in our story because they facilitate processes of enrolment and translation of CMS.

Since their arrival at Saint Mary's University, Albert J. Mills and Jean Helms Mills have received a number of grants from the Canadian Council that supports post-secondary research in the social sciences and humanities—namely, the Social Sciences and Humanities Research Council (SSHRC). Having economic support, Albert and Jean, both enacting particular nuances of criticality, are able to translate CMS and to enrol students in assisting them in their research projects. Here translations of CMS take place and criticalities start to be enacted by new actors and, in turn, translated.

44 *Bettin et al.*

SSHRC funds are also very important because they contribute, in this particular case, to the enrolment of other crucial non-human actors through access to data archives. Albert and Jean's research involves archival research. The research focuses primarily on the gendering of airline cultures over time— amassing material from the archives of British Airways, Air Canada, Pan American Airways and Qantas, but they have also gathered materials from other sources for studies on the dissemination of management knowledge. In this latter case, they have gathered material from the Academy of Management archive housed at Cornell University and a large collection (six hundred plus) of business textbooks published between 1928 and today. They have also created an in-house archive on the local Atlantic Schools of Business (ASB) conference. In the process, Albert and Jean have collected a considerable number of materials and artefacts since the early 1990s. Those archives (i.e. the materials amassed from several airline and other archives) are part of a crucial process of translation. Currently, Sobey PhD students can use these archives to write the papers required to complete their coursework. This translation inevitably features dynamics of power (Callon and Law, 1982; Latour, 1992): students have to get a grade to complete their coursework, and in order to do so, they have to conform to the norms of the "more powerful" actors, such as professors, research grants and archives. All these are "durable" actors that oscillate into networks, and their presence contributes to the growth of the CMS actor. Most importantly, they create "continuity" and "permanence" (Law, 1992). We identify in the presence of these durable networks one of the conditions of possibilities for criticality to be enacted.

On Othering as a Condition of Possibilities

"What are the other conditions of possibilities that allow for local performances of CMS?" We asked this questions to our human actors, and one recurrent theme emerged: "othering". The process of othering is broadly associated with hierarchical dynamics in which essential "subjects" identify the "others" as "different", in the sense of not belonging to their group. This conceptualization of "othering" is somehow problematic in an ANT context because, as mentioned before, ANT is committed to go beyond the dualities and dualisms typical of positivism (Alcadipani and Hassard, 2010) and sees trials diffused with politics of power in continuous renegotiation. Hence informing our analysis in terms of "subjectification versus objectification" would be inconsistent, because it would speak to an "essential" understanding of reality that we are trying to avoid.

This is why we prefer to use De Beavoir's conceptualization of "othering" as "mutually validating reciprocity" (Kruks, 2006, p. XXIII). This is a further elaboration of the idea of ANT as "material semiotics" (Law, 2009). Here we are looking at the emergence of the social as networks of relations and differences. As stated at the beginning, CMS in general could be seen as an outcome of processes of "othering", both in active and passive voice (being the one who others and being on the receiving end). We think that tracing the theme of "othering" in this context could help us investigate these specific dynamics of enrolment and—equally important—resistance to enrolment that are enacted in the Sobey School of Business and that contribute to its specific enactment of criticality.

As mentioned previously, the Sobey PhD programme is in management, not in critical management. It is up to the student to decide which *discipline* (in a Foucauldian sense) to pursue. Roughly half of us decide for the "critical" route, the other half does not. Nevertheless, the point that we want to highlight is that the programme offers *a choice*.

How does "othering" contribute to the emergence of a space for choices? In the Sobey PhD programme, multidisciplinarity is translated when first year students receive the outline for the course "Management Thought and the Management Environment". Here new students are exposed to a very powerful non-human actor, Gibson Burrell and Gareth Morgan's work, *Sociological Paradigms and Organizational Analysis*. At this stage, we could argue whether what is being translated is "critical management" or only the general idea that positivism is a possibility among others. This is not really our point here (it would drag us on to an essentialist discussion about how to categorize CMS, which we are not interested in dealing with now). What we are trying to point out is the idea that Burrell and Morgan translate possibilities of ontological positioning.

Drawing on our personal experiences and on the conversations we had with our actors, it emerged that in every cohort,[8] there are students that have no familiarity with concepts such as ontology or epistemology, and Burrell and Morgan's book is their first encounter with ontological possibilities other than positivism. This exposition does not necessarily turn into an enrolment; however, it constitutes a condition of awareness that cannot be ignored throughout the courses, because of the interaction that the classes require. Ontological stances keep on being enacted, affirmed and reinforced—more or less passionately—during class discussions in the cohorts. In this manner, classes become one of the locations of enactments of criticality or resistance to it, with continuous attempts of translations and enrolments and reactions to those attempts.

Other possibilities of translation and enrolment are the papers that students are required to write to pass the courses. Here "provisional translations" (Callon and Law, 1982) take place, as students have to conform to norms in order to pass to the next stage of the programme. In the first year, every student must write at least one paper each of the three core courses— two that usually require the use and thought style of positivist methods (e.g. statistical analyses) and usually one that requires the use of qualitative postpositivist (P. Prasad, 2005) methods (e.g. applying Critical Discourse Analysis). In the second year, the requirement usually centres on one paper using positivist thinking and methods, one that utilizes postpositivist thinking and methods and one that could go either way. This means that students

46 Bettin et al.

have to speak the language of positivism *and* postpositivism at the same time. As a consequence, "provisional orders"(Durepos and Mills, 2012c, p. 104) emerge and "conditional translations" happen in virtue of power relations. In other words, who self-identifies with criticality has to become temporarily "positivist" and, conversely, who does not identify with critical positions has to practice postpositivist methodologies.

This translation of different ontological languages creates and reinforces the idea of the existence of different intellectual spaces to explore or inhabit, even if only temporarily. Students can *choose* to enact criticality, but they *do not have* to.

We will now address two questions:

1. How do conditions of possibilities of an intellectual space that allows for enactments of criticality come to be?
2. What is the role of intentionality in practices of enrolment?

On Intellectual Spaces of Possibilities

So far we have portrayed the Sobey PhD programme as constituted by structures of relations. In this context, the possibilities to perform criticality are the effects of the acknowledgement of the existence of a distinction between something that is "positivist" management studies and something that is not. This "awareness of discrepancy" does not perform inferiority, because the legitimacy of CMS is granted by "durable" networks that help return the "othering gaze" (Sartre, 1957).

Our actors networks (grants, archives, students, PhD graduates and professors) contribute to the translation of CMS as a "legitimate" and "powerful" actor network in the Sobey PhD programme. As a network, CMS grows to the extent that it acquires "durable" actors. The "critical edge" is an effect of the constant negotiations occurring with other types of enactments.

However, non-critical enactments still shape performances of criticality because non-Critical Management Studies are identified as such only as an effect of their interaction with CMS. Many PhD programmes do not facilitate (consciously or not) the enactment of criticality, because the relationships with CMS is not performed and negotiated on a local level. In other words, CMS is not enacted in the social on a daily basis. Hence distinctions are not performed because there is no breeding ground for other possibilities of ontological positioning. The translation of CMS is weak, unstable and there is no durable network to lean on locally. In the Sobey PhD programme, mutually intervalidating processes of "othering" are constantly part of the conversation. Students, graduates and faculty members are familiar with both positivist and postpositivist territories. This awareness is continuously renovated and reinforced in daily enactments. Moreover, it constantly creates the condition of possibilities for an intellectual space that allows for the choice of whether to enact criticality or not.

"CMS, Canada & the Network" 47

Of course, these reciprocally intervalidating relationships are not necessary peaceful and tensions do exist. The enactment of respectful "intervalidation" varies dramatically. We look at "othering" processes as reactions and resistance to enrolment. Sometimes they happen to be performed as confrontations and less frequently they can take the form of open conflicts. Still, even the fiercest enactments of opposition participate in enacting CMS in our programme. Intense hostilities or attempts of diminishing the legitimacy of CMS still contribute to the performances of criticality that happen in our context.

The Halifax School: Monitoring a Punctuation?

The idea that the so-called "Halifax School" is a punctuation, or very close to becoming one, emerged during our interviews. In one way or another, all interviewees either spontaneously referred to it or, when asked, were very clear on what it is. Moreover, three participants recalled having heard this "label" used in two occasions by different people and at very different times over the years.[9]

In ANT, a punctuation or the "blackboxing" (Whitley, 1972) of a network into an actor happens when there is a strong alignment of actions and interests among actors constituting a network. Punctuations occur when the presence of actor networks as singular entities disappear by virtue of being perceived as acting as one.

Arguably, CMS is now constituted as a "durable" actor network in the context of the Sobey School of Business. Professors, students, archives, research grants, PhD graduates, faculty members and so on all come to be included in the CMS network, and they are very aligned in how they enact their critical edge. A specification is needed here: the particular enactment of criticality performed by the actors can be rooted in different and even conflicting ontologies, but the alignment that we are considering here is an outcome of the particular understanding of academic engagement and a latent criticality that has found in the programme chances to be performed. Altogether, this network can be seen as an ensemble oscillating from its constitution as a network to a new single actor: the "Halifax School".

Clearly when attempting to write ANT stories, we need to artificially reduce the complexity of the networks that we are trying to trace. Our task here is to detect themes and narratives, and sometimes this necessarily happens at the cost of oversimplification, portraying as clear-cut something that is in continuous and constant renegotiation, hence inherently unstable and uncertain (Singleton and Michael, 1993). So let us phrase this as a question: are we monitoring a punctuation? Perhaps. We are oscillating, and we surely are enacting a particular flavour of criticality as part of the global network of CMS. There is some evidence that a blackboxing is about to happen. Maybe this chapter is contributing in conveying a narrative. If so, it will mean that our enactments of CMS are being successfully translated and that we will have enrolled other actors. It ultimately depends on their intentions.

48   *Bettin et al.*

Self-Enrolment: Identity Projects and Existential Questions

What we have so far outlined is the emergence of conditions of possibilities that enable enactments of criticality. In particular, ANT has helped us trace the emergence of CMS in our programme as an intellectual space that enables choices.

Unfortunately, the existential dimension of choices has not been explicitly discussed by ANT and/or the "ANT and after" scholarship. This is not really surprising, for at least two reasons. The first one is a consideration that is valid for organizational studies in general: the individual in organizations is largely undertheorized (Nord and Fox, 1996; Yue and Mills, 2008). Individuals are indeed present in organizational analysis, but they (we) tend to be assumed and not problematized. The second reason is specifically related to ANT. The human being, from an ANT perspective, should not enjoy a special position in analytical terms, because the human is part of the heterogeneous network of the social, exactly like all the other non-human actors (Law, 1992). In particular, for ANT scholars, the power of the humans and the non-humans is to be seen as equally uncertain and ambiguous. This implies that, *in principle*, humans do not have more agency than non-humans (Whittle and Spicer, 2008) in the enactments of the social.

While elaborating on the role of interests in enrolment processes, Callon and Law (1982) do bring up the idea of "choices", but they do not really problematize it. They suggest that actors are constantly engaged in constructing interest maps, with interests as "articulated and explored in terms of choices between courses of action" (Callon and Law, p. 617). In ANT, the concept of enrolment tends to be conceived in a transaction between something/someone that is active in wielding power and something/someone that is passive and accepting. The actor that is getting enrolled is assumed to be docile and manageable (Durepos and Mills, 2012a). The problem is that this assumption of the human actor is a translation of the essentialist and positivist assumption of the human being as a receptor of stimuli. By not questioning the role of intentionality of the human actors, we run the risk of imposing a pre-existent conceptualization of the human being that inevitability gets enacted.

The term "intentionality" is not to be confused with "agency". When we talk about "intentionality", we are thinking of what existentialism refers to as the possibility of the human being to make choices in every situation.

Here we are suggesting a combination of almost opposite points of view. On the one side there is ANT with a focus on relational structures. On the other side, there is existentialism committed to subjectivism and intentionality. The outcome is a concept that we think can be relevant, "self-enrolment".

Let us go back to our case. The enactments of criticality that emerged from our interviews are different in many ways, ranging from ontological stances to emotional investments to enactments of activism.[10] But in all cases, we noticed that the critical ontological positioning is not confined

"CMS, Canada & the Network"   49

to enactments of professional academic activities, it goes beyond, and it becomes a constituting part of the identity project. According to our interviewees, the enactment of a critical edge is intentional because it enables a specific existential project to be enacted. Of course, the extent to which one's identity comes to be constituted by intentional performances of criticality varies and here we will not investigate the topic further. But still, our question remains: when does enrolment become self-enrolment?

When entering the Sobey PhD programme, we are all constituted in particular ways. Some of us may have a latent criticality that is waiting to find a space to be enacted, and some of us may not be familiar with concepts such as ontology or epistemology. Maybe some have never been previously presented the opportunity to problematize the functionalist paradigm (and frankly this is not really surprising given the dominance of positivist-managerialism in US and Canadian business schools). By provisionally enrolling students in both the positivist and the nonpositivist paradigm, the Sobey PhD programme offers the opportunity to operate from a different ontological positioning, giving the *choice* to those who have a critical edge to enact their criticality by providing the intellectual tools developed by the global CMS network.

Is the choice of enacting criticality only an effect of the relations diffused with politics that articulate the network? Is it possible to think of a *self-enrolment* process as a translation of an identity project that resonates with criticality? As suggested by Latour, after all, all there is "a set of associations [. . .] made of shifting compromises" (1999, p. 163). Can this apply to human actors as well? Should we pay attention to processes of enrolment and disenrolment that take place *inside* of us?

Conclusions

In the book *The Postmodern Condition: A Report on Knowledge* (1984), Lyotard discusses how knowledge should be constituted in "small stories", located in time and space and, because of this, very unstable and discrete. In this chapter, we did our best to avoid considering CMS as a label or a definition that had to be substantiated and verified. On the contrary, we looked at CMS as an effect of performances. Following this intuition, it was not possible to discuss CMS in general terms. We provided a general overlook at the Canadian network, but we decided to mainly focus on our own enactments of CMS in a context that we know, the Sobey School of Business. Our aim in this chapter was to reflect on how CMS *as a phenomenon* is produced rather than identify who is (and who is not) in the Canadian CMS community.

We have also questioned if such a thing as "the Halifax School" exists. If translation is what happens at the sides of oscillation, then the CMS network in the Sobey PhD is oscillating in the process of timidly becoming a "blackboxed" actor.

50 *Bettin et al.*

In following our actors, two fascinating themes emerged as part of how CMS is enacted: the idea that CMS is constituted by processes of othering and the role of intentionality in choosing to enact criticality as part of one's identity project.

Both are still unexplored territories in ANT. ANT is not geared specifically to grapple with questions of identity. But we think that there is a space of possibility. As it happened with history (Durepos and Mills, 2012a, 2012b; Weatherbee et al., 2012), ANT and "ANT and After" can provide some intellectual tools to problematize the assumption that we have on the individual, one of the last topics that still remains unquestioned in organizational studies (Nord and Fox, 1996).

NOTES

1. Jean Helms Mills and Albert J. Mills, for instance, are former divisional chairs of the Academy of Management's Critical Management Studies Division, and Albert is currently the co-chair of the International Board for Critical Management Studies and the CMS Series editor for Emerald books.
2. This is not to suggest that critical studies of management did not exist prior to the 1990s. One only has to think of the work of Acker (Acker and van Houten, 1974), Braverman (1974), Clegg (1981), Burrell and Morgan (1979) and various other exemplars.
3. The term was first enacted in print by Corrigan (2015) to refer to a pattern of thought associated with a range of publications—on the relationship between history, organization, identity and actor networks—by authors from the Sobey doctorate in management.
4. "Labelling" ANT is an oxymoron. Readers will not be surprised that among scholars a common agreement on how to refer to ANT is still to be found. Alcadipani and Hassard (2010, p. 249) use the word "approach", Callon and Latour (1981, p. 292) and Law (1999, p. 4) prefer "method".
5. In the development of this paper, Albert Mills and Jean Helms Mills served as co-authors in a particular way. Cognizant of their power (as faculty members) to influence translation of the various human and non-human actors involved in the narrative, they restricted their contributions to the broad presentation of the storyline on ANT. Not without its problems, this approach reduced if not eradicated some of the power influences on Caterina Bettin's ability (as a PhD student) to develop a narrative of the Sobey PhD programme. For similar reasons, the selection of people to interview and the interviewing itself was left entirely to Caterina Bettin.
6. Retrieved from the Sobey School of Business institutional website on September 19, 2014, http://www.smu.ca/academics/sobey/phd-management-program-overview.html.
7. Ibid.
8. The Sobey PhD programme works on a cohort system. Around five to six students enter the program on May 1 of a given year and are expected to complete three of the core courses in the first year and the remaining three core courses in the second year. It is only the independent studies that are completed individually, but even then the programme offers a multivariate statistics course that usually involves two or more students.

9. The Sobey PhD was established in the late 1990s, and 2000 was its first year of operation.
10. For other examples of the emotional attachment to the idea of CMS, see Cunliffe (2008).

REFERENCES

Acker, J. and van Houten, D.R. (1974). Differential Recruitment and Control: The Sex Structuring of Organizations. *Administrative Science Quarterly*, 9(2): 152–163.
Alcadipani, R. and Hassard, J. (2010). Actor-Network Theory, Organizations and Critque: Towards a Politics of Organizing. *Organization*, 17(4): 419–435.
Alvesson, M. and Willmott, H. (1992). *Critical Management Studies*. London; Newbury Park: Sage.
Boothman, B. (2000). The Development of Business Education in Canada. In B. Austin (Ed.), *Capitalizing Knowledge*, 11–86. Toronto: University of Toronto.
Braverman, H. (1974). *Labor and Monopoly Capital*. New York: Monthly Review Press.
Burrell, G. and Morgan, G. (1979). *Sociological Paradigms and Organizational Analysis*. London: Heinemann.
Calás, M.B. and Smircich, L. (1999). Past Postmodernism? Reflections and Tentative Directions. *Academy of Management Review*, 24(4): 649–671.
Callon, M. (1986). Some Elements of a Sociology of Translation: Domestication of the Scallops and the Fishermen of Saint Brieuc Bay. In J. Law (Ed.) *Power, Action and Belief: A New Sociology of Knowledge? Sociological Review Monograph*, 196–233. London, Routledge and Kegan Paul.
Callon, M. (1987). Society in the Making: the Study of Technology as a Tool for Sociological Analysis. In W. E. Bijker, T. P. Hughes and T. J. Pinch (Eds.) *The Social Construction of Technical Systems: New Directions in the Sociology and History of Technology*, 83–103. Cambridge, MA and London: MIT Press.
Callon, M. and Latour, B. (1981). Unscrewing the Big Leviathan: How Actors Macro-Structure Reality and How Sociologists Help Them To Do So. In K. Knorr-Cetina and A.V. Cicourel (Eds.), *Advances in Social Theory and Methodology: Towards an Integration of Micro and Macro-Sociologies*, 277–303. Boston: Routledge & Kegan Paul.
Callon, M. and Law, J. (1982). On Interests and their Transformation: Enrollment and Counter Enrollment. *Social Studies of Science*, 12: 615–625.
Clegg, S. (1981). Organization and Control. *Administrative Sciences Quarterly*, 26: 532–545.
Coller, K., McNally, C. and Mills, A.J. (in press). The Inner Circle: Towards a 'Canadian' Management History—Key Canadian Contributors to New Institution Theory. In P. Genoe McLaren, A.J. Mills and T.G. Weatherbee (Eds.), *The Routledge Companion to Management and Organizational History*, 342–360. London: Routledge.
Corrigan, L.T. (2015). *Budget Theatre: a Postdramaturgical Account of Municipal Budget Making*. PhD, Saint Mary's, Haifax, Nova Scotia.
Cunliffe, A.L. (2008). Will You Still Need Me . . . When I'm 64? The Future of CMS. *Organization*, 15(6): 936–938.
Derrida, J. (1978). *Writing and Difference*. Chicago: University of Chicago Press.
Durepos, G. and Mills, A.J. (2012a). Actor Network Theory, ANTi-History, and Critical Organizational Historiography. *Organization*, 19(6): 703–721.

52   Bettin et al.

Durepos, G. and Mills, A.J. (2012b). *ANTi-History: Theorizing the Past, History, and Historiography in Management and Organizational Studies*. Charlotte, NC: Information Age Publishing.

Durepos, G. and Mills, A.J. (2012c). *ANTi-History: Theorizing the Past, History, and Historiography in Managment and Organization Studies*. Charlotte, NC: Information Age Publishing Inc.

Foucault, M. (1977). Histories of Systems of Thought. In D.F. Bouchard (Ed.), *Language, Counter-Memory, Practice: Selected Essays and Interviews*, 199–204. Ithaca, NY: Cornell University Press.

Foucault, M. (1979). *Discipline and Punish: The Birth of the Prison*. New York: Vintage Books.

Fournier, V. and Grey, C. (2000). At the Critical Moment: Conditions and Prospects for Critical Management Studies. *Human Relations*, 53(1): 7–33.

Genoe McLaren, P. and Mills, A.J. (2015. History and the Absence of Canadian Management Theory. In P. Genoe McLaren, A.J. Mills and T.G. Weatherby (Eds.), *Routledge Companion to Management & Organizational History*, 319–331. London: Routledge.

Kruks, S. (2006). Reading Beauvoir with and Against Foucault. In L.J. Marso and P. Moynagh (Eds.), *Simone De Beauvoir's Political Thinking*, 55–71. Chicago: University of Illinois Press.

Latour, B. (1986). The Powers of Association. In J. Law (Ed.), *Power, Action and Belief: A New Sociology of Knowledge?*, 264–280. London: Routledge Kegan Paul.

Latour, B. (1987). *Science in Action: How to Follow Scientists and Engineers Through Society*. Cambridge, MA: Harvard University Press.

Latour, B. (1992). Where are the Missing Masses? The Sociology of a Few Mundane Artifacts. In W. Bijker and J. Law (Eds.), *Shaping Technology/Building Society: Studies in Sociotechnical Change*, 225–258. Cambridge, MA: MIT Press.

Latour, B. (1993). *We Have Never Been Modern*. Cambridge, MA: Harvard University Press.

Latour, B. (1999). The Historicity of Things. In B. Latour (Ed.), *Pandora's Hope*, 87–113. Cambridge, MA: Harvard University Press.

Latour, B. (2005). *Reassembling the Social: An Introduction to Actor-Network-Theory*. Oxford: Oxford University Press.

Law, J. (1986) *Power, Action, and Belief: A New Sociology of Knowledge?* London: Routledge & Keagan Paul.

Law, J. (1987). On the Social Explanation of Technical Change: The Case of the Portuguese Maritime Expansion. *Technology and Culture*, 28(2): 227–252.

Law, J. (1992). Notes on the Theory of the Actor-Network: Ordering, Strategy and Heterogeneity. *Systems Practice*, 5(4): 379–393.

Law, J. (1999). After ANT: Topology, Naming and Complexity. In J.O. Law and J. Hassard (Eds.), *Actor Network Theory and After*, 1–14. Oxford and Keele: Blackwell and the Sociological Review.

Law, J. (2009). Actor Network Theory and Material Semiotics. In B. Turner (Ed.), *The New Blackwell Companion to Social Theory*, 141–158. Oxford: Blackwell.

Law, J. and Hassard, J. (1999). *Actor Network Theory and After*. Oxford; Malden, MA: Blackwell/Sociological Review.

Law, J. and Urry, J. (2004). Enacting the Social. *Economy and Society*, 33(3): 390–410.

Lee, N. and Brown, S. (1994). Otherness and the Actor Network. *American Behavioral Scientist*, 37(6): 772–790.

Lyotard, J.-F. (1984). *The Postmodern Condition: A Report on Knowledge*. Minneapolis: University of Minnesota Press.

Mills, A.J. and Helms Mills, J. (2013). CMS: A Satirical Critique of Three Narrative Histories. *Organization*, 20(1): 117–129.

Mol, A. (2005). Ontological Politics. A Word and Some Questions. In J. Law and J. Hassard (Eds.), *Actor Network Theory and After*, 74–89). Oxford: Blackwell.

Nord, W. and Fox, S. (1996). The Individual in Organizational Studies: The Great Disappearing Act? In S.R. Clegg, C. Hardy and W.R. Nord (Eds.), *Handbook of Organizational Studies*, 148–175. Thousand Oaks, CA: Sage.

Prasad, A., Prasad, P., Mills, A.J. and Helms Mills, J. (2015). *The Routledge Companion to Critical Management Studies*. London: Routledge.

Prasad, P. (2005). *Crafting Qualitative Research. Working in the Postpositivist Traditions*. Armonk, NY: M.E. Sharpe.

Sartre, J.P. (1957). *Being and Nothingness: An Essay on Phenomenological Ontology*. New York: Philosophical Library.

Singleton, V. and Michael, M. (1993). Actor-Networks and Ambivalence: General Practitioners in the UK Cervical Screening Programme. *Social Studies of Science*, 23: 227–264.

Tatli, A. (2012). On the Power and Poverty of Critical (Self) Reflection in Critical Management Studies: A Comment on Ford, Harding and Learmonth. *British Journal of Management*, 23: 22–30.

Weatherbee, T.G., Durepos, G., Mills, A.J. and Helms Mills, J. (2012). Theorizing the Past: Critical Engagements. *Management & Organizational History*, 7(3): 193–202.

Whitley, R. (1972). Black Boxism and the Sociology of Science: A Discussion of the Major Developments in the Field. *Sociological Review Monographs*, 18: 61–92.

Whittle, A. and Spicer, A. (2008). Is Actor Network Theory Critique? *Organization Studies*, 29(4): 611–629. doi: 10.1177/0170840607082223.

Yue, A.R. and Mills, A.J. (2008). Making Sense Out of Bad Faith: Sartre, Weick and Existential Sensemaking in Organizational Analysis. *Tamara: Journal for Critical Organization Inquiry*, 7(1): 67–81.

4 CMS with a Local Accent
Is Critical Management Education Possible in China?

Shih-wei Hsu

CMS has flourished as a scholarly activity for more than three decades, especially in the UK and Scandinavia. However, it has hitherto had little impact on the management education in China, where more than 20 per cent of the world's population lives. On the one hand, this may reflect the fact that, at an institutional level, business schools in China are dominated by a modernist project of progress that values pro-managerial research, often appearing in quantitative forms. In this process, research and intellectual practices that are incompatible with the corporate interest of performance are usually marginalized. On the other hand, I suggest that CMS, as a well-established discipline, may itself pose some obstacles to scholars who have a critical outlook on the Chinese context. With Zizek (2011) warning that the world system seems to converge towards either Anglo-Saxon neo-liberalism or Chinese-Singaporean capitalism with Asian values, it is an important task for us to develop and inspire critical management pedagogy in the Chinese context.

Historically speaking, the Chinese social system, rooted in collectivism, seems to privilege a non-critical attitude to reality, while critical thinking may be presented as negative or as something that violates harmony. On the Chinese mainland, the academic milieu is clearly dominated by "scientism"; thus management, in order to survive or compete for funding, has to present itself as "soft science". Many highly ranked Chinese business schools are currently gradually trying to adopt "Western" (especially North American and UK) business school models and highlight the significance of quantifiable publication indexes such as SSCI, FT45, Dallas, ABS or a combination of these indices and the Chinese journal ranking system appearing in the so-called "A-Plus" lists by different schools. Management scholars, under such a structure, can hardly develop an interest in a critical approach to management. Despite these structural factors, however, we should note that this does not mean that critical thinking is an unappreciated value in Chinese-speaking societies. For instance, Taiwan in recent years has witnessed a series of social movements led by social activists, environmentalists and university students, which have successfully forced the Taiwanese government to withdraw several neo-liberal policies. What is intriguing is the fact that, at this point, business schools in Taiwan are still dominated by a neo-liberal approach that prioritizes the managerial interest of performance. Business practitioners, even those with critical inclinations, can obtain little help from critical management research. The absence of CMS in the Chinese context may have a dual implication. First, it denotes the institutional difficulties in developing CMS, which in turn imply a general absence of CME (critical management education) in the Chinese context. In terms of CMS, I refer to theories or practices that are oppositional to mainstream management. Second, it also foreshadows the need for CMS to develop a critical engagement with local realities, and I suggest that CMS should be epistemologically and a theoretically pluralized.

I developed an interest in CMS in the UK and have experiences of teaching management in China. Based on my teaching experiences and empirical research in China, I will illustrate the challenges and opportunities of CME in China. It should be noted that, as both CMS and CME are underdeveloped and face similar difficulties in the Chinese context, I will not discuss CME and CMS separately. The chapter is structured as follows. First, I articulate the structural factors that may pose barriers to CME. Second, I will discuss some "silent" issues relating to CMS in the Chinese academic milieu and also briefly introduce the critical impulse in the Chinese world views. Third, I shall try to portray a potential picture of CME with a Chinese "accent"; nevertheless, this does not mean that I seek to either "westernize" management education in China to fit the interest of CMS (developed and defined in terms of Anglophone writings) or to "easternize" CMS to fit the Chinese requirements. What I seek to propose is that critical pedagogy should be viewed as something inherent in the local context. As such, CMS, as an academic discipline, also needs to be more epistemologically pluralized while retaining its critical impulse, as a possible tentative criterion for action in a (future) civil society.

THE CONTEXT OF CMS IN CHINA

Business Schools in China

At first glance, critical thinking is not a culturally and politically preferred value in the Chinese societies, especially in China. One of the major reasons is that historically, the Chinese educational system has been dominated by exams; among others, the well-known (national) college entrance exam plays an important role. As a Chinese scholar commented in a recent conversation: ". . . embracing the off-the-main-stream ideas is a hazardous way of learning deeply buried in the psychological fibre of Chinese students", because "alternative ideas may imply zero-score in the exam". In such a context, students are expected and encouraged to offer (or predict) "correct" answers in the exam. In particular, before 2012, for many Chinese students, a university degree implied the opportunity to become urban citizens

56   Shih-wei Hsu

who enjoyed much better social and economic benefits compared to rural citizenship.

At the level of higher education, recent years have witnessed the increased popularity of business education in China. Although it is difficult to offer an overall picture of what Chinese business schools look like, it seems to be clear that there is a tendency to adopt the mainstream curricula and privilege the Anglo-American approach to business schools. Broadly speaking, business/management education is often understood as a subfield of "science" and represented as "soft science" wherein objectivity, rationality, performance and control are considered as underlying assumptions in the Chinese context. This tendency is more observable in the funding system, as one of the major criteria of successful application is its "scientific value". While many first-tier business schools, in order to survive and compete with others in the global ranking system, tend to adopt objective criteria such as SSCI, FT45, ABS and/or the A-Plus (a combination of different indexes) to evaluate their academic publications, other business schools in China seem to be less affected by the Western business school system. Yet in recent years, there has been a systematic requirement for the internationalization of business schools; hence more and more Chinese business schools currently also privilege ABS and FT45 publications. Nevertheless, the process is usually power-laden and reflects different interests. Taking the cue from the so-called "A-Plus" journal list can have different significance to different business schools and may be flexibly defined in different institutions.

The "scientification" of management education in China seems to be an institutionalized obstacle to CMS. Nevertheless, while postmodernism has had certain impacts upon academic disciplines such as philosophy, a critical approach to management that questions issues like rationality, objectivity and one-dimensional views of (economic) progress is barely recognized in the Chinese context. Apart from this, CME/CMS in China also faces some "macro" difficulties.

Is Critical Thinking Unthinkable in China?

Since a decade ago, we have witnessed the rise of the "harmonious society", and the concept of harmony has become a somewhat hegemonic discourse in China. The discourse of harmony also appears in the field of education, and the outcome seems to be that critical thinking has become a marginalized value, as it may be considered as something violating harmony. Historically, the idea of harmony has its roots in the ancient Confucian philosophy, which highlights the importance of a peaceful relationship between people, between different social classes and between humankind and its environment. Superficially, the notion of harmony is in contradiction with a Chinese Marxist tradition that privileged conflicts, as Marxism implies that conflicts are an important source of class struggle and emancipation. Nevertheless, we should note that there also exists a different understanding of harmony, i.e. harmony-with-difference, which means "peaceful coexistence" of different voices. In Callahan's (2004) view, harmony-with-difference is, perhaps, closer to the Confucian ideal, although the definition of harmony is itself very ambiguous (an issue we will return to).

In order to get a grip on how the idea of harmony affects CMS/CME in China, I conducted 12 informal and open-ended interviews with 12 business school undergraduate Chinese students and asked them to briefly illustrate their understanding, feelings and expectations of a harmonious society. As the concept of harmony is politically sensitive in China, all the interviews (and discussions) were restricted to issues relating to business and management. The interviews were conducted in an office, and all interviewees were studying in a business school in China. All interviews lasted around 30 minutes. The empirical material shows that the participants in general tend to see harmony as an abstract and vague concept, and their understanding of the very notion of "harmony" also varies. Nevertheless, it is possible to identify two general attitudes to harmony: a top-down view of harmony (10 out of 12 interviewees), and a bottom-up view of harmony (2 out of 12 interviewees).

Those holding a top-down view believed that the concept of harmony should be defined by those who have the authority in society, while entertaining a somewhat negative attitude to conflicts. Some of them also retained a unitarist belief, seeing conflicts as the outcome of poor communication. However, when asked to illustrate their attitude towards conflicts in the business contexts, only one of them thought that economic progress should be the priority in society. That is, most of them thought that a harmonious society should refer to a society wherein all interests should be "balanced", such as interests of economic growth and environmental health. Those who retained a bottom-up view seemed to view harmony as a political and "conflicting" concept. For instance, one of them argued that the discourse of harmony might silence alternative voices. When asked to explain their attitudes towards conflicts in the business context, they believed that harmonious discourse only privileges employers' interests, while devaluating employees' interests. It is also important to note that all of the participants recognized that the work environment in China is not only getting worse but also that interests that are incompatible with the corporate interest in performance may be silenced by the hegemonic discourse of harmony. They were also aware of the fact that under the current system, industrial action might cause trouble in China, such as strikes. This observation is not at odds with my teaching experience. While I found that many Chinese students are well aware of the deteriorating work (and natural) environment caused by the rapid economic progress, they were not sure how to protect employees' rights without violating the harmonious discourse, especially at a political level. I suggest that such awareness implies both a challenge and an opportunity for CME in China. However, to the extent that there should be a "market" for the critical pedagogy of management, the current state of

58 Shih-wei Hsu

CMS seems to have offered little help. To understand this, it may be useful to first look into what happened in another Chinese-speaking society, Taiwan.

The Absence of CME

The absence of CME seems to be a general phenomenon in Chinese societies, including the Chinese mainland, Taiwan and Hong Kong. However, it is interesting to note that critical thinking has become an important value in Taiwan, which has also played a significant role in recent years (Abbott, 2012). While social activists and NGOs (non-governmental organizations) are increasingly playing an important role in the decision-making process at a political level, many of the activities were also led by university students. This rise of civil action in Taiwan seems to be in line with Beck's (e.g. 1992, 1999, 2008) thesis of a risk society, that neo-liberal projects can be the source of reflexive awareness, as neo-liberal projects often generate different kinds of risks and culminate in crises, such as the financial crisis and environmental disasters. For Beck, the combined risk and crisis may lead to "enforced enlightenment" and civil action at a societal level. Conventionally, the neo-liberal ideology has dominated the governmental decision-making process in Taiwan. But in recent years, this neo-liberal environment has itself triggered a huge reaction and a public concern over issues such as social inequality, environmental crisis, corporate/managerial misdeeds and deteriorating working conditions. Plainly, many of these issues are related to management. However, while such an environment may offer fertile soil for critical management pedagogy, CMS is virtually absent in Taiwan. Perhaps this is because the current state of CMS may itself pose some obstacles to the critical pedagogy of management, especially for non-western academics. In this chapter, non-Western academics refer to scholars/researchers who receive their education in the Chinese-speaking world and/or academics who do not have much experience in European culture.

While it seems to be the case that the Anglophone tendency of CMS may pose a linguistic difficulty to scholars/students outside the UK and Scandinavia, it is also possible that CMS, as a well-established academic discipline, has become so established and institutionalized that it has little external effects other than to ensure the continued existence of the discipline. The latter seems to be more problematic, as with the seemingly overwhelming process of neo-liberalization within higher education; CMS scholars have to play the "boys club" (Clark and Knights, 2014) game in order to survive in the highly competitive academic arena, the ABS publication regime. Under this process, non-Western intellectual and epistemological traditions can hardly enter the CMS/CME discourse. Let us take the issue of objectivity as an example. For many CMS scholars (e.g. Willmott, 1997; Boje and Al-Arkoubi, 2009), the obsession with objectivity reflects a modernist agenda of rationality rooted in the Enlightenment project of progress; as such, the concept of objectivity has been a long-standing target of critique

CMS *with a Local Accent* 59

in CMS. While to a large extent, I agree that adopting a sceptical attitude based on objectivity to any truth claims is an important step to becoming aware of how the existing power structures shape our understanding of the world, it should also be pointed out that, for many Chinese people, the belief in objectivity and the critique of objectivity are both imported products. One striking example is that in Confucianism most of the literature was written in a highly subjective way; it is also well known that Confucius himself often offered different answers to the same question. For instance, when asked the meaning of the key Confucian concepts such as Ren and Yi (literally meaning "kindness" and "righteousness"), Confucius provided different answers to different disciples, because Confucius believed that no universal answers exist in the world. Taoism, the other major source of wisdom in the Chinese context, also shares a similar character, as much Taoist literature is also written in a highly subjectivist way. Although the discourse of objectivity seems to have dominated management education in current China, Chinese people, culturally, do not have much belief in it. Thus the belief in objectivity and the critique of it are both imported concepts from a Chinese cultural perspective.

The issue of power is another example. While in the field of CMS, power is an important subject of critique which is largely informed by the Foucauldian thesis of power/knowledge, in the Chinese context, the understanding of power is very different. Within CMS, the critical examination of power, for instance, reveals the fact that human realities are always power-laden, and the process of information and decision making are subject to power structures in a particular context (e.g. Foucault, 1980). Hence, from a postmodern sensibility, bureaucracy should not be understood as a matter of how (value-free) rational-legal authority shapes human reality, but rather a matter of how the construction of bureaucracy can be ideologically driven within the relations of power. However, in Chinese, the term "bureaucracy" has a fundamentally different implication. I suggest that the difference is not just a linguistic issue, but rather a philosophical one because the Chinese definition of bureaucracy denotes a different world view. For many Chinese people, the term bureaucracy refers to the use of arbitrary power to serve sectarian interests, and it also implies corruption. Perhaps this is mainly owing to the fact that Chinese people, historically, did not have a strong belief in the rational or that humankind is even capable of being rational; thus they are well aware that human realities can never be free from emotion, intuition, subjectivity and arbitrary power, which are seen as integral parts of the "Guanxi" structure. The concept of Guanxi also has some implications of "Yuan", a Chinese Buddhist notion that refers to a kind of fate or otherworld connection that may bring people together. In this regard, it may be difficult, from a Chinese cultural perspective, to comprehend the "Western" understanding of bureaucracy, as well as its critique.

The argument here is not that CMS-related issues such as power, objectivity and rationality are unappreciated in the Chinese-speaking context or

60 Shih-wei Hsu

that some ancient Chinese wisdom shows better explanatory power of those CMS-related concepts. What I intend to argue is that while the mainstream modernist agendas such as objectivity, control and rationality are add-on concepts in the Chinese context, the criticisms of them are, equally, imported notions. Moreover, after the economic reforms since 1979, a "mantra" of progress seems to have appeared in public that dominates the practice and directions of Chinese business schools; at its core is a pragmatist interest in corporate performance. A telling example is that the management-related journal ranking system tends to be very practitioner-oriented in China. As such, CME may look distant to Chinese-speaking academics.

Critical Thinking in Chinese Wisdom

It is suggested that CME has virtually not entered the Chinese higher educational system, but we should recognize that critical thinking is not an unappreciated value in the realm of Chinese wisdom. Nor does it imply that CME is impossible in the Chinese context. In this section, I will briefly introduce the critical impulse embedded in some major Chinese wisdom and world views. But, the ultimate purpose is to envision a tentative and localized approach to CME in China.

Confucianism

While many believe that the discourse of harmony is rooted in the ancient Confucian ideal of "Great Harmony", it is also recognized that harmony is a vague and ambiguous concept (Callahan, 2004). Our empirical observation also shows this ambiguity, as most of the interviewee students tended to see harmony as an abstract notion and could hardly offer a clear definition of the term. As one student said, "Harmony is an ancient ideal of a peaceful society but I think it has a different meaning in today's world". Yet when asked to further explain the contemporary meaning of harmony, he could not answer the question.

In Chinese, "Great Harmony", often embodying the concept of *Datong*, may refer to a kind of utopia where people could live in peace with other people, as well as with their environment. However, it is important, at this point, to explore how Confucianism views the term harmony, because it is believed that harmony has a double sense, i.e. sameness-without-harmony and harmony-with-difference. In the pre-Qin Confucian classics (i.e. before the seventeenth century), harmony-with-difference was a more prevalent concept. Literally, harmony-with-difference implies an ideal type of people: "the exemplary person harmonizes with others, but does not necessarily agree with them [*he er bu tong*]" (Confucius, 1979, pp. 13–23). By contrast, "the mean person always agrees with others but is not harmonious with them [*tong er bu he*]" (Confucius, 1979, pp. 13–23). While the former denotes an ideal type of being: harmony-with-difference, the latter implies a highly problematic state of being: sameness-without-harmony. For Confucius, harmony and sameness are opposite concepts.

The ideal form of harmony is closer to harmony-with-difference that is able to generate a state of coexistence of different voices and a kind of order that is not generated "through unity and universality, but through an appeal to difference and ambiguity." (Callahan, 2004, p. 586). Harmony-with-difference is a philosophy that recognizes the inevitability of different interests in a given context. Yet it does not seek to unify different voices, but rather to maintain a state of mutual respect in society. Hence there is a famous aphorism in ancient Confucianism: "The people are the most important element; the state is the second; the least is the emperor" (translated by the author). Confucianism, to some extent, implied a radical ideal in the sense that it sought to restrict the ruler's power, while assuming that the ruler should serve the people. Such a critical impulse may be exemplified in the Confucian ideal of harmony-with-difference, which denotes a different mode of social order that recognizes the fact that the human world inevitably contains conflicting voices and that each individual is unique. It also implies that abolishing differences is a task of preserving "sameness" which is, perhaps, ethically problematic. In Confucius's own mind, to maintain sameness-without-harmony was a "mean" person's project. Although there are good reasons to explore the Chinese understanding of harmony/sameness, a fuller study is outside the scope of this chapter. I shall now return to the topic of CMS/CME.

In contemporary China, harmony-with-difference is, at times, promoted at a political level (Liu, 1992). For instance, harmony-with-difference has been used to legitimize the idea of "One country; two systems" (Luo, 1997; Tang, 1997; Li Tianchen, 1997; Li Changdao, 1999; Tong, 1999; Xiang, 2003) as a political approach to Hong Kong. At an individual level, while many view harmony as a vague concept, their understanding of harmony seems to reflect that, practically, the distinction between sameness and harmony is not clear. For example, an interviewee contended that harmony implies that "those who have authority should try to unify different interests", because "different interests may lead to conflicts which are not good for a society". Nevertheless, another interviewee claimed:

> It is important to raise our awareness of voices and interests that were marginalized in the past, such as environmental protection and workers' rights. But people do not know what to do, as some acts might violate harmony.

From the perspective of CMS, the latter interviewee revealed a more critical understanding of the discourse of harmony, but his views also reflect that many Chinese people seem to adopt a pragmatist attitude towards (controversial or politically sensitive) issues while they are also mindful of "politically incorrect" behaviours in China.

Taoism

The other intellectual tradition in the Chinese context is Taoism. Taoism, as ancient wisdom, was especially associated with the works *Tao Te Chin* and *Chuang Tzu*. While the former was written by Lao Tzu (fifth century BCE?), the reputed founder of Taoism, the latter was written by Chuang Tzu (369–286 BCE), who reinterpreted and developed this ancient tradition of nature worship and divination. Lao Tzu and Chung Chou, at a time of social disorder and great religious scepticism, developed the notion of the Tao (i.e. the reason, the way and the other way) as the origin of all creation and the force, unknowable in its essence, that lies behind the changes in the natural world. Although Taoism offered a range of alternatives to the Confucian world view, these two strands of thought, at a metaphysical level, were not mutually exclusive (allegedly, Confucius and Lao Tzu had a discussion on etiquette). Taoism has coexisted alongside the Confucian tradition throughout Chinese history. However, historically, most Chinese empires tended to be in favour of Confucianism, and the Confucian tradition was therefore the dominant philosophy. It is possible to identify two reasons for this.

First, Taoism was radical and somewhat "subversive" in essence. It implied a path of liberation from this world; it was, in this respect, comparable to Buddhism. In the Chinese cultural context, this liberation meant, more specifically, a liberation from the strict (social) rules of convention (Capra, 1992, p. 125); therefore, it encouraged a "classless" society, whereas Confucianism meant just the opposite. Second, from a Confucian perspective, the Taoist view of knowledge was mystically oriented, for Taoists acknowledged the limitations and relativity of all knowledge or, more precisely, they challenged the possibility of "logical reasoning". Taoists believed that knowledge could never be learned. As Chuang-Tzu (1968, p. 239) argued:

> Breadth of learning does not necessarily mean knowledge; reasoning does not necessarily mean wisdom—therefore the sage rids himself of these things.

Logical reasoning and learning were considered by Taoists as part of the artificial world of man, along with etiquette and moral codes, and these were what Taoists mistrusted. As such, the Taoist approach to action, or to knowledge, is what they called *wu-wei* (i.e. non-action). While the Confucian "sage" (i.e. a metaphor used to describe the exemplary person) was wise, an intellectual and a moral paragon, Taoist sages were usually lowly artisans, such as butchers and woodcarvers. For ancient Taoists, only the artisans understood the secret of art and the art of living. To be skilful and creative, they had to have inner spiritual concentration and put aside concern for externals, such as monetary rewards, fame and praise. Art, like life, followed the creative path of nature, not the values of human society. While the Confucian scholars attempted to maintain a static, paternalist norm based on aristocratic blood, knowledge and etiquette, Taoism offered a potential transformation, unaffected by artificial norms, for Taoists recognized that nature itself comprises change and transformation. In the words of Chuang Tzu:

> Spring and summer precede, autumn and winter follow—such is the sequence of the four seasons. The ten thousand things change and grow, their roots and buds, each with its distinctive form, flourishing and decaying by degree, a constant flow of change and transformation.
>
> (Chuang-Tzu, 1968, p. 146)

For Taoists, since our world is in essence a process of transformation, any social hierarchy is unnatural and therefore unnecessary. Contrary to the dominant man/nature dualism inherent in the Enlightenment world view, Taoism provides a holistic world view that is exemplified, particularly, in the notion of Tao, though the meaning of Tao can always be shifting. However, it should be noted that such a holistic world view also implies a kind of harmony: humankind should always act in harmony with its environment, as Taoism assumes that humankind is an integral part of nature. While Taoism recognizes the fact that our world is always in a state of change, the Taoist harmony by no means implies a kind of sameness-without-difference, but it rather implies that human reality is chaotic, unpredictable and full of conflicting interests. It is in this regard that the Taoist world view is not at odds with Confucius's harmony-with-difference, in the sense that both recognize the problematic nature of "sameness".

In addition, the Taoist notion of harmony also implies a radical environmental awareness that shows a strong respect for Nature: the Taoist harmony implies that humankind has no right to "manage" its environment, including Nature, other species and people. In this regard, it is also an anti-managerial stance.

Envisioning the Future: A Showcase of Two Possible Approaches

Critical thinking has been an important value in ancient Chinese wisdom but, as we have seen, it is somewhat repressed under the current predominant discourse of harmony. Despite the institutionalized obstacles to critical thinking and CME, based on my teaching experiences in the area, I suggest that there is still space for educators to deliver the critical pedagogy in management in China. In this chapter, I propose and conclude with two possible and tentative approaches to CME in China, as both seem to share some features with Chinese world views. However, the purpose of this section is not to identify how CME should be conducted but to show how existing CME, as well some obstacles to CME, might appear in the Chinese context.

64 *Shih-wei Hsu*

The Unlearning Approach

In the area of education, much attention has been focused on the positive effect of learning but, from the perspectives of CME, I suggest that "unlearning" could be an important approach to the critical pedagogy in the Chinese context. The concept of unlearning is not new. For instance, drawing upon the Foucauldian concept of governmentality, Chokr (2009, pp. 71–77) views unlearning as a way and capacity, for individuals, to question the dominant social paradigms and knowledge. Hence unlearning, as "the art of not being governed", is a positive and liberating process that helps to unmask, discover and re-rediscover what Foucault (e.g. 1980) called "subjugated knowledges", i.e. the knowledges are repressed under the predominant social/political presumptions and are often represented as insufficiently elaborated, naïve knowledges or hierarchically inferior knowledges that are below the required level of erudition and scientificity (Foucault, 2003, p. 7). In Chokr's (2009) mind, unlearning has the potential to resist a highly problematic state of education, identified by Dewey (1954; quoted in Chokr, 2009, p. 68):

> . . . certain collections of fixed, immutable subject matter that they were taught which in turn they transmit to students under them. The educational regimen thus consists of authorities at the upper end handing down to the receivers at the lower end what they must accept. This is not education but indoctrination, propaganda.

In China, the college entrance exam seems to have formulated a prior commitment to "knowledges" that have a scientific, technical or practical value, and this (ideological) commitment is, perhaps, more observable in the context of business schools. As one of the interviewed scholars depicted:

> . . . students often asked me whether the theory is applicable, or whether the argument is scientific. But when they realized that the theory is for the sake of a critical understanding of business reality, many seemed to lose their interest.

I suggest that unlearning is a helpful approach to CME in the Chinese context because unlearning, as a liberating process, may help learners to critically reflect upon the dominant social presumptions and how these presumptions shape and reshape their understanding of reality. As I proposed elsewhere (Hsu, 2013), Foucault-Chokr's stance is also somewhat in line with a Taoist attitude towards learning: "Learning consists in daily accumulating; the practice of Tao consists in daily diminishing" (Lao-Tzu, 1989, p. 99; translated by John C. H. Wu). Nevertheless, the concept of unlearning here should not be taken to mean a process of destroying existing knowledge, but rather a process of revisiting and unmasking knowledge that is

CMS *with a Local Accent* 65

repressed within the theory and practice of management. It is also a reflexive process, for both instructors and students, to question and understand the institutionalized interest and silenced voices in the discourse of management in the Chinese context.

The Harmony-with-Difference Approach

It was suggested earlier that harmony-with-difference [*he er bu tong*] is an important value in Confucianism. However, while harmony-with-difference contains a critical impulse, many seem to adopt a pragmatist approach to harmony; hence "sameness-without-harmony" often appears to be a more prevalent (political) discourse in China. However, the concept of "harmony-with-difference" is, perhaps, a bridge that potentially connects the Chinese world views to CMS/CME. It may also be a way for instructors to help students to learn the conflicting nature of human reality while localizing CME in Chinese society. In a way, harmony-with-difference captures the spirit of Hardt and Negri's (2000) immanent utopia that look to "various different alternative subjectivities joined in a decentralized network, rather than transcendent utopia's arithmetic equality and homogenous happiness" (Callahan, 2004, p. 588). As such, harmony-with-difference implies an environment wherein people can freely and openly express their voices and interests. It does not seek to identify a universal principle that informs human action, but rather seeks to liberate the "bio-politics of the everyday" (Callahan, 2004, p. 594). To some extent, harmony-with-difference implies Deleuze and Guattari's (e.g. 1988/2004) philosophical notion of multiplicity and is also implicated in the Foucauldian "archaeology of knowledge" that shows how knowledge could be in the services of different values and interests in a given context (e.g. Foucault, 2003).

The implication here is that the harmony-with-difference approach to management pedagogy may make it easier for Chinese students to comprehend the potential consequences from different perspectives. The harmony-with-difference approach may also pluralize (or problematize) the hegemonic interpretation of harmony that is embedded in the Chinese educational system. Practically, instructors could try to generate a decentralized learning environment and guide students to reflect how management knowledge is power-laden and subject to certain social interests. Instructors may also help students to critically reflect on their own knowledge base and values and how different stakeholders may look at issues, such as well-being, performance and progress. Nevertheless, this requires instructors to be reflexive of their own interests and values, as harmony-with-difference implies a decentred network, wherein different subjectivities freely express their voices and defend their own position. Certainly this implies the fact that CMS instructors should also be open to any debates on their own identity as CMS scholars or even problematize CMS itself.

Concluding Remarks

We have reached the point where it is time to answer the ultimate question in the chapter: is CME possible in China? The answer is "possibly", although certain obstacles to CME do exist. First, at an institutional level, management education in China is usually dominated by mainstream pedagogy of management, while at a political level the discourse of harmony seems to marginalize critical thinking. Second, CMS, as a well-established discipline, seems to formulate a boundary for non-Western academics. The possibility of CME exists to the extent that CMS has to show a recognition of different intellectual and epistemological traditions, while CMS educators may also need to develop a localized pedagogy of management that makes itself comprehensible to Chinese learners/students who are used to learning how to fit themselves to the institutionalized requirements but are not encouraged to critically question this reality. However, this should not be taken to mean that the Chinese people are less capable of critical thinking, because the Chinese world views (and much Chinese wisdom) contain implicit critical impulses, even including the discourse of harmony. For CMS educators, what is required is to recognize the implicit critical impulse embedded in the Chinese social system and to develop "understandable" CMS pedagogy for students. I believe that the rapid economic growth in China will bring certain silenced issues to light and that a reflexivity concerned with management will also appear on the scene. While there is a potential market for CME, CMS should be better equipped with a local accent to meet the local expectations.

REFERENCES

Abbott, J. (2012). Democracy@internet.org Revisited: Analyzing the Socio-Political Impact of the Internet and New Social Media in East Asia. *Third World Quarterly*, 33(2): 333–357.

Beck, U. (1992). *Risk Society: Towards a New Modernity*. London: Sage.

Beck, U. (1999). *World Risk Society*. Cambridge: Polity Press.

Beck, U. (2008). Reframing Power in the Globalized World, *Organization Studies*, 29(5): 793–805.

Boje, D.M. and Al-Arkoubi, K. (2009). Critical Management Education Beyond the Siege, In S.J. Armstrong and C.V. Fukami (Eds.), *The Sage Handbook of Management Learning, Education and Development*, 104–125. London: Sage.

Callahan, W.A. (2004). Remembering the Future: Utopia, Empire and Harmony in 21st Century International Theory, *European Journal of International Relations*, 10(4): 569–601.

Capra, F. (1992). *The Tao of Physics: An Exploration of the Parallels Between Modern Physics and Eastern Mysticism*. London: Flamingo.

Chokr, N. (2009). *Unlearning: Or How Not to be Governed?* Exeter: Societas Imprint Academic.

Chuang Tzu (1968) *The Complete Works of Chuang Tzu*, trans. B. Waston. New York: Columbia University Press.

CMS *with a Local Accent*   67

Clark, C. and Knights, D. (2014). *Reconfiguring Resistance: Gendered Subjectivity and New Managerialism in UK Business Schools*. Corfu: 9th OS Workshop.

Confucius (1979). *The Analects*, trans. D.C. Lau. London: Penguin.

Deleuze, G. and Guattari, F. (2004/1988). *A Thousand Plateaus: Capitalism and Schizophrenia*. London: Continuum.

Dewey, J. (1954). *The Public and Its Problems*. Chicago, IL: The Swallow Press.

Foucault, M. (1980). Truth and Power. In C. Gordon (Eds.), *Michel Foucault: Power/Knowledge*, 109–113. London: Prentice Hall.

Foucault, M. (2003). *Society Must be Defended: Lectures at the College de France 1975–76*. New York: St Martin's Press.

Hardt, M. and Negri, A. (2000). *Empire*. Cambridge, MA: Harvard University Press.

Hsu, S. (2013). Alternative Learning Organizations. In A. Ortenblad (Eds.), *Handbook of Research on the Learning Organization*, 358–371. Cheltenham, UK: Edward Elgar.

Lao Tzu (1989). *Tao Teh Chin*, trans. J.C.H. Wu. Boston, MA: Shambhala.

Li, C. (1999). Datong xiaoyi, geju tese: Xianggang jibenfa yu Ao'men jibenfa bijiao (Great Harmony with Small Differences, Each Having Its Special Characteristics: A Comparison of the Basic Laws of Hong Kong and Macau). *Fudan xuebao*, 6: 86–91.

Li, T. (1997). Harmony: A Prescription to Build a Better World in the 21st century, in *Confucian Thought and the 21st Century, International Conference Volume*, 147–150. Hong Kong: Confucian Academy.

Liu, Z. (1992). *Dongfang heping zhuyi: yuanqi, liubian ji zouxiang (Oriental Pacificism: Its Origins, Development and Future)*. Changsha, Hunan: Hunan chubanshe.

Luo, C. (1997). "Harmony but not uniformity" and "one country, two Systems". In *Confucian Thought and the 21st Century, International Conference Volume*, 130–133. Hong Kong: Confucian Academy.

Tang, W. (1997). Kongzi sixiang yu Xianggang heping huigui (Confucian Thought and Hong Kong's Peaceful Return). In *Confucian Thought and the 21st Century, International Conference Volume*, 525–529. Hong Kong: Confucian Academy.

Tong, Y. (1999). Ruxue zai shiji zhi jiaode huigui yu zhanwang (Confucianism at the Turn of the Century: Returning and Looking to the Future). In *The 2nd International Confucian Studies Association Conference Volume*, 3–8. Beijing.

Willmott, H. (1997). Critical Management Learning. In J. Burgoyne and M. Reynolds (Eds.), *Management Learning: Integrating Perspectives in Theory & Practice*, 161–176. London: Sage.

Xiang, S. (2003). Rujia chuantong sixiang zai dangdai Zhongguo de jiezhi he yinxiang (On the Value and Influence of Traditional Confucian Thought in Contemporary China), Paper Presented at the *Regional Governance: Greater China in the 21st Century International Conference*. Durham, UK.

Zizek, S. (2011). Capitalism with Asian Values. Retrieved from access 23 August 2014 http://www.aljazeera.com/programmes/talktojazeera/2011/10/201110281 3360731764.html

5 The Awakening of Critical Management Studies in France
Mimicry or a Process of Coming Out?

Isabelle Huault and Véronique Perret

INTRODUCTION

In contrast to Scandinavia and countries like the United Kingdom and Australia, the emergence of Critical Management Studies (CMS) in France is a relatively recent phenomenon. This rather delayed development is made all the more enigmatic by the fact that CMS is a field that has drawn on French critical theory, as is clear, for example, from the heavy reliance on the work of Bourdieu, Foucault, Deleuze, Lacan and Derrida in research from the English-speaking world. And a structured community of French critical researchers has yet to fully emerge.

Nonetheless, for a few years now, we have seen an awakening of critical research in France and a kind of normalization of this field, which now forms a more explicit component of academic CMS programmes worldwide. Is this simply a mimetic strategy to mirror the international community, or are French researchers "coming out"—reappropriating the rich critical tradition of France's social sciences and asserting an authentic identity? This is the question that will be addressed in this chapter.

We begin by explaining the recent eruption of Critical Management Studies in France as part of the history of the formation of management science, which from the outset tended towards a "managerialist" perspective, the search for consensus and the marginalization of critical thinking. We go on to show how changing socio-economic conditions and a context of academic globalization favoured the awakening of critical theory in France in the mid-2000s. More than mere mimicry, this theory draws on the rich tradition of social sciences that developed in France over time, allowing it to claim its own specific features. Finally, we suggest that by fitting in with the broader CMS research agenda, French researchers can make an original contribution to the emancipation efforts made in this discipline on a global level.

THE CONSTRUCTION AND INSTITUTIONALIZATION OF A DISCIPLINE: FAR REMOVED FROM CRITICAL APPROACHES[1]

The relatively recent emergence of Critical Management Studies in France can be understood by looking at the key phases in the formation of "management science"[2] as a discipline in this country. This is a process that was marked by a delay in structuring management research and teaching in universities. As a result, management science in France was from the outset characterized by a functionalist and "managerialist" perspective, whereby knowledge-based legitimacy repeatedly clashed with managerial legitimacy. This state of affairs ensured that the discipline was far removed from a critical perspective as understood by CMS scholars.

THE INSTITUTIONALIZATION OF MANAGEMENT SCIENCE AND THE INFLUENCE OF THE AMERICAN MODEL

The period between 1965 and 1975 saw the institutionalization in France of higher-level management teaching and the progressive formalization of research. The shift towards a more "academic" discipline and more "scientific" knowledge took place against the backdrop of a more favourable international context, university reforms in the 1970s and the intervention of a few senior civil servants, high-profile business leaders and academics (Pavis, 2003). The objective during that period, as formulated by the public authorities and company directors, was to bestow upon the country's future managers the methods they would need to face the economic challenges associated with internationalization, build a more competitive society and bridge the gap between French-style management and that adopted in North America. The Americans, who boasted complex bureaucratic technologies, were considered to be more rational and professionalized and in a position to enable large companies to cope with the strategic challenges they faced.

In 1968, the creation in France of a national foundation for management teaching, Fondation Nationale pour l'Enseignement de la Gestion des Enterprises (FNEGE) reflected a desire to make up for lost ground. The FNEGE's mission was to prepare French companies for increasingly open borders and to bring the corporate and teaching worlds closer together. To achieve this, in the 1970s, it provided grants for students to travel to the US, thereby contributing to the formation of a body of permanent teaching staff in the field of management science.

It should be pointed out that two competing conceptions operated within the FNEGE, indicative of the tensions with which management science repeatedly surfaced in the French context. The first underscored the need to develop teaching and research in a way that closely reflected the professional world by determining what companies expected from management science and by developing a learning approach based on action and case studies, drawing inspiration from Harvard. The second represented a desire to develop autonomous academic research built on an international culture of scientific knowledge by training teaching staff through doctoral studies with a view to establishing new knowledge within the field of management science (Chessel and Pavis, 2001). The aim was to move beyond the

70   Isabelle Huault and Véronique Perret

dominant empiricism (Pavis, 2003) by applying mathematical and statistical methods to organizational and managerial problems.

It was around the same time that the experimental Paris-Dauphine centre was set up, later becoming the *Université Paris IX Dauphine* in 1970. This move reflected a clear policy to encourage the development of management teaching in France. The founder of Dauphine, Pierre Tabatoni, took inspiration from the US model adopted by Carnegie Tech in structuring the new university.

It was also during this period that the leading French engineering schools set up management research centres. The centre for scientific management (CGS) within the *Ecole des Mines de Paris* was established in 1967 under an initiative by Claude Riveline, an engineer with the *Corps des Mines*. The name of the centre itself (*Centre de Gestion Scientifique*) was a French translation of "scientific management", a term used by Wharton School. In 1973, a management research centre, Centre de Recherche en Gestion (CRG) was also set up in the *Ecole Polytechnique* by Bertrand Collomb, an engineer with the *Corps des Mines* who had written an operational research thesis in United States (Aggeri and Labatut, 2010).

Management teaching and research in France were therefore heavily influenced by the North American model under which the first research and teaching staff were trained. This Americanization was matched by an increasing shift towards "scientific" knowledge in the field of management, largely influenced by the positivist logic used in economics from where this knowledge to a large extent originated. This period of institutionalization can therefore be described as the shift from an educational project to a scientific project in need of consolidation and unification (Hatchuel, 2000).

THE SEARCH FOR CONSENSUS AND THE MARGINALIZATION OF CRITICAL THEORY

Inspired by the model of the English-speaking world, management science research in France developed around the search for performance, the preponderance of the market and utilitarian dimensions, and the universalization of the manager's point of view. Its primary objective was to move beyond conflict and the diverging interests between parties and to promote the ideology of consensus.

As in the dominant paradigm borrowed from the English-speaking world, management science research in France is generally presented as being ideologically neutral. Those who hold this view consider that which is beneficial for companies to be beneficial for society as a whole. From this perspective, consensus constitutes and remains a key value. As a discipline, management science is part of a dynamic that seeks to transcend class struggle. Performance, therefore, is in no way considered in terms of performance benefiting a specific group of stakeholders, shareholders, for example, but rather in terms of performance benefiting the "organization".

Mimicry or a Process of Coming Out? 71

Besides, in a breakaway from more established social sciences such as sociology or economics, the commercial and utilitarian dimensions were emphasized in particular. Although this initially limited the academic legitimacy of the discipline, it is also indicative of its identity and explains why it was so successful as a discipline used to train students, who were anxious about their career prospects, how to become future managers (Pavis, 2003). The conception of this discipline as an amalgam of instruments and technical specialist knowledge undeniably facilitated its expansion and increasing professionalization, but it also exposed it to epistemological critiques and a crisis of identity (Hatchuel, 2000). Despite benefiting from professional legitimacy, the discipline suffered as it was dragged into repeated controversies relating to the effectiveness of its techniques or its borrowings from many of the other sciences. Beginning in the 1990s, several publications calling for an epistemological project specific to management science (Martinet, 1990; Le Moigne, 1995; David et al., 2000) sought to respond to this identity crisis. Although the position being advocated (a form of pragmatic constructivism that was clearly distinct from positivism) remained very much a minority viewpoint, these reflections caused the French community to become acutely sensitive to the epistemological question and the need to clarify and lay down the academic project underpinning management science.

However, throughout this period, although critiques of organizational and social changes were not totally absent, they were formulated almost entirely outside of management science, which was continuing to become institutionalized. While studies in management science endeavoured to move beyond dialectical readings that opposed employers and employees, exploiters and the exploited, subjugators and the subjugated, critical analysts from other social sciences insisted on the contrary on the importance and permanence of these dialectics. But critical theory was not allowed to penetrate the gates of management science. Kept at bay, critical and reflective thinking was for a long time provided by other disciplines, which observed the development of management with circumspection. There was virtually no dialogue between these approaches and management science, as management was considered to be a discipline that contributed to the implementation and reproduction of the structures in question. More focused on theory or interested in studying the big social issues, most French sociologists, largely inspired by Marxism, tended to see these studies as a form of applied industrial sociology serving the interests of employers (Chanlat, 1992).

It was in this hostile sociological environment that, in 1962, Michel Crozier founded the Centre for the Sociology of Organizations (CSO), whose mission was to study French institutions against the backdrop of rapid social change. This desire to understand the dynamics of organizations was a new feature in the French context. The studies to emerge from this new school, including authors such as Michel Crozier and Jean-Claude Thoenig, while recognizing the intellectual debt they owed to the US, displayed original approaches that were to have a crucial influence on the development of

72   Isabelle Huault and Véronique Perret

management science in France. It is important to note the extent to which the work of Crozier, who in the US is often known only for his analysis of the bureaucratic phenomenon, was responsible for developing an acute awareness of the micropolitical dimensions of organizations and nurtured the development of monographic studies in the field of management science.

However, for a long time, this research was considered by French sociologists to belong to the American tradition and was therefore judged accordingly (Chanlat, 1992). Critical social scientists in France viewed management science as a form of social engineering whose purpose was to provide managers with a rationale for their practical knowledge. It therefore appeared to serve the established order by looking for "techniques with which to accommodate and facilitate it" and by placing "rational instruments of knowledge at the service of ever more rationalised domination" (Bourdieu, 1997, p. 121). For the critical sociologists, however, such a scientific discipline could never truly pose a radical challenge, yet the very function of any form of social science is not to serve something—or someone—but rather to understand the social and organizational world.

These analyses suggest that efforts to keep critical approaches at bay corresponded to a specific cultural, economic, social and political context at a specific stage in the institutionalization of management science. The 1990s marked a turning point, which gained momentum during the first decade of the twenty-first century and saw the awakening of CMS in France.

A PLACE FOR CRITICAL THEORY: TOWARDS A RECONFIGURATION OF THE MANAGEMENT RESEARCH LANDSCAPE IN FRANCE?

Changing socio-economic conditions, as well as the academic legitimacy now accorded to management science, provided a new context that was more favourable for Critical Management Studies in France to "come out". Here we will consider the main features of this development.

NEW CONTEXTS AND THE LEGITIMIZATION OF CRITICAL STUDIES

A new context emerged in the last decade of the twentieth century, one which was more conducive to the development of critical approaches within the field of management science in France. Two dimensions seem to have influenced this process: changes in economic activities, which rattled the foundations on which management research had been built, and the internal dynamics of the academic world.

Changing economic conditions and the turndown challenged the social consensus on which management research had initially been founded.

During the 1980s and 1990s, the economy underwent radical change. Increasing financialization, the central importance of "value creation for shareholders", and heightened globalization formed the ingredients of this change. On the strength of widespread liberalization and deregulation, the financial markets took on ever greater importance. Financial resources were now allocated via the markets to those companies that performed the best. In this context, production evaluated using standardized financial norms came to be subordinate to the creation of shareholder value and short-term investment policies. Mergers and acquisitions, relocation and restructuring became the preferred strategic directions in a system of corporate governance that centred on the shareholder.

Against this backdrop, as returns on capital investment took up an increasingly large proportion of value creation, it became ever more difficult to support the view that the search for consensus within organizations formed the basis of management methods. The social foundations of French-style consensus on which management research had been built began to crumble. The sudden emergence of social and environmental issues and challenges to the legitimacy of business provided a favourable context for the development of critical studies in France. Its proponents began to study power relations and systemic forms of domination in an effort to comprehend the full scope of social relations in organizational and collective terms.

Added to this socio-economic context was another, even more decisive factor in the development of critical studies: the internal dynamics of the academic world and the changes taking place in French management research. Researchers in France increasingly took an interest in the academic studies being produced in North America as well as Europe. Around the mid-2000s, research which had primarily developed in the UK under the label Critical Management Studies began to attract the attention of the academic community in France. And with the help of academic globalization, this trend became increasingly widespread.

A dialogue was initiated with the international community, and, as the number of exchanges and shared contacts increased, research management in France was effectively "normalized". Like their overseas counterparts, French researchers began to participate in major international conferences in the field, such as EGOS, AoM (within the CMS division) and the Critical Management Conference, and they published in international journals such as *Organization, Organization Studies, Human Relations, Management Learning, Accounting and Organization and Society*, to mention just a few. They also sat on the editorial committees of critical journals. It is interesting to note that, paradoxically, as a discourse was being formed within the critical school against the dictatorship of excellence and the dominant criteria used for evaluation purposes, the emergence of formal procedures to meet the requirements of accreditations and international rankings produced a favourable context in France for the legitimization of critical studies. The publication of articles in international journals came to be a factor of recognition in the field. What had

74 *Isabelle Huault and Véronique Perret*

once been seen as "off topic" or "ideological" by mainstream thinkers now came to be, if not fully accepted, then at least partially recognized. In general terms, the analysis of management mechanisms as historical artefacts and as vectors of ideology and power relations was now no longer considered to be the sole preserve of sociologists. From this perspective, the move to contest the alignment between knowledge, truth and effectiveness (Fournier and Grey, 2000), favouring knowledge *of* management over knowledge *for* management (Alvesson and Willmott, 2003), constituted a notable change in direction from the hegemony of the managerialist perspective that had dominated during the discipline's early years. The epistemological debates intensified and the contours and ultimate aims of the discipline were increasingly questioned and opened up to more diverse views (Allard-Poesi and Perret, 2014). Attention no longer focused on managers alone, as researchers began to include analysis of countermovements and resistance (Blanc, 2010; Peton, 2011; Yousfi, 2014), and ultimately a more diverse set of players were affected by the managerial phenomenon (Huault and Perret, 2009).

Within France itself, in universities and business schools in cities such as Paris, Lyon, Lille and Montpellier, groups and research teams imbued with a critical perspective began to emerge, explicitly describing themselves as proponents of this view. Doctoral theses in this field were successfully defended and recognized, and international critical workshops were held at regular intervals. In 2009, the journal *Economies et Sociétés* launched a series dedicated to critical approaches (Allard-Poesi and Loilier, 2009).

Although overall the French critical school remains in the minority, it is gradually becoming more widespread and now forms part of research programmes in Critical Management Studies at an international level. Should this be seen as opportunism on the part of an academic community eager to prove itself internationally and publish in English? Is it merely an act of mimicry by researchers following a research agenda that is largely set beyond their borders? There is a certain level of irony, sometimes met with bitterness by French researchers, in the fact that the work of France's leading critical thinkers has only received recognition within the management community in France after it has led to English-language publications, often written by non-French-speaking researchers!

We would argue, however, that this movement cannot be reduced to a mere strategy of opportunism or mimicry. It can also be seen to represent the efforts of a community to voice some of its specific views in an environment that is less hostile to this form of thinking.

MORE THAN MIMICRY: IDENTITY ASSERTION

The context that we have just described, and in particular the increased visibility that comes with international exposure, paradoxically seems to have facilitated French critical management research in "coming out". Although it remains a minority field, Critical Management Studies as it has developed

Mimicry or a Process of Coming Out? 75

in France appears to have benefited from this momentum. Its proponents have had to openly recognize their roots in the critical tradition of French social science and emphasize some of the specific features that can be traced back to this tradition, features which up until recently had remained on the margins of the discipline.

Ancestry: Reappropriating the Critical Tradition of French Social Sciences

It is noteworthy that French management research, until recently, had not for the most part drawn on the cultural legacy of French social science, despite its rich critical tradition.

In his assessment of French-language publications on the analysis of organizations between 1950 and 1990, generally speaking, Jean-François Chanlat (1992) charted a tradition that was clearly distinct from the English-language model that dominated management science at the time. He described this tradition as follows:

> The long-standing tradition of critical analysis found among French thinkers from Proudhon to Foucault and from Gurvitch to Sartre, to mention only a few, the conflictual nature of social relations [. . .], and the desire for social emancipation fuelled by many intellectuals, [. . .]. By presenting a more radical vision of power [. . .], a large number of studies can be clearly distinguished from the dominant functionalist vision that has so far been put forward by most North American studies [. . .].
>
> (Chanlat, 1992, p. 111)

It is clear—and we agree with the author on this point—that this shared intellectual and linguistic context resulted in a heightened sensitivity among French management researchers. For example, the anthropological approach (Chanlat, 1990), drawing on the work of Mauss (1968), distances itself from a vision of management science that is too utilitarian in its intentions and clearly bears the hallmarks of ethnocentrism. For Chanlat (1990, p. 7), this critique is particularly valid in the field of management science, where the dominant conception of the rational *homo economicus* responding to external stimuli and whose universality goes unchallenged is a pure ideological construct with the objective of legitimizing the actions of companies and preserving the established organizational order. This epistemological and theoretical position is in line with that of other French researchers who tried to account not only for human complexity in general (e.g. Morin, 1986) but also that of organizations (Girin, 1982).

Research in France has also placed great importance on the political dimension of organizations. Many studies depict power relations, conflicts and processes of legitimization as being paramount. Contemporary critical analyses that re-emphasize the importance of power and organizational

76 Isabelle Huault and Véronique Perret

resistance can be said to belong to this research tradition to a certain extent (see for example Courpasson and Dany, 2003; Courpasson and Thoenig, 2010).

Within the tradition of French social science, political phenomena and domination have often been analysed in light of macro-social factors and the socio-historical moulds by which they are determined. Up to the end of the 1970s, most of the social sciences in France were driven by a desire to transform both organizations and society itself. Although not directly descended from the same ideological ancestry, today's management research agenda now reflects a desire to develop alternative organizational governance models that are more democratic and free from the diktat of economic growth by integrating the human, social, political and moral dimensions (Gomez and Harry, 2009; Segrestin and Hatchuel, 2012).

However, it was not until the late 1990s that French management science researchers began to "discover" authors whose work had been lauded by US academics since the 1970s under the label French Critical Theory (Cusset, 2003). Ironically, it was the controversy initiated by Sokal and Bricmont's *Impostures intellectuelles* (1997), in which they denounced what they termed the "French imposture", that brought French Critical Theory into the limelight in France. This branch of theory may be defined as a corpus of philosophical, literary and social theories that began to appear in French universities in the 1960s[3] and which enjoyed considerable success in American humanities departments from the 1970s onwards. Beginning in the 1980s, it largely contributed to the emergence of Cultural, Gender and Postcolonial Studies. Although the categorization of such a wide range of authors under the single term "post-structuralist" appeared to be artificial and to blur the existing theoretical specificities and divergences, French Critical Theory nonetheless gave voice to radical critiques that raised questions about the subject, representation and historic continuity.

It was at the beginning of the 2000s that research began to emerge within France's management research community, addressing the work of these authors and the theoretical and ideological views they defended. Examples— by no means exhaustive—include studies that considered the scope of Derrida's post-modernist project in terms of management science (Allard-Poesi and Perret, 2002) or those that tried to outline the French perspective on critical approaches in management (Golsorkhi et al., 2009). It is also worth citing studies by Florence Allard-Poesi (2010), who draws on the work of Foucault and Deleuze to describe strategic management as a control technique through which strategists are made to "unfold", as well as reflections on the contributions made by Jacques Rancière to the question of emancipation (Huault and Perret, 2011; Huault et al., 2014).

The critical tradition of French social science that is now overtly recognized appears to serve a form of research that can assert some of its specific features and give them greater visibility within the management science community.

Specificities: Contributing to a Renewal of the Critical Research Agenda

The affirmative action that can be seen as French management researchers *come out* in a renewed academic landscape seems to express itself through certain intellectual and cultural ties that have long been cultivated and which now offer new possibilities for the critical research agenda. This point of view is defended, for example, in a recent publication by Rendtorff (2014), who develops the notion that France's philosophical and sociological tradition fuels original and critical thinking in the field of business ethics and corporate social responsibility.

For our part, we have identified two themes—suffering in the workplace and the *instrumentation* of management—which, while they may not account for all of the critical research currently being done in France, appear to be very much part of this movement.

Suffering Rather Than Stress in the Workplace

It should be noted that French researchers began to pay considerable attention to phenomena that fall under human subjectivity, symbolism or the unconscious. This manifested itself in particular as part of a research tradition that is critical of the concept of corporate culture. The harmonious and instrumental vision of this concept has often been analysed as a technique of symbolic manipulation. It has largely been supplanted by a more complex understanding that identifies the primordial role of affective relations and unconscious dimensions in organizations (Pagès et al., 1979; Reitter and Ramananstsoa, 1985). Psycho-sociological analysis in the 1970s, fed in particular by the work of Castoriadis (1975), resulted in rather subversive and disturbing interventions in the corporate world (Lapassade, 1970; Lourau, 1970). Although these radical experiments did not last long, it is interesting to note the renewed interest in the work of Castoriadis within the field of CMS today. The author's notions of a social imaginary, the instituting/instituted duality and heteronomy seem to have fuelled new reflections on the themes of radical creativity (Komporozos-Athanasiou et al., 2014), autonomy and emancipation.

Various studies at the crossroads of psychoanalysis and management (see for example Amado, 1980; Aubert et al., 1986; Enriquez, 1997) emphasize the technical failings and political malpractice found in companies: repeated failures to implement strategy, irrational resistance to change, ineffective management, etc. From a psychoanalytical perspective, these phenomena are not "dysfunctions", but rather indicative of "another scene" that is radically different—that of the unconscious (Arnaud, 2002). The crossover between psychoanalysis and social science, particularly fertile ground among French researchers, has also drawn heavily on the work of Jacques Lacan. These researchers aim to explore the contribution made by the

78 Isabelle Huault and Véronique Perret

French psychoanalyst to questions relating to work, management and organizations (see for example Vidaillet, 2007; Faÿ, 2008; Arnaud, 2012). These contributions led to a rejection of the "psychologization" of contemporary management and the corollary ideology of "becoming oneself".

The singularity of the psychosociological approaches that have developed in France is marked by efforts to associate the symbolic and unconscious dimensions with the organizational and institutional mechanisms that produce them and to resituate them in their sociopolitical contexts. The theme of "suffering in the workplace" is an example of this singularity. It is a concept that was developed in the 1980s, based on the work of the psychiatrist and psychoanalyst Christophe Dejours. It is distinct from the stress (or burnout) theory more typical of research in the English-speaking world. Psychopathology in the workplace, predominantly a French area of research, developed around this concept. With the objective of considering the subject's personal experience in relation to his/her work situation, this approach seeks to shed light on the organizational conditions that result in subjects in the workplace sliding towards creative or pathogenic suffering (Dejours, 1990). Distinct from the dominant approaches to stress in the workplace, for which the evaluation criteria are above all somatic and biological, studies on suffering in the workplace shift the line of enquiry away from "mental illness" towards the defensive strategies developed by individuals for coping mentally with their work situation. Here it is normality that is seen as an enigma: how do a majority of individuals, despite the constraints of their work situation, manage to maintain their psychic equilibrium and remain in a state of normality (Dejours, 1990)? Several studies based on this approach have offered particularly critical reflections on contemporary organizational models, asking if there is a need to extend the scope of the human, social and political responsibilities borne by organizations (Dejours, 1998; Pérezts et al., 2011).

Certain studies, for example on the question of evaluation (e.g. Allard-Poesi and Hollet-Haudebert, 2012; Vidaillet, 2013), show that there is an alignment between research on suffering in the workplace and reflections on the instrumentation of management, which also contribute to the unique nature of French management research rooted in the critical tradition of social science.

The Instrumentation Rather Than the Tools of Management

There is nothing new about the interest shown in the tools of management, a perfectly natural feature of a growth discipline essentially intended as a form of "engineering" in the service of performance. In this vein, research in the area has been largely oriented by an instrumental and mechanist vision in which tools are seen as ideologically neutral objects used to serve the rational objectives of an organization (Aggeri and Labatut, 2010; Chiapello and Gilbert, 2013).

Mimicry or a Process of Coming Out? 79

However, in the 1980s, an original approach was developed in France following the work of the CGS and CRG. Michel Berry (2003) offered an overview of this approach, marking the shift from theory based on management tools to a political theory based on the instruments of management. This new conception uprooted the idea that tools were loyal servants of those in power, arguing instead that they are veritable operators which, acting together, form an "invisible technology" that can have harmful effects. Although it was not overtly cited at the time, the idea developed by Michel Foucault that contemporary forms of government operate at a detailed level of instrumentation significantly influenced this emerging research approach (Aggeri and Labatut, 2010).

However, over the course of the last decade, the input of Foucault's work in terms of structuring management science research has been clearly identified by the academic community (Hatchuel et al., 2005). Examples include the studies on biopower and governmentality that have been applied to the tools of human resources management (e.g. Lambert and Pezet, 2011). In the fields of accounting and management control in particular, we are seeing the formation of a critical community inspired by the work of Foucault (e.g. Ramirez, 2001; Pesqueux, 2005; Morales and Pezet, 2012).

Chiapello and Gilbert's typological analysis of research on management *instrumentation* (2013) nonetheless demonstrates that the work being done on this topic draws on several other traditions of French social science. The authors point out that, taken together, the studies that form part of this particularly fertile area of research offer reflections that are anthropological in nature, addressing all of the dimensions of managerial actions and considering management tools as a "complete social reality" (Mauss, 1968). Without trying to be exhaustive, the following is an illustration of the diverse contributions that have fuelled the reflective and critical perspective of the *instrumentation* of management.

For example, the large number of studies that draw on the sociology of translation and Actor Network Theory (ANT) (Callon and Latour, 1981) contribute to the analysis of management tools as social constructs. This perspective defines tools as sociotechnical mechanisms, as complex human/non-human arrangements that are the (forever provisional) result of a network of relations and actions. ANT offers us a new understanding of the way in which management tools are disseminated and adopted. It also allows us to rethink the performativity of mechanisms and its role in the construction of markets (Blanchet, 2013; Muniesa, 2014). By reintegrating the corporal and material dimensions of our social lives into the analysis, ANT is seen as a means of returning to a form of materiality, although without regressing to the determinism of Marxist approaches (Allard-Poesi and Loilier, 2009).

It is also worth noting that studies produced using a conventionalist approach (Boltanski and Thevénot, 2006) provide an analytical framework that is conducive to the denaturalization of management tools. Here the *instruments* of management are seen as the result of efforts to frame and

80 Isabelle Huault and Véronique Perret

shape the managerial environment; through the conventions which they construct and perpetuate, they make it easier to manage affairs and the people involved. Several studies refer to the contributions of pragmatic sociology developed by Luc Boltanski and Eve Chiapello (2005/1999), offering an updated perspective on the framing, categorization and commensuration at work in management tools and market mechanisms (e.g. Bourguignon, 2005; Berland and Chiapello, 2009; Huault and Rainelli, 2011, 2013). Researchers have also focused on Boltanski's recent work (2011) on domination and emancipation, highlighting the institutional mechanisms through which credit rating agencies in the financial sector preserve their prerogatives and the permanence of the system (Taupin, 2012).

Lastly, certain studies inspired by Marx and Bourdieu consider management tools to be part of a wider economic and social system. The apparent technical neutrality of management tools is denounced in favour of the view that they serve the interests of the most dominant groups and a capitalist model that tends to overdetermine the way in which they operate (Djelic and Quack, 2012; Chiapello and Gilbert, 2013). Studies on international accounting standards (Capron, 2005) or on globalization and global value chains (e.g. Palpacuer et al., 2010) offer examples of empirical research that supports this view. Tools become one of the indicators of the wider economic and social system and an instrument of the power relations that run through it. Contemporary Western society is witnessing the proliferation and sophistication of management instruments, and their expansion into ever wider domains. Under the pressure of new public management (NPM), these instruments have colonized public policy and the functions of the State (Lascoumes and Le Galès, 2004). Part of the trend towards a "managerialized" society, *instrumentation* now has an increasingly strong presence in the private sphere of our daily lives. This observation is a reminder of the importance for society of studying contemporary management in a critical way.

CONCLUSION

Between mimicry and a process of coming out, the awakening of Critical Management Studies in France we outlined is certainly more a "both" than an "either/or" story. On the one hand, it is now easier to be enrolled into the CMS community because of its international recognition. In this sense, the CMS brand could be viewed today as a legitimation channel option for an academic career in France. On the other hand, however, the conviction expressed in this chapter is that management research as it is currently developing in France is in a position to make an original contribution to the emancipatory project of the Critical Management Studies movement, by the reappropriation of its intellectual history and the assertion of its cultural sensitivity.

NOTES

1. This paragraph constitutes a reworked and enriched version of Golsorkhi, D., Huault, I. and Leca, B. (2010) 'Introduction', in Golsorkhi D., Huault I. and Leca B. (Eds.), *Les études critiques en management. Une perspective française*, Presses universitaires de Laval, pp. 1–29.
2. Management science in France is broadly structured around the main functions of a company. It covers the following fields: finance, marketing, human resources management, strategy, information systems, accounting and auditing.
3. The following authors are regularly associated with French Critical Theory: Jean Baudrillard, Cornélius Castoriadis, Hélène Cixous, Gilles Deleuze, Jacques Derrida, Michel Foucault, Félix Guattari, Julia Kristeva, Jean-François Lyotard, Jacques Lacan and Jacques Rancière.

REFERENCES

Alvesson, M. and Willmott, H. (Eds.) (2003). *Studying Management Critically*. London: Sage.

Aggeri, F. and Labatut, J. (2010). La gestion au prisme de ses instruments. Une analyse généalogique des approches théoriques fondées sur les instruments de gestion. *Finance Contrôle Stratégie*, 13(3): 5–37.

Allard-Poesi, F. (2010). A Foucauldian Perspective on Strategic Practice: Strategy as the Art of (un) Folding. In D. Golsorkhi, L. Rouleau, D. Seidl and E. Vaara (Eds.), *Cambridge Handbook of Strategy as Practice*, Chapter 11, 168–182. Cambridge University Press.

Allard-Poesi, F. et Hollet-Haudebert, S. (2012). La construction du sujet souffrant au travail au travers des instruments scientifiques de mesure. *@GRH*, 4(5): 45–74.

Allard-Poesi, F. and Loilier, T. (2009). Qu'est-ce que la critique en Sciences du Management ? Que pourrait-elle être ? Introduction à la Série "Etudes Critiques en Management". *Économies & Sociétés série KC*, 1(12): 1975–1999.

Allard-Poesi, F. and Perret, V. (2002). Peut-on faire comme si le postmodernisme n'existait pas ? In N. Mourgues et alii (Dir), *Questions de méthodes en sciences de gestion*, Chapter 10, 255–291. Caen: EMS.

Allard-Poesi, F. and Perret, V. (2014). Fondements épistémologiques de la recherche. In Thiétart (Coord), *Méthodes de Recherche en Management*, Chapter 1, 14–46, Paris: Dunod.

Amado, G. (1980). Psychoanalysis and Organization. A Cross-Cultural Approach. *Sigmund Freud House Bulletin*, 4(2): 17–20.

Arnaud, G. (2002). The Organization and the Symbolic: Organizational Dynamics Viewed from a Lacanian Perspective. *Human Relations*, 55(6): 691–716.

Arnaud, G. (2012). The Contribution of Psychoanalysis to Organization Studies and Management: An Overview. *Organization Studies*, 33(9): 1121–1135.

Aubert, N., Enriquez, E. and de Gaulejac, V. (1986). *Le sexe du pouvoir*, Paris: Epi.

Berland, N. and Chiapello, E. (2009). Criticisms of Capitalism, Budgeting and the Double Enrolment: Budgetary Control Rhetoric and Social Reform in France in the 1930s and 1950s, *Accounting, Organizations and Society*, 34(1): 28–57.

Berry, M. (2003). *Une technologie invisible ? L'impact des instruments de gestion sur l'évolution des systèmes humains*, CRG-Ecole polytechnique, Rapport pour le ministère de la Recherche et de la Technologie. Retrieved from http://crg.polytechnique.fr/publications/popup.php?idtitrebase=1133&LangueInterface=F RBl (viewed in September 2015).

82 Isabelle Huault and Véronique Perret

Blanc, A. (2010). *Les formes de pouvoir dans la reproduction institutionnelle: Le cas de la licence globale en France.* Thèse de doctorat, Paris-Dauphine, DRM.

Blanchet, V. (2013). *Le commerce équitable à l'épreuve de la mode: Le rôle de la critique dans la formation des marchés.* Thèse de doctorat, Paris-Dauphine, DRM.

Boltanski, L. (2011). *On Critique: A Sociology of EmancipationPrécis de sociologie de l'émancipation.* Paris: Gallimard. Polity (Originally, 2009. *De la critique. Précis de sociologie de l'émancipation.* Paris: Gallimard).

Boltanski, L. and Chiapello, E. (2005/1999) *The New Spirit of Capitalism.* London: Verso

Boltanski, L. and Thévenot, L. (2006). *On Justification. Economies of Worth.* Princeton, NJ: Princeton University Press (Originally 1991, *De la justification, Les économies de la grandeur,* Paris: Gallimard).

Bourdieu, P. (1997). *Méditations Pascaliennes.* Paris: Seuil.

Bourguignon, A. (2005). Management Accounting and Value Creation: The Profit and Loss of Reification. *Critical Perspectives on Accounting,* 16(4): 353–389.

Callon, M. and Latour, B. (1981). Le grand Léviathan s'apprivoise-t-il? In M. Akrich, M. Callon and B. Latour (Eds.), *Sociologie de la traduction. Textes fondateurs,* 11–32. Paris: Ecoles des mines de Paris. 2006.

Capron, M. (Dir.) (2005). *Les normes comptables internationales, instruments du capitalisme financier.* Paris: La Découverte.

Castoriadis, C. (1975). *L'institution imaginaire de la société.* Paris: Seuil.

Chanlat, J.-F. (dir) (1990). *L'individu dans l'organisation: les dimensions oubliées.* Les Presses de l'Université Laval, Editions ESKA.

Chanlat, J.-F. (1992). L'analyse des organisations: un regard sur la production de langue française contemporaine (1950–1990). *Cahiers de recherche sociologique,* 18–19: 93–138. (Translation 1994, Francophone Organizational Analysis (1950–1990): An Overview. *Organization Studies,* 15(1): 47–80).

Chessel, M.-E. and Pavis, F. (2001). *Le technocrate, le patron et le professeur. Une histoire de l'enseignement supérieur de gestion.* Paris: Belin.

Chiapello, E. and Gilbert, P. (2013). *Sociologie des outils de gestion. Introduction à l'analyse sociale de l'instrumentation de gestion.* Paris: La Découverte, Col. Grands Repères.

Courpasson, D. and Dany, F. (2003). Indifference or Obedience? Business Firms as Democratic Hybrids. *Organization Studies,* 24(8): 1231–1260.

Courpasson, D. and Thoenig, J.-C. (2010). *When Manages Rebel,* Basingstoke, UK: Palgrave MacMillan (Originally, 2008, *Quand les cadres se rebellent,* Paris: Vuibert).

Cusset, F. (2003). *French Theory. Foucault, Derrida, Deleuze & Cie et les mutations de la vie intellectuelle aux Etats-Unis.* Paris: La Découverte.

David, A., Hachtuel, A. and Laufer, R. (Coord) (2000). *Les nouvelles fondations des sciences de gestion.* Paris: Vuibert.

Dejours, C. (1990). Plaisir et souffrance dans les organisations. In J.-F. Chanlat (dir), *L'individu dans l'organisation: les dimensions oubliées,* 77–94. Les Presses de l'Université Laval, Editions ESKA.

Dejours, C. (1998). *Souffrance en France.* Paris: Seuil.

Djelic, M.-L. and Quack, S. (2012). *Transnational Communities. Shaping Global Economic Governance.* Cambridge: Cambridge University Press.

Enriquez, E. (1997). *Les jeux du pouvoir et du désir dans l'entreprise.* Paris: Desclée de Brouwer.

Fournier, V. and Grey, C. (2000). At the Critical Moment: Conditions and Prospects for Critical Management Studies. *Human Relations,* 53(1): 5–32.

Faÿ, E. (2008). Derision and Management. *Organization,* 15(6): 831–850.

Girin, J. (1982). Langage en actes et Organisations, Économies et sociétés, série. Sciences de gestion, 3: 1559–1591.

Mimicry or a Process of Coming Out? 83

Golsorkhi, D., Huault, I. and Leca, B. (Dir) (2009). *Les études critiques en management. Une perspective française.* Québec: Presses de l'Université de Laval.

Gomez, P.-Y. and Harry, K. (2009). *L'entreprise dans la démocratie. Une théorie politique du gouvernement des entreprises.* Louvain-la-Neuve, Belgium: De Boeck col. Ouvertures économiques.

Hatchuel, A. (2000). Quel Horizon Pour les Sciences de gestion ? Vers une théorie de l'action collective. In A. David, A. Hachtuel and R. Laufer (Coord), *Les nouvelles fondations des sciences de gestion*, 7–43. Paris: Vuibert.

Hatchuel, A., Pezet, E., Starkey, K. and Lenay, O. (Eds.) (2005). *Gouvernement, Organisation et gestion: l'héritage de Michel Foucault.* Quebec: Presses universitaires de Laval.

Huault, I. and Perret, V. (2009). Extension du domaine de la stratégie. Plaidoyer pour un agenda de recherche critique. *Economies & Sociétés série KC*, 1(12): 2045–2080.

Huault, I. and Perret, V. (2011). Critical Management Education as a Vehicle for Emancipation. Exploring the Philosophy of Jacques Rancière. *M@n@gement*, 14(5): 281–309.

Huault, I., Perret, V. and Spicer, A. (2014). Beyond Macro- and Micro-Emancipation: Rethinking Emancipation in Organization Studies. *Organization*, 21(1): 22–49.

Huault, I. and Rainelli, H. (2011). A Market for Weather Risk? Conflicting Metrics, Attempts at Compromise and Limits to Commensuration. *Organization Studies*, 32(10): 1395–1419.

Huault, I. and Rainelli, H. (2013). The Connexionist Nature of Modern Financial Markets. From a Domination to a Justice Order? In P. du Gay and G. Morgan (Eds.), *New Spirits of Capitalism? Crises, Justifications and Dynamics*, 181–206, Oxford University Press.

Komporozos-Athanasiou, A., Mainemelis, B. and Pérezts, M. (2014). Organizations and the Imagined Life: Perspectives on Imagination, Creativity and Novelty, *Call for Paper Egos 2015.* Athens, Sub-theme 48.

Lambert, C. and Pezet, E. (2011). The Making of the Management Accountant—Becoming the Producer of Truthful Knowledge. *Accounting, Organizations and Society*, 36(1): 10–30.

Lapassade, G. (1970). *Groupes, Organisations et institutions.* Paris: Gauthier-Villars.

Lascoumes, P. and Le Galès, P. (2004). *Gouverner par les Instruments.* Paris: Sciences Po Les Presses.

Le Moigne, J.-L. (1995). *Les épistémologies constructivistes.* Paris: PUF.

Lourau, R. (1970). *L'analyse institutionnelle.* Paris: Minuit.

Martinet, A.-C. (Coord) (1990). *Epistémologies et Sciences de Gestion.* Paris: Economica.

Mauss, M. (1968). *Sociologie et anthropologie.* Paris: PUF.

Morales, J. and Pezet, A. (2012). Financialization through Hybridization: The Subtle Power of Financial Controlling. In I. Huaultand, C. Richard (Eds.), *Finance: The Discreet Regulator. How Financial Activities Shape and Transform the World*, 19–39. Basingstoke, UK: Palgrave Macmillan.

Morin, E. (1986). *La Méthode: La Connaissance de la Connaissance* (t. 3). Paris: Le Seuil.

Muniesa, F. (2014). *The Provoked Economy. Economic Reality and the Performative Turn.* London: Routledge.

Pagès, M., Bonetti, M., de Gauléjac, V. and Descendre, D. (1979). *L'emprise de l'organisation.* Paris: PUF.

Palpacuer, F., Leroy, M. and Naro, G. (Dir.) (2010). *Management, mondialisation, écologie: regards critiques en sciences de gestion.* Paris: Hermès.

Pavis, F. (2003). L'institutionnalisation universitaire de l'enseignement de gestion en France (1965–1975). *Formation Emploi*, 83: 51–63.

84   Isabelle Huault and Véronique Perret

Pérezts, M., Bouilloud, J.-P. and Gaulejac, V. (2011). Serving Two Masters: The Contradictory Organization as an Ethical Challenge for Managerial Responsibility. *Journal of Business Ethics*, 101: 33–44.

Pesqueux, Y. (2005). Corporate Governance and Accounting Systems: A Critical Perspective. *Critical Perspective on Accounting*, 16: 797–823.

Peton, H. (2011). Organisation frontière et maintien institutionnel. Le cas du Comité permanent amiante en France. *Revue Française de Gestion*, 217: 117–135.

Ramirez, C. (2001). Understanding Social Closure in its Cultural Context: Accounting Practitioners in France (1920–1939). *Accounting Organizations and Society*, 26(4–5): 391–418.

Reitter, R. and Ramanantsoa, B. (1985). *Pouvoir et politique: au-delà de la culture d'entreprise*. Paris: McGraw-Hill.

Rendtorff, J.D. (2014). *French Philosophy and Social Theory: A Perspective for Ethics and Philosophy of Management*. Springer, Col: Ethical Economy.

Segrestin, B. and Hatchuel, A. (2012). *Refonder l'entreprise*. Paris: Seuil, Col. La république des idées.

Sokal, A. and Bricmont, J. (1997). *Impostures Intellectuelles*. Paris: Odile Jacob.

Taupin, B. (2012). The More Things Change . . . Institutional Maintenance as Justification Work in the Credit Rating Industry. *M@n@gement*, 15(5): 528–562.

Vidaillet, B. (2007). Lacanian Theory's Contribution to the Study of Workplace Envy. *Human Relations*, 60(11): 1669–1700.

Vidaillet, B. (2013). *Évaluez-moi ! Évaluation au travail: les ressorts d'une fascination*. Paris: Seuil.

Yousfi, H. (2014). Rethinking Hybridity in Postcolonial Contexts: What Changes and What Persists? The Tunisian Case of Poulina's Managers. *Organization Studies*, 35(3): 393–421.

6 Critical Scholarship in Management and Organization Studies in German-Speaking Countries
An Overview and Historical Reconstruction

Ronald Hartz

This contribution aims to enrich the discourse about Critical Management Studies (CMS) through reconstruction and 'writing in' of selected endeavours of critical scholarship in German-speaking countries. Besides early references to the 'Frankfurt School' (Alvesson and Willmott, 1992), there is still a lack of knowledge about precursors and recent work done in the spirit of CMS in Organization Studies in German-speaking countries. To fill this gap, at least partially, I will first outline some main contributions to critical scholarship. Second, I will focus on three distinct strands of thinking: 'labour-oriented business administration' (Arbeitsorientierte Einzelwirtschaftslehre or AOEWL), the 'critique of the political economy of organization' associated with the organizational scholar Klaus Türk and, finally, the development of gender studies, exemplified through the pioneering work of Gertraude Krell. Krell's research is relatively well known in the German scientific community, especially in the field of personnel management. The approach of Türk is gradually 'written out'. This 'fate' happened to the AOEWL too, which nowadays is merely a 'footnote' in the history of business administration. Indeed, there are other critical scholars and projects that are in need of reconstruction and a 'writing in' into the tradition of critical scholarship. Other academics can probably tell other stories about heterodox accounts. This account is limited to the field of management and organization studies and pertains to my own academic socialization, including the books I have read and the people I have had the opportunity to meet. Thus I will not discuss critical traditions in, for example, 'critical psychology' in the tradition of Holzkamp (2013), organizational pedagogy (Engel and Sausele-Bayer, 2014) or industrial sociology with its strong links to Marxism and the Labour Process Debate (e.g. Deutschmann, 2002).

CMS IN GERMAN-SPEAKING COUNTRIES: AN OVERVIEW

To write about CMS in the German context is not an easy task. In contrast to, for example, Anglo-Saxon or Scandinavian countries, I have the impression that the label CMS does not function very well as an umbrella term for critical scholars. It appears that explicit references to critical management

86 Ronald Hartz

or organization studies are broadly framed as stigmatizing the 'non-critical' scientific community and seen as a kind of hubris. With notable exceptions (Nienhüeser, 2004b, 2011; Sieben, 2007; Costas, 2010; Hartz, 2011; Hartz and Rätzer, 2013a; Weik 2014), the explicit reference to questions of 'critique' is more or less a lacuna. However, looking at the history and present state of the field of management and organization studies in Germany, it is possible to identify a number of critical strands of thinking, which can be linked (but not subsumed) to the programmatic orientation of CMS: 'denaturalizing', 'non-performative intent' or 'reflexivity' (Fournier and Grey, 2000). Reflecting on the history of business administration, management and organization studies, we can find a number of authors addressing critical issues within the field. Sönke Hundt (1977) points to a number of authors and critical traditions in his historical reconstruction of business administration. Besides 'labour-oriented business administration', he mentions the writings of Ekkehard Kappler (e.g. Kappler, 1980) in the tradition of critical theory; the work of Hans Raffée, which was influenced by the critique of consumerism; authors in the tradition of Marxism (Sönke Hundt, Günther Ortmann, Axel Zerdick); protagonists of methodological constructivism (Horst Steinmann); and, finally, Hartmut Wächter and Wolfgang Staehle, who argue for an institutional or normative framing of business administration. From the 1980s, there was a growing awareness of gender issues in the field of business administration (for an overview, see Bendl, 2006). Finally, from the 1990s, we can observe a reception of post-structuralist thinking in the field of management and organization studies (Weik, 1998, 2014; Schreyögg, 1999). Here important contributions have been made by Richard Weiskopf (e.g. Weiskopf, 2003b, 2005), Günther Ortmann (e.g. Ortmann, 2003, 2004) and Costas (e.g. Costas and Taheri, 2012; Costas and Grey, 2014). Weiskopf refers to the writings of Foucault, Derrida, Deleuze and Guattari and addresses issues of control and discipline (e.g. Laske and Weiskopf, 1996; Weiskopf, 2005), the temporality and fragility of the process of organizing (Weiskopf, 2003a), ethics as 'critical practice', drawing on Derrida's notion of responsible decision making and Foucault's conceptualization of 'truth-telling' (Weiskopf and Willmott, 2013). Ortmann's theoretical work gets its inspiration from the writings of Derrida (Ortmann, 2003). Furthermore, he addresses the intersection of language and organization, i.e. the performativity of language (*sensu* Austin) in the process of organizing (Ortmann, 2004). His recent contributions address questions of morality and organizations (Ortmann, 2010). The studies of Jana Costas and other researchers (e.g. Costas and Taheri, 2012; Costas and Grey, 2014) draw on the writings of, for example, Foucault and Lacan, focusing on power relations, fluidity and organizational secrecy. Other efforts include those of Werner Nienhüser in strengthening issues of political perspective on Human Resource Management (Nienhüeser, 1998, 2004b, 2011, 2015) and in developing a 'Political Personnel Economy' (Nienhüeser, 2004a), the socio-analytic perspective on organizations developed by Burkard Sievers (Sievers, 1994, 2006) as well as our own attempts in establishing a biannual conference

Critical Scholarship in Management   87

on 'critical organization studies' (Forum 'Kritische Organisationsforschung', see http://www.kritische-organisationsforschung.de/) for German-speaking scholars. While addressing issues of critique and CMS, one of the workshops has been turned into a publication entitled *Organisation Studies after Foucault* (Hartz and Rätzer, 2013b).

Given this broad overview, I will turn to three critical approaches formulated and developed before the explicit development of CMS. First, the reconstruction of the concept of 'labour-oriented business administration' (AOEWL) highlights the most prominent heterodox approach in business administration in the 1970s. Second, the 'political economy of organization' of Klaus Türk and colleagues presents a comprehensive approach of the problematization of the modern form of organization as a form of domination. Finally, I would like to highlight the pioneering work of Gertraude Krell and her collaborators in the field of gender studies in German-speaking countries. While Türk developed a consistent theoretical framework for an understanding of the modern organization, the work of Krell signalled a change in the field, varying from women's studies to issues of gender studies and the early anchoring in critical theory to post-structuralism. In addition, the history of the AOEWL points to some discursive mechanisms of 'writing out' and consequently the 'forgetting' of critical approaches. I will turn to these discursive strategies in the remainder of this chapter.

TOWARDS AN 'EMANCIPATORY RATIONALITY': LABOUR-ORIENTED BUSINESS ADMINISTRATION

The concept of 'labour-oriented business administration' (Arbeitsorientierte Einzelwirtschaftslehre/AOEWL) was introduced as an alternative or counter concept to the 'capital-oriented' business administration model at the beginning of the 1970s. The initial idea to develop an alternative form of business administration came from the unions. In 1972, the WSI (Institute of Economic and Social Research at the Hans Böckler Foundation) asked a group of nine scientists from the fields of business administration, economics, sociology and political science to critically examine the interests of employees and unions in business administration. The AOEWL was the subject of discussion by a number of scientists in business administration (e.g. Chmielewicz, 1973; Kappler, 1973; Wächter 1976; Wächter and Metz 2010; Krell 2013) but was mostly ignored or criticized (e.g. Hax, 1974; WSI, 1973, p. 273). Despite a recent publication on 'labour orientation' (Laske and Schweres, 2014), the concept of AOEWL is a historical footnote in the context of the discipline (Wächter and Metz, 2010) and is written out of handbooks on business administration too (the chapter of Schanz (1992) in a textbook on business administration was removed in later editions).

The starting point of the AOEWL was a general critique of the basic premises of neoclassical economy, which were seen as the guiding principles of

88 *Ronald Hartz*

traditional business administration. For proponents of AOEWL, these guiding ideas centre on the principle of individualism and its linkage to private property, competition as a basic mechanism of assertions of interests and the orientation of economic action based on capital-oriented rationality (Projektgruppe im WSI, 1974, pp. 25–27). The hegemony of these principles leads to the privileging of property-owning classes, whereas the autonomy and personal development of wage earners or employees are strongly restricted. It seems that the AOEWL was positioned as a counterweight to this assumed alliance of capitalism and business administration and was explicitly presented as a political project. With this backdrop, the protagonists of the AOEWL called for an 'emancipatory rationality' to overcome the dominating capital-orientation in business administration. 'Capital-oriented rationality' was framed as focusing on quantification, a one-dimensional orientation towards efficiency and profitability and an obscuring of decision making as a political process. In contrast, 'emancipatory rationality' targets the 'quality of life' and its plural character. Instead of individualism and competition, it is necessary to develop a 'collective and solidarity orientation and a democratic coordination of interests about ends and means of work' (Projektgruppe im WSI, 1974, p. 28, all quotations are translated by the author).

The question remains: what are the interests of the employees? In the context of single organizations, the protagonists of AOEWL point to three areas that require measures to 'increase the scope for emancipation' (Koubek, 1973, p. 84):

(1) 'Relative' job security, including occupational and regional mobility and questions of qualification and further training;
(2) Income security and raises;
(3) Working conditions to enable 'opportunities for personnel development at the workplace' (Projektgruppe im WSI, 1974, p. 116), including the reduction of hierarchies and participation in the decision-making processes.

Beyond these areas and interests at the individual and organizational levels, the authors point to necessary societal and socio-economic changes and actions to realize 'emancipatory rationality':

(1) First, there is focus on *the control of production*, where the authors differentiate between necessary goods (i.e. 'goods') which serve the needs of people and 'bads' which have negative impact on people and the environment or show bad quality (planned obsolescence). In principle, a control of production should focus on a sanctioning of bads and a promotion of goods.
(2) Next, *the provision of private and public goods* problematizes the capital- or market-oriented distribution of goods in education, health care or the housing market and pleads for a stronger political control

of these fields (Projektgruppe im WSI, 1974, p. 146). In addition, the authors claim a strengthening of community-based usage of goods, e.g. common facilities or houses, more transparency in pricing, product quality and a limitation of planned obsolescence.

(3) Finally, there is a plea for a *fair distribution of income and wealth* even though an increase of income may mean lower profits. Further recommendations include the extension of co-determination to investment issues and the introduction of profit-sharing models at the supra-company level. The development of a 'collective property fund' aims–due to its powerful property rights–both at regulation and control of production.

To realize these more or less programmatic claims, the protagonists of the AOEWL finally propose a number of concrete measurements. First, what is necessary is a reconceptualization of the foundational concepts of business administration ('costs and services', 'assets and liabilities') to integrate social or ecological costs. Second, any functional area of an organization needs an assessment of its role, actual functioning and any necessary changes to realize labour-oriented business administration. Personnel departments need to pay special attention to the core needs of labour and are in need of emancipation from other functional areas as far as possible (Koubek, 1973, p. 90). Third, the authors suggest the development of a combination of economic, social and ecological calculations to 'operationalize' the construct of 'emancipatory rationality'. Furthermore, the authors propose the implementation of a multi-staged procedure of co-determination, ranging from practical changes at the workplace level to a co-determined economic and social policy. The aim is 'to establish co-determination in every societal sphere, where the interests of the dependent employees are affected' (Projektgruppe in WSI, 1974, p. 266). Finally, the authors suggest a differentiated model of social technologies, ranging from political planning at the societal or macro level to the regulation of production via prohibitions and requirements and last but not the least, market coordination of issues of importance at the company level.

KLAUS TÜRK: TOWARDS A 'CRITIQUE OF THE POLITICAL ECONOMY OF ORGANISATION'

The writings of the organizational scholar Klaus Türk focus on the development of a 'critique of the political economy of organisation' in the following 'critique'. This critical approach was formulated in a number of book chapters and monographs, sometimes written and published in cooperation with Thomas Lemke, Michael Bruch and Hans-Jürgen Stolz. Türk was a professor of organizational sociology at the Bergische Universität Wuppertal. His 'critique' retains a more or less singular status in the development of organizational scholarship in Germany.

90   *Ronald Hartz*

Türk's point of departure in formulating his 'critique' is twofold. First, he points to the rather ephemeral status of organizational scholarship in the context of a theory of society. Despite the recognized importance of organizations in everyday life and to the social fabric, prominently labelled as 'a society of organisations' (Perrow, 1991), reflections about the importance of the construct of organization for modern society are rather scarce (e.g. Türk, 1995a). What is needed is a conceptualization of the interrelated structuration of organization and society, or 'a theory of the organisational social formation that identifies the modern era' (Türk, 1999, p. 7). As noted, the 'critique of the political economy of organization' is also a critique of the distinction between organization and society (commonly labelled as 'environment') and an extension of the critique of political economy formulated by Marx. For Marx, capital and capitalist relations are the pivotal aspects to understand the 'anatomy' of modern society and to critique it. Türk states that organization and organizational relations are fundamental to modern society and that 'without organisation, there is no capital' (Türk, 1999, p. 8). Moreover, he claims that '[o]rganisation is neither a neutral nor an ambiguous social form for the coordination of human co-operation. Rather, it is a historically specific form of domination' (Türk, 1999, p. 6). To give evidence of this repositioning and the focal (and problematic) role of the organization in modern society, Türk points first to the historical rise of the modern form of organization prior to markets. First, there was disciplinary action, barracking, subsumption and the production of surplus value; then there were markets, rule of law and liberalization (Türk, 1995b, p. 13). Following empirical observations, Türk states,

> that not only does production in the narrower sense take place in a form of organization, but more importantly, crucial areas of society are in the hands of organisationally-backed elites: one need only mention the state, the military, associations, trade unions, political parties, hospitals, schools, universities, churches, and charity organisations.
>
> (Türk, 1999, p. 8)

On the backdrop of this argument, Türk proposes a concept of organization, which allows an exploration of the entanglement of domination, rationality and the structure of modern organizations. To conceptualize the form of organization as a 'specific form of domination', Türk differentiates between power and domination. Whereas power 'is an *interactive* phenomenon, domination is an *institutional* phenomenon' (Türk, 1999, p. 10). Any concept of domination which focuses on exploitation or command models is insufficient due to the probable resort to the feudal logic of masters and slaves to understand organization as a form of domination. For example, political parties function via the shaping of consciousness and 'domination in school derives . . . from the hegemonic socialisation and classification of individuals' (Türk, 1999, p. 10). In fact, domination is obscured by

Critical Scholarship in Management 91

deep-seated belief that 'organisations appear to nearly everyone to be necessary and as productive social instruments for the achievement of specific ends' (Türk, 1999, p. 10). However, organizations are not totalitarian forms of domination. Their existence depends on the commitment and the contribution of cooperating people. Thus '[e]very process of organization is . . . contingent on subjects that consent to being organised' (Türk, 1999, p. 11). Organizations are a double structure of domination and cooperation—the term 'political' refers to the aspect of regulation, whereas the term 'economy' can be linked to any kind of cooperation.

To explore the organizational reproduction of domination, Türk proposes a concept that analytically distinguishes three interrelated dimensions of organization (Türk, 1995b, 1999, pp. 12–19, Türk et al., 2002, pp. 19–37). The question of interest is 'what people do when they produce something they call "organization"' (Türk, 1999, p. 12).

(1) The Dimension of 'Order'

The dimension of order points to the process of organizing, which is the 'production of ordered sequences of events' (Türk, 1999, p. 13). This dimension encompasses the discourses of rationality, discipline and normalization. It has three more or less implicit aspects or imperatives of order. First, it is concerned with the structuring of social relations towards an end-oriented rationality as a dominant form of reason. Second, organizational structures are linked to expectations in terms of effectiveness and productivity. Finally, the pursuit of a common purpose requires discipline. The dimension of order points to the entanglement of rationality and domination, as prominently discussed by Weber, entangled with the constitution of both obedience and a productive subject, conceptualized as factors of production or human capital.

(2) The Dimension of the 'Structured Entity'

As Türk (1999, p. 15) puts it, 'Every order requires a locus to which it refers, a *social space* for which it strives to prescribe a structure. The creation of any order . . . entails the construction of a unit with clear boundaries'. The idea of an organization as a 'structured entity' creates organizations as accountable units, both in legal and economic terms. In legal terms, the construct of a 'legal person' allows first the accumulation of wealth and power without any reference to concrete persons and secondly creates a legal space besides family and the state, with its own rules and regulations. In economic terms, the dimension of the 'structured entity' enables the accountability of productivity to organizations. This promotes a 'fiction of productivity' which simultaneously de-symbolizes forms of cooperation and obscures human cooperation as a productive force. The construction of an entity further enables internalization and externalization of resources or costs, institutionalized through balance sheets and accounting principles.

(3) The Dimension of 'Collectivity' (Vergemeinschaftung)

Finally, the dimension of 'collectivity' points to an 'us and them' perspective. Related terms for this dimension are 'esprit de corps', 'team spirit', 'corporate culture' or 'loyalty'. It aims at the construction of a social body which points to aspects of discipline and organizational socialization; furthermore, the construction of a corporate identity goes hand in hand with the process of social closure. This social closure is linked to processes of social discrimination. In following Weber, Türk highlights the function of organizations in terms of social stratification via the ascription of attributes such as race, gender or ethnicity.

To sum up, Figure 6.1 binds together the three dimensions of the modern form of organization and highlights some important demarcations in the process of organizing. In short, the question, 'what people do when they produce something they call "organization"' can be answered by an exploration of these processes of demarcation in relation to the three dimensions described earlier. Producing an 'organization' means to (Türk, 1999, p. 20, Türk et al., 2002, p. 37):

- Sort what is relevant and not in the dimension of order (rational–irrational)
- Select attributions via the construct of a structured entity (internal–external)
- Distinguish between belonging and not belonging in the dimension of collectivity (us–them)

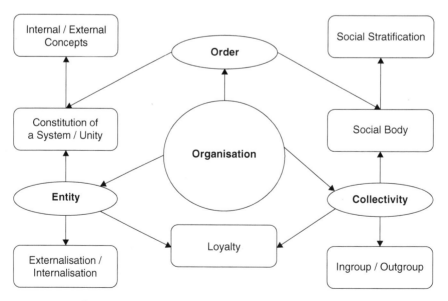

Figure 6.1 The Construct 'Organization' (Türk et al., 2002, p. 36, own translation)

Critical Scholarship in Management 93

GERTRAUDE KRELL: FROM WOMEN'S POINT OF VIEW TOWARDS THE (DE-)CONSTRUCTION OF GENDER

In a personal conversation, Gertraude Krell described her own work and her writings as starting with women's studies, going on with gender studies and finally focusing on the field of diversity studies. As a professor of business administration at the Freie Universität Berlin, Gertraude Krell maintained a special interest in personnel policies (Personalpolitik). She published a number of monographs and articles, sometimes in cooperation with colleagues, for example, Renate Ortlieb and Barbara Sieben (Krell et al., 2011), Margit Osterloh (Krell and Osterloh Margit, 1993a), Richard Weiskopf (Krell and Weiskopf, 2006) or Daniela Rastetter (Krell et al., 2012). The work of Krell can be situated in the context of the development of business administration in Germany. Her pioneering attempt to introduce 'the women's point of view' into this field of research is also a story about 'male stream' efforts to dominate in the field (Krell, 2013).

Following are three directions or stages of Krell's work, which point both to her personal story and to the general development of the field of gender studies as a critical endeavour in the field of business administration in Germany.

Her first major work was a genealogical reconstruction of the 'image of women in work science' (Krell, 1984). Starting with a historical construction of woman as housewife and mother, Krell presents an in-depth exploration of numerous German articles and monographs in work science written in the 1980s, focusing the construction of women as 'second-class' employees in physiological, psychological and gynaecological (menstruation and motherhood) terms. Physiologically, women are constructed as a 'deficit model' in comparison to the male role model, e.g. in relation to muscularity, weariness or a postulated 25 per cent reduction of performance during menstruation. In psychological terms, Krell identifies typical characterizations of women (in contrast to men), where, for example, women follow a kind of 'logic of the heart' and are equipped with a weak will (Krell, 1984, p. 86). Looking at the ascribed attitudes towards work, women are constructed as family-oriented, motivated by income and interested in the work atmosphere. On the contrary, men are described as work-oriented and overtly motivated by the content of work (Krell, 1984, p. 98). The overall picture indicates that the construction of women in contrast to men goes along with and reproduces societal division of labour. Moreover, Krell argues that the 'deficit model' of women indicates a general discrimination of vitality in work science. Referring to Adorno, Horkheimer, Theweleit and Marcuse, she states that work science in the tradition of Taylor and Gilbreth is dominated by an instrumental rationality, which consequently suppresses questions of meaning or the necessity of work or delegates them to other sciences. Under this tradition, humans are 'anachronistic' beings. Finally, Krell outlines a 'critique of male productivity', which links her analysis of work science to studies about suppression and violence against women

94   Ronald Hartz

together. Her final thesis echoes the diagnosis of the 'dialectic of enlightenment' by Adorno and Horkheimer: 'Violence against women, suppression of women . . . is caused by the permanent suppression, exclusion and fight by the civilized man against the male's inner nature and its identified female parts . . . It is terribly hard to be a "whole man"' (Krell, 1984, p. 210).

Together with Margit Osterloh, in 1993, Krell published a special issue on 'Personnel Policies from Women's Point of View–Women from the View of Personnel Policies' in *Zeitschrift für Personalforschung (German Journal of Research in Human Resource Management)* (Krell and Osterloh Margit, 1993a). This publication, consisting of around 20 articles, can be understood as a landmark in establishing the category of gender in the field of business administration in Germany. First, Krell, Osterloh and a number of colleagues conducted a survey on the relevance of gender and women's issues in research and teaching of HRM chairs in the German-speaking countries (Krell and Osterloh Margit, 1993b). Moreover, they analysed 19 HRM textbooks, published between 1978 and 1992, in terms of the appearance and depiction of women in textbooks (Gerhard et al., 1993). It was obvious that women or gender issues were more or less absent until the mid-1980s. The books were implicitly oriented towards the male model of work and lifetime. From the 1980s, women as employees began to get recognized in the books. However, they were overtly constructed as 'trouble makers' or as a 'special group'. Female employees are associated with topics such as absenteeism from work, turnover, health problems, maternity leaves, unemployment, etc. Furthermore, the textbooks reproduced stereotypes of 'typical' male or female jobs. In case studies or examples, women were shown in roles such as secretaries, shorthand typists or in the personnel department. On the contrary, men worked as heads of departments, electricians, or pilots. The results of the studies were followed by a plea for systematic inclusion of 'gender as a differentiating category', which allows both the addressing of differences in HRM (Gerhard et al., 1993) and the analysis of structural discrimination of women (Krell, 1993).[1]

From the 1990s, it is possible to observe a growing recognition of poststructuralist strands of thinking in the field of business administration, which also become visible in the work of Krell and her collaborators. The introduction of Foucault and Butler into the analyses allowed a reframing and shaping of previous work and a new theoretical anchoring of the 'women's point of view' (e.g. Krell, 2003, 2013, Krell and Weiskopf, 2006). To reconstruct the 'fabrication of gender', Krell draws first on Foucault's *Order of Things* and the 'principle of classification', crystallized in the idea of the tableau. Second, she applies Foucault's reconstruction of the 'art of distribution' in *Discipline and Punish*, i.e. closure, parcelling and classification in terms of position and rank, to explore the gendered 'ordering of human resources' (Krell, 2003). In applying the 'principle of classification', Krell discusses the 'polarization of gender characteristics' from the eighteenth century onwards and its 'naturalizing' effects. Even recent ideas of androgyny, e.g. in leadership, perpetuate this polarization. Despite this inertia, it seems obvious that the polarization is fluid too. Nowadays, women are confronted with a number of identity offers, which potentially allow for breaking with the 'attitude of clarity'. The history of polarization has co-evolved with the 'art of distribution'. Krell discusses the closure of (the bourgeois) woman as housewife and mother related to the discursive fabrication of 'motherly love'. Alongside other physiological and psychological ascriptions, the 'work of love' gets echoed in the gendered construction of female and male work as a form of parcellation. For example, service work in the care sector is constructed as a 'service of love'. Finally, Krell points to some aspects of classification of female work. Typically, female work is described as 'easy work', whereas male work is considered 'hard work'. In consequence, the misrecognition (or invisibility) of specific demands of, for example, care work, leads finally to an economic stratification between female and male workers.

For Krell, gender is a pivotal modus of classification both in society and organizations. A genealogy and deconstruction of the 'fabrication of gender' does not only allow one to '[explain] relations of power' (Krell, 2003, p. 87) but can also help to change them (Krell et al., 2011).

CONCLUDING REMARKS

The three distinct critical approaches presented point to precursors of CMS in need of further recognition. Reconstruction leads to the question of their having partially been 'written out' of critical traditions. Turning back to AOEWL, it seems that from the viewpoint of traditional business administration and that of mainstream management and organization theory, the addressing of societal and macroeconomic issues and the focus on regulation, control and social technologies is irritating and an expression of hubris and utopian thinking. The writings of Klaus Türk, Gertraude Krell and other critical scholars mentioned earlier, however, can be reconstructed as a way to transgress the limits of their subsequent fields. In effect, the discussion of critical scholarship reminds us of the limits of what can be said in the field of business administration, management and organization. Finally, in focusing on the discourse surrounding AOEWL, it is possible to identify at least three forms of discursive demarcation. The first demarcation is drawn between *truth*, i.e. objectivity and neutrality and ideology or science driven by interests. Thus Karl Hax states in his critique of labour-oriented business administration, 'True science serves the truth and should not be a simple instrument for the enforcement of particular interests' (Hax, 1974, p. 800). In the forefront of any politics, there exists 'scientific research devoted to the recognition of objective causalities' (Hax, 1974, p. 800). A second demarcation functions as the rejection of the reflection of societal issues in the realm of business administration. Thus this demarcation points to the *object*

96   Ronald Hartz

of study and consequently pleads for a normative indifference with socio-economic issues. For example, Wolfram Engels argues,

> Business administration is done within a specific economic frame. [. . .] Consequently, our task is to solve problems within that frame and not to pay attention to fantasies. Just give me an economic frame and I will create a respectable form of business administration.
>
> (WSI, 1973, p. 237)

The third line addresses the question: who is speaking? For example, Hax points to the issue of *legitimate authorship* in the following way:

> One has to ask about the legitimation of the group to come to such negative judgments. Unfortunately, this group is part of the academic youth. They have grown up in the time of the 'economic miracle.' They do not know what wage-labour, hard physical work and dependency on a weekly wage really means.
>
> (Hax, 1974, pp. 805–806)

It can be argued that these demarcations play an important role in the defence of the traditional ways of doing research in the field. In the case of AOEWL, it seems paradoxical that nowadays a number of topics, e.g. ecological balance sheets, planned obsolescence or the role of commons are recognized as relevant and have a certain impact on the field. However, these topics are coming from outside the field and one can be sceptical about their impact on discussions about the direction and aims of business administration in particular and for management and organization studies in general in German-speaking countries.

NOTE

1. The contributions of Krell, Osterloh and colleagues were echoed by statements of the editors of the journal, mostly pointing to the relevance of the addressed topic. However, the critical status of a 'women's point of view' is made visible in one comment where one of the editors showed complete misunderstanding of the topic and the analysis of his own textbook, where female employees were overtly constructed as 'trouble makers' (Krell, 2013).

REFERENCES

Alvesson, M. and Willmott, H. (Eds.) (1992). *Critical Management Studies*. London: Sage.

Bendl, R. (Ed.) (2006). *Betriebswirtschaftslehre und Frauen- und Geschlechterforschung: Teil 1. Verortung geschlechterkonstituierender (Re-)Produktionsprozesse*. Frankfurt am Main [u.a.]: Lang.

Critical Scholarship in Management 97

Chmielewicz, K. (1973). Interessen in der Betriebswirtschaftslehre aus wissenschaftstheoretischer Sicht. In WSI (Ed.), *Arbeitsorientierte Einzelwirtschaftslehre contra kapitalorientierte Betriebswirtschaftslehre. WSI-Forum am 6. u. 7. Juni 1973*, 4–25. Köln: Bund-Verlag.

Chmielewicz, K. (1975). *Arbeitnehmerinteressen und Kapitalismuskritik in der Betriebswirtschaftslehre.* Reinbek (bei Hamburg): Rowohlt.

Costas, J. (2010). Unveiling the Masks: Critical Management Studies. *Organization*, 17(6): 789–792.

Costas, J. and Grey, C. (2014). The Temporality of Power and the Power of Temporality: Imaginary Future Selves in Professional Service Firms. *Organization Studies*, 35(6): 909–937.

Costas, J. and Taheri, A. (2012). 'The Return of the Primal Father' in Postmodernity? A Lacanian Analysis of Authentic Leadership. *Organization Studies*, 33(9): 1195–1216.

Deutschmann, C. (2002). *Postindustrielle Industriesoziologie. Theoretische Grundlagen, Arbeitsverhältnisse und soziale Identitäten.* Weinheim: Juventa.

Engel, N. and Sausele-Bayer, I. (Eds.) (2014). *Organisation. Ein pädagogischer Grundbegriff.* Münster and New York: Waxmann.

Fournier, V. and Grey, C. (2000). At the Critical Moment: Conditions and Prospects for Critical Management Studies. *Human Relations*, 53(1): 7–32.

Gerhard, B., Osterloh, Margit and Schmid, R. (1993). Wie kommen Frauen in deutschsprachigen Personallehrbüchern vor? In G. Krell and Osterloh Margit (Eds.), *Personalpolitik aus der Sicht von Frauen—Frauen aus der Sicht der Personalpolitik. Was kann die Personalforschung von der Frauenforschung lernen?*, 28–49. Munich: Hampp.

Hartz, R. (2011). Die 'Critical Management Studies'—eine Zwischenbilanz in kritischer Absicht. In M. Bruch, W. Schaffar and P. Scheiffele (Eds.), *Organisation und Kritik*, 211–246. Münster: Westfälisches Dampfboot.

Hartz, R. and Rätzer, M. (2013a). Einführung. In R. Hartz and M. Rätzer (Eds.), *Organisationsforschung nach Foucault. Macht—Diskurs—Widerstand*, 7–15. Bielefeld: Transcript.

Hartz, R. and Rätzer, M. (Eds.) (2013b). *Organisationsforschung nach Foucault. Macht—Diskurs—Widerstand*, 1st ed. Bielefeld: Transcript.

Hax, K. (1974). Das Projekt "Arbeitsorientierte Einzelwirtschaftslehre". Eine kritische Betrachtung. *Schmalenbachs Zeitschrift für betriebswirtschaftliche Forschung: Zfbf*, 26(12): 798–809.

Holzkamp, K. (2013). *Psychology from the Standpoint of the Subject. Selected Writings of Klaus Holzkamp.* Basingstoke: Palgrave Macmillan.

Hundt, S. (1977). *Zur Theoriegeschichte der Betriebswirtschaftslehre.* Köln: Bund-Verlag.

Kappler, E. (1973, July 13). Warum nicht AOGWL? *Wirtschaftswoche*, 38–40.

Kappler, E. (1980). Brauchen wir eine neue Betriebswirtschaftslehre? Vorbemerkungen zur kritischen Betriebswirtschaftslehre. In N. Koubek, H.-D. Küller and I. Scheibe-Lange (Eds.), *Betriebswirtschaftliche Probleme der Mitbestimmung*, 177–201. Köln: Bund-Verlag.

Koubek, N. (1973). Grundelemente einer Arbeitsorientierten Einzelwirtschaftslehre. In WSI (Ed.) *Arbeitsorientierte Einzelwirtschaftslehre contra kapitalorientierte Betriebswirtschaftslehre. WSI-Forum am 6. u. 7. Juni 1973*, 69–102. Köln: Bund-Verlag.

Krell, G. (1984). *Das Bild der Frau in der Arbeitswissenschaft.* Frankfurt/Main and New York: Campus.

Krell, G., (1993). Wie wünschenswert ist eine nach Geschlecht differenzierende Personalpolitik?—Ein Diskussionsbeitrag. In G. Krell and Osterloh Margit (Eds.), *Personalpolitik aus der Sicht von Frauen—Frauen aus der Sicht der Personalpolitik.*

98 Ronald Hartz

Was kann die Personalforschung von der Frauenforschung lernen?, 2nd ed., 50–61. München: R. Hampp Verlag.

Krell, G., (2003). Die Ordnung der 'Humanressourcen' als Ordnung der Geschlechter. In R. Weiskopf (Ed.), *Menschenregierungskünste. Anwendungen poststrukturalistischer Analyse auf Management und Organisation*, 65–90. Wiesbaden: Westdt. Verlag.

Krell, G. (2013). "Widerstandspunkte im Machtnetz". Facetten (m)einer Diskursgeschichte der BWL-Kritiken. In R. Hartz and M. Rätzer (Eds.), *Organisationsforschung nach Foucault. Macht—Diskurs—Widerstand*, 61–83. Bielefeld: Transcript.

Krell, G., Ortlieb, R. and Sieben, B. (Eds.) (2011). *Chancengleichheit durch Personalpolitik. Gleichstellung von Frauen und Männern in Unternehmen und Verwaltungen; rechtliche Regelungen—Problemanalysen—Lösungen*, 6th ed. Wiesbaden: Gabler.

Krell, G. and Osterloh, Margit (Eds.) (1993a). *Personalpolitik aus der Sicht von Frauen—Frauen aus der Sicht der Personalpolitik. Was kann die Personalforschung von der Frauenforschung lernen?*, 2nd ed. München: R. Hampp Verlag.

Krell, G. and Osterloh, Margit (1993b). Welchen Stellenwert haben Frauenthemen an Personallehrstühlen im deutschsprachigen Raum?—Eine Bestandsaufnahme. In G. Krell and Osterloh Margit (Eds.), *Personalpolitik aus der Sicht von Frauen—Frauen aus der Sicht der Personalpolitik. Was kann die Personalforschung von der Frauenforschung lernen?*, 2nd ed., 11–27. München: R. Hampp Verlag.

Krell, G., Rastetter, D. and Reichel, K. (Eds.) (2012). *Geschlecht Macht Karriere in Organisationen. Analysen zur Chancengleichheit in Fach- und Führungspositionen*, 1st ed. Berlin: Edition Sigma.

Krell, G. and Weiskopf, R. (2006). *Die Anordnung der Leidenschaften*. Wien: Passagen.

Laske, S. and Schweres, M. (Eds.) (2014). *Arbeitsorientierung in den Wirtschaftswissenschaften. Vielfalt als Krisenindikator oder als Potenzial?* München und Mering: Hampp.

Laske, S. and Weiskopf, R. (1996). Personalauswahl—Was wird denn da gespielt? Ein Plädoyer für einen Perspektivenwechsel. *Zeitschrift für Personalforschung*, 10(4): 295–330.

Nienhüser, W. (1998). Die Nutzung personal- und organisationswissenschaftlicher Erkenntnisse in Unternehmen. Eine Analyse der Bestimmungsgründe und Formen auf der Grundlage theoretischer und empirischer Befunde. *Zeitschrift für Personalforschung*, 12(1): 21–49.

Nienhüser, W. (2004a). Political (Personnel) Economy—a Political Economy Perspective to Explain Different Forms of Human Resource Management. *Management Revue*, 15(2): 228–248.

Nienhüser, W. (2004b). Politikorientierte Ansätze des Personalmanagements. In E. Gaugler, W.A. Oechsler and W. Weber (Eds.), *Handwörterbuch des Personalwesens*, 1671–1685. Stuttgart: Schäffer-Poeschel.

Nienhüser, W. (2015). Sozialökonomische Personal- und Organisationsforschung. In R. Hedtke (Ed.), *Was ist und wozu Sozioökonomie?*, 311–336. Wiesbaden: Springer VS.

Nienhüser, W. (2011). Empirical Research on Human Resource Management as a Production of Ideology. *Managementrevue*, 22(4): 367–393.

Ortmann, G. (2003). *Organisation und Welterschließung. Dekonstruktionen*, 1st ed. Wiesbaden: Westdt. Verlag.

Ortmann, G. (2004). *Als ob. Fiktionen und Organisationen*, 1st ed. Wiesbaden: VS Verlag für Sozialwissenschaften.

Ortmann, G. (2010). *Organisation und Moral. Die dunkle Seite*, 1st ed. Weilerswist: Velbrück.

Perrow, C. (1991). A Society of Organizations. *Theory and Society*, 20(6): 725–762.

Critical Scholarship in Management 99

Projektgruppe im WSI (1974). *Grundelemente einer arbeitsorientierten Einzelwirtschaftslehre. Ein Beitrag z. polit. Ökonomie d. Unternehmung.* Köln: Bund-Verlag.

Schanz, G. (1992). Wissenschaftsprogramme der BWL. In F.X. Bea, E. Dichtl and M. Schweitzer (Eds.), *Allgemeine Betriebswirtschaftslehre*, 18–30. Stuttgart: Fischer.

Schreyögg, G. (Ed.)(1999). *Organisation und Postmoderne. Grundfragen—Analysen—Perspektiven.* Wiesbaden: Gabler.

Sieben, B. (2007). *Management und Emotionen. Analyse einer ambivalenten Verknüpfung.* Frankfurt/Main [u.a.]: Campus-Verlag.

Sievers, B. (1994). *Work, Death, and Life Itself. Essays on Management and Organization.* Berlin and New York: Walter de Gruyter.

Sievers, B. (2006). The Psychotic Organization: A SocioAnalytic Perspective. *Ephemera*, 6(2): 104–120.

Türk, K. (1995a). Einleitung. In K. Türk (Ed.), *"Die Organisation der Welt". Herrschaft durch Organisation in der modernen Gesellschaft*, 9–17. Opladen: Westdeutscher Verlag.

Türk, K. (1995b). Zur Kritik der politischen Ökonomie der Organisation. In K. Türk (Ed.). *"Die Organisation der Welt". Herrschaft durch Organisation in der modernen Gesellschaft*, 37–92. Opladen: Westdeutscher Verlag.

Türk, K. (1999). The Critique of the Political Economy of Organization. A Contribution to the Analysis of the Organizational Social Formation. *International Journal of Political Economy*, 29(3): 6–32.

Türk, K., Lemke, T. and Bruch, M. (2002). *Organisation in der modernen Gesellschaft. Eine historische Einführung*, 1st ed. Wiesbaden: Westdeutscher Verlag.

Wächter, H. (1976). Die Arbeitsorientierte Einzelwirtschaftslehre—eine Herausforderung an die Betriebswirtschaftslehre. *Wirtschaftswissenschaftliches Studium: Wist; Zeitschrift für Ausbildung und Hochschulkontakt*, 5(7): 310–316.

Wächter, H. and Metz, T. (2010). Das kritische Vermächtnis der AOEWL. In W. Baumann, U. Braukmann and W. Matthes (Eds.), *Innovation und Internationalisierung. Festschrift für Norbert Koubek*, 29–44. Wiesbaden: Gabler.

Weik, E. (1998). *Zeit, Wandel und Transformation. Elemente einer postmodernen Theorie der Transformation.* München: R. Hampp Verlag.

Weik, E. (2014). Interpretative Theorien: Sprache, Kommunikation und Organisation. In A. Kieser and M. Ebers (Eds.), *Organisationstheorien*, 346–385. Stuttgart: Kohlhammer.

Weiskopf, R. (2003a). Management, Organisation, Poststrukturalismus. In: R. Weiskopf (Ed.), *Menschenregierungskünste. Anwendungen poststrukturalistischer Analyse auf Management und Organisation*, 9–33. Wiesbaden: Westdeutscher Verlag.

Weiskopf, R. (Ed.) (2003b). *Menschenregierungskünste. Anwendungen poststrukturalistischer Analyse auf Management und Organisation*, 1st ed. Wiesbaden: Westdeutscher Verlag.

Weiskopf, R. (2005). Gouvernementabilität: Die Produktion des regierbaren Menschen in post-disziplinären Regimen. *Zeitschrift für Personalforschung*, 19(3): 289–311.

Weiskopf, R. and Willmott, H. (2013). Ethics as Critical Practice: The "Pentagon Papers", Deciding Responsibly, Truth-Telling, and the Unsettling of Organizational Morality. *Organization Studies*, 34(4): 469–493.

WSI (Ed.) (1973). *Arbeitsorientierte Einzelwirtschaftslehre contra kapitalorientierte Betriebswirtschaftslehre. WSI-Forum am 6. u. 7. Juni 1973*, 2nd ed. Köln: Bund-Verlag.

7 From Anti-Managerialism to Over-Managerialism

How Critical Management Studies in Israel Were Exiled from Local Business Schools and Emerged Elsewhere

Michal Frenkel

INTRODUCTION

Israel could have been the ideal greenhouse for the cultivation of a lively and innovative Critical Management Studies (CMS) community. The anti-managerial sentiment that characterized Israeli society in its first decades, a dynamic post-Marxist intellectual discourse, the explicit and widely discussed interlocking of business management and the political sphere, and the many internal and geopolitical conflicts that have clearly and openly affected the evolution of the country's business system (Frenkel, 2005) could have inspired an extended adoption and innovative development of a critical theoretical lens for the understanding of management theories and practices in Israel's booming business education system. Such a lively critical management discourse has indeed evolved since the early 1990s (e.g. Shenhav, 1992, 1995, 2013; Shenhav, 1999; Shenhav and Gabay, 2001; Darr, 2003; Frenkel, 2005; Frenkel and Shenhav, 2006; Ailon, 2008; Frenkel, 2008a; Ailon and Kunda, 2009; Belhassen and Caton, 2011; Katz, 2013) in parallel to the emergence and institutionalization of Critical Management Studies as a differentiated field within organization and management studies but, paradoxically (or maybe not), this emergence has been exiled from the institutionalized disciplinarian environment of Israeli business schools and is taking place, for the most part, in departments of sociology and anthropology and in labour studies. Only one of the 14 business schools that offer master of business administration (MBA) or management degrees, and none of the numerous other undergraduate and graduate programmes in management studies in Israel, has offered a course openly dedicated to "critical management thought" (that single exception is the course offered by Yaniv Belhassen at Ben-Gurion University). In personal communication, some business professors in Israel, who introduce critical management theories as part of their general organization theory (OT) courses, often report hostile responses from students and the need to rhetorically justify such deviation from mainstream management thinking. In the current chapter, I apply a *critical approach of glocalization* to account

Anti-Managerialism to Over-Managerialism 101

for the exclusion of Critical Management Studies from Israel's formal management education industry.

A critical approach to glocalization integrates insights from critical theories of globalization, which focuses on the ways in which centre-periphery geopolitical and postcolonial power dynamics affect the cross-national transfer of ideas, theories, and practices with critical theories focusing on local power dynamics and the ways in which the adoption, translation, and implementation of foreign ideas play a role in the construction of new groups' identities and securing their exclusive jurisdiction and political domination.

Applying this theoretical approach, I argue that the exclusion of CMS from the Israeli business school system reflects the success of the US neocolonial project aimed at exporting "the American way" after World War II (for a detailed description of this process in Israel, see Frenkel and Shenhav, 2003; Frenkel, 2005; Frenkel, 2008b). Since the outset of the Marshall Plan in post-World War II Europe, the development of management and business studies and the exportation of managerialism have been seen as ways to secure the legitimation of the free market, consumerism, and the preference toward private capital and entrepreneurship ideologies and institutions in countries leaning toward the Communist Bloc (Bu, 1999; Djelic, 1998; Kipping and Bjarnar, 2002). The evolution of management institutions, including management education in Israel, is closely associated with this project, thus constructing not only a close tie between the local business schools and U.S.-based ones, but also a strong tendency on the part of these schools top resist everything that might be associated with "leftism" and the critique of the free market and managerialism (Frenkel, 2001). Reinforced by the desire to gain academic and scientific legitimacy at the global centre through the publication of papers in mainstream, prestigious journals (especially in the United States), this inclination has resulted in the rejection of any scholarship that has the potential to undermine the legitimacy of managerialism in Israel.

Simultaneously, the professionalization project of the business leadership in Israel and its attempt to secure its exclusive jurisdiction vis-à-vis professional politicians who lead many of the state- and union-owned business enterprises has been grounded in the presentation of management studies as scientific, objective, and rational (Frenkel, 2001). The ostensive ostensible de-politicization and, to a large extent, the decontextualization of management studies in Israel may be seen as a means to an end in this project. I argue here that the de-politicization, decontextualization, and reliance upon generalizable positivist research methods and epistemology are key components of the ability of management scholars and students to shed their confining parochial-peripheral Israeli identity and replace it with a transnational and cosmopolitan one.

The juxtaposition of geopolitical pressures and local interests, I contend, has led to the marginalization of any attempt to develop an innovative and critical theoretical perspective as part of the management education system.

102 *Michal Frenkel*

Yet the same conditions that led to the marginalization of CMS in Israeli business schools are at least partially responsible for the flowering of critical management theoretical and empirical efforts in other academic scenes in Israel, especially in departments of sociology, anthropology, and labour studies.

After a short theoretical section in which I outline the premises for a critical approach to understanding glocalization processes, this chapter presents the historical roots of management studies in Israel and the present state of this discipline, which has led to the common rejection of CMS in this system. I conclude the chapter by reviewing some of the contributions made by Israeli scholars to Critical Management Studies and by pointing to the role of the institutionalization of CMS at the global level as a context within which this development in Israel has been afforded.

TOWARDS A CRITICAL APPROACH TO GLOCALIZATION: A THEORETICAL NOTE

Emerging as a critique of the common understanding of globalization as homogenization, theories of glocalization point to the "complex process that fuses the global and the local, and interlaces worldwide similarity with cross-national variation" (Drori et al., 2013, p. 3). Coined by Robertson in 1994, the notion of glocalization" has inspired a series of studies in sociology, anthropology, cultural studies, and organization and management studies that provide a detailed picture of the transformations that ideas, theories, and practices undergo when they travel across borders. While studies of homogenous globalization often present the process as a top-down and agency-free diffusion in which ideas travel and are implemented because they are either inherently rational or have been socially constructed as rational and effective, studies of glocalization have highlighted the role of specific social actors (or agents) in the exportation, importation, translation, and implementation of these ideas and practices. Yet while power and interests on both ends of the process (exporters and importers) have been identified in some historical studies of glocalization (whether they apply the notion itself or not) (Boltanski, 1987; Guillen, 1994; Djelic, 1998; Kipping and Bjarnar, 1998), until recently very little effort had been made in *theorizing* the ways in which power and interests were involved in the process.

Evolving alongside the intensification of the globalization process, Critical Management Studies have pointed to the importance of studying the process of cross-national transfer and translation of management practices and ideologies, as well as to the potential social influence of managerialism and neo-liberalization in the receiving societies. Understanding management "as a political, cultural and ideological phenomenon" (Alvesson and Willmott, 1992, p. 6), this general school of thought has called for research to pay closer attention to the geopolitical power relations within

Anti-Managerialism to Over-Managerialism   103

which management theory has emerged and been institutionalized (Calas and Smircich, 1999; Cooke, 2003; Frenkel and Shenhav, 2006) in a way that has marginalized and undermined indigenous and local systems of knowledge and organizing practices (e.g. Mir et al., 2009; Alcadipani et al., 2012). In line with previous historical studies of the exportation of "American" models of management to Europe (Guillen, 1994; Djelic, 1998; Kipping and Bjarnar, 1998), which have already noted the geopolitical interests invested in this effort, critical studies in this field have mostly adopted a postcolonial perspective, presenting the introduction of management studies and models as part of the colonial domination system that reinforce, reproduce, and legitimize the economic domination of the Global North over the Global South, even after the end of the formal colonial rule (Frenkel and Shenhav, 2003; Jack and Westwood, 2009; Alcadipani and Rosa, 2011). More recently, CMS scholars have also pointed to the structure of the global academic publication and evaluation industries—situated in the Global North and reproducing its logic of action and epistemological priorities—as an additional means through which the marginalization of alternative "non-Western" epistemologies, methodologies, and organizational practices remain marginalized, even when the corporations applying them and the economies within which they have emerged are being celebrated as the new "tigers" of the global economy (Frenkel, 2014). While obviously important and inspiring, these studies tend to focus their analysis on the geopolitical power relations among states, blocs, hemispheres, or between international organizations and local societies depending upon them. Local actors operating at the receiving end and their interests are largely overlooked in these studies, which present them as agency-less victims of globalization.

In another (less visible) stream of critical writing, local acceptance or resistance toward imported management studies and practices are analysed, with a little more attention paid to local power relations (e.g. Frenkel, 2005). This line of study usually highlights local interest groups and elites, as well as marginalized and exploited groups, as they struggle to negotiate the implementation of managerial ideas. The global-structure positions of local actors and their interests at the global geopolitical level are rarely discussed.

Despite this growing interest of CMS in the role of power and politics in the cross-national glocalization of management studies and ideas, this theoretical effort remains somewhat limited and unsatisfactory. With a few exceptions, the ways in which power dynamics within the nation-state and other local units are (and to a certain extent always have been) intertwined with a more global power dynamic remain undertheorized.

In the present chapter, I call for the development of a more comprehensive critical approach to glocalization, arguing that a better understanding of the spread—or lack thereof—of both managerialism and its critics depends upon a simultaneous exploration of power dynamics at the local and transnational fields of management and the interrelations between them. Moreover, in line with the way the notion of power is articulated and understood

104 *Michal Frenkel*

in CMS, power should be defined in ways that go beyond the narrow understanding of power as coercion. (For a critique of this conceptualization of power, see Alvesson and Willmott, 1992).

THE UNCRITICAL CRITIC: THE EMERGENCE OF AN ISRAELI FIELD OF MANAGEMENT STUDIES

The field of Critical Management Studies calls for an understanding of the emergence and evolution of management theories and concepts in their broadest context, taking into account the power relations, agency, and interests of those involved in the production and dissemination of these ideas. Recently, Alvesson (2008) has offered a distinction between "light" and "heavier" versions of CMS, seeing the introduction of nonpositivist and reflexive qualitative methods as proxies of a light critical approach. A heavier critical approach, in his view, requires the questioning of the underlying assumptions of managerialism and a heightened focus on the role of management theories and practices in the production and reproduction of social inequalities and exploitive relations. In this chapter, I trace the evolution of both approaches in Israel and argue that while the lighter version has left some imprint on Israeli business and management schools (especially at the Hebrew University and Ben-Gurion University), the heavier version has been developed in exile.

Tracing the history of the path not taken is naturally a complicated mission. No open archive can provide the story of critical management scholars who were not hired, and no document explicitly reveals a decision not to develop CMS in Israel. At the same time, the centrality of the pro-managerialist approach to the development of business education in Israel and the struggles to legitimize this approach in the country's early days is documented in archival materials and contemporary media coverage. (For an extended review of this archival material, see Frenkel, 2001, 2005). Thus my explanation of the rejection of CMS in Israeli management schools starts with a genealogical enquiry into the introduction of management ideas and theories to Israeli society right after statehood, in the 1950s and 1960s. In line with the critical approach to glocalization outlined earlier, my study of the emergence of Israel's field of management research and education takes into consideration the geopolitical and global academic dynamics characterizing the global field of management research and education; the local Israeli fields of power and management; and the asymmetric, intertwined co-evolution of the two. The uncritically managerialist tendency of Israeli management studies, I argue, owes its DNA to three main power dynamics surrounding its foundation: the geopolitical Cold War dynamic, the local struggle for professional-managerial exclusive jurisdiction, and the Israeli academy's struggle for international recognition.

My point of departure for an understanding of the rejection of Critical Management Studies in the Israeli management education system goes back

Anti-Managerialism to Over-Managerialism 105

to its foundation, to a context in time when managerialism itself was considered a harsh critique of the local anti-managerialist dominant discourse led by the political Zionist-Socialist elite of the labour movement, which then dominated Israel's political economy. Before statehood (in 1948), under British Mandatory rule, Israel's project of state and nation building was administered through the various institutional arms of the local labour movement. The different factions of this movement, each of which adhered to slightly different versions of socialist ideology, simultaneously controlled prestate (and state) apparatuses and the powerful General Federation of Jewish Workers (the *Histadrut*) (Shalev, 1992). Because there was a lack of privately owned capital, the construction of physical, economic, and industrial infrastructures for the new society drew upon "national capital" contributed by world Jewry and was administrated by the prestate political apparatuses dominated by the labour movement (Frenkel, 2005).

Given this unique social structure, it is easy to understand why the main (collective) social actors involved in the shaping of practical management were the state, the *Histadrut*, and a weaker group of private capital holders. While the capital holders were indeed interested in promoting increased productivity and reducing the power of the labour unions, there is much evidence from the prestate era and the 1950s that capitalists in Israel were quite sceptical about the contribution that professional management could make to their businesses. They saw management as an art that was passed down from father to son, and they were anxious about relinquishing control of their businesses (Sobel, 1959).

Viewing industrial and economic enterprises as political tools, the leadership of the *Histadrut*-owned corporations also held an anti-managerialist ideology. In the 1950s, prominent managers of *Histadrut*-owned industries even rejected the very term "manager". Hillel Dan, by far the most influential manager in the first decade of Israel's existence, refused to see his position as a manager as implying any kind of professional identity and presented himself instead as a leading worker or an economic leader. It was against this backdrop that the US operation Mission to Israel designed its aid programme, identifying the introduction of "American-like" business and management institutions as its priority list.

Arriving in Israel as part of the Point Four Programme—a Marshall Plan–like program intended for developing countries—the United States Operations Mission to Israel (USOM) articulated its mission in terms of securing Israeli affiliation with the Western Bloc and turning its political system from a socialist to a free market–oriented one. An internal document that summarizes the programme's activities up until 1959 shows that 118 American experts visited Israel over those years. Eighteen of them were directly or indirectly involved with promoting the institutionalization of the field of management, diffusing methods for increasing productivity, advancing the professionalization of production and marketing, and creating and teaching programmes for training managers.[1] The foundation of the first two

106 Michal Frenkel

programmes in management studies, the department of industrial engineering at the Technion in 1954, and the school for management and administration at the Hebrew University of Jerusalem (in 1957) constituted critical parts of this project. Management professors from the US came to Israel for short and long missions both to teach in schools and to shape their curricula. Later on, promising Israeli students were sent to US business schools such as Harvard and Columbia to acquire the type of American business education that would allow them to establish additional business schools and spread the gospel of managerialism and professionalism. Yair Aharoni and Teddy Weinshall, who later established the business school at Tel Aviv University, were part of this group (Frenkel, 2001).

It is important to note that the role of the new management training programmes in constructing an alternative to the dominant "labour-centred" one did not go unnoticed by the local elite. In fact, the USOM's plans faced much criticism and resistance, and several leading political figures explicitly condemned the establishment of the business training institutions as an American attempt to intervene in Israel's internal political affairs. This political turmoil surrounding the foundation of business schools and departments of management expressed itself most vividly during the establishment of the school of management at Tel Aviv University in the early 1960s, when *Histadrut* leaders demanded that the school adopt a labour-relations rather than a managerialist perspective. A compromise was eventually reached, and while the school of management emulated the "American" model in its structure and curriculum, a department of labour studies was established simultaneously to promote labour-relations research and training for managers and leaders in *Histadrut*-owned corporations (Frenkel, 2001).

Thus, from its very foundation, a division of labour was institutionalized between schools of management, in which North American managerialist ideology became a core identity component, and the department of labour studies (and, later on, departments of sociology and anthropology as well), in which alternative, labour-oriented thinking has been legitimated.

PROFESSIONAL BOUNDARY WORK AND THE DELETION OF THE "POLITICAL"

While extensively influenced by American pressure to introduce an alternative to the statist and *Histadrut*-owned economy, the institutionalization of the overmanagerialist character of Israeli schools of management has also been associated with the struggle of serving managers to demarcate their professional jurisdiction and delegitimize politicians' intervention in their decision making. In his brief review of the Israel Management Center, Teddy Weinshall lent support to this notion when he noted that "one of the serious problems in Israeli society is that until a few years ago the managers did not know that they were managers" (Weinshall, 1969). The shift to self-representation as managers with professional expertise and the beginnings of a distinct identity that called for recognition and legitimation in Israeli society were part of the process of the institutionalization of a distinct field, not a condition for its emergence. Until then, making a proven contribution to the collective—such as through lengthy service in the labour movement and the ability to creatively and convincingly deploy arguments from the Socialist-Zionist arsenal—was the kind of cultural capital that enabled those who possessed it to act as legitimate players in the local field. Thus, in the mid-1950s, concurrently with the initial implementation of USOM's managerializing project—and when, thanks to their control over the country's economic means, managers of *Histadrut*-owned corporations accumulated enough political power to threaten the country's political leadership—a war was declared against them. The assault took the form of corporate restructuring aimed at weakening these corporations and their managers' political influence (Dan, 1963; Frenkel, 2001). The availability of the new managerialist discourse allowed these managers to embark upon a collective identity demarcation. Since the adversary party in this struggle was the political leadership, much of the discursive effort was built upon early twentieth-century American progressive ideology, demarcating professionalism from politics. Politicians were accused of making irrational decisions and favouring their political interests over those of the corporation and its prosperity. Throughout this debate, the demarcation of boundaries between management and politics became the main building block of professional management and administration and of the emerging professional identity of managers in Israel. Given this professional heritage, the repoliticization of management, as promoted by Critical Management Studies, still constitutes a threat to this budding professional identity project.

SCIENCE IN A SMALL COUNTRY

The third aspect contributing to the uncritical essence of business schools in Israel is the strong affiliation that local academia has developed with its American counterpart. In his 1964 article entitled "Science in a Small Country", sociologist of science Joseph Ben-David of the Hebrew University and the University of Chicago articulated the ideology that forced most Israeli social scientists to turn their backs on the contextual study of Israeli society, including that of Israeli organization and management. According to Ben-David, in a small academic system where everyone knows each other personally, a peer-review academic system is meaningless. To prevent nepotism and scientific stagnation, scientists in small countries should direct their work toward the international scientific community and be evaluated based on their publications abroad. Due to the rising global centrality of US academia after World War II and the exchange programmes offered to students and professors by US-based agencies, international affiliation after statehood

108   *Michal Frenkel*

meant mostly an affiliation with US universities and publication in North American journals and publishing houses. From a critical management perspective, this strong affiliation had three main outcomes: (1) precedence in hiring and promotion of US-trained scholars, who brought in positivist methodology and managerialist epistemology; (2) decontextualization of research questions and writing to allow for publication in mainstream North American journals; and (3) marginalization (almost eradication) of Hebrew writing and publications, leading to the absence of a local journal of management within which a local academic perspective could emerge and gain influence.

The establishment of Israeli business schools in opposition to the anti-managerialist and pro-labour dominant ideology, the importance of the distinction between management and politics as part of managers' professional boundary work, and the heavy dependency of Israeli scholars in general and of management scholars in particular on being published in leading mainstream North American journals have worked in combination to turn Israel's schools of management into a rather hostile environment for CMS.

DISCIPLINE AND PUNISH: ISRAEL'S MANAGEMENT STUDIES BETWEEN INTERNATIONAL "QUALITY CONTROL" AND LOCAL POLITICS

In addition to the three historical characteristics of the business education system in Israel, which hinder the institutionalization of CMS, three additional and interrelated features have materialized since the 1990s in combination with the emergence and institutionalization of CMS in Britain, Scandinavia, and Australia: the integration of the Israeli economy into the global economy; the restructuring of Israel's academic system with the foundation of privately owned, for-profit colleges that have turned to management studies as a major source of income; and the institutionalization of the global ranking system of business schools (Guri-Rozenblit, 1993).

The integration of Israel into the global economy has been accompanied by a weakening of the *Histadrut* and its economic enterprises to the point that they have been almost entirely privatized and by the growing influence of North American–based multinationals. These multinationals expect their Israeli managers to be acquainted with cutting-edge management techniques and to accept managerialism at face value, contributing to the growing decontextualized identity of business schools and their constituencies. The expansion of the academic system has led to the founding of additional business schools and undergraduate programmes in management that compete for a rather small candidate pool by highlighting the applicability of the training they offer rather than by appealing to students' general intellectual interests. Finally, the global business school ranking (and general university ranking) has added to the pressure for mainstreaming and decontextualization,

Anti-Managerialism to Over-Managerialism   109

making it even harder for scholars interested in CMS to develop careers in this field within Israeli business schools that offer courses in it.

As a result, of the 14 business schools that offer graduate education in management and MBA programmes, only one has offered an elective course devoted entirely to Critical Management Studies. None of the colleges offering undergraduate programmes in management offers such a course. Business school faculty members who introduce critical theories in their courses report the need to justify the discussion of this perspective and sometimes face strong opposition from their students, which may lead, in turn, to low student evaluations and difficulty in justifying their curriculum choices to their colleagues.[2] One faculty member who presented a paper about the importance of introducing Critical Management Studies as part of a specific training programme was told that such a topic does not belong in management studies but might better be applied to labour studies.

Another obstacle to the introduction of Critical Management Studies into the business school curriculum is general concern about the eruption of a political debate in the classroom. In the shadow of the continuous Arab-Israeli conflict, several civic organizations have taken it upon themselves to "monitor" what they define as the political and anti-Zionist bias that university professors bring to their classrooms. These organizations publish reports and appeal to university authorities to push back against the targeted professors. While most universities have so far refrained from taking measures against their faculties for these reasons, the general political climate discourages teachers from engaging their students in such controversial debates.

To be sure, some "light" aspects of Critical Management Studies have been integrated into the mainstream curriculum in some Israeli management schools. For instance, qualitative methodology and constructivist epistemology have gained some prominence in several schools of management, including those of the Hebrew University, Tel Aviv University, Haifa University, and others, and a growing number of organizational behaviour graduate students now apply these methods in their doctoral research. In most cases, however, their application of ethnographic and other qualitative methods is not framed as a critique of more conservative methods. But, with few exceptions, less attention is given even in these research projects to the role of conflicts (such as the Israeli-Palestinian one) in shaping organizational lives and management practices, and critical theories are rarely discussed in these studies.

A preliminary review of Israeli business school syllabi in organizational theory pointed to a single Hebrew text through which management students encounter critical studies in the management field: Yehouda Shenhav's book *The Organization Machine: A Critical Inquiry into the Foundations of Management Theory* (1995). Not surprisingly, this text—which provides a Foucauldian genealogy of the emergence of the first organizational theories and fundamental concepts—was not conceived in an Israeli business school environment, but rather in that of a department of sociology and anthropology.

110 *Michal Frenkel*

MINDING THE GAPS: THE EMERGENCE OF CRITICAL MANAGEMENT THINKING IN SOCIOLOGY, ORGANIZATION, AND LABOUR STUDIES[3]

The 1980s constituted a turning point in Israel's political economy. The political domination of the labour parties ended in 1977, opening the way for a new economic policy heavily influenced by Milton Friedman's neoclassical economic ideology. The collapse of the old economic system was publicly blamed on the "political management" that characterized *Histadrut-* and state-owned corporations, and the demand for professional management training increased. The rigid academic system in Israel at the time did not allow for the expansion of management training in the existing schools of management and business, and the departments of labour studies and sociology and anthropology have gradually become alternatives to the formal business school education, offering a curriculum that combines studies of organizational and management theories with sociological, social psychological, historical, and legal perspectives on management, labour, and organizations. Under the rules of science in a small country, these departments, much like the local business schools, have affiliated themselves with the North American academic industry, giving preference in hiring to graduates of major American universities and promoting those scholars who are able to publish their work in major American journals. However, thanks to the renewed interest of North American social sciences in their European critical roots since the late 1960s (see Kunda, 2013), as well as the long-lasting tradition of historical and critical (mostly Marxist) research in both labour studies and sociology in Israel, a critical body of research and teaching in the field of organization and management theory could have emerged in these departments. The evolution of this critical tradition in Israel can be traced back to the intellectual work of two leading Israeli scholars: Yehouda Shenhav and Gideon Kunda. As I shall argue, Shenhav's work leans toward the heavy critical tradition, combining the development of a critical theory inspired by writing about management with social activism. Kunda's highlights the merit of ethnographic studies. In different ways, they are both socially active in fields related to their critical writing.

Since completing his doctoral studies in sociology at Stanford University, Shenhav has specialized in both sociology of organizations and sociology of science. Writing his doctoral dissertation under Bernard Cohen and Richard Scott, he developed an interest in the historical evolution of American management theory. After he joined the Tel Aviv University Department of Sociology and Anthropology in 1987, he began teaching a course in organizational sociology. Yet the introduction of North American theories of organization and management in the Israeli context soon revealed the differences in the underlying assumptions of students in the US and Israel about organizations, management, rationality, and politics. This forced Shenhav to rethink the basic notions of this theoretical school and encouraged him to further explore the historical roots of American management theory in its exceptional social

Anti-Managerialism to Over-Managerialism   111

and historical context. The growing popularity of neo-Marxist and post-structuralist theories in Israeli academia at the time also fed his conceptualization of his research project, leading to the publication of two books: a popular book summarizing a series of radio lectures titled *Managerial Ideologies in the Age of Rationality* (1991) and the academic book mentioned earlier, *The Organization Machine* (1995b). The former mainly reconceptualized existing knowledge about the evolution of managerial ideologies (Bendix, 1956) using a Foucauldian perspective of power-knowledge. The latter, by contrast, combines a more extensive neo-Marxist and post-structuralist critique of the different theoretical paradigms in management with a meticulous historical study of the origins of scientific management, also published in the *Administrative Science Quarterly* (Shenhav, 1995) and in his later book *Manufacturing Rationality: The Engineering Foundations of the Managerial Revolution* (Shenhav, 1999). This growing interest in critical thinking about management and organizations has coincided with Shenhav's growing role as a public intellectual and social activist interested specifically in ethnic inequality within the Jewish population in Israel and the marginalization of the Asian and African cultures associated with Jews who immigrated to Israel from those countries. The lack of critical writing on management and organizational theories in Hebrew, as well as Shenhav's desire to advance the discussion on organization and management among students and the general public, has led to the publication of his first two books in Hebrew, despite the general tendency of Israeli universities to undervalue Hebrew publications.

The Organization Machine has met with harsh criticism among management scholars in Israeli business schools, who have accused Shenhav of misunderstanding and misrepresenting management theories and practices.[4] Yet, as is often the case in peripheral society, the publication of the research project by prestigious journals and a book publisher has legitimized the Hebrew publication as well. The availability of the book in Hebrew and its compelling presentation of management theories in their historical context have made this book a popular starting point for any discussion of management theories in Organization and Management Theory (OMT) courses in most programmes of management and business studies. A preliminary review of 15 online syllabi of courses in organization and management theory at the undergraduate and graduate levels reveals that nine individual chapters from the two books are required reading. While most courses introduce the book as a heuristic device aimed at introducing the theories and not the critical perspective through which Shenhav understands them, this theoretical framework comprises many students' first encounter with management thinking.

Writing his doctoral dissertation under John Van Mannen at the Massachusetts Institute of Technology, Gideon Kunda was one of the most successful protagonists of the reintroduction of qualitative and ethnographic methodologies in management research. His study of the implementation of organizational culture theory in a high-tech firm in the 1980s highlighted the role of this popular managerial model as a mode of organizational control

112 Michal Frenkel

(Kunda, 1992). While Kunda's book *Engineering Culture: Control and Commitment in a High-Tech Corporation* eventually became very popular in business school curricula around the globe, according to his own testimony, his interest in pursuing an ethnographic study encountered much scepticism among many American and Israeli academicians (Kunda, 2013). The more open and critically oriented intellectual environment in the social sciences has allowed him to find an academic home at Tel Aviv University's departments of Labor Studies and Sociology and Anthropology. Beyond the introduction of qualitative ethnographic research methods in organizational studies in Israel, Kunda has also worked on the history of management ideologies in their general social and economic contexts (Barley and Kunda, 1992) and on questions of control and exploitation at work (Barley and Kunda, 2006).

While Shenhav and Kunda have never engaged in a collaborative study of organizations or management theories,[5] and while their theoretical perspectives and methodological approaches differ, throughout the 1990s, they inspired each other's work. Individually and together, they sponsored a stream of critical master's and doctoral students applying a critical theoretical framework to the understanding of the evolution of management ideologies, theories, and models in the US (see, e.g. Shenhav and Weitz, 2000; Weitz and Shenhav, 2000; Ailon and Kunda, 2003; Landau, 2006;) and Israel (Darr, 1999).

Shenhav, Kunda, and their critical graduate students, who now serve as faculty members in several departments of sociology and anthropology and in graduate programmes in organizational studies, have kept pushing critical management theory forward in Israel. While, with some exceptions, Kunda and his students and colleagues have adhered to the "light" version of CMS and have kept developing the understanding of Israeli organizations in their conflictual context by applying an ethnographic methodology to the study of Israeli-American and Jewish-Palestinian relations in the workplace, Shenhav and his students have taken a heavier and more historical and theoretically explicit perspective, highlighting the more macro complex political and geopolitical power relations within which models of management are imported and translated across borders.

A critical development in the flourishing of critical management thinking and research in Israel has been the founding of the Hebrew journal *Theory and Criticism*, which Shenhav edited from 1999 to 2009. Sponsored by the Van Leer Jerusalem Institute, which sought to encourage a critical and diversified democratic discourse in and about Israel, *Theory and Criticism* (established in 1991)[6] is an interdisciplinary journal that brings together critical thinkers in philosophy, art, literature, history, sociology, and law, allowing them to develop a critical approach that cuts through disciplinary boundaries. It was through this journal that many cutting-edge critical studies and theoretical writings were translated into Hebrew, inspiring an interdisciplinary study of Israeli society. While in its first years the journal focused more on classic critical and postmodern theory, Shenhav, in his capacity as editor in chief,

Anti-Managerialism to Over-Managerialism 113

has promoted the introduction and development of postcolonial studies that also corresponded with his political activism in the field of ethnic and racial identity and inequality in Israel. The result has been a long list of studies stressing the roots of the Zionist project in the colonial era and under British rule, the complex relations between European Jews and Jews of Arab origin, and the relations between Jews and Arabs in the Israeli context. The growing prominence of postcolonial studies in other fields has eventually come to inspire a string of postcolonial writings on organization and management, both in the context of Israel and in a broader theoretical context (e.g. Frenkel and Shenhav, 2003, 2006; Frenkel, 2008a, 2014; Shenhav, 2013).

It is important to note that while Critical Management Studies in Israel was not directly inspired (at least at first) by the emergence of CMS in the UK, Scandinavia, and Australia, the institutionalization of this paradigm in management studies abroad has helped legitimize the field in Israel and opened up publication opportunities in established international outlets. This has made academic career building for CMS scholars possible even in the generally inhospitable context of Israeli academia.

NOTES

1. USOM American Personnel to Israel, Cumulative List, 1950–1959, State Archives, box 43, file 5366, file 175.
2. This observation is based on personal communication with colleagues in several management departments and business schools conducted in October 2014. The exception to this rule is the experience of a colleague from the Hebrew University's school of management who reported openness and interest in critical thinking among her students.
3. This section is grounded mostly in my own observation as a participant in the events depicted; continual conversations with many of the figures involved; and my reading of books, journal papers, and chapters published by Israeli scholars in the field of organization studies. Given the snowballing essence of my data collection, Israeli scholars who are not part of the critical management circles or the local unofficial network may have escaped my attention.
4. Hebrew readers can review this critique at http://people.socsci.tau.ac.il/mu/yshenhav/publications/academic-publications-in-english/booksinhebrew/
5. Shenhav and Kunda's only co-authored publication is the 1992 "Fertile Western Imagination: How Israel's Ethnic Problem is Represented", *Theory & Criticism*, 2, 137–146 [Hebrew].
6. http://theory-and-criticism.vanleer.org.il/en/AboutJLS.aspx

REFERENCES

Ailon, G. (2008). Mirror, Mirror on the Wall: Culture's Consequences in a Value Test of Its Own esign. *Academy of Management Review*, 33(4): 885–904.

Ailon, G. and Kunda, G. (2003). The Local Selves of Global Workers: The Social Construction of National Identity in the Face of Organizational Globalization. *Organization Studies*, 24(7): 1073.

114 Michal Frenkel

Ailon, G. and Kunda, G. (2009). "The one-company approach": Transnationalism in an Israeli-Palestinian Subsidiary of a Multinational Corporation. *Organization Studies*, 30(7): 693–712.

Alcadipani, R., Khan, F.R., Gantman, E. and Nkomo, S. (2012). Southern Voices in Management and Organization Knowledge. *Organization*, 19(2): 131–143.

Alcadipani, R. and Rosa, A.R. (2011). From Grobal Management to Glocal Management: Latin American Perspectives as a Counter-Dominant Management Epistemology. *Canadian Journal of Administrative Sciences/Revue Canadienne des Sciences de l'Administration*, 28(4): 453–466.

Alvesson, M. (2008). The Future of Critical Management Studies. In D. Barry and H. Hansen (Eds.), *The Sage Handbook of New Approaches in Management Organization*, 13–26. London: Sage.

Alvesson, M. and Willmott, H. (1992). *Critical Management Studies*. London: Sage.

Barley, S.R. and Kunda, G. (1992). Design and Devotion: Surges of Rational and Normative Ideologies of Control in Managerial Discourse. *Administrative Science Quarterly*, 37(3): 363–399.

Barley, S.R. and Kunda, G. (2006). *Gurus, Hired Guns, and Warm Bodies: Itinerant Experts in a Knowledge Economy*. Princeton: Princeton University Press.

Belhassen, Y. and Caton, K. (2011). On the Need for Critical Pedagogy in Tourism Education. *Tourism Management*, 32: 1389–1396.

Bendix, R. (1956). *Work and Authority in Industry: Ideologies of Management in the Course of Industrialization*. New York: Wiley.

Boltanski, L. (1987). *The Making of a Class: Cadres in French Society*. Cambridge, UK: Cambridge University Press.

Bu, L. (1999). Educational Exchange and Cultural Diplomacy in the Cold War. *Journal of American Studies*, 33(3): 393–415.

Calas, M.B. and Smircich, L. (1999). Past Postmodernism? Reflections and Tentative Directions. *Academy of Management Review*, 24(4): 649–671.

Cooke, B. (2003). The Denial of Slavery in Management Studies. *Journal of Management Studies*, 40(8): 1895–1918.

Dan, H. (1963). *The Unpaved Road: The Story of Solel Boneh*. Tel Aviv: Am Oved.

Darr, A. (1999). Conflict and Conflict Resolution in a Cooperative: The Case of the Nir Taxi Station. *Human Relations*, 52: 279–301.

Darr, A. (2003). Control and Autonomy Among Knowledge Workers in Sales: An Employee Perspective. *Employee Relations*, 25: 31–41.

Djelic, M.-L. (1998). *Exporting the American Model: The Post-War Transformation of European Business*. Oxford and New York: Oxford University Press.

Drori, G.S., Höllerer, M.A. and Walgenbach, P. (2013). The Glocalization of Organization and Management: Issues, Dimensions, and Themes. In G.S. Drori, M.A. Höllerer and P. Walgenbach (Eds.), *Global Themes and Local Variations in Organization and Management Perspectives on Glocalization*, 3–24. New York and London: Routledge.

Frenkel, M. (2001). *The Invisible History of the Visible Hand: The Emergence of Israel's Field of Management*. Unpublished PhD Thesis, Department of Sociology, Tel-Aviv University, Israel.

Frenkel, M. (2005). The Politics of Translation: How State-Level Political Relations Affect the Cross-National Travel of Management Ideas. *Organization*, 12(2): 275–301.

Frenkel, M. (2008a). The Multinational Corporation as a Third Space: Rethinking International Management Discourse on Knowledge Transfer Through Homi Bhabha. *Academy of Management Review (AMR)*, 33(4): 924–942.

Frenkel, M, (2008b) The Institutionalization of Israel's Field of Management as a Dynamic in Overlapping Fields, *Israeli Sociology*, 10(1): 133–159. [Hebrew]

Frenkel, M. (2014). Can the Periphery Write Back? Periphery-to-Centre Knowledge Flows in Multinationals Based in Developing and Emerging Economies. In R.

Anti-Managerialism to Over-Managerialism 115

Westwood, G. Jack, F.R. Khan and M. Frenkel (Eds.), *Core-Periphery Relations and Organization Studies*, 32–52. London: Palgrave Macmillan.

Frenkel, M. and Shenhav, Y. (2003). From Americanization to Colonization: The Diffusion of Productivity Models Revisited. *Organization Studies*, 24(9): 1537–1561.

Frenkel, M. and Shenhav, Y. (2006). From Binarism Back to Hybridity: A Postcolonial Reading of Management and Organization Studies. *Organization Studies*, 27(6): 855–876.

Guillen, M.F. (1994). *Models of Management: Work, Authority, and Organization in a Comparative Perspective*. Chicago: University of Chicago Press.

Guri-Rozenblit, S. (1993). Trends of Diversification and Expansion in Israeli Higher Education. *Higher Education*, 25(4): 457–472.

Jack, G. and Westwood, R. (2009). *International and Cross-Cultural Management Studies: A Postcolonial Reading*. Basingstoke: Palgrave Macmillan.

Katz, I. (2013). *Organizations in a Post-Modern World*. Tel Aviv: Resling. [Hebrew]

Kipping, M. and Bjarnar, O. (1998). *The Americanisation of European Business: The Marshall Plan and the Transfer of US Management Models*. London: Routledge.

Kipping, M. and Bjarnar, O. (2002). *The Americanisation of European business*. New York and London: Routledge.

Kunda, G. (1992). *Engineering Culture: Control and Commitment in a High-Tech Corporation*. Philadelphia, PA: Temple University Press.

Kunda, G. (2013). Reflections on Becoming an Ethnographer. *Journal of Organizational Ethnography*, 2(1): 4–22.

Landau, O. (2006). Cold War Political Culture and the Return of Systems Rationality. *Human Relations*, 59(5): 637–663.

Mir, R., Banerjee, S.B. and Mir, A. (2009). From the Colony to the Corporation: Studying Knowledge Transfer Across International Boundaries. In S.B. Banerjee and V. Chio (Eds.), *An Anthropology of Globalization*, 150–169. Cheltenham, UK: Edward Elgar Publishing.

Robertson, R. (1994). Globalisation or Glocalisation? *Journal of International Communication*, 1(1): 33–52.

Shalev, M. (1992). *Labour and the Political Economy of Israel*. Oxford and New York: Oxford University Press.

Shenhav, Y. (1992). Taylorism Transformed—Scientific Management Theory Since 1945—Waring, Sp. *Administrative Science Quarterly*, 37(4): 676–679.

Shenhav, Y. (1995). From Chaos to Systems: The Engineering Foundations of Organization Theory, 1879–1932. *Administrative Science Quarterly*, 40(4): 557–585.

Shenhav, Y.A. (1999). *Manufacturing Rationality: The Engineering Foundations of the Managerial Revolution*. Oxford and New York: Oxford University Press.

Shenhav, Y. (2013). Beyond "instrumental rationality": Lord Cromer and the Imperial Roots of Eichmann's Bureaucracy. *Journal of Genocide Research*, 15(4): 339–359.

Shenhav, Y. and Gabay, N. (2001). Managing Political Conflicts: The Sociology of State Commissions of Inquiry in Israel. *Israel Studies*, 6: 126–156.

Shenhav, Y. and Weitz, E. (2000). The Roots of Uncertainty in Organization Theory: A Historical Constructivist Analysis. *Organization*, 7(3): 373–401.

Sobel, I. (1959). Management in Israel. In F. Harbison and A.C. Myers (Eds.), *Management in the Industrial World: An International Analysis*, 185–206. New York: McGraw-Hill.

Weinshall, T. (1969). The Problems of Israel's Management Reserve. *Nihul*, 3, 13–22 [Hebrew].

Weitz, E. and Shenhav, Y. (2000). A Longitudinal Analysis of Technical and Organizational Uncertainty in Management Theory. *Organization Studies*, 21(1): 243–266.

8 Italian Voices from the Outside
The Context for CMS in Italy

*Maria Laura Toraldo, Gianluigi Mangia,
Paolo Canonico, Stefano Consiglio and
Riccardo Mercurio*

INCIPIT

It was a bright sunshine day as usual in Naples in summertime and at the University Federico II the opening plenary lecture of the Critical Management Studies Conference was taking place. Maurizio Lazzarato, an Italian philosopher working in Paris was invited as keynote speaker, and he was giving a speech entitled 'The Pastoral Power: Self Entrepreneurship as Subjectivity Control Mechanism in the Neoliberalism'. Among the general praise for his words, an Italian colleague asked me, "Gianluigi, why did you invite an Italian 'scientist' living abroad, whose name is associated with Marxism and delivering a speech on social relations structuring capitalism? I thought this was a Management Conference, what are we supposed to manage, here"?

This ironic vignette is an expedient to describe the 'state of the art' of Critical Management Studies in Italy, exploring barriers encountered by the movement in this country as well as the contribution of Italian researchers to the development of CMS. The debate around CMS in Italy has been no doubt received with certain interest by Italian managerial scholars and yet with an elusive understanding of its potential for advancing studies of management.

Organizing the Seventh International Critical Management Studies Conference at the University Federico II of Naples has been seminal for the inception of Critical Management Studies within more traditional managerial academic circles in Italy and for reinvigorating it among those scholars with a critical orientation. With a certain surprise, the Seventh CMS Conference was organized by a university somehow peripheral with respect to the European business school circuit. Wasn't this a way for giving voices to bordering and silent actors in tune with the progressive spirit of the CMS community? Being external to the major business school ranking systems and geographically located in a Southern Europe city, the University Federico II was certainly an unusual venue for hosting the CMS Conference.

It was the first—and so far the last—time, that the CMS Conference was held outside the UK. It was doubtless successful for the number of participants

Italian Voices from the Outside 117

and the academic connections generated, with around 750 participants from 30 universities across Europe and with about 70 participants coming from Italian universities. Organizing this event seemed to signal that the terrain was fertile in Italy for the introduction of critical management perspectives, in line with the increasing interest displayed on criticality in management studies (Mercurio, 2012).

In the wake of the CMS Conference, reformist reflections also originated from the Accademia Italiana di Economia Aziendale (AIDEA). The 2012 annual meeting hosted at the University of Salerno was emblematic. Prof. Alessia Contu from UMass Boston—a well-known thinker in the area of CMS—was invited by AIDEA for discussing and talking about boundaries and limits of management studies and managerial practices and theories. The title of the plenary section was illustrative: 'Towards a new, distinctive, European management scholarship'. Prof Contu's participation at the traditional Italian Academy of Management Conference seemed to point in the direction of a critical rethinking of managerial studies within the Italian context. However, even if the country has been recently exposed to critical reflections, questions remain as to the extent to which critical orientations have only partially aroused interest in the country.

This chapter is driven by the quest for understanding the extent and scope of Critical Management Studies activism in Italy. Why and how have the CMS Conference and, more generally, critical events contributed to shape a critical research agenda in Italy? In which ways are Italian theorists and thinkers contributing to CMS theoretical groundings?

We present our arguments as follows. First, we engage in a brief description of the Italian academic system, with particular reference to the organization of economics and management departments. Next, we present some of the features of the Italian academia that, to our understanding, have influenced the diffusion of CMS in this country. Building on a qualitative survey undertaken with Italian scholars who participated at the Seventh International CMS Conference, we finally provide a discussion on the contribution of the Italian intellectual tradition to CMS, exploring future directions for CMS in Italy.

A SHORT JOURNEY WITHIN THE ITALIAN ACADEMY

The organization of the Seventh International Critical Management Studies Conference in Naples has certainly marked a new time for management studies in Italy, allowing a bridgehead into the problem of promoting different ways of thinking about organizing and organizations. Soon after the CMS Conference, we carried out a qualitative survey with the aim of understanding the extent to which scholars who participated at the 2011 CMS Conference continued research within CMS. The survey instrument was emailed, together with a cover letter explaining the aims of the research, to Italian scholars who participated at the Seventh CMS Conference in Naples

Institutions	CMS areas of interest	Academic sources perceived as "critical"	Researchers working on CMS
University of Naples "Federico II"	Post-fordism; organizational control; identity; diversity management	– Alvesson, A., Bridgman, T., Wilmott, W. 2009. The Oxford Handbook of Critical Management Studies, Oxford: Oxford University Press. – Knight, D., Wilmott, H. 2007. Introducing Organizational Behaviour and Management. Thomson Learning	Yes
University of Naples "Parthenope"			No
Second University of Naples	Post-fordism; organizational control	– Alvesson, A., Bridgman, T., Wilmott, W. 2009. The Oxford Handbook of Critical Management Studies, Oxford: Oxford University Press. – Knight, D., Wilmott, H. 2007. Introducing Organizational Behaviour and Management. Thomson Learning	Yes
University of Benevento	Diversity Management		Yes
University of Salerno "Fisciano"	Organizational Culture; Organizational symbolism; inter-organizational relations	– Alvesson, A., Bridgman, T., Wilmott, W. 2009. The Oxford Handbook of Critical Management Studies, Oxford: Oxford University Press – Alvesson, M. 2011. Classics in Critical Management Studies. Edward Elgar Publishing	No
University of Catanzaro "Magna Graecia"		– Alvesson, A., Bridgman, T., Wilmott, W. 2009. The Oxford Handbook of Critical Management Studies, Oxford: Oxford University Press	Yes
University of Ferrara	Control; Organizational Change	– Alvesson, A., Bridgman, T., Wilmott, W. 2009. The Oxford Handbook of Critical Management Studies, Oxford: Oxford University Press	Yes

University of Calabria	The importance of different values, interests and perspectives; power; conflict	– Alvesson, M., Spicer, A. 2011. Organizational Behavior; Metaphors We Lead By: Understanding Leadership in the Real World. New York: Routledge	No
University of Bologna	Organizational Change; Organizational analysis of networks different to SNA	– Adler, P.S., Forbes, L.C., Willmott, H., 2008. Critical management studies: premises, practices, problems, and prospects. Academy of Management Annals, 1, pp.119-79. – Canonico P., Söderlund J. 2010. "Getting control of multi-project organizations: combining contingent control mechanisms", International Journal of Project Management, 28 (8) pp.796-806; – Pezzillo Iacono M. Esposito, V., Mercurio, R. 2012.Controllo manageriale e regolazione dell'identità organizzativa: la prospettiva dei Critical Management Studies (Managerial control and identity regulation: a critical perspective), FrancoAngeli, Milano.	Yes
University of Molise			No
University of Verona			No
Polytechnic University of Marche	Control; Culture; Post-bureaucracy	– Alvesson, M. Willmott. 2000. Doing Critical Management Research. London: SAGE – Boje, D. and Winsor, R. 1993. The resurrection of Taylorism: Total quality management's hidden agenda, Journal of Organizational Change Management, 6 (4): 57–70- – Buchanan, D. A. (2003). Getting the story straight: Illusions and delusions in the organizational change process. TAMARA: Journal of Critical Postmodern Organizational Science, 2, 7–21	No
University of Pisa	Work-group; knowledge and learning	Knights, D., Willmott, H. 2007. Introducing Organizational Behaviour and Management. Thomson Learning.	No

Figure 8.1   List of Institutions Taking Part in the Survey and Their Perception of CMS

120 *Toraldo et al.*

Topic	No. of researchers
Political dimension and decision making processes	9
Individual motivation & teamwork	8
Organizational culture	7
Organizational change	7
Leadership	6
Technology and information systems	6
Organizational structure and design	2

Figure 8.2   Topics That Participants Perceive as Needing to Be Critically Approached

and to researchers who did not participate in the conference but who had shown research interest in CMS. Follow-up mailings to nonrespondents were undertaken. The survey was composed of 12 items, and it contained both open and closed questions. It consisted of three sections: (1) general information about the respondent (position in the department, research area, teaching course), (2) the extent and degree of individual and collective research adopting CMS approaches (specific teaching course based on CMS materials, members of the research groups, including PhD students, working from a CMS perspective, recent research themes approached through a critical lens), and (3) the perceived relevance of CMS studies for the Italian managerial community and its diffusion in the future.

Of the 50 universities contacted, a total of 13 universities responded to the survey (see Figure 8.1). It emerged that scholars working on topics from CMS perspectives are active in six universities in Italy.

We received information about topics that participants perceived as needing to be critically approached (see Figure 8.2).

Moreover, it is interesting to observe the perception of Italian scholars with regard to the diffusion of CMS in Italy. All researchers responding to the survey and working in the 13 universities observed the relevance of adopting a critical perspective. The common thinking is that CMS represents an alternative way for writing about management, as it provides a reflexive perspective on economics and managerial topics. However, what does this picture tell us regarding Italian scholars' commitment to CMS? And how such evidence can be interpreted?

THE CONTEXT FOR CMS IN ITALY

To illuminate on the diffusion of critical approaches in Italy, we can probably start with an analysis of the broader institutional context, shedding light on some of the features that can be plausibly considered as having slowed down its dissemination.

Italian Voices from the Outside 121

As we were drafting the chapter, we asked ourselves: what is the most effective way to paint a picture of the Italian academia? And with which characteristics shall we start off?

As the CMS phenomenon originated from within business schools, a good way is probably to look into the configuration of schools of business in Italy. Compared to the European landscape, business schools appear less diffuse in Italy. With the exception of a few renowned and highly ranked business schools—such as SDA Bocconi School of Management and Luiss Business School—and more recently, the advent of international business schools (e.g. ESCP campus in Turin), managerial education in Italy has been traditionally undertaken within management departments. This means that managerial research has mainly been unfolded within public-funded universities, where competitions for funding, restricted independence in terms of research policy, as well as governance aspects of departments have certainly influenced the nature of research.

Furthermore, the traditional distinction among academic departments, based on specialisms, has contributed to some sort of disciplinary closure. As an example of the division among disciplines (and subdisciplines!) within management department, we can consider the sectorial codes, the so-called 'code SECS-P'.

SECS-P stands for Scienze Economiche, and this is the disciplinary sector for the area of economics and management in Italy. Different numbers identify specific functional disciplines (accounting, organization studies, marketing, etc.) of management practice. For example, within the totality of departments of management and economics in Italy, about 755 researchers (here including assistant, associate and full professor) work in the area of accounting, about 577 researchers are employed in the area of management and 164 in the area of organization studies (MIUR, 2014). It is difficult to define the extent to which boundaries among disciplinary sectors have impacted on the CMS diffusion in Italy, but it is plausible to believe that an effect of mimeticism can be seen in place here. In fact, scholars tend to conform to research traditionally conducted within their departments. Moreover, their research is further influenced by how evaluation procedures for career advancement are carried out, where criteria of evaluation tend to privilege homogeneity amongst lines of research and themes. However, reforms, amendments and new regulation for recruitment of professors have been introduced, changed and replaced several times with the aim to counterbalance dysfunctional aspects of recruitment, research policy and similar aspects.

For example, a disappointing mechanism introduced in 1999 and based on 'vacancy specific concorsi' (Perotti, 2002) was supplanted by a new system of recruitment, heralded as a radical change of approach, based on meritocracy and transparency: in 2010, the Abilitazione Scientifica Nazionale was introduced. Candidates became 'qualified' for associate and full professor positions with the hope that a vacant position in universities would become available soon after. This was celebrated as a way to accord prizes to the quality of individual research output. But was this a step towards flattening

122 *Toraldo et al.*

the pompous administrative machine? After two years of experimentation, the result was that the Abilitazione was finally changed in 2014. Despite a remarkable effort to introduce new rules and procedures, it is intuitive that one of the main criticalities concerns academic policies and the organization of recruitment within academic departments.

In general terms, it can be noted that drawing boundaries among disciplines limits the potential for developing criticism. Considering the genesis of Critical Management Studies, it can be noted that the movement has been informed by a plurality of intellectual tradition from social sciences (Fournier and Grey, 2000) drawing upon a range of different orientations, including Marxist tradition (Labour Process Theory, Frankfurt School of Critical Theory, Post-Operaismo), feminism, cultural studies, post-structuralism, psychoanalysis and several other theoretical traditions. In actual fact, the theoretical pluralism has created a space of freedom for thinkers interested in exploring the limit of management studies and to bringing new lens and perspectives. Such variety and the deep theoretical engagement is also evident in the fact that many scholars working within Critical Management Studies write notably from diverse backgrounds, including sociology, anthropology, humanities and philosophy.

We might reasonably argue that organizing events such as the Seventh International CMS Conference, as well as more recent initiatives, including the AIDEA Capri Summer School, have gradually engendered interest and general awareness of the CMS approaches. Alongside the research axis, events such as the AIDEA Capri Summer School have also promoted critical approaches in teaching and learning where students have been confronted with critical application of diverse methodologies of research. Furthermore, some of these events have also contributed to the creation or reinforcement of networks with international scholars. For instance, lecturers of the AIDEA Capri Summer School came from some of the most important business schools in Europe (e.g. Cardiff Business School; Keele University; HEC Paris; University of Innsbruck; Grenoble Ecole de Management, ESSEC Business School, Paris; Stockholm University).

In this vein, collaboration with international business schools and international scientific networks with critical scholars have certainly been pivotal for the diffusion of CMS in the country. To a certain extent, international collaborations can also be interpreted as stimuli to nuance the strong disciplinarization. Opportunities to publish in international journals, to co-write with international scholars on alternative topics have certainly urged the Italian academia to rethink consolidated approaches towards research. For example, in 2008, AIDEA published a ranking list of journals on which some of the 'top' international journals were featured. Even if questions can be raised on the discrepancy amongst the different lists across countries, and although the Italian ranking tends to classify its journals on the basis of sectors, there is no doubt that this can be interpreted as a sign of reformism.

In the next section, we will look more concretely at the contribution of Italians to the critical movement.

EXPLORING THE ITALIAN CONTRIBUTION: STIMULI FROM WITHIN AND OUTSIDE

In light of what we have portrayed regarding the institutional context in Italy, it can be observed that the intellectual questioning, the critique of various elements of managerialist ideology and the interest towards aspects related to organizational power have only partially found a place for discussion in Italy. Even if organizing CMS-related events since the beginning of 2011 signals a certain activism of Italian scholars within the critical debate, the diffusion of Critical Management Studies can not to be said to have fully occurred in Italy. It seems that Italians have the potential to contribute even more.

To further understand the extent and contribution of Critical Management Studies activism in Italy, we can reflect on an additional orientation that characterizes the Italian academia and that might be interpreted as an input that Italians can give to Critical Management Studies.

The research/practice connection and a solid collaborative partnership between academia and industry is a distinguishing feature of Italian universities. In this sense, management studies exhibit a pragmatic orientation in Italy. On the one hand, this anchorage with the practice can rebalance one of the limits that have been traditionally associated with CMS: not actively engaging with concrete social problems and social practices (Voronov et al., 2009; Spicer et al., 2009; King and Learmonth, 2014). Along these lines, the pragmatic inclination of Italian management scholars might contribute to the CMS debate by injecting a practical facet. This was also the challenge characterizing the organization of the CMS Conference in Naples: to interpenetrate practice-oriented knowledge with theory, moving away from the self-referential sphere of scholarship (Willmott, 2008).

The second aspect concerns the influence of Italian thinkers over CMS. To some extent, this would seem counterintuitive. So what is the explanation? In effect, several Italian scholars working abroad have deeply contributed to shape and inform Critical Management Studies. A particular prominent aspect is that these are Italian thinkers, living and working outside the Italian academia. In some cases, they are distinguished professors in some of the best universities worldwide and have deeply shaped the field with influential books. For instance, this is the case for the Italian political philosopher Antonio Negri with his book *Empire* (2000), co-authored with Michael Hardt. Previously engaged in political activism in Italy, he escaped to France and he is now a professor at the European Graduate School in Switzerland. Theories elaborated from Marxists scholars associated with the theoretical strand known as Operaismo (or post-Operaismo, in its most recent transformation) have been especially influential on CMS in the last years. Alongside Antonio Negri, post-Operaismo has included the work of Paolo Virno and Maurizio Lazzarato. Their work has been particularly significant for studying new forms of work associated with information technology, which

124   Toraldo et al.

emerged in late capitalism. The journal *Ephemera*—a journal on theory and politics in organizations—has published several articles on this, dedicating an entire special issue to the Italian workerist in 2007 with the title 'Immaterial and Affective Labour: Explored'.

The Italian Marxist tradition has thus played an important role on the development of CMS. The aforementioned Professor Maurizio Lazzarato, invited as keynote speaker at the Seventh International CMS Conference in Naples, is working in France. He has been an inspiring source for CMS scholars, authoring books such as *Governing by Debt* in 2015, *Signs and Machine* in 2014 and the well-known booklet *Immaterial Labour* in 1997.

In some sense, reflecting on the significance of Italian thinkers outside the Italian academia offers the prospect of deepening our understanding of the limits of Italy in retaining her scholars; they are only appreciated the moment in which they step into institutions outside of Italy.

In short, if we ask the question of whether Italian theorists and thinkers have been able to contribute to the CMS theoretical foundations, our reflection would suggest that their contributions could be framed as 'from the outside'—that means that it has come from those who found a space to engage in political reflection outside the boundaries of the Italian academia.

CONCLUSION AND FUTURE PROSPECT FOR CMS IN ITALY

The ongoing crisis affecting Italy has enlivened the debate regarding the knowledge produced from within academic circles and the extent to which classic managerial models, theories and practices might partially be responsible for such situations. Returning to the initial question related to why and how critical events have contributed to shaping a critical research agenda in Italy, first, we can respond that one of the main contributions of the Italians needs to be traced back to the influence of Italian thinkers working outside this country. We have noticed that the contribution of Italians working abroad has been particularly important. Italian scholars, in fact, have variously informed critical thinkers and they have contributed to enriching the theoretical foundations of CMS. Second, we can argue that the Critical Management Studies Conference in 2011 and the three editions of the AIDEA Capri Summer School are evidence of critical reflections on management activism in Italy. It is worth mentioning that some stimuli already existed. For example, during the '50s, a training school was active in Naples, so-called CESAN, providing training courses on production, market and industry analysis and developing *pari passu* with European schools. CESAN trained a new managerial class, also providing financial expertise to Small and Medium-sized Enterprise (SME) companies such as Alfa Romeo, Cirio, Motta, Alemagna, Star, and it trained managers for multinational companies, such as Ferrero.

The purpose of this chapter has also been to understand why CMS in Italy has not developed at the same pace as in other European countries. To spot

Italian Voices from the Outside   125

relations between the Italian higher education system and the poor diffusion of the CMS in this county is a difficult task that could easily engender inaccurate descriptions of the Italian academy. To avoid the risk of providing a misleading account, we have not provided a comprehensive description of the Italian academy. Rather, we have mainly focused on some of the characteristics of the institutional context of the Italian academia, looking at some of the features that have limited potential for critique among Italian researchers.

We have attempted to paint a picture of the Italian academia as a context somehow characterized by rigidity of formal rules. First, we have found that boundaries among different disciplines within Italian management departments have represented one of the reasons for limiting the potential of cross fertilization among fields of study. Demarcation among disciplines has played an important role since it has deeply influenced recruitment processes of researchers. The direct consequence is that researchers have experienced strong difficulties in bringing in new perspectives or in launching themselves into novel research topics.

The time is now ripe to ask whether Italy is open for changes within its 'elephantic' academia. Many doctoral programmes are becoming increasingly international, and mobility among young scholars is increasingly becoming more diffuse. In such a context, we would expect Critical Management Studies to acquire popularity and interest among the managerial community in Italy in the near future. We hope that these are early manifestations of a new way of conceiving research, researchers and the part they can play in producing critical thinking and knowledge for society.

REFERENCES

Fournier, V.E. and Grey, C. (2000). At the Critical Moment: Conditions and Prospects for Critical Management Studies. *Human Relations*, 53(1): 7–32.
Hardt, M. and Negri, A. (2000). *Empire*. Cambridge, MA: Harvard University Press.
King, D. and Learmonth, M., (2014). Can Critical Management Studies Ever be 'practical'? A Case Study in Engaged Scholarship. *Human Relations*, 68(3): 353–375.
Mercurio, R. (2012). *Critical Management Studies: temi di ricerca nel dibattito internazionale*. Napoli: Editoriale Scientifica.
MIUR. (2014). Retrieved from http://cercauniversita.cineca.it/php5/docenti/vis_docenti.php
Perotti, R. (2002). *The Italian University System: Rules vs Incentives*. In Annual Report on Monitoring Italy 2002. Roma: Istituto di Studi e Analisi Economica (ISAE).
Spicer, A., Alvesson, M. and Karreman, D. (2009). Critical Performativity: The Unfinished Business of Critical Management Studies. *Human Relations*, 62(4): 537–560.
Voronov, M., Wolfram Cox, J., LeTrent-Jones, T.G. and Weir, D. (2009). Introduction: Intersections of Critical Management Research and Practice: A Multi-Domain Perspective. In J. Wolfram Cox, T.G. LeTrent-Jones, M. Voronov and D. Weir. (Eds.), *Critical Management Studies at Work: Negotiating Tensions Between Theory and Practice*, 1–14. Cheltenham, UK: Edward Elgar.
Willmott, H. (2008). Critical Management and Global Justice. *Organization*, 15(6): 927–931

9 Self-Problematization and Relational Problematization
A Critical-Constructive Approach in the Japanese Context

Toru Kiyomiya

INTRODUCTION

The aim of this chapter is to consider the relevance of Critical Management Studies (CMS) to the Japanese context. In particular, how can CMS contribute to the construction of a critical dimension to management studies in Japan and hereby contribute to shaping a better world? It is not difficult to imagine that CMS has not been popular in Japan. On the contrary, it may come as a surprise to learn that there is a strong Marxist tradition in Japanese history, to the extent that by the 1980s, Japanese academia was largely dominated by a variety of left-wing scholars. In this respect, it is natural for the reader to understand why CMS had not developed in the Japanese context. To begin with, therefore, this chapter analyses how capitalism and various critical perspectives have been interdiscursively translated from Western concepts into the Japanese context, which has ensured that CMS has not been widely welcomed in Japanese culture and history. We emphasize how the translation of both capitalism and critical perspectives is co-constructed socially, which in turn has shaped reality. In other words, interdiscursive processes of translation were never neutral; instead, they shaped the power relations of domination and marginalization. Second, this chapter illustrates how the cultural context of Japanese discourses with regard to Buddhism and Confucianism may possibly offer an alternative and meet the need in Japan for a more positive, constructive approach to CMS. Finally, we conclude with a discussion of the potential for a Japanese contribution to the CMS literature, such as self-cultivation as a methodology to emancipate oneself in the face of the ontological distortions brought about by commodification. To this end, we propose the concepts of 'self-problematization' and 'relational problematization'. Lastly, future avenues of research are suggested from a Japanese contextual point of view.

CRITICAL PERSPECTIVES IN HISTORICAL CONTEXT

Japanese Modernization, Westernization, and Capitalism

When looking at the Japanese context in terms of how capitalism and a critique thereof have developed historically, they were initially imported from two

Self-Problematization   127

quite distinct contexts, the USA and Europe. Until the middle of the eighteenth century, important knowledge and culture (including religions) had come to Japan from China and Korea. However, from the late Edo Period (1603–1868) and the start of the Meiji Period (1868–1912), the influence of Western civilization became dominant and was central to Japanese modernization.

In particular, the Meiji Period saw a deliberate policy of social and political modernization, which involved abandoning traditional Japanese ways of living and customs. In this respect, many aspects of the Western lifestyle were introduced: bread, milk, beef and other Western foodstuffs; Western clothes and fashion; Western architectural styles and materials, such as bricks and steel; or a switch from the traditional Japanese lunar calendar to the Gregorian calendar. In addition, Western institutional systems were adopted in the name of modernization. Such drastic social and cultural changes were supported and legitimized by the Meiji government's policies of modernization. In other words, the historical turning point in Japan was the transition from the Edo Period to the Meiji Period, and modernization was used as a rhetorical discursive device that legitimized and facilitated westernization. In this sense, Japanese modernization is significantly different from Western modernization. Japanese modernization did not arise from civil war, for example, but rather it was imported mainly from the West. It must also be acknowledged that modernization in Japan involved the concomitant introduction of economic capitalism and the westernization of the Japanese military, too. Until now, Japanese people have taken for granted that modernization means westernization, so capitalism is naturally accepted as a part of the modern lifestyle. However, westernization was legitimized by modernization during a transitional period of the Meiji Period, and capitalism was synchronized with modernization in Japan.

In this sense, translation played an important role in the westernization of Japan, since many discourses about modernization were translated from Western languages (mainly English, German and French). For instance, a new political system was introduced under the discourse of *minshu-shugi* (民主主義), which is translated from 'democracy', so that Japanese people struggled to understand new imported systems in politics. Japanese people could only understand new institutional systems through the translation of Western discourses. Similarly, capitalism and business were imported and translated into Japanese, and such discourses sidelined traditional Japanese commercial activity, such as *sanpo-yoshi*, which is discussed later. It is important to emphasize that the emergence of capitalism in Japan was different from that in the West, and its generation was due to it having been imported from Europe as a part of modernization and westernization, which had to be introduced as translated discourses. The uniqueness of Japanese capitalism has thus developed because of historical processes that are markedly different than the West.

Critical Perspectives in Japan

In contrast, critical perspectives on capitalism have developed in Japan through the introduction of Marx and other Western philosophers.

128 *Toru Kiyomiya*

Historically, there has been a strong tradition of critical perspectives[1] in social science (economics and politics) and other disciplines. Scholars, however, have struggled with the translation of critical Western concepts. In this section, we discuss a Japanese critical philosopher, Wataru Hiromatsu, who is a highly regarded post-Marxism scholar in Japan. He is known for his work on the relationship between the concept of reification and commodification. Hiromatsu (1969, 1974, 1987) advocates the former concept through the philosophy of Lukács (1972) and questions why Marx starts with the commodity as a fundamental form of capital in the first chapter of *Capital*, while emphasizing the differentiation of a 'commodity' from a 'product' and focusing on a dialectic process of value form development. Hiromatsu attempts to reveal the fundamental contradiction between exchange value and use value, which exists in everyday life and leads to a distortion of communication through the fetishism of capitalistic reification; social relations are treated as a thing-like entity. In other words, Hiromatsu's philosophy focuses on how capitalism distorts social relations due to the social (dialectical) process of reification (not as a general effect of psychological perception). He stresses that, because reification is embedded as one of the fundamental contradictions of capitalism, it must be criticized and be a central target of emancipation. Hiromatsu expands the concept of reification beyond mere economic activities into every dimension of social life. In particular, he criticizes the fact that people are not aware of this reified relationship, which leads to a blind acceptance of the reified/commodified world. This is particularly important in the Japanese context, since human relations are considered to be one of the central concerns in Japan. In this chapter, I would like to connect Hiromatsu's concept of reification to commodification, which fetishize market discourses and created wag-the-dog relations in society. The latter occurs through discursive interactions that trivialize use values and prioritize exchange values in business and organizational settings. In addition, Holiday (2011, p. 197) defines commodification from a postmodern perspective with regard to intercultural communication studies: he treats something as though it has a commercial value and can be bought and sold. In this regard, it is central to critique insofar as it is an important concept embedded in modern capitalism.

The concept of commodification is appropriate to analyse various ways of exploitation, especially in relation to Japanese capitalism, which is embedded in collaboration, harmony and tacit understandings and practices, whereas economic exploitation in Western capitalism typically derives from competition and individualism. Although there are many common features in capitalist systems across countries, capitalism is neither monolithic nor universal (Hall and Soskic, 2001; du Gay and Morgan, 2014). In this sense, CMS needs to pay more attention to the ways in which different forms of exploitation are embedded in local contexts. Typically, Japanese management emphasizes internal communication and in-group relationships. The relationship between employee and employer is reified, such that the former's identification with an organization is considered as commodified (identity commodification). Traditional Japanese management exploits employees through identity commodification. This hegemonization of the workplace is considered locally as 'relational exploitation'. For instance, there have been many problems of business scandals or corporate misconduct in Japan. Since the Japanese possess a strong cultural tendency to follow the norms of the community to which they belong (i.e. *uchi*), in a typical *uchi* community, the members strive to assimilate themselves into the group (Kiyomiya et al., 2006). The primary goal in such a group is to maintain and enhance the harmony within the group, which ensures the mutual success of the individual and the group itself so that the more involved people are in an *uchi* community and the more they internalize the community's values and norms, the narrower their perspective is likely to be (Furuta, 1996). As a result, although no one orders or ordains misconduct, employees are spontaneously committed to a focus on the good of the *uchi* and the good of the company. Thus, rather than speak of errors or mistakes, misconduct is an inevitable consequence of intensive, hegemonic control and identity commodification (Kiyomiya et al., 2006; Kiyomiya, 2011, 2012). Business scandals are a form of exploitation that is linked with the tradition of organizations in Japan, and therefore identity commodification and corporate hegemony must be studied in Japanese firms. Similarly, emancipatory goals must be considered from a different methodological perspective that is connected to traditional Japanese discourse and wisdom.

Critical Perspectives Dwindle

The popularity of critical perspectives in Japan waned with the collapse of the Soviet Union and other socialist countries, and it dwindled even further in the late 1980s and the early 1990s. We might explain the decline in the fortunes of critical perspectives in one of (at least) two ways: the domination of Japanese management studies by a mainstream discourse that has its origins in American/foreign business schools and the failure of socialism as mentioned earlier. The proliferation of Japanese management discourses emerged in the period of rapid economic growth and the international expansion of the Japanese economy during the 1980s, whereas discourses about the end of the Cold War and the collapse of socialist political and economic systems served to enhance criticism in Japan of the possibility of a socialist or communist alternative. These two types of discourses became hegemonic to the extent that any critical perspectives in Japan became well-nigh impossible.

Moreover, the proliferation in Japanese management studies emerged within the context of the local corporate culture discussed earlier, which

130 *Toru Kiyomiya*

obviously distinguishes it from other countries. Historically, for example, Ouchi (1981) and Abegglen (1958) were first to highlight the specific features of Japanese organizations, and they attempted to understand how Japanese management had been successful from Western perspectives. Their studies resulted in an emphasis on the cultural differences between Japanese and Western organizations. They treat Japanese management as exotic and peculiar, and in so doing, Japanese management practices gained widespread attention against the background of the strong Japanese economy. At the same time, however, a proliferation of discourses about the peculiarity of Japanese culture segregated and marginalized Japanese management, which merely served to legitimate Western management practices as essential and central. Consequently, the burgeoning discourses of Japanese management excellence became blind to the social dimension of organizations. These discourses on socialism's failure and Japanese management excellence have worked together as rhetorical devices to demotivate Japanese scholars to adopt CMS in their study of management and organizations.

In addition, today's problems are exacerbated by market competition in higher education for economic advantages and survival, which has resulted in world ranking systems in universities and business schools (typically linked to research output). The problems are also related to competitiveness in job markets or how universities contribute to higher employment rates. These free-market discourses might be seen as a rhetorical device that makes people blind to the purpose of education, which in turn reinforces market competition in education. These discursive interactions entail the commodification of education, which is embedded in market competition and embodied as the fetish nature of education.

In the field of management studies, therefore, many scholars are concerned about their ranking in the educational hierarchy, rather than social problems in business settings and critical perspectives in management. They have lost their educational purpose through the commodification of education. Therefore, Japanese management scholars do not pay attention to social theories, which could be applied to management. They usually do no more than pick up the issues that are studied from a managerial point of view, which seldom sheds light on the social dimensions of management.

TRANSLATION AND JAPANESE TRADITIONAL DISCOURSE

From Critical Negative to Critical Constructive

When the Japanese context is considered in terms of the current state of CMS, there is a further difficulty of the problem of translating concepts between distinct cultures and attitudes. In the Japanese context, there may be two reasons for the difficulty of practicing CMS in everyday life and the negative image of the activity itself. One reason comes from the study

Self-Problematization 131

of intercultural communication. In comparison to cultures that emphasize individual independence, the Japanese tend to avoid conflict and therefore dislike criticizing others. According to the literature of intercultural communication, Japanese people tend to prefer collaboration and harmony in small-group communities. Criticism is interpreted as inconsiderate and rude (Gudykunst and Nishida, 1994). The assumption in Japan is that criticizing others will rebound against one, while it also has a bad influence on personal relationships. A critical discourse is therefore recognized not in the philosophical sense, but at the level of personal, affective relationships within the group only.

The other difficulty is to understand certain words within critical discourses, such as emancipation. This is not only a problem of translation but also a matter of religion and culture. CMS scholars generally acknowledge that CMS focuses on emancipation. In the Western tradition and context of Christianity, there is a Messianic logic that implies change and salvation. When CMS scholars used the term of emancipation to imply a necessary solution, it involves an approach from a monotheistic religion, which Lennerfors (2014) points out is at the centre of the relationship between Christianity and Marxism. If a discourse of emancipation is related to such a specific cultural and religious context, it becomes difficult to understand in a different religious context, such as polytheism. In this sense, a discursive relationship between critique and emancipation does not fit the Japanese perspective. Given the polytheistic religious context of Japan, it may be more suitable to consider that emancipation is related to a process (or methodology) of self-cultivation and personal inner revolution, which is supported by the fact that traditional Japanese ways of thinking are related to Buddhism and Confucianism and emphasize a process-oriented approach.[2]

According to Tsuda (1994), for example, Japanese management philosophy was shaped through its historical development of interacting with Chinese culture. He points out that Japanese indigenous culture has been transformed, yet it was over a long period of time (a thousand years) that Chinese culture and thought (typically, Buddhism and Confucianism) were adopted and digested. In the historic period of the *samurai*, namely, during the Japanese feudal period, Confucianism was the most important discipline to study in every social class. Moreover, when Japanese history is analysed, we see that Buddhism was adopted from the sixth century and became widespread in culture and thought. Confucianism and Buddhism have influenced and become the fundamental Japanese ways of thinking, and they are embodied in Japanese management and organizations.

Japanese business leaders draw on a strong religious influence in their management styles, such as compassionate management and the attempt to improve Japanese economy and society. For example, Konosuke Matsushita (the so-called "father of management" in Japan), a founder of Panasonic, and Kazuo Inamori, a founder of Kyocera and a former president

132 Toru Kiyomiya

of Japan Airlines, were heavily influenced by Buddhist morality and ethics (Kotter, 1997). Matsushita emphasized welfare for the entire Japanese society through business activities, and he strongly addressed the improvement of Japanese life by overcoming the devastation of World War II. Moreover, Eiichi Shibusawa, who was recognized as a role model in Japanese business during the Meiji Period, emphasized business activities that were based on moral principle that strongly reflected Confucianism. His perspective has had a great impact on business leaders in contemporary Japanese industry (Yui, 2008). Many ideas that emerged in business and management are embodied in Japanese discourses that are influenced by traditional Eastern thought.[3]

Thus the discursive devices of Buddhism and Confucianism are used for management control in Japan. However, they may have a possible path to CMS by facilitating a way of self-enhancing, 'autogenous' growth as an alternative methodology for emancipation. Lennerfors (2014, pp. 5–6) argues that it is necessary and possible to construct "critical Buddhist economics, rather than Buddhism as a way of coping or harmony". He advocates the possibility of Buddhism not as a critical-negative approach, but as a critical-constructive approach and claims that Buddhism can indeed be critical if its principles go against the ideology of the society into which Buddhism is imported, not through a total critique but incrementally through the autogenous practice of each individual who avoids disturbing or directly confronting or questioning the harmony of the group (Lennerfors, 2014). His claim embodies the same idea that this chapter suggests. The following sections take a closer look at how some conceptualizations of Japanese moral discourses may be linked with CMS.

Buddhist Methodology for CMS

On the surface and from the outside, Buddhism operates as an important religion in Japanese culture and society. However, strictly speaking, "Buddhism is neither a philosophy nor a religion" (Jacobson, 1986, p. 9) in the Western sense of these terms, but the teachings of Buddha and "a method of awakening to what is really real in the world". Indeed, unlike Christianity, Buddhism does not talk about a god or gods, an absolute being that governs the world. Japanese people historically strive for ways of awakening and emancipating themselves through Buddhism. We therefore focus on Buddhist's term of 'enlightenment', which is comparable to the Western notion of Enlightenment, which is often discussed with regard to emancipation.

Buddha is "not a personal name[4] but an epithet of those who have achieved enlightenment, the goal of the Buddhist religious life" (Keown, 2003, p. 42). The Buddha are those who have awakened to the nature of things and attained 'nirvana' by destroying defilements, such as desire for material goods (Keown, 2003). In Buddhism, enlightenment and nirvana are closely linked with each other, but they emphasize slightly different aspects of Buddhist's achievement. Nirvana is the ultimate goal for Buddhists. When an enlightened person achieves nirvana, which is called *gedatsu* (解脱)[5] in

Self-Problematization   133

Japanese, it indicates the destruction of corrupting influences, the absence of mental suffering, the possession of wisdom, and so on. In this sense, nirvana seems to equate with the English term of (negative) freedom from pain and (positive) freedom from suffering in the world, and it invokes personal emancipation through an inner revolution. "To achieve nirvana in life is to effect permanent change in wisdom and in moral character, and to make possible certain kinds of experience, both in general terms and as the attainment of specific meditative and spiritual states" (Collins, 1998, p. 152). Such a process of permanent change for nirvana is an essence of *gedatsu* for Japanese self-cultivation.

The Buddhist term of enlightenment is often confused because of the same term of Enlightenment in the West. The original word of Buddhist enlightenment is 'bodhi'; literally, enlightenment means awakening and awakened (Collins, 1998). Buddhist enlightenment is "the state that marks the culmination of the Buddhist religious path" (Keown, 2003, p. 87). Buddhist enlightenment or Awakening[6] results from the process of self-cultivation and *gedatsu* so that wisdom and knowledge based on personal experiences are the most important means for awakening. Buddhist enlightenment or Awakening is the means to achieve nirvana, and it is obvious that the methodology of Awakening strongly relies on everyday practices of mastering various kinds of desire. For training, Zen emphasizes meditation to empty one's mind for the purpose of controlling the general desires of human being. Thus Buddhist enlightenment is a continuous form of awareness present through every activity, achieved by and embodied in the practice of mindfulness. It is an internal dialogue of the individual with him or herself, which produces inner revolution and permanent change of *gedatsu* through reflecting on one's own experiences.

In contrast, from a CMS point of view, Western Enlightenment is "the critique and replacement of earlier belief systems grounded in tradition, common sense, superstition, religion, etc., with ostensibly more rational forms of thought and practice" (Alvesson and Willmott, 1996, p. 74).[7] The different emphasis of enlightenment between the East and the West indicates an interesting contrast in ways of learning and personal development. The Buddhist approach to Awakening by emphasizing experiences and meditation may be related to self-reflection for the purpose of self-improvement. Thus a Buddhist methodology is strongly connected with a process of self-cultivation and autogenous growth (which is a more recent view of *gedatsu*), and therefore I would like to relate this point with a methodology of emancipation, which may be effective for deconstructing identity commodification.

Confucian Methodology for CMS

Confucianism provides a similar view that emphasizes the process of Awakening. In Japanese history, Confucianism and Buddhism have the same roots in ancient Chinese thought. They are not mutually exclusive, but rather Confucianism complements Buddhism in the Japanese context; in this respect, the Buddhist term of enlightenment is compatible with *toku* (徳) in Confucianism.

134 *Toru Kiyomiya*

An important point in the *Analects of Confucius* is '修己治人', which means that "you should train yourself and then you are able to manage others" (see Figure 9.1). In other words, and with echoes of Socrates' dictum in Plato's *Apology* that the "unexamined life is not worth living", you should examine and develop yourself before commanding others. This suggests that the *Analects of Confucius* sees the importance of self-cultivation in relation to creating a good relationship with others. It aims at developing *kun-shi* (君子), which resembles the idea of the 'gentleman' in English, and Confucius taught people to achieve *kun-shi* as the goal of self-cultivation. In order to reach the level of *kun-shi*, people have to obtain various types of *toku* (徳), which implies virtues or goodness. As Table 9.1 shows, there are seven types of *toku* (Moriya, 2009).

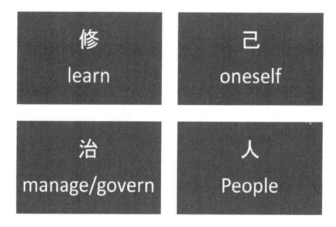

Figure 9.1 Basic Idea of Confucianism Self-Cultivation

Figure 9.2 Basic Framework of Confucianism *Toku*

Self-Problematization 135

Table 9.1 Seven Types of *Toku* (徳)

仁 (jin)	warm-hearted mind, compassion and benevolence
智 (chi)	talent, wisdom or intelligence
勇 (yu)	strong faith, brave, decisiveness
信 (shin)	Trust, promise, never tell a lie
寛 (kan)	Broad-mindedness, generous attitude
礼 (rei)	principle of social life and formal and informal manner of social behaviours
義 (gi)	justice, legitimacy, manner or rule of human relationship

Here, four of them are described. *Jin* (仁) is the most important virtue in Confucianism. *Jin* is related to leadership and indicates a warm-hearted soul who displays compassion and benevolence. If you are a manager, you should not treat your subordinates merely as abstract labour, but consider them as equals and trustworthy partners (Moriya, 2009). Since ancient Japan, *jin* has been the core spirit to maintain good relationships between people. Second, *chi* (智) literally means wisdom or intelligence. It is an important ability; it allows people to deeply read and understand context-dependent situations. Therefore, this type of insight is related to communication competence in decision making and the perception of issues. The other two virtues are *rei* (礼) and *gi* (義). The former is the principle of social life and embodies both formal and informal manners necessary for social behaviour. Using *rei*, Japanese make human relationships run smoothly and harmoniously. If you don't show *rei* in some contexts, you will lose trust and good personal relationships. *Rei* is therefore always accompanied with politeness, which explains why politeness is one of the most important virtues in Japanese life. Finally, *gi* (義) is almost the same word as *gi-ri* (義利). It means a sense of 'justice' that people have to uphold. If Japanese people do not conduct *gi*, they will definitely lose trust and personal relationship. As a whole, people are encouraged to gain various virtues of *toku*, and those who work on self-cultivation for interpersonal relationships are highly respected in Japanese society. On the contrary, those who don't have these virtues of *toku*, nor attempt to work on self-cultivation, will lose social trust and meaningful human relationships within the Japanese group community. Confucianism, which is widely understood, has become the common denominator in Japanese social life, with its influence on business styles and management philosophy of hierarchical social order. In particular, it fosters lifetime learning to gain *toku*, which must reflect the relationship between oneself and others. From the CMS point of view, self-cultivation as a methodology in Confucianism may be useful in terms of reflecting upon the relationship with others.

Needless to say, neither Buddhism nor Confucianism directly connects to CMS. Also, it doesn't mean that old lifestyles and traditional Japanese culture are better. Rather, as it may be easier to identify characteristics of Confucianism

136 *Toru Kiyomiya*

and Buddhism in Japanese management and business (compassionate/welfare management with employee-centred perspective), it stands to reason that traditional local wisdom has been more influential in managerial control than CMS. However, these discourses provide a point to align CMS with the Japanese context, as Lennerfors (2014) proposes with his 'critical-constructive' approach rather than a 'critical-negative' approach. Traditional Japanese discourses embedded in Buddhism and Confucianism are crucial not only in terms of meanings and content but also in terms of methodology to construct a new self through permanent change in daily practices. In this regard, there might be two important implications. First, it may be possible to apply a Japanese methodology of self-cultivation into CMS by connecting problematization, which would allow us to deal with daily communication that has been commodified by the market discourses. Second, it may be effective to conduct a discursive strategy that actively deploys a non-English language set of concepts. These would be related to a self-cultivation methodology and require implementing a reverse translation from Japan to the West. These two implications must be strategized for the critical-constructive approach.

ALTERNATIVE METHODOLOGIES FOR EMANCIPATION

Self-Cultivation Methodology and Problematization

In order to explore alternative forms of emancipation relevant to the Japanese context, I would like to integrate critical perspectives with self-cultivation methodology based on Japanese discursive practices of *gedatsu* and *toku* that reflect Buddhism and Confucianism, respectively. Exactly how self-cultivation methodologies might enrich the CMS and promote emancipation as self-cultivation and autogenous moral growth (what we might call 'self-cultivation methodologies') may be relevant to finding an alternative pathway for a critical-constructive approach (Lennerfors, 2014). I would like to propose that it is possible to connect self-cultivation methodologies with problematization in order to deconstruct market discourses that shape the fetish nature of commodification. Buddhism's *gedatsu* and Confucianism's *toku* are traditionally used as methods to overcome general personal issues, such as personal desire and material success. Yet they can also be applied to the overwhelming nature of capitalism and the problem of distortion, such as commodification in identity, family, education, workplace and other various contexts in business. Self-cultivation methods in everyday life practices should be linked with methodologies of problematization that Foucault and Alvesson[8] advocate. This approach offers two ways to complement critical-constructive approaches, and, particularly, it may be more suitable in non-Protestant Christian societies. One is the Buddhist notion of *gedatsu* that might be translated as 'self-problematization', and the other is the Confucian notion of *toku* that could be translated as 'relational problematization', as we will now explain in the following section.

Gedatsu as Self-Problematization

Self-cultivation in *gedatsu* is the core of human life and is historically rooted in the Japanese cultural context; a life is training for *gedatsu*. For example, Japanese people emphasize personal development in a business setting, and they are always willing to study and learn through on-the-job and off-the-job training. People try to change themselves and/or tend to refine themselves. In other words, their personal emancipation is achieved by self-discipline and self-cultivation. Therefore, Japanese people often emphasize how to achieve, not what is achieved. Self-cultivation methodology can be connected with self-problematization; it must be effective in terms of the aspects of the self that are distorted by market discourses and capitalist relationships.

In order to deconstruct market discourses of commodification, therefore, a self-cultivation methodology of *gedatsu* should embrace problematizing capitalism's commodification of desire (that distorts the self). In other words, *gedatsu* should be integrated with the Foucauldian concept of problematization so that it aims at problematizing one's self. The Foucauldian notion of problematization is generally described as questioning how people govern themselves and others through the production of truth (Foucault, 1976). In other words, problematization questions how and why certain phenomena are made into a problem, analysed and regulated at specific time and under specific circumstances, while others are not. In terms of 'self-problematization', the production of capitalistic truth should be problematized and deconstructed by self-cultivation of *gedatsu* for the purpose of emptying capitalist self-desire. Whereas *toku* targets deconstruction of interpersonal relationships, *gedatsu* targets the domain of self. The Buddhist notion of Awakening should be linked with problematizing one's self, which is blinded by capitalism's regimes of truth, or market discourses of commodification and its normalization. As a result of self-problematization methodology, people may be able to attempt and accomplish *gedatsu* as both consumers and producers in economic activities.

In particular, crisis moments may provide a chance of self-problematization. A crisis often changes people's way of viewing the world and their lifestyle itself, and it might result in an inner revolution. For example, Japan experienced a tragic natural disaster when a tsunami struck on March 11, 2011, which caused approximately 20,000 casualties in the Tohoku area, the northern part of Japan. This incident had a significant impact on people's mindsets and social relations in Japan. Japanese people who suffered the tsunami first-hand realized that they lost everything but learned a lot, and it led to an inner revolution in their lifestyles. According to discourses in the devastated area, they realized their lives were distorted by deep embeddedness in the market system and competition, and therefore an alternative mode of organizing can be identified in communities under crisis, which contrasts starkly with a capitalist mode of organizing. While evacuated people denied their own self-desire, they shared their food and other materials necessary

138   *Toru Kiyomiya*

with other people. They often stated that human relationships and collaboration were more central and effective for overcoming difficulty and paid more attention to values used in the crisis context. People want to survive under the crisis of the absence of electricity, heating in the cold of winter, money, credit cards and the market more generally. It is a moment of their inner revolution with deconstructing 'commodification' through problematizing distortion oneself. A crisis experience makes people realize the fine line between life and death, with the tsunami having taken everything as well as destroyed the capitalist system, albeit only for brief a moment. They became aware that relational ties enable survival, whereas market competition is less helpful in the efforts of resilience. It implies that people became aware that they are overwhelmed by their focus on exchange value and realize the centrality of use value under crisis and resilience.

Toku as Relational Problematization

The Confucian notion of *toku* emphasizes the accumulation of personal practices in respect of relational virtue in daily life. In contrast with *gedatsu*, which centres on self-discipline, *toku* tends to focus more on interpersonal relationships with others. For our purposes, it can be linked to organizational communication by acting as a transformative methodology for emancipation due to it reflecting and questioning interpersonal relationships. In the name of a critical-constructive approach, *toku* should accentuate a perspective of 'relational problematization', which questions how people govern the communicative relationship with others through the production of truth. It implies that a capitalist regime of truth on the internal and external aspects of organizing should be problematized by asking how certain relationships of domination come to be seen as natural at specific times and under specific circumstances, while others do not. Therefore, a self-cultivation methodology of *toku* indicates that dialectical struggles and the socially constructed aspects of antagonism are considered as discursive processes for the accumulation of *toku* practices through relational problematization. By enhancing *toku* in interpersonal communication settings, internal organizing must develop more democratic relationships for various types of minority groups. By enhancing *toku* in corporate communication settings, corporate virtue in external organizing is obtained in terms of corporate reputation and branding. Although this may seem to correspond with a capitalist marketing strategy, *toku* as relational problematization is associated with relational democracy among different stakeholders; in other words, it can be underpinned by multiple-stakeholder communication[9].

These methodologies fit the Japanese collaborative approach of doing business, which is a set of discursive practices of expanding 'relational' co-construction for benevolent objectives, facilitating cohesiveness in the community and harmonizing in-group members by adopting the others'

Self-Problematization 139

perspectives. At the micro level of interpersonal relationships, business relations get critically considered and problematized. People often reflect upon previous relationships and problematize what was normal when they face problems and crisis. In the example of the 2011 natural disaster, people described how they changed their world view and problematized their conventional business style centred on market competition. Realizing that market competition did not allow them to overcome the crisis or facilitate resilience, they emphasized respecting human relationships and collaborating through co-constructed partnerships. Thus relational problematization is practiced through co-constructing collaboration in the context of human relationships.

In the domain of external organizing, various types of stakeholder relationships must be critically reviewed and problematized for the purpose of a critical-constructive approach to emancipation. The balance offered by the multiple-stakeholder approach in mainstream corporate communication studies would seem to provide an alternative management model.[10] If it is treated as a strategy for gaining competitive advantages through controlling corporate governance, this is a fetish and wag-the-dog relationship between an organization and its stakeholders. However, from a *toku* perspective, multiple-stakeholder communication is crucial for a critical-constructive approach. Balancing conflicting interests and communicating stakeholders is a complicated process, which includes understanding the socially constructed aspect of stakes and deconstructing identity and social relations that have been distorted by market discourses.

A historical example of multiple-stakeholder balance can be found in ancient Japanese business activities. Historically, virtue in business had been shaped through various practices of merchants. One of the classic business models is *Oumi-shonin* (a group of merchants who lived in the Oumi area [the east side of Kyoto] and travelled as ambulant vendors[11]). It emphasized *sanpo-yoshi*; literarily, vendors practiced good business in respect of the three parties (*sanpo*) of sellers, buyers and *seken* (society). This philosophy of *sanpo-yoshi* emphasizes balancing mutual benefits among these three parties. In terms of *sanpo-yoshi*, the objective of their business transactions is not profit, but social welfare (Suenaga, 2004). The discourse of *sanpo-yoshi* embraces a meaning of self-cultivation through activities of ambulant vendors. Therefore, their own business style emphasized maintaining trust with stakeholders and upholding good relationships over a long period of time. *Sanpo-yoshi* came to define virtue in the Japanese classical business model. From a CMS point of view, emphasizing the long-term relationship with multiple stakeholders can be a key in a critical-constructive approach, which in turn should be related to relational problematization and review the business relationships that are distorted by market competition in the short run. Thus the discourse of *sanpo-yoshi* was practiced in order to overcome conflicts and different interests, and it should be applicable as an important process of a critical-constructive approach.

140 *Toru Kiyomiya*

Future Studies

In concluding this chapter, it is useful to recapitulate the issue of translation in the Japanese context. Because much of our knowledge and discourses came from other countries, notably, from China and Korea in ancient times and from the West in modern times, discourses about both capitalism and critical perspectives have been understood through the translation of Western languages. It is important to confirm that translation is never conducted in a neutral context, but it is practiced through a historical and cultural context of power relations. Under the transition from the Edo Period to Meiji Period, westernization was legitimized by modernization once the Meiji government implemented its new policy. In a similar way of assimilating knowledge, capitalism as well as critical perspectives were imported from the West but were translated into a local context, which facilitated the development of Japanese capitalism. Critical perspectives have been marginalized, while a tremendous number of conceptualizations have been translated for developing managerialism. In this sense, for the purpose of considering a future study, it is crucial for scholars in non-English-speaking cultures to analyse how the translation of some discourses have been socially constructed and reified (dominated, normalized, trivialized and legitimized); in particular, this chapter implies that commodification by market discourses has affected Japanese academia and pejoratively shaped the prospects of CMS in Japan.

Moreover, on the basis of the earlier discussion, we might suggest a future orientation for CMS would be to situate itself with a particular cultural context by paying attention to traditional and local discourses, many of which have been made obsolete and dwindled away by the forces of free-market discourses. In other words, it is suggested that CMS refocus on indigenous discourses that have not been contaminated by commodification and which harbour important meanings that are distinct from dominant market discourse. What we have in mind here is what Foucault called the recovery of forgotten knowledges for the purposes of a counter-history of the present.[12] This chapter implies how some Japanese discourses that have Buddhist and Confucian connotations have the potential to enhance critical perspectives, such as *gedatsu* and *toku*, and it is necessary to deconstruct such discourses by questioning how they are expelled or marginalized by the domination of the market discourses. Also, it is necessary to find the kernel of an alternative critical view within traditional discourses, which hereby can contribute to reshape the reinvigorated discourse of emancipation in a local context. In this sense, two approaches might be significant for future studies. One is to excavate indigenous discourses, which shed light on self-cultivation implied by *gedatsu* and *toku* and use them to fuel critical-constructive approaches. The other is to inquire how such indigenous discourses are expelled by dominant discourses of managerialism. In this chapter, *sanpo-yoshi* has been compared with multiple-stakeholder communication, as the former emphasizes a *moral sense*, whereas the latter has an information strategy of public relations, as well as balance of power in corporate governance. Critical-constructive approaches should pay attention to the

Self-Problematization 141

local history of indigenous business and commerce, such as the discourse of *sanpo-yoshi*, which reshapes the meaning for local emancipation.

Third, when considering future studies, I would like to stress the strategy of reverse translation for a critical-constructive objective. Here it may be defined as a boomerang effect of discursive transformation of an original foreign term with additional or alternative meanings by translation and local understandings. This chapter has attempted to illustrate the Japanese discourse of *gedatsu* and *toku* by translating them via the Western notions of self-problematization and relational problematization, respectively. To be sure, these are far from perfect translations; to take another example, the Japanese discourse of *kaizen* (改善), which is a workplace practice, is typically translated by the English term, 'continuous improvement'. However, kaizen is not exactly synonymous with continuous improvement. Kaizen has important meanings beyond the words 'continuous improvement'. It originally has a connotation of self-cultivation, while carefully considering and reflecting their work environment, which includes cleaning up, workplace safety, self-discipline and so on. However, it is used as a management tool by emphasizing efficiency of lean management and organizational learning for effectiveness, and therefore it is trivialized and distorted through its linkage to managerialism. In this chapter, I have argued that the Japanese discourse of *gedatsu* and *toku* translated by self-problematization and relational problematization are crucial components in a critical-constructive approach. A renewed discursive strategy should make a point to use the Japanese discourse of *gedatsu* and *toku*, which imply the ongoing process of everyday practices for self-cultivation. In so doing, reverse translation facilitates understanding of ambiguous terms for an alternative methodology that is relevant to local emancipation.

Lastly, a future study should shed more light on the problem of commodification. It should seek to demonstrate how market discourses distort social relations and make them wag-the-dog via a fetish relationship. This chapter facilitates discussion about self-cultivation methodologies that may effectively deconstruct commodification, because self-cultivation is process oriented and it requires lifelong practices in daily life. It means that a critical-constructive approach takes time and relies on continuous efforts that are embedded in everyday practices of problematization in the domain of self and its relationships. Commodification can never be solved by an instant remedy, but it can be overcome by continuous efforts. As a future study, therefore, the extension of this argument should lead to questioning people's daily consumption. Namely, from a critical-constructive point of view, the morality of consumers must become central for deconstructing commodification. In order to overcome (empty) market prioritization of exchange value, consumer morality must be related to use value. In the resilience of the 2011 natural disaster in Japan, people became aware of the limitations of the market system and realized the importance of use value as well as relational collaboration. These people are in the process of reshaping their identities through awareness of use value. Thus important future study should consider consumer morality that must be related with consumer identity.

142 *Toru Kiyomiya*

This chapter indicates that analysis about CMS in Japanese context leads to the contribution of developing a critical-constructive approach. Alternative methodology of self-cultivation to local emancipation may provide a hint to CMS scholars.

NOTES

1. Critical perspectives in this chapter indicate the Western tradition of critiques in general; it may include Kant, Nietzsche, Weber, Foucault and others. CMS is related but not directly connected.
2. This perspective may be shared with a concept of 'becoming' that Tsoukas and Chia (2002) advocates.
3. Lennerfors (2014) points out that the Western understanding of Buddhism, which focuses on 'coping and harmony' as a means to instal hegemonic control in organizations actually emerged in Japanese management.
4. Siddhartha Gautama is the name of the historical Buddha.
5. *Satori* (悟り) is similar in meaning and may be used as an everyday discourse in Japanese.
6. 'Awakening' that is symbolized in the capital A indicates Buddhist term of enlightenment.
7. However, this vision of the 'Enlightenment' is the source of contestation within the Western tradition itself, which dates back to the Romantic reaction against it in the eighteenth century and, more recently, Nietzsche, Weber, Foucault and others (Dalgliesh, 2013).
8. Alvesson proposed a notion of problematization as a research method in order to create effective research questions. However, the essence of this approach is effective not only for scholars but also for people (including scholars) who have discursive interaction and communication in everyday life.
9. Deetz (1995) has a similar perspective of organizational democracy from the stakeholder point of view.
10. As Cornelissen (2014) points out, a contemporary perspective in corporate communication studies has more of a social democratic flavour on the relationship between organization and society.
11. The Japanese discourse of *sanpo-yoshi* embraced important notions of Buddhism and Confucianism, since early Oumi-merchants were devout Buddhists (Suenaga, 2004).
12. Foucault (2003, p. 9 and p. 179) spoke of the idea of "the insurrection of subjugated knowledges" as a way to write a counter-history, the aim of which is an "immense and multiple battle between knowledges in the plural—knowledges that are in conflict because of their very morphology, because they are in the possession of enemies, and because they have intrinsic power-effects".

REFERENCES

Abegglen, J.C. (1958). *The Japanese Factory: Aspects of its Social Organization.* Glencoe, IL: Free Press
Alvesson, M. and Willmott, H. (1996). *Making Sense of Management: A Critical Introduction.* London: Sage Publications.
Collins, S. (1998). *Nirvana and Other Buddhist Felicities: Utopias of the Pali Imaginarire.* Cambridge: Cambridge University Press.

Self-Problematization 143

Cornelissen, J. (2014). *Corporate Communication: A Guide to Theory and Practice* (4th ed.). London: Sage Publications.

Dalgliesh, B. (2013). Critical History: Foucault After Kant and Nietzsche. *PARRHE-SIA: A Journal of Critical Philosophy*, 18: 68–84

Deetz, S. (1995). *Transforming Communication, Transforming Business: Building Responsive and Responsible Workplaces*. Cresskill, NJ: Hampton Press.

du Gay, P. and Morgan, G. (2014). *New Spirits of Capitalism?: Crises, Justifications, and Dynamics*. Oxford University Press.

Furuta, G. (Ed.). (1996). *Ibunka Komyunikēshyon (Intercultural communication)* (2nd ed.). Tokyo: Yuuhikaku.

Foucault, M. (1976). *Discipline & Punish*, trans. A. Sheridan. New York: Vintage.

Gudykunst, W.B. and Nishida, T. (1994). *Bridging Japanese/North American Differences*. Thousand Oaks, CA: Sage Publications.

Hall, P.A. and Soskic, D.W. (2001). *Varieties of Capitalism: The Institutional Foundations of Comparative Advantage*. Oxford University Press.

Hiromatsu, W. (1969). *Marukususyugino Chihei (Horizon of Marxism)*. Tokyo: Keisou Shobo.

Hiromatsu, W. (1987). *Shihonron no Tetsugaku (Philosophy in Marx's Capital)*. Tokyo: Keiso Shobo.

Holiday, A. (2011). *Intercultural Communication and Ideology*. London: Sage Publications Jacobson, 1988.

Jacobson, N.P. (1986). *Understanding Buddhism*. Carbondale: Southern Illinois University Press.

Keown, D. (Ed.). (2003). *A Dictionary of Buddhism*. Oxford: Oxford University Press.

Kiyomiya, T. (2011). Corporate Hegemony in Japanese Collaborative Management: A Case Study of Corporate Misconduct in Japan. *Studies in English Language and Literature*, 51: 113–135.

Kiyomiya, T., (2012). Collaborative Organizational Communication in Ethical Problems: The Dark Side of Japanese Management. *International Studies of Management and Organization*, 42(3): 51–70.

Kiyomiya, T., Matake, K. and Matsunaga, M. (2006). Why Companies Tell Lies in Business: A Japanese Case in the Food Industry. In S. May (Ed.), *Case Studies in Organizations: Ethical Perspectives and Practices*, 287–304. Thousand Oaks, CA: Sage Publications.

Kotter, J.P. (1997). *Matsushita Leadership*. New York: The Free Press.

Lennerfors, T.T. (2014). A Buddhist Future for Capitalism? Revising Buddhist Economics for the Era of Light Capitalism. *Futures* 68, 67–75.

Lukács, G. (1972). *History and Class Consciousness: Studies in Marxist Dialectics*, trans. R. Livingstone. London: Merlin Press.

Moriya, H. (2009). Manejya-no Rongo-Nyumon (The Managerial Lessons from Confucius). *Diamond Harvard Business Review (October)*, 24–36.

Ouchi, W.G. (1981). *Theory Z: How American Business Can Meet the Japanese Challenge*. Reading, MA: Addison-Wesley Publishing Company.

Suenaga, K. (2004). *Oumi-shonin-gaku Nyumon: CSRnogenryu Sanpoyoshi* (Introduction of Oumi-Merchants Studies: Orignin of Sanpoyoshi of CSR). Hikone, Japan: Sanraise-syuppan.

Tsuda, M. (1994). *Nihon no Keieibunka* (Japanese Management Culture). Kyoto: Mineruba-shobo.

Tsoukas, H. and Chia, R. (2002). On Organizational Becoming: Rethinking Organizational Change, *Organization Science*, 13(5): 567–582

Yui, T. (2008). The Significance of Management Philosophy in SHIBUSAWA Eiich Left, Japan Academy of Management Philosophy (Eds.), *Practice of Management Philosophy*, 3–22. Tokyo: Bunshindo.

10 CMS in Scandinavia
A Hitchhiker's Guide to the Realm of the Scandocrits

Rasmus Koss Hartmann, Dan Kärreman and Mats Alvesson

INTRODUCTION

It is often claimed that CMS is an Anglo-Scandinavian project. This is flattering and reflects the impact of some early key writings (e.g. Alvesson and Willmott, 1992, 1996/2012; Alvesson and Deetz, 2000), but it may be overstating the case quite dramatically, both as regards the contributions of Scandinavian scholars and the extent of critical thought in the region. It is certainly true both that critical scholarship on management does not live the embattled existence here that it does elsewhere and that Scandinavians have been quite vocal in some branches of CMS. This should not, however, give anyone the impression that Scandinavian business schools are frothing at the mouth with revolutionary fervour. To some parts of the world, Scandinavia may well be the poster boy of in-practice, first-world socialism and our voice in CMS loud, but there is quite some way from the lived experience of doing CMS here to the description of Scandinavian CMS as a particularly potent force.

In many ways, Scandinavian-style CMS conforms to the reformist call in Spicer et al. (2009) in mostly rejecting or questioning the explicit antiperformative intent of the standard or pure form of CMS, on the grounds that Scandinavia historically has been a place where socially progressive movements have been unusually successful and that this contribution to social progress shouldn't be discounted completely. Hence the endemic impulse in CMS to satisfy itself with asking questions about the 'ends' of any social formation from a safe distance is treated with suspicion. Scandinavia also has a long tradition of stewardship (Davis et al., 1997), rather than managerialism, as the prevailing model for manager-worker interaction. Thus the almost caricature version of management often found in CMS studies is perceived to have little or no validity in the Scandinavian context. The authoritarian and mechanistic form of managerialism exercised at some metrics-driven UK business schools (e.g. Parker, 2014) would be almost inconceivable at a Scandinavian university or business school.

Furthermore, what distinguishes Scandinavia as a context for (critical) management and organization studies, more than anything, is the welfare

CMS in Scandinavia 145

state and everything that this form of social organization implies: societies with high levels of taxation and public provision of welfare service, hence also societies with relative equality and some kind of 'social justice'; workplaces with relatively good working conditions that are also less hierarchical and more democratic than tends to be the case internationally; and politics hinging on a commonsensical appreciation of social democracy. Social democracy is the crux here: Scandinavian democracies are by international comparison social, not liberal, democracies. Taken together, organization studies in Scandinavia happen in quite a privileged social context, as regards both the social milieu of the researcher and the organizations that we study.

Against this background, this chapter proposes that in Scandinavia, CMS gets interpreted in five different ways and that these interpretations have some geographical correlate. Even if people do move around and ideas travel within the region, we can meaningfully talk about CMS research as organized in two 'schools' in Copenhagen and Lund and three smaller 'clusters' in Helsinki, Stockholm and Gothenburg.

The Copenhagen School (associated primarily with the Department of Management, Politics and Philosophy at Copenhagen Business School) tends to be driven primarily by strong readings of postmodernism and is theoretically informed by French sources. Here there is a focus on expanding 'what we think about' in the business school. Various branches of the humanities play a key role in inspiring this expansion. By contrast, the Lund School (associated with the LUMOS group at Lund University but also with some representation in smaller environments at Copenhagen Business School) tends to be more pragmatically oriented than the Copenhagen School. Here there is a greater reliance on empirical work (especially ethnographically inspired studies) and less on specific theorists, with the exception of some Frankfurt School–inspired theoretical work (Alvesson and Willmott, 1996/2012). The focus is on changing 'how we think' in the business school by engaging 'mainstream' discussions, rather than dwelling within specific debates about specific theorists. As a matter of transparency, we count ourselves as representatives of this approach, with a genuine interest in management and organizational phenomena—somewhat different from the 'no management' style of philosophers in exile, making up a part of the overall CMS community.

The Helsinki Cluster (associated with Janne Tienari and Eero Vaara) has been inspired by theories of practice, narrative, sensemaking, discourse and gender, applying them in various contexts. The Stockholm cluster (scattered groups at Kungliga Tekniska Hogskolan [Royal Institute of Technology] and Stockholm University) applies critical themes to project management and gender as well as health in organizations, among other things. The Gothenburg cluster (associated with Barbara Czarniawska) is known for a particular stylistic and boundary-spanning approach to management studies emphasizing bricolage as a vehicle for thinking creatively, rather than a particular commitment to critique.

146 *Hartmann et al.*

As we go about mapping the realm and domains of the Scandocrits, we rely on a definition of CMS that includes both 'heavy' and some 'light' versions of critical thought (Alvesson, 2008). Taking a 'heavy', 'strong' or 'hard-core' approach to CMS would involve not only standing by doing CMS and being explicit about a critical normativity, a political agenda and a desire for social change (Spicer et al., 2009). We would probably also need people to be open to describing management in terms of 'dark metaphors' as well as ambiguous ones and to calling management by its 'true names': oppression, control, exploitation, etc. Doing heavy CMS would therefore involve doing things that are fundamentally critical, i.e. that can actually be distinguished from mainstream work (Parker, 2013).

Lighter versions of CMS could take several forms. It could involve claiming an identity as CMS, but without really throwing the most critical punches. Then there is talk of 'branding' efforts more than anything, provided there are no underlying tactics at work (e.g. Hartmann, 2014; Wickert and Schaefer, 2015). It could also involve eschewing an identity as CMS, but doing things that in practice might be indistinguishable from or strongly inspired by CMS work. Then there is perhaps talk of 'unaffiliated CMS'. Finally, it could involve just doing CMS in less edgy versions, which of course is where the boundaries become most blurred. We could perhaps talk of 'watered-down CMS'. For the purpose of this chapter, we adopt somewhat of a definitional middle ground and cover the scholarship that is either 'heavy' or 'unaffiliated' CMS. We do not include work that is too opaquely connected to CMS, merely seems like branding efforts or is so light as to be indistinguishable from mainstream work.

The definition is important, because we can either make CMS in Scandinavia a really marginal phenomenon or a completely mainstream one. If we delimit CMS to mean 'heavy CMS', there really may only be one school, namely that in Lund. A sizable proportion of the heavy CMS in Scandinavia might even be said to come from just one of the chapter's authors. If, however, we relax the term—probably needed in order to be able to produce this chapter—and let CMS describe 'pretty critical studies', 'kind-of-critical studies' or 'CMS on helium', it is easy to make the case that CMS is absolutely mainstream here: a journal like *Organization* is a completely normal thing for business students and academics to read and appreciate, the same almost going for *Ephemera*; many people work with theories and theorists that are considered highly critical and play marginal roles elsewhere; qualitative methods and those associated with a CMS tradition are immensely common.

Irrespective of how we draw the boundaries in this chapter, a scholar 'doing CMS' would most likely find many people to talk to in this region, many people to appreciate his or her work and many people doing similar things, but very few who would confess to a critical orientation or (even fewer) to belonging to CMS. It is some of this sense of 'appreciating CMS' that we try to capture in our definition and overview. It is also the paradox

CMS *in Scandinavia* 147

of Scandinavian CMS: at once, it is everywhere and nowhere, mainstream and marginal. In the discussion that closes the chapter, we offer some reasons for this apparent paradox and suggest that welfare state politics play a major role. While it is easy to be disillusioned with the welfare state, it makes life so privileged that really strong critique may seem overdone to many, even if it also makes one very open to questioning the social purpose of organizations. It also has a considerable impact on the empirical world that we observe.

SCANDINAVIA AS A RESEARCH CONTEXT

It is somewhat odd to be writing about CMS in Scandinavia for the simple reason that 'Scandinavia' is one of those terms that it is easy for CMS to critique. To the outside observer, this most northern of the Global North seems to cover countries that are very alike and tend to get treated as a unit. However, the unity of the region is relatively historically tenuous, very political and not as altogether wholesome as many prefer to believe. The ethnic and cultural kinship of particularly Norway, Sweden and Denmark (the 'original' Scandinavia, if you will) has something to do with Iron Age commonalities: Vikings, a particular branch of paganism, somewhat similar languages, etc. On closer examination, this historic kinship is also one of quite considerable conflict, intra-regional wars and pursuit of independence from one another. The positive understanding that dominates today owes a lot to the political movement of Scandinavianism of the 1800s, which emphasized common cultures and heritage. These ideas gained considerable traction not just in Scandinavia but also in Europe (especially Germany) and produced a general fascination with Vikings and Nordic culture. In the early twentieth century and the interbellum, this came to inspire ideas about racial purity in both Germany and Scandinavia itself with disastrous consequences to follow.

This deconstruction notwithstanding, there are certainly commonalities in contemporary Scandinavian countries (Norway, Sweden, Finland and Denmark). The most central one (and indeed what seems to define the area internationally) is the social model: the welfare state, which empowers all individuals, and the strong consensual norms, which moderates authoritarian leanings.

Politically, the inherently social democratic vision of the welfare state tends to shape the discourse and place discussions to the left of what would be the centre in many other Western countries. This is important in the sense that it makes us think about Scandinavian countries as *social democracies* and not *liberal democracies*. To be sure, the Scandinavian countries are characterized by many of the same features as liberal democracies, but they also include more expansive social 'rights' than is the case elsewhere. While these rights do come under increasing pressure from international

148 Hartmann et al.

neo-liberal currents (e.g. Pedersen, 2011), there remains a sense across the political spectrum and in large parts of the electorate that the welfare state is desirable and should be preserved.

Socially, it entails high levels of taxation to finance extensive public provision of social, educational and health-related services. Along with quite high levels of economic re-distribution and socialized insurance (e.g. against unemployment), this contributes to societies with limited income disparities and large middle classes. The welfare state not only provides a social 'safety net' but also allows for greater social mobility than tends to be the case elsewhere. It is hardly surprising, then, that in in statistics claiming to examine such things, Scandinavian countries generally come out to high levels of happiness, trust and perceived social justice.

Organizationally, a history of strong, government-supported unionization means that work is generally well compensated and wages not as exorbitantly skewed as is the case elsewhere. Working conditions are also generally good, at least in the physical sense of being regulated in ways that make them less hazardous and unhealthy to be in. Thinking in terms of national culture, workplaces tend to be relatively informal and 'low-hierarchy', just as there is a general idea that work should be relatively democratically organized. Scandinavians might like to think that they can 'talk about it' with their colleagues and superiors. Carmaker Volvo famously introduced self-managing groups, airline SAS claimed to tear down the pyramids of hierarchy in the 1980s and hearing-aid manufacturer Oticon made some efforts to abolish them outright by introducing the Spaghetti Organization. The Scandinavian countries and their companies also tend to consider themselves progressive as regards many of the things CMS scholars would tend to be concerned about: gender equality, nonfinancial performance (things like the triple bottom line come out of Scandinavian corporate practices), corporate social responsibilities, etc. In popular renditions, some talk about all of this as related to a particularly Scandinavian way of doing business.

Before there was anything called 'CMS', Scandinavia was associated with a particular branch of sociological enquiry emphasizing various forms of action research. Known by different names (working life research, sociology of work, etc.), this form of enquiry has certain similarities to Labour Process Theory and industrial relations research in seeing management as a problematic feature of work to be overcome through democratization, although conflicts were generally toned down compared to UK labour process studies. It was also a research tradition that was driven primarily from outside of the university context, being grounded in smaller 'institutes', formally independent but often connected to labour unions. This strand of research still exists and is strongly connected to the labour movement. Because of this connection the research is treated with some suspicion of being partisan and policy oriented more than scholarly, and in many ways, it nowadays operates more as a think tank for the labour movement than as an independent research stream. It is quite different from most versions

CMS in Scandinavia 149

of CMS, the latter being independent, socially and politically isolated, often seen as esoteric and irrelevant and located at business schools rather than in sociology or education departments or in independent institutes of working life studies.

SCHOOLS AND CLUSTERS

In this section, we describe the two schools and three clusters of CMS in Scandinavia: the Copenhagen School, the Lund School, the Helsinki Cluster, the Stockholm Cluster and the Gothenburg Cluster. We call it a school when a sizable group of scholars seem to practice and advocate similar kinds of research, but this should not be taken too literally: we are not talking about schools in the sense of a 'Frankfurt School' or 'Chicago School' here, but more of groups of people interested in related things and engaged to advancing distinct approaches in publication and doctoral training, i.e. 'schools' rather than Schools.

THE COPENHAGEN SCHOOL

The Copenhagen School is organizationally located at Copenhagen Business School's Department of Management, Politics and Philosophy (MPP). This rather large department (around 80 faculty including PhD students) contains people working within a range of social science disciplines with the particular variation of Critical Management Studies being done in two research groups: Management and Entrepreneurship and Management Philosophy. In the first group, we find researchers such as Timon Beyes, Daniel Hjorth and Pierre Guillet de Monthoux, while the latter houses people such as Bent Meier Sørensen, Sverre Raffnsøe, Michael Pedersen and Ole Bjerg. Topics of central interest here concern the nature of contemporary work and modern capitalism, philosophy and entrepreneurship.

Relating to work and capitalism, questions of interest here concern self-management (e.g. Lopdrup-Hjorth et al., 2011) and the organization of work (e.g. Muhr et al., 2012) as well as financial markets, crises and the role of money (Bjerg, 2014). Concerning philosophy, there is an interest in interpretations of particular thinkers and their oeuvres (e.g. Raffnsøe et al., 2008) and in applying philosophical analyses to management topics and to the development of new styles of theorizing (e.g. Helin et al., 2014). The philosophical inspiration is also evident in the interest in aesthetics and the role of art in understanding and teaching management (e.g. Beyes and Steyaert, 2011). Researchers at the department have also been associated with the development of a European School of Entrepreneurship set on questioning our understandings of entrepreneurship, innovation and organizational creation (Hjorth, 2012; Barinaga, 2013).

150 Hartmann et al.

As is evident from the scope of topics being dealt with here, the Copenhagen School draws on many sources, although some are, of course, more influential than others. The critical work being done in the department is often influenced by rather strong understandings of postmodernism and draws on a theoretical canon emphasizing primarily French thinkers such as Foucault, Derrida, Deleuze and De Certeau, all of whom are highly influential in the Copenhagen School. Considerable conceptual work gets done in applying their analytics to question and exoticize our ideas about management. The same is the case of classical philosophers, who also play a substantial role.

More generally, however, the Copenhagen School is characterized by the aspiration to bring ideas typically associated with the humanities into the business school context. As such, it is not just philosophy that is used as an inspiration but also business history, art history and theology (e.g. Sørensen et al., 2012). This effort to draw on ideas from fields that are noncanonical in the business school very much reflects the Copenhagen School's interest in expanding what it is that we think about in the business school and of legitimizing alternative perspectives in management research and education. In management education, the *bildung* and intellectualization of managers is emphasized. The general sense of this effort is that empirics play a somewhat limited role relative to theories: empirical material is inspirational, not formative; deep engagement and experimentation with theories and specific theorists, as well as an appreciation of 'classics' is highly valorized.

The work relating to the European School of Entrepreneurship provides an illustrative case of this approach. Associated particularly with Hjorth's research, this represents an effort to critically question contemporary notions of entrepreneurship. This is done by exploring the intellectual origins of the concept and highlighting how it has been annexed, skewed and narrowed by 'enterprise discourse' (Hjorth, 2001). Revisiting classic meanings through readings of Schumpeter's work and connecting the idea to European intellectual traditions and styles of theorizing contributes to affording the concept some of its lost richness. Unconventional and artful mobilizations of illustrative, but limited, empirical material (Sørensen, 2006, 2010a, 2010b) are similarly employed. Of course, students who sign up thinking that they will learn about starting a business will come away from such a perspective either inspired or deeply disappointed.

THE LUND SCHOOL

Across the Öresund to the east from Copenhagen, one finds Lund University and in it the group Lund University Management and Organizations Studies (LUMOS). This is where one finds the Lund School of CMS most clearly represented. Scholars associated with this group include Mats Alvesson, Nick Butler, Tony Huzzard, Roland Paulsen, Jens Rennstam, Katie Sullivan, Sverre Spoelstra and Stefan Sveningsson. Moreover, Lund School 'alumni'

CMS in Scandinavia   151

such as Dan Kärreman and Sara Louise Muhr can also be found at CBS in departments other than MPP. During the years, many of the more prominent Anglo-Saxon CMS researchers have been affiliated and co-worked with the Lund group, e.g. Karen Ashcraft, Stan Deetz, Yiannis Gabriel, André Spicer and Hugh Willmott.

The central topics that this school engages with include leadership (Alvesson and Spicer, 2011, 2012a; Alvesson et al., 2016), culture, identity, branding and other issues related to meaning and symbolic manipulation in organizations (Ashcraft et al., 2012; Alvesson, 2013;), gender (Muhr, 2011), organizational control (Alvesson and Kärreman, 2004; Rennstam, 2012; Costas and Kärreman, 2013) and, recently, 'functional stupidity' (Alvesson and Spicer, 2012b) as well as 'empty labour' (Paulsen, 2014). Work is also done on issues of method (Alvesson and Sköldberg, 2009; Alvesson and Kärreman, 2011; Alvesson and Sandberg, 2011; Jeanes and Huzzard, 2014) and on the practice of CMS (Spicer et al., 2009; Alvesson and Spicer, 2012b; Butler and Spoelstra, 2014; Wickert and Schaefer, 2015). It is quite common for knowledge-intensive firms to provide the empirical context for the Lund School, be that consultancy or engineering work, but this is far from always the case.

Compared to the Copenhagen School, the Lund School can be characterized as pragmatic and empirically oriented, although the work with developing the theoretical foundation of CMS is also associated with Lund writers (primarily Alvesson). Generally, Lund School research builds on a less purist interpretation of social constructionism and postmodernism than is the case in Copenhagen. We could say that there is less 'epistemological paranoia' in Lund than in Copenhagen and also a less French flavour in theorizing. The central difference that this entails is regarding the role of empirical material: the Lund School frequently relies on in-depth ethnographic studies of organizations and places greater faith in the ability of such studies to illuminate theoretical issues and create starting points for interesting insights. These studies tend to take an explorative approach, looking into what people actually do at work as opposed to what management theories say that they do. What the natives themselves think they are up to, if you will.

Rather than data being used to illustrate theoretical arguments, data is used as a basis for developing theoretical arguments. This also means that other ethnographic studies coming from American traditions, such as Goffman, Geertz, Van Maanen, Kunda or Orr, serve more strongly to inform the Lund School than the Copenhagen School. The inspiration for the Frankfurt School of critical theory is also quite strong here, particularly Habermas's ideas about communicative interaction (Spicer et al., 2009; Alvesson and Spicer, 2012a) and the critique of consumer society associated with Marcuse (Alvesson, 2013).

The pragmatism also extends to the understanding of the conduct of critical research, where the idea of critical performativity (Spicer et al., 2009) informs some of the engagement with CMS. The argument this puts forth is for researchers to accept and engage with CMS as a political project and

152 *Hartmann et al.*

being explicit about their critical intentions. It also suggests that realizing a political project might depend on engaging in ways that accept the contexts of management and, within them, pursue and contribute to forms of micro-emancipation. This in itself is in contrast to the more opaque and convoluted politics of literal interpretations of postmodernism. Another implication here is that there is a much greater willingness to being explicit about one's critical position and about doing CMS, more so than in Copenhagen.

The general sense of the Lund School approach is to focus on contesting established ways of thinking in the business school context, more than carving out new niches. The central means for doing this is in-depth empirical enquiry, rather than established theoretical positions, and a general ethos of relating critically to management and organizations. Arguments are generally directed not only to other scholars in CMS or critical organization studies but also at a mainstream audience in organization and management studies. More than convincing other critical scholars that they have gotten things right, it is about convincing mainstream scholars, and to some extent the broader public, that they have gotten things slightly or sometimes really wrong. The allegiance to CMS, while pronounced, has two purposes here. It serves as a means for doing management research that is interesting and provocative—if critical theories can help open up a space for creative reflection, they can be mobilized but so can a range of other theories that help us understand what people are up to in their working lives. CMS also serves as a normative basis for wanting to make organizations better, even if it entails being somehow torn between being very critical and caring for the participants we study.

THE HELSINKI CLUSTER

The dramatis personae of the Helsinki Cluster are, centrally, Janne Tienari of Aalto University and Eero Vaara at Hanken School of Economics. Organizational change is of general interest here, while more specific topics include mergers and acquisitions (Tienari and Vaara, 2012), strategy (Vaara and Whittington, 2012), gender and diversity (Tienari et al., 2009). These issues are often studied in relation to organizations working, or merging, across borders and cultures. The construction of the pan-Scandinavian banking corporation Nordea has been central to their work.

Theoretically, discourse analysis plays a key role in the work being done here, as does various theorizations of narrative and practice. Discourse analysis is often applied in moderately critical ways and takes an empirical focus, for instance, to understand organizational strategy (Vaara, 2010; Vaara et al., 2010) and legitimization of particular courses of action (Mantere and Vaara, 2008; Vaara and Tienari, 2008). Related to this, narrative analysis has also been applied to study such legitimization and the construction of organization. Theorizations of practice are applied in the analysis

CMS in Scandinavia 153

of strategy, and Vaara has been central in the recent movement of studying strategy as practice (Golsorkhi et al., 2010; Vaara and Whittington, 2012). While the Helsinki Cluster draws on CMS research and does things that both theoretically and thematically fall under the umbrella of CMS, the sense here is less of contributing to CMS itself than to challenging mainstream notions, as is evident, for instance, in the work on strategy as practice, which is more about expanding a general understanding of strategy than of deliberately and openly being critical. So while there is a self-description as critical, participation under the 'banner' of CMS, frequent publications in critically inclined journals and an obvious indignation in their work, there is little in the way of directly claiming a CMS identity. CMS is perhaps seen more a springboard and the intention is more of spanning beyond the boundaries of CMS than to argue about them.

THE STOCKHOLM CLUSTER(S)

The Stockholm cluster is very scattered. One orientation is primarily organized around Monica Lindgren and Johann Packendorff at KTH (Royal Institute of Technology), particularly though their commitment to the "Making Projects Critical" set of conferences, special issues and workshops that intend to provide a platform for critical perspectives on all aspects of projects, including project management, project-based organizing and the 'projectification' of society. This strand of research draws on an eclectic mix of influences that includes work inspired by Labour Process Theory, Critical Theory, Actor Network Theory, Environmentalism, Feminism, Postmodernism and other traditions related to Critical Management Studies. The common denominator here is the application of CMS on a particular field: projects and project management. Key publications from this cluster includes Lindgren and Packendorff (2006a, b) and Lindgren et al. (2014). In a separate environment at Stockholm University, we find a group of scholars inspired by Foucauldian ideas and having done work on health issues in organizations, including the use of disciplinary power. Salient here are Mikael Holmqvist, Christian Maravelias and Thorkild Thanem (e.g. Maravelias et al., 2013).

THE GOTHENBURG 'CLUSTER'

The Gothenburg Cluster of CMS is not so much a cluster, given that it is associated primarily with Barbara Czarniawska. Barbara Czarniawska's work is characteristically hard to pin down and is certainly at or across the boundaries of critical management research. While obviously critical of mainstream research, she has also questioned whether research actually gets better by being critical (Czarniawska, 2010). It is, however, also illustrative of a very distinct style of engaging with and contesting management and

154   Hartmann et al.

management theory that makes it too interesting to omit here. A hallmark of this work, which spreads across a range of management subfields and into methodology, is notable for its effort to draw things together and create bricolages that open up new questions.

This effort is closely connected to the inspirations that underpin it. Actor Network Theory is one central source providing concepts such as 'translation' and 'overflows' (Czarniawska and Hernes, 2005), as are ideas about narratives (Czarniawska, 2004a), but her work really draws on many different traditions and could be seen as an exercise in mobilizing very diverse perspectives. Hybridity is a virtue. Empirically, the effort is similarly one of pushing at the stylistic boundaries and of finding methods for studying modern and very mobile organizations (Czarniawska, 2004b, 2007), as well as how to draw on literary sources. The general drift of this boundary-spanning, cross-cutting and hard-to-pin-down approach is less to be critical, it seems, than to be creative; to carve out a space for more creative and unconventional management research that can help us exoticize and think differently.

DISCUSSION: A SCANDINAVIAN ACCENT IN CMS?

Our mapping of the territories of CMS in Scandinavia has taken a definitional middle ground in delimiting CMS: had we taken a hard-core definition, most of the scholars in this review would have been omitted and some of our own work would probably have gone the same way (in some cases by intention—Hartmann, 2014); had we taken a more open one of looking at critically inclined scholars, we would have had representatives of critical thought across the map. This is, of course, also a general paradox of CMS that is at once marginal and mainstream. This paradox can have many causes (some more mundane than others, e.g. career concerns, philosophical allegiances, etc.). If there is a Scandinavian accent, it is perhaps in the cause of the paradox. In Scandinavia, welfare state politics may play an important role in forming the impetus for critique, albeit in different ways. For the Lund School (the most 'hard-core' critical of the groupings), it may well be disillusion with the welfare state and the 'pseudo' quality of democratization, collaboration and democracy. Contrast this to the Copenhagen School, where the welfare state may also be a driver: it creates the 'surplus' and affluence required to question the social purposes of organizations while also delegitimizing a really strong critique and fundamental indignation (which may seem overdone when life, after all, is quite privileged).

More important than the impetus for critical scholarship, the welfare state also provides a quite unique empirical setting for doing critical studies. This is something that we think requires more reflection on the part of researchers doing empirical work in the area: one should perhaps be more explicit about the particular influence that Scandinavia presents and what this context is good at showing and what it is not good at showing. Being

CMS *in Scandinavia* 155

afraid of losing one's job, for instance, is an existential issue much more than a really dramatic economic one that could make a family lose access to things such as health insurance. Starting a company is often likely to be about self-realization and self-determination more than about desperately struggling to make ends meet in the wake of some creative destruction. In the best of all worlds, this reflection will make critical empirical work in Scandinavian contexts much more interesting. Without it, critical studies here might easily become both myopic and solipsistic, which would of course be a shame.

A second characteristic of Scandinavian CMS is the relative downplaying of power and resistance and the playing up of the role of language and representation. In this sense, it can be argued that Scandinavian CMS is more modelled around discourse analysis and post-structuralist influences than the Frankfurt School and Foucault, although the most cited works are, paradoxically, inspired by these (e.g. Alvesson and Willmott, 1992, 1996/2012; Alvesson and Deetz, 2000). One possible reason for that is the main sources of power, the state and big corporations, are considered to be mostly benign and reasonably responsive to citizens, employees and other stakeholders. The Lund group, and parts of the Copenhagen one, are exceptions to this and have more sceptical takes, as noted earlier, and it seems that the strong faith in governmentality is a genuine phenomenon worthy a critical examination, and it seems clear that this is an under-researched area in the Scandinavian context.

A puzzling feature of CMS in Scandinavia is the lack of Norwegian representation. If one accepts that the Scandinavian countries have much in common, why is it that Norwegian business schools host so little critical scholarship? One major difference is, of course, the economic one afforded by Norway's offshore oil deposits and the freedom this affords the Norwegian state. Does this make life so privileged that critique becomes all the more contrived? Does it mean that the welfare state here does not experience the disillusioning breakdowns of its neighbours? Is there simply no institutional support (e.g. funding) for dissident and subversive research? Or is it because the role played by CMS is fulfilled by the older and more established tradition of 'work life research'? To be sure, this type of research is still being done in Norway, but associates itself less with business and management research than with action research and critical sociology. Even though critical scholars often emphasize broader societal conditions, it is likely that the personal interest or disinterest of very active individual senior researchers affects the presence of a tradition such as CMS in a country, and one needs to recognize the role of the individual level.

CONCLUSION

In this chapter, we have argued that CMS in Scandinavia is rather unevenly distributed and concentrated geographically in two schools and three 'clusters' with their distinct accent vis-à-vis one another: the humanist theorists

156 Hartmann et al.

of Copenhagen, the avowedly critical ethnographers in Lund, the boundary spanners in Helsinki, the projectification sceptics in Stockholm and the bricoleur in Gothenburg. Of these it is only the Lund group that has a strong focus on CMS in its heavy version. We have also proposed that welfare state politics, particularly in relation to the dominant schools, plays a role in creating a particular impetus for critical scholarship. Apart from this, the interest and local shape of various heavy and—in particular—light versions of CMS are probably more a reflection of various person's interests and orientations than any clear outcome of something distinctive associated with Scandinavian society.

REFERENCES

Alvesson, M. (2008). The Future of Critical Management Studies. In D. Barry and H. Hansen (Eds.), *The Sage Handbook of New Approaches in Management and Organization*. London: Sage.

Alvesson, M. (2013). *The Triumph of Emptiness. Consumption, Higher Education and Work Organization*. Oxford: Oxford University Press.

Alvesson, M., Blom, M. and Sveningsson, S. (2016). *Reflexive Leadership*. London: Sage.

Alvesson, M. and Deetz, S. (2000). *Doing Critical Management Research*. London: Sage.

Alvesson, M. and Kärreman, D. (2004). Interfaces of Control. Technocratic and Socio-Ideological Control in a Global Management Consultancy Firm. *Accounting, Organizations and Society*, 29(3–4): 423–444.

Alvesson, M. and Kärreman, D. (2011). *Qualitative Research and Theory Development: Mystery as Method*. London: Sage.

Alvesson, M. and Sandberg, J. (2011). Generating Research Questions Through Problematization. *Academy of Management Review*, 36(2): 247–271.

Alvesson, M. and Sköldberg, K. (2009). *Reflexive Methodology: New Vistas for Qualitative Research*. London: Sage.

Alvesson, M. and Spicer, A. (Eds.) (2011). *Metaphors We Lead By: Understanding Leadership in the Real World*. Abingdon: Routledge.

Alvesson, M. and Spicer, A. (2012a). Critical Leadership Studies: The Case for Critical Performativity. *Human Relations*, 65(3): 367–390.

Alvesson, M. and Spicer, A. (2012b). A Stupidity-Based Theory of Organizations. *Journal of Management Studies*, 49(7): 1194–1220.

Alvesson, M. and Willmott, H. (Eds.) (1992). *Critical Management Studies*. London: Sage.

Alvesson, M. and Willmott, H. (1996/2012). *Making Sense of Management*. London: Sage.

Ashcraft, K.L., Muhr, S.L., Rennstam, J. and Sullivan, K. (2012). Professionalization as a Branding Activity: Occupational Identity and the Dialectic of Inclusivity-Exclusivity. *Gender, Work and Organization*, 18(5): 467–488.

Barinaga, E. (2013). Politicizing Social Entrepreneurship—The Social Entrepreneurial Rationalities Toward Social Change. *Journal of Social Entrepreneurship*, 4(3): 347–372.

Beyes, T. and Steyaert, C. (2011). Spacing Organization: Non-Representational Theory and Performing Organizational Space. *Organization*, 19(1): 45–61.

Bjerg, O. (2014). *Making Money: The Philosophy of Crisis Capitalism*. London: Verso.

CMS *in Scandinavia* 157

Butler, N. and Spoelstra, S. (2014). The Regimes of Excellence and the Erosion of Ethos in Critical Management Studies. *British Journal of Management*, 25(3): 538–550.

Costas, J. and Kärreman, D. (2013). Conscience as Control—Managing Employees Through CSR. *Organization*, 20(3): 394–415.

Czarniawska, B. (2004a). *Narratives in Social Science Research*. London: Sage.

Czarniawska, B. (2004b) On Time, Space and Action Nets. *Organization*, 11(6): 773–791.

Czarniawska, B. (2007). *Shadowing: And Other Techniques for Doing Fieldwork in Modern Societies*. Malmö: Liber.

Czarniawska, B. (2010). How Critical Does the Management Research Need to be? *Critical Policy Studies*, 4(4): 417–418.

Czarniawska, B. and Hernes, T. (Eds.) (2005). *Actor-Network Theory and Organizing*. Malmö: Liber.

Davis, J.H., Schoorman, F.D. and Donaldson, L. (1997). Toward a Stewardship Theory of Management. *Academy of Management Review*, 22(1): 20–47.

Golsorkhi, D., Rouleau, L., Seidl, D. and Vaara, E. (Eds.) (2010). *Cambridge Handbook of Strategy as Practice*. Cambridge, UK: Cambridge University Press.

Hartmann, R.K. (2014). Subversive Functionalism: For a Less Canonical Critique in CMS. *Human Relations*, 67(5): 611–632.

Helin, J., Hernes, T., Hjorth, D. and Holt, R. (Eds.) (2014). *The Oxford Handbook of Process Philosophy and Organization Studies*. Oxford: Oxford University Press.

Hjorth, D. (2001). *Rewriting Entrepreneurship: For a New Perspective on Organizational Creativity*. Copenhagen, Denmark: Copenhagen Business School Press.

Hjorth, D. (Ed.) (2012). *Handbook on Organizational Entrepreneurship*. Cheltenham, UK: Edward Elgar Publishing.

Jeanes, E. and Huzzard, T. (2014). *Critical Management Research*. London: Sage.

Lindgren, M. and Packendorff, J. (2006a). What's New in New Forms of Organizing? On the Construction of Gender in Project-Based Work. *Journal of Management Studies*, 43(4): 841–866.

Lindgren, M. and Packendorff, J. (2006b). Projects and Prisons. In: D. Hodgson and S. Cicmil (Eds.), *Making Projects Critical*, 111–131. London: Palgrave.

Lindgren, M., Packendorff, J. and Sergi, V. (2014). Thrilled by the Discourse, Suffering Through the Experience: Emotions in Project-Based Work. *Human Relations*, 67(11): 1383–1412.

Lopdrup-Hjorth, T., Gudmand-Høyer, M. Bramming, P. and Pedersen, M. (Eds.) (2011). Editorial: Governing Work Through Self-Management. *Ephemera*, 11(2): 97–104.

Mantere, S. and Vaara, E. (2008). On the Problem of Participation in Strategy: A Critical Discoursive Perspective. *Organization Science*, 19(2): 341–358.

Maravelias, C., Thanem, T. and Holmqvist, M. (2013). March Meets Marx: The Politics of Exploitation and Exploration in the Management of Life and Labour. *Research in Sociology of Organizations*, 37: 129–160.

Muhr, S.L. (2011). Caught in the Gendered Machine—on the Masculine and Feminine in Cyborg Leadership. *Gender, Work and Organization*, 18(3): 337–357.

Muhr, S.L., Pedersen, M. and Alvesson, M. (2012). Workload, Aspiration, and Fun: Problems of Balancing Self-Exploitation and Self-Exploration in Work Life. *Research in the Sociology of Organizations*, 37: 193–220.

Parker, M. (2013). 'What is to be done?' CMS as a Political Party. *Dialogues in Critical Management Studies*, 2: 165–181.

Parker, M. (2014). University, Ltd: Changing a Business School. *Organization*, 21: 281–292.

Paulsen, R. (2014). *Empty Labour*. Cambridge: Cambridge University Press.

158 Hartmann et al.

Pedersen, O.K. (2011). *Konkurrencestaten*. Copenhagen, Denmark: Hans Reitzel.

Raffnsøe, S., Gudmand-Høyer, M.T. and Thaning, M. (2008). *Foucault*. København, Denmark: Samfundslitteratur.

Rennstam, J. (2012). Object-Control: A Study of Technologically Dense Knowledge Work. *Organization Studies*, 33(8): 1071–1090.

Sørensen, B.M. (2006). Identity Sniping: Innovation, Imagination and the Body. *Creativity and Innovation Management*, 15(2): 135–142.

Sørensen, B.M. (2010a). St Paul's Conversion: The Aesthetic Organization of Labour. *Organization Studies*, 31(3): 307–326.

Sørensen, B.M. (2010b). The Entrepreneurial Utopia: Miss Black Rose and the Communion. In D. Hjorth and C. Steyaert (Eds.), *The Politics and Aesthetics of Entrepreneurship: A Fourth Movements in Entrepreneurship*, 202–220. Cheltenham, UK: Edward Elgar.

Sørensen, B.M., Spoelstra, S., Höpfl, H. and Critchley, S. (2012). Theology and Organization. *Organization*, 19(3): 267–279.

Spicer, A., Alvesson, M. and Kärreman, D. (2009). Critical Performativity: The Unfinished Business of Critical Management Studies. *Human Relations*, 52(4): 537–560.

Tienari, J., Holgersson, C., Meriläinen, S. and Höök, P. (2009). Gender, Management and Market Discourse: The Case of Gender Quotas in the Swedish and Finnish Media. *Gender, Work and Organization*, 16(4): 501–521.

Tienari, J. and Vaara, E. (2012). Power and Politics in Mergers and Acquistions. In D. Faulkner, S. Teerikangas and R.J. Joseph (Eds.), *The Handbook of Mergers and Acquisitions*, 495–516. Oxford: Oxford University Press.

Vaara, E. (2010). Taking the Linguistic Turn Seriously: Strategy as a Multifaceted and Interdiscursive Phenomenon. *Advances in Strategic Management*, 27: 29–50.

Vaara, E., Sorsa, V. and Palli, P. (2010). On the Force Potential of Strategy Texts: A Critical Discourse Analysis of a Strategic Plan and its Power Effects in a City Organization. *Organization* 17(6): 685–702.

Vaara, E. and Tienari, J. (2008). A Discursive Perspective on Legitimation Strategies in Multinational Corporations. *Academy of Management Review*, 33(4): 985–993.

Vaara, E. and Whittington, R. (2012). Strategy as Practice: Taking Social Practices Seriously. *Academy of Management Annals*, 6(1): 285–336.

Wickert, C. and Schaefer, S.M. (2015). Towards a Progressive Understanding of Performativity in Critical Management Studies. *Human Relations*, 68(1): 107–130.

11 CMS in the Periphery
A Look at South America

Ernesto R. Gantman

INTRODUCTION

Throughout the twentieth century, social scientists in South America have developed theoretical perspectives for understanding the social and economic problems of their countries, which emerged as independent nations after several centuries of colonial rule and became part of the periphery of the global economy. Dependency theory, which gained international scholarly recognition in the 1970s, is a clear example in this regard. However, in terms of management and organizations studies (MOS), South American countries have had basically a role of importers of knowledge produced mainly in the US. Since these concepts, models, and theories were elaborated for a different economic and cultural environment, they may not be easily adapted to the domestic context of Latin American public and private organizations, nor apt solutions for these different organizational realities (Ibarra Colado, 2006). While most South American indigenous knowledge in MOS can be considered derivative from US theories, there were a few attempts at original elaborations. Some of these are critical approaches to MOS, and the goal of this chapter is to provide an overview of such intellectual contributions. In this regard, following Adler et al. (2011, p. 120), I use the term "critical" to express a sense of "radical critique", which problematizes "the socially divisive and ecologically destructive broader patterns and structures—such as capitalism, patriarchy, imperialism, and so forth—that condition local action and conventional wisdom".

The chapter is organized as follows. In the first section, I review the main aspects of critical management thought on a country-by-country basis. Only five countries are considered (Argentina, Brazil, Chile, Colombia, and Venezuela), since the rest of them have a very low production of management knowledge.[1] In the second section, I make a brief comparative analysis to explain some of the differences observed. In the concluding section, I summarize the basic findings and provide some reflections about the prospects for the development of CMS in the countries analysed.

160   *Ernesto R. Gantman*

THE NATURE AND EXTENT OF CMS IN SOUTH AMERICA

Argentina

Argentina has a long tradition of critical thinking in MOS, which dates back to the pioneering works of Alfredo Palacios and Jose Angel Gilli. In his book *Fatigue and Its Social Projections*, Palacios (1922), a scholar and socialist politician, developed a critique to Taylor, indicating that his scientific management system with its detailed time and motion standards affected the workers' health, also harming the natural solidarity that should reign among them. Years later, Gilli (1944) made a critical evaluation of the contribution of Fordism to improve production in factories from a Marxian frame of analysis.

In the seventies, when management was already institutionalized as an academic discipline in the country (Fernández Rodríguez and Gantman, 2011), the thoughts of US authors dominated Argentine business education in the field. However, in a widely read management textbook, Bernardo Kliksberg (1971) discussed the problems and pitfalls of orthodox US theories. In particular, he pointed out the limitations of March and Simon's thought due to its ahistorical dimension and its legitimation stance towards the process of economic concentration. In those years, the rise of dependency theory in the social sciences had some influence on management thinking, as evidenced by Kliksberg's (1973) analysis of technological backwardness in Latin American companies as a result of their subordinate incorporation into the global capitalist system. In addition, Gallart et al. (1973) studied the relationship between organizations and their environment, not with the goal of determining how the latter affected the former, but examining how organizations contribute to building their environment and recognizing them as active participants in a society marked by class conflict. Acknowledging the influence of dependency theory, they argued that the three basic dimensions of dependence—economic, cultural, and institutional—should be emphasized in order to understand organizational problems in peripheral countries. Finally, the concern about the distribution of power in capitalist firms is exemplified by the work of Martinez Nogueira (1975), who discussed the forms of workers' participation in organizations.

With the rise of a military government in 1976, which took power in a time of social violence and economic crisis, the social sciences suffered a great blow, and many scholars were forced to exile abroad for reasons of ideological persecution. The possibilities for critical thinking in MOS, which gained momentum at the beginning of the decade, fell drastically. The development of the social sciences have had a positive political environment since the return of democracy in 1983, but MOS was still marked by the dominance of mainstream approaches during the 1990s, when there was a boom in the pop management literature aimed at a professional audience (Gantman and Parker, 2006). Despite the growth of business higher

CMS *in the Periphery* 161

education, critical thinking in MOS was largely absent in public and private universities. However, an example of critical thought was Gantman's (1994, 2005) work, which associates the evolution of management thinking with phases of capitalist development.

The big economic crisis of 2001, which resulted from the unsustainable debt-led economic growth model of the 1990s, caused new organizational problems that provided abundant empirical material for social science research framed within critical perspectives. These problems were mainly addressed by sociologists, psychologists, and political scientists who examined issues such as the emancipatory possibilities of the so-called recovered factories, a form of self-management that emerged from the massive bankruptcies that occurred during the crisis. These were studied by several authors, among them Magnani (2003), Fernández (2008), and Rebón (2007). Moreover, other scholars dealt with the issue of the construction of subjectivities in the new world of work, such as Zangaro's (2011) Foucauldian analysis of the recent management literature and Pierbattisti's (2008) study of workers in the national telecommunication company privatized in the '90s. However, these critical works are not based on the contributions of British CMS scholars, which is not surprising, because Argentine political scientists and sociologists rarely use scholarly management publications as bibliographical sources. There seems to be a clear epistemic divide according to which critical approaches to MOS are not part of the academic interests of researchers in business schools and universities' Faculties of Economics but do appeal to scholars in academic units of other social sciences, a divide that did not exist in the early '70s.

Interestingly enough, the country has been ruled since 2003 by a populist left-wing government, which a priori would seem a favourable environment for the development of critical thinking in the social sciences; but this aspect of the political environment, specially significant in a higher education system with a large weight of the public sector, has had no influence on the development of CMS by scholars working in Faculties of Economics or business schools. Possibly because of their proximity to the business world and the concerns of management professionals, Argentine business schools appear to be only interested in the mainstream approaches to the discipline or simply in the practitioner-oriented literature.

Brazil

Brazil is the Latin American country with the highest productivity in the social sciences (Olaverrieta and Villena, 2014). Regarding critical perspectives to MOS, Brazilian social scientists have had an important role. In this regard, three academic pioneers should be especially mentioned: Mauricio Tragtenberg, Fernando Prestes Motta, and Alberto Guerreiro Ramos. Mauricio Tragtenberg, who defined himself as a Marxist anarchist (Paes de

162   Ernesto R. Gantman

Paula, 2008), made a central contribution to the study of bureaucracy as a form of domination (Tragtenberg, 1971, 1974). In the words of Prestes Motta (2001, p. 64), this Brazilian scholar was "one of the world founders of critical organization theory". In his book *Bureaucracy and Ideology*, framed in the Marxist tradition, Tragtenberg analysed bureaucracy from its origins dating back to the Asiatic mode of production up to the present and denounced the oppression inherent in bureaucratic forms of domination, including the Soviet state apparatus. For Tragtenberg, management theories are ideologies and their function is to legitimize the interests of the ruling class, posing as technical literature, while actually constituting a discourse that distorts reality. In particular, he argued that the management theories of the twentieth century tried to achieve administrative harmony and to avoid the existing class conflict between capital and labour. Tragtenberg (1980) discussed the theories of workers' participation as a new incarnation of the search for harmony and therefore as an ideological construct with a manipulative intent, although he believed that self-management could also be the basis for an emancipatory project.

Fernando Prestes Motta's work has some parallels with Tragtenberg's, particularly in its criticism of bureaucracy (Prestes Motta, 1980; Prestes Motta and Bresser Pereira, 1980), which Prestes Motta understood in terms of three basic aspects: power, control, and alienation (de Faria and Meneghetti, 2011). In his book *Bureaucracy and Self-Management*, Prestes Motta (1981) reassessed the contribution of utopian socialist thought for MOS, shifting the emphasis from critical thinking that denounces existing organizational arrangements to the construction of viable alternatives. According to Prestes Motta, organizations based on Proudhon's self-management theory are a real possibility for radical transformation of society, rather than a mere utopia. While this organizational logic greatly alarms the ruling class, it holds unprecedented possibilities for liberation from the modern forms of alienation in contemporary society. In a later work, he analysed the phenomenon of workers' participation and co-determination in European countries (Prestes Motta, 1982). In addition, Prestes Motta authored one of the most widely used management textbooks in Brazil, as well as other works that raised issues clearly germane to the critical tradition of MOS. For example, he highlighted the role of the business enterprise in the transmission of the dominant ideology of capitalism (Prestes Motta, 1984, 1986). While in later years he focused on topics such as the national character of organizational cultures and the relationships between anthropology, psychoanalysis, and organization theory (Bresser Pereira, 2003), he always maintained a basically critical orientation.

Another eminent exponent of critical thinking was Alberto Guerreiro Ramos, considered one of the major Brazilian sociologists. Beyond pioneering works such as *The Sociological Reduction* and *Management and Development Strategy*, written in 1955 and 1966, respectively, Guerreiro Ramos made a very significant contribution to CMS with his *The New Science*

CMS in the Periphery 163

of Organizations, published in both Portuguese and English in 1981. In this book, Guerreiro Ramos (1981) went beyond the conceptualization of management theories as legitimating ideologies that emerge in particular historical moments, although he also discussed this topic when analyzing the "cognitive politics" of the human relations school and claiming that speaking about issues such as authenticity, de-alienation, and self-actualization in the context of the human problems of "economizing organizations" was theoretically indefensible. His great contribution was his warning about the instrumental nature of the rationality underpinning organizational theories and his emphasis on the need to move towards a substantive rationality to overcome it. To develop this formulation, Guerreiro Ramos drew on the thought of Horkheimer and Habermas, thus anticipating the concern about instrumental reason of some British CMS scholars. Guerreiro Ramos believed that economic organizations were only one type of possible human forms of organizing and elaborated a paraeconomic paradigm that includes other types of organizations or "social systems" in his terminology. Unlike Tragtenberg's and Prestes Motta's, Guerreiro Ramos's work gained some recognition beyond Brazil (Ventriss and Candler, 2005), possibly because one of his books was published in English, although paradoxically this recognition was not from CMS theorists, but from scholars in public administration—the discipline he taught since 1966 in the US. According to Ventriss et al. (2010), the reception of Guerreiro Ramos's contribution was not what it really deserved, which they attribute to the epistemic parochialism of Anglophone scholars.

The development of critical MOS continued in Brazil, not only under the influence of these three pioneers but also due to the diffusion of the theories of some foreign authors. In a bibliometric study, Davel and Alcadipani (2003) assessed the extent of critical approaches in Brazilian management literature. To this end, they analysed the period 1990–2000, considering all articles published in the five leading Brazilian academic journals in the discipline, as well as all papers presented at the congresses of ANPAD (the Brazilian Academy of Management). Davel and Alcadipani categorized an article or paper as critical if (1) it had a denaturalized view of management (i.e. a conception of the discipline as socially and historically constructed), (2) a theoretical interest unrelated to concerns about organizational performance, and (3) an emancipatory intent. From 3,702 articles and papers, they identified 27 papers and 53 articles as critical. These were mostly theoretical in nature and generally had a strong influence from early critical Brazilian MOS, although 20 items were framed within the post-analytical tradition. Paes de Paula et al. (2010) performed a similar analysis, covering a greater period of time. Of a total of 4,896 articles and conference presentations from 1980 to 2008, they identified 515 as critical. The number of critical articles and papers shows an increasing trend with 187 published in 2005–2008 (12 per cent of the total output for this period). Among the most cited authors were Guerreiro Ramos, Marx, Habermas, Foucault, Tragtenberg, and, to a lesser

164 Ernesto R. Gantman

extent, European CMS theorists (Willmott, Alvesson, Parker, etc.). There was also some influence of French scholars (Pages, Enriquez, and Dejours).

Given the remarkable growth of Brazilian critical MOS production in recent years, I will not mention all the scholars who have worked in this tradition, but only some of the main contributions. For example, in a three-volume work entitled *Political Economy of Power*, José Henrique de Faria (2004a, 2004b, 2004c), drawing on the Marxist tradition, the psychosociology of Eugène Enriquez, and the Frankfurt School, developed a critique of management theory as ideology and analysed the specific ways in which power and control are exercised in organizations. Rafael Alcadipani examined the relevance of Foucault for organizational studies (Alcadipani, 2005), the fallacies of the Brazilian literature on organizational culture (Alcadipani and Crubelatte, 2007), and the critical potential of Actor Network Theory (Alcadipani and Hassard, 2010), while Maria Ceci Misoczky studied the struggles of the environmental movement (Misoczky, 2010; Misoczky and Böhm, 2013).

At present, Brazilian MOS scholars work within several critical approaches (de Faria, 2009), but a recent development within Brazilian CMS is particularly important: the emergence of a new approach informed by postcolonialism, which emphasizes the problems of Latin American nations as a result of the domination to which they were historically subject. In this regard, Misoczky and Amantino (2005) considered that British CMS theorists only provide a "domesticated criticism". As an alternative to it, Misoczky (2011) and Misoczky and Flores (2012) proposed to delve into the ideas of Latin American social thinkers and revolutionary intellectuals as analytical frameworks for studying the particular problems that affect the societies of the region and for exploring emancipatory possibilities. Similarly, the marginalization of Latin American scholarly production in MOS has been an ongoing concern in publications by Rafael Alcadipani and Alex Faria (Alcadipani and Reis Rosa, 2011; Alcadipani and Faria, 2014). In addition, the need for a postcolonial perspective has been highlighted regarding issues such as family firms (Faria and Wanderley, 2013) and international management (Faria et al., 2010; Guedes and Faria, 2010a, 2010b; Alcadipani and Faria, 2014) and the relevance of indigenous models of organizing, such as the Brazilian Solidarity Economy (Alcadipani, 2010). To sum up, Brazil has not only developed an autonomous tradition of critical thinking in MOS, even prior to the emergence of CMS in England, but some of its scholars are currently pursuing a line of enquiry inspired by postcolonialism that, by provincializing Anglo-Saxon approaches, may contribute a new perspective on critical thinking in the discipline.

Chile

In recent decades, Chile has achieved significant levels of economic growth and is currently considered one of the most dynamic economies in the region. After several years of military dictatorship, a healthy democratic

CMS *in the Periphery* 165

regime has been established in Chile. The Chilean government has strongly promoted scientific activities, which can be observed in the growth in the number of articles in international scientific databases (Olaverrieta and Villena, 2014). Chile's economic success is associated with a positive business climate generated by a free market–oriented economy. At present, many of the top-ranked public and private business schools of Latin America are located in Chile. Consistent with this, there is a relatively high level of production of management knowledge, which is basically framed within the mainstream approaches to the discipline. Interestingly enough, two Chilean scientists, Humberto Maturana and Francisco Varela, have pioneered the study of autopoietic systems, and their contributions were used in MOS by Chilean authors, most notably Fernando Flores, and scholars from other Latin American countries, such as the Argentine Jorge Etkin. While this undoubtedly constitutes indigenous knowledge production in the field, such knowledge does not belong to the critical tradition in MOS. Within this tradition, Chilean scholarly output is low.

However, a few recent contributions must be mentioned. In a similar line to the Brazilian postcolonialist approach, Marcela Mandiola (2010) proposed to reformulate the concept of liberation in Latin American critical social thought associated, for example, with the Brazilian Paulo Freire and the Argentine Enrique Dussel—in terms of the colonizing threat represented by management thinking. Mandiola's reflection aims to overcome the monopoly of CMS by Eurocentric traditions of thought. In this regard, she posited that the idea of emancipation was exclusively interpreted from a Eurocentric philosophical perspective, which should be widened by considering the forms of oppression that happen within Latin American societies. Drawing on Laclau's discourse theory, Mandiola considered CMS as an empty signifier. Specifically, she argued, what is "critical" and what is "resistance" outside the Anglo-Saxon context must be filled with content, and this redefinition should take into account local social problems and struggles. To this end, Mandiola questioned the concept of liberation from Latin American critical philosophy and suggested the need to enlarge the notion of the "oppressed" in the face of new contemporary issues arising from the colonization by contemporary management thinking. In her view, the "oppressed" are no longer merely the "poor", but a category that includes both managers and students of management who are subject to a managerial discourse imported from developed countries, a discourse that reproduces the antagonism between the Global North and the Global South. Moreover, another Chilean scholar doing research framed within CMS is Miguel Imas, who is currently residing in the UK. He analysed management not as a technocratic discourse, but as a tool of oppression under authoritarian dictatorships in Argentina and Chile (Imas, 2010); and he also explored the organizational processes that occurred in slums and favelas (Imas and Weston, 2012), showing how, despite their lack of material resources, the poor were able to organize themselves around an entrepreneurial logic (Imas et al., 2012).

166 *Ernesto R. Gantman*

Colombia

Although the social sciences output of Colombia is lower than that of other countries, such as Argentina and Chile (Olaverrieta and Villena, 2014), Colombian scholars have produced much work in MOS from 2000 onwards (Malaver Rodríguez, 2006). Two Colombian management journals are indexed in the Social Science Citation Index, and there are many other publications recognized for their quality in Latindex Catálogo (an Iberoamerican scientific journals database). However, like in other Spanish-speaking South American country, critical perspectives in management have not received much attention.

Some contributions in the critical tradition have been carried out. Colombian researchers, drawing on Omar Aktouf and Jean Francois Chanlat (some of whose writings were translated into Spanish in Colombia), have developed a line of enquiry that has been termed critical humanism (Saavedra Mayorga, 2009). Among them, I can mention Rojas's (2003) and Cruz and Rojas's (2008) works on inhumanity in business practices and Saavedra Mayorga's (2006) critique on the role of management in the instrumental conception of man in contemporary society. In a similar vein, López Gallego (2008) elaborated a critique of ontological coaching, and Vélez and Dasuky (2008) analysed the negative consequences of the discourse of contemporary capitalism and consumerism in organizational life. From the psychology of work, Pulido Martinez (2010a) argued in favour of critical perspectives to the dominant discourse in his discipline and suggested that psychological interventions on workers were an ideological control mechanism adapted to the new conditions of flexible and precarious work (Pulido Martínez, 2010b). In addition, Saavedra Mayorga (2009) contributed to diffuse in his country the thought of key figures in contemporary British CMS and of the Spanish sociologist Carlos Fernández Rodríguez (2007), and Saavedra Mayorga et al. (2013) discussed the applicability of the Foucaultian tradition to the analysis of leadership in organizations. These and other recent contributions (e.g. Carvajal Baeza, 2013) suggest that Colombia has some potential for further development of critical perspectives on MOS.

Venezuela

Venezuela has some degree of development in management studies, and a Venezuelan management journal was even indexed in the Social Sciences Citation Index; but regarding critical approaches to MOS, the contributions of Venezuelan scholars are scarce. This is striking because of the political and ideological context in Venezuela, which has been governed since 1999 by a regime that has been characterized as left-wing populism (Weyland, 2013). This regime, led by Commander Hugo Chavez, introduced large economic and political reforms, nationalizing mass media and other businesses enterprises in what has been denominated by the Bolivarian Revolution. Chavist

CMS in the Periphery   167

ideology, which evolved over the years, has an anti-capitalist, anti-American and nationalist orientation—or, more broadly, a regionalist one, since it advocates the union of the Latin American peoples. Its economic policy is largely similar to that of early Peronism in Argentina, with an omnipresent state in the economy and active distributive policies in favour of the poor. This context, which a priori seems favourable to the development of social science sympathetic to the government ideology, was, nevertheless, not sufficient to stimulate the appearance of critical MOS.

Among the few critical contributions, I can mention Barboza Pérez (2007), who discussed some concepts of British CMS in her analysis of Michael Burawoy's theory of the relationship between conflict and consent within work. More recently, Díaz de Mariña (2012) questioned the neutrality of management theory and suggested the need to develop a "political administrative science" that does not concern itself solely with the study of the actors' actions and orientations in the world of work, as does the hegemonic episteme, but rather focus on how their actions affect the economic, social, and political contexts in which they are embedded in order to provide socially and ecologically responsible orientations for those who rule organizations.

Finally, and just as in the Argentine case, empirical reality provided Venezuelan social scientists with an object of study especially suited for a critical perspective of analysis. I refer to the "community councils", a Chavist organizational creation to promote participatory democracy (López Maya, 2004; Salazar Borrego and Rivas Torres, 2004). The basic goal of these civil society organizations is that citizens themselves request funding from the State and then collaborate in the planning, implementation, and monitoring of community projects. Some scholars viewed these organizational innovations in a favourable light, such as Yanez Medina et al. (2012), who emphasized the importance of the affective component that binds organizational members together, while others warned about the risk that they become instruments of political clientelism (Córdoba Jaimes, 2012).

Some Comparative Remarks

The creation of scientific knowledge depends largely on the characteristics of the community that produces it, which, in turn, is strongly influenced by the institutional, political, and cultural environments. One of the main conclusions from the previous section is that Brazil has the greater development of CMS in the region. In my opinion, this can be explained by the greater institutionalization of the academic profession in Brazilian higher education (Schwartzman and Balbachevsky, 1997), which is associated with this country's high scientific productivity. The reform of Brazilian higher education in the 1960s granted special importance to postgraduate studies and research activities (Schwartzman, 1991). University teaching became mostly a full-time occupation; while in other South American countries, especially

168 Ernesto R. Gantman

in professional disciplines such as law, medicine, and administration, it is still a basically part-time occupation. Although Wood and Paes de Paula (2003, p. 15) suggest that being a full-time management professor "is relatively uncommon in Brazil", the proportion of those who hold full-time appointments at universities and business schools is higher than in other countries of the region. For example, comparing the two largest public universities of Brazil and Argentina, the figures indicate that the Faculty of Economics of the University of Buenos Aires had 2,208 professors in 2004, of which only 52 had full-time dedication, while in the same year, the Faculty of Economics, Administration and Accounting (campus São Paulo and Ribeirão Preto) of the University of São Paulo had 236 professors, of which 152 had full-time dedication (Gantman, 2010). It can thus be expected that there is greater dedication to knowledge creation from Brazilian scholars than from those in other countries where full-time dedication to academia is rare. In addition, better postgraduate education is often associated with a more rigorous training in the social sciences and, therefore, with greater exposure to critical social thought. Hence not only is there a greater level of scholarly management knowledge creation in Brazil but also an increased attention to critical thinking in the discipline. In Colombia, there appears to be a growing interest in the institutionalization of the academic profession (Malaver Rodríguez, 2006), which may be associated with the scholarly productivity in the critical MOS of Colombian authors during the first decade of this century.

Another interesting point pertains to the effect of the political environment upon knowledge creation in MOS. In this regard, it can be observed that political authoritarianism in Brazil, Argentina, and Chile had a different impact on the production in social sciences, and particularly of critical knowledge in MOS, in these countries. The military dictatorships in Argentina and Chile were more repressive than the Brazilian regime, which had a more moderate level of ideological repression (Domínguez, 2011). Whereas the social sciences were seriously affected in Argentina and Chile with a remarkable number of exiled scholars, academic exiles were fewer in Brazil—Alberto Guerreiro Ramos, however, self-exiled to the US after the military coup of 1965. Also in relation to the political environment, it is somewhat surprising that in countries ruled for many years by political parties of a left-wing radical persuasion, such as Venezuela (1999 to date) and Argentina (2003 to date), scholars sympathetic to such political perspectives have not developed a significant production in the discipline. This may be due to the very nature of business higher education in many countries in the region, which is mainly focused on practical-normative issues and on gaining legitimation by training practitioners for business enterprises (Mandiola and Ascorra, 2010).

However, this does not mean that there were no critical approaches to the study of organizational phenomena. They did exist but came from social scientists trained in other disciplines in which exposure to traditions of critical thinking is the norm. As seen in Argentina and Venezuela, reality itself

CMS *in the Periphery* 169

provided researchers with interesting material for study. In these cases, critical enquiry was basically empirically driven by the emerging problems of the local economic and political environment. It is not surprising that after a situation similar to the Argentine economic crisis of 2001, the phenomenon of worker-recuperated factories appeared in Greece and stimulated the interest of CMS researchers (eg. Kokkinidis, 2014). The particularity of these research works in some Latin America countries is that indigenous critical thinking makes little use of the wealth of theoretical elaborations advanced by CMS scholars from core countries.

Conclusion: Prospects for CMS in South America

The development of scholarly MOS in South American countries is overwhelmingly framed within the mainstream approaches to the field. The diffusion of CMS was very limited, except in the case of Brazil, a country that has developed an indigenous tradition in the 1970s and 1980s and in which a strong interest in postcolonial thought has informed some recent contributions to CMS. In Argentina and Venezuela, the few critical works in MOS are mostly linked to concerns with domestic issues, being empirically driven, and mainly developed by social scientists outside business schools and Faculties of Economics. Interestingly enough, there is no significant development of indigenous critical management thought in these two countries whose leftist governments show, at least at the level of discourse, a radical position against global capitalism.

Regarding the future prospects for CMS, I must again distinguish between Brazil, with a significant local presence, and other countries with isolated contributions. In the Brazilian case, CMS development prospects are very positive. First, its higher education system offers opportunities to those interested in engaging in research activities, and this line of thinking in MOS is a possible specialization in this regard. Second, and unfortunately, the reality of a growing economy with marked social inequalities will continue to pose empirical concerns for social scientists, which will surely receive scholarly attention. To what extent Brazilian CMS theorists will gain the status of public intellectuals and achieve a position of influence that allows them to contribute to solving their country's organizational problems is an open question. In other countries, the development of CMS will continue to be primarily the result of isolated individual efforts; and the invisible walls between the Faculties of Social Sciences and the Faculties of Economics (and business schools) are unlikely to fall down. If this divide is still in place, CMS will lose the possible benefit of significant intellectual synergies. The barriers of expertise, associated to academic communities with very different theoretical and research traditions, are a serious obstacle to the development of CMS in most South American countries.

Despite these problems, there are still opportunities for CMS in the region. An interesting avenue in this regard is the Latin Americanist postcolonial

170   Ernesto R. Gantman

line of authors such as Ibarra Colado, Faria, Alcadipani, Misockzy, and Mandiola, a path that may also help to overcome disciplinary barriers (Ibarra Colado, 2008). But there are other possibilities as well, since there are particular organizational arrangements in the region, mostly associated to situations of poverty and economic malaise, that are specially apt for the gaze of the critical scholar. While local production of CMS knowledge should be stimulated in Spanish-speaking South American countries, scholars must also try to internationalize their production, as this may lead to further institutionalization of CMS as a legitimate domain of enquiry within local business schools and Faculties of Economics. Something that is needed is more collaborative work among researchers from different Latin America countries, especially from Brazil, which already has a critical mass of scholars. This will greatly strengthen the critical tradition in the region and also enrich CMS at the international level simply because new voices are added to the global choir of this field of study.

NOTE

1. Since Latin American countries outside South America are not reviewed here, I must briefly mention that some CMS contributions have been done in México. In this regard, the work of Eduardo Ibarra Colado is noteworthy (Fernández and Ramírez Martínez, 2014).

REFERENCES

Adler, P., Forber, L. and Willmott, H. (2011). Critical Management Studies. *Academy of Management Annals*, 1(1): 119–179.
Alcadipani, R. (2005). *Michel Foucault. Poder e a Analise das Organizacoes*. Rio de Janeiro: Fundacao Getulio Vargas.
Alcadipani, R. (2010). From Latin America to the World: Notes on the (Possible) Latin America Management Styles. In A. Guedes and A. Faria (Eds.), *International Management and International Relations: A Critical Perspective from Latin America*, 136–158. London: Routledge.
Alcadipani, R. and Crubelatte, J. (2007). The Notion of Brazilian Organizational Culture: Questionable Generalizations and Vague Concepts. *Critical Perspectives on International Business*, 3(2): 150–169.
Alcadipani, R. and Faria, A. (2014). Fighting Latin American Marginality in 'International' Business. *Critical Perspectives on International Business*, 10(1/2): 107–117.
Alcadipani, R. and Hassard, J. (2010). Actor-Network Theory, Organizations and Critique: Towards a Politics of Organizing. *Organization*, 17(4): 419–435.
Alcadipani, R. and Reis Rosa, A. (2011). From Grobal Management to Glocal Management: Latin American Perspectives as a Counter-Dominant management Epistemology. *Canadian Journal of the Administrative Sciences*, 28(4): 453–466.
Barboza Pérez, M. (2007). De actores cooptados a actores suprimidos: Desde Burawoy a la teoría crítica de la gerencia. *Revista Venezolana de Gerencia*, 12(37): 66–79.
Bresser Pereira, L.C. (2003). O Sociólogo das Organizações: Fernando, C. Prestes Motta. *Revista de Administração de Empresas*, 43(2): 116–118.

CMS in the Periphery   171

Carvajal Baeza, R. (Ed.) (2013). Estudios críticos de la organización: qué son y cuál es su utilidad. California: Editorial Universidad del Valle.

Córdoba Jaimes, E. (2012). Los desafíos de la política comunitaria en Venezuela. *Revista Venezolana de Gerencia*, 18(4): 670–683.

Cruz, F. y Rojas, W. (2008). La noción de inhumanidad y culturas híbridas en algunas organizaciones colombianas. In F. Cruz (Ed.), *Racionalidad instrumental y gestión*, 13–66. California: Universidad del Valle.

Davel, E. and Alcadipani, R. (2003). Estudos críticos em administração: aprodução científica brasileira nos anos 1990. *Revista de Administração de Empresas*, 43(4): 72–85.

de Faria, J.H. (2004a). *Economia Política do Poder: fundamentos*. Curitiba: Juruá.

de Faria, J.H. (2004b). *Economia Política do Poder: uma crítica da Teoria Geral da Administração*. Curitiba: Juruá.

de Faria, J.H. (2004c). *Economia Política do Poder: As práticas do controle nas organizações*. Curitiba: Juruá.

de Faria, J.H. (2009). Teoria crítica em estudos organizacionais no Brasil: o estado da arte, *Cadernos Ebape.Br*, 7(3): 509–515.

de Faria, J.H. and Meneghetti, F. (2011). Burocracia como organizaçaõ, poder e controle, *Revista de Administração de Empresas*, 51(5): 424–439.

Díaz de Mariña, N. (2012). Hacia una ciencia administrativa política hoy. *Revista Venezolana de Gestión Pública*, 3(3): 145–177.

Domínguez, J.I. (2011). The Perfect Dictatorship? South Korea versus Argentina, Brazil, Chile, and Mexico. In K. Byung-Kook and E. Vogel (Eds.), *The Park Chung Hee Era: The Transformation of South Korea*, 573–602. Cambridge, MA: Harvard University Press.

Faria, A, Ibarra Colado, E. and Guedes, A.L. (2010). Internationalization of Management, Neoliberalism and the Latin America Challenge. *Critical Perspectives on International Business*, 6(2/3): 97–115.

Faria, A. and Wanderley, S. (2013). Fundamentalismo da gestão encontra a descolonialidade: repensando estrategicamente organizações familiares. *Cadernos Ebapr. Br*, 11(4): 569–587.

Fernández, A.M. (2008). *Política y subjetividad: asambleas barriales y fábricas recuperadas*. Buenos Aires: Biblos.

Fernández, M.M. and Ramírez Martínez, G. (2014). Administración y Estudios Organizacionales: de las orillas a las orillas, *Administración y Organizaciones*, 17(32): 55–70.

Fernández Rodríguez, C.J. (2007). *El discurso del management: tiempo y narración*. Madrid: Centro de Investigaciones Sociológicas.

Fernández Rodríguez, C.J. and Gantman, E.R. (2011). Spain and Argentina as Importers of Management Knowledge (1955–2008): A Comparative Analysis. *Canadian Journal of Administrative Sciences*, 28(2): 160–173.

Gallart, M.A., Ortega, E.H. And Suárez, F. (1973). *La inserción de las organizaciones en los procesos sociales*. Buenos Aires: El Coloquio.

Gantman, E.R. (1994). La evolución de las ideologías gerenciales. Tesis doctoral, Universidad de Buenos Aires, Argentina.

Gantman, E.R. (2005). *Capitalism, Social Privilege and Managerial Ideologies*. Aldershot: Ashgate.

Gantman, E.R. (2010). Scholarly Management Knowledge in the Periphery: Argentina and Brazil in Comparative Perspective (1970–2005). *Brazilian Administration Review*, 7(2): 115–135.

Gantman, E.R. and Parker, M. (2006). Comprador Management? Organizing Management Knowledge in Argentina (1975–2003). *Critical Perspectives on International Business*, 2(1): 25–40.

Gilli, J.A. (1944). *La fábrica. De Marx a Ford*. Buenos Aires: Librería Hachette.

172 Ernesto R. Gantman

Guedes, A.L. and Faria, A. (2010a). Bringing the International into International Management: New Challenges. In A.Guedes and A. Faria (Eds.), *International Management and International Relations: A Critical Perspective from Latin America*, 231–242. London: Routledge.

Guedes, A.L. and Faria, A. (2010b). International Management, Business and Relations in Latin America. *Critical Perspectives on International Business*, 6(2/3): 145–161.

Guerreiro Ramos, A. (1981). *The New Science of Organizations: A Reconceptualization of the Wealth of Nations*. Toronto: University of Toronto Press.

Ibarra Colado, E. (2006). Organization Studies and Epistemic Coloniality in Latin America: Thinking Otherness from the Margins. *Organization*, 13(4): 463–488.

Ibarra Colado, E. (2008). Is there any future for Critical Management Studies in Latin America? Moving from Epistemic Coloniality to 'Trans-Discipline'. *Organization*, 15(6): 932–935.

Imas, J.M. (2010). Dirty Management': The Legacy of Chile and Argentina. In A.Guedes and A. Faria (Eds.), *International Management and International Relations: A Critical Perspective from Latin America*, 185–200. London: Routledge.

Imas, J.M. and Weston, A. (2012). From Harare to Rio de Janeiro: Kukiya-Favela Organization of the Excluded. *Organization*, 19(2): 205–227.

Imas, J.M., Wilson, N. and Weston, A. (2012). Barefoot Entrepreneurs. *Organization*, 19(5): 563–585.

Kliksberg, B. (1971). *El pensamiento organizativo: del taylorismo a la moderna teoría de la organización*. Buenos Aires: Depalma.

Kliksberg, B. (1973). *Administración, subdesarrollo y estrangulación tecnológica: introducción al caso latinoamericano*. Buenos Aires: Paidós.

Kokkinidis, G. (2014). Spaces of Possibilities: Workers' Self-Management in Greece. *Organization*, 22(6): 847–871.

López Gallego, F. (2008). El coaching ontológico: o una arremetida de gestión totalitaria. In R. Carvajal (Ed.), *Gestión crítica alternativa*, 249–265. California: Editorial Universidad Del Valle.

López Maya, M. (2004). Democracia participativa y políticas sociales en el gobierno de Hugo Chávez Frías. *Revista Venezolana de Gerencia*, 9(28): 1–22.

Malaver Rodríguez, F. (2006). El despegue de la investigación colombiana en administración: análisis de sus avances en el período 2000–2006. *Cuadernos de Administración*, 19(32): 71–109.

Magnani, E. (2003). *El cambio silencioso: empresas y fábricas recuperadas por los trabajadores en la Argentina*. Buenos Aires: Prometeo.

Mandiola, M. (2010). Latin America's Critical Management? A Liberation Genealogy. *Critical Perspectives on International Business*, 6(2/3): 162–176.

Mandiola, M. and Ascorra, P. (2010). Chilean Management Education: Rhetoric of Pragmatism, Consumerism, Individualism and Elitism. *Cadernos Ebape.br*, 8(2): 371–387.

Martínez Nogueira, R. (1975). *Redistribución del poder y participación en las empresas: demandas para la reforma de la empresa*. Buenos Aires: El Coloquio.

Misoczky, M.C. (2010). Green Deserts in the South of Latin America: The Role of International Agencies and National States. In A. Guedes and A. Faria (Eds.), *International Management and International Relations: A Critical Perspective from Latin America*, 201–228. London: Routledge.

Misoczky, M.C. (2011). World Visions in Dispute in Contemporary Latin America. *Organization*, 18(2): 345–363.

Misoczky, M.C. and Amantino, J. (2005). Uma crítica à crítica domesticada nos estudos organizacionais. *Revista de Administração Contemporánea*, 9(1): 193–212.

Misoczky, M.C. and Böhm, S. (2013). Resisting Neocolonial Development: Andalgalá's People. *Cadernos Ebape.br*, 11(2): 311–339.

CMS in the Periphery 173

Misoczky, M.C. and Flores, R. (2012). Contributions of Latin American Revolutionary Intellectuals. *Revista Brasileira de Estudos Latino-Americanos*, 2(1): 1–18.

Olaverrieta, S. and Villena, M. (2014). Innovation and Business Research in Latin America: An Overview. *Journal of Business Research*, 67(4): 489–497.

Paes de Paula, A.P. (2008). Maurício Tragtenberg: contribuições de um marxista anarquizante para os estudos organizacionais críticos. *Revista de Administração Pública*, 42(5): 949–968.

Paes de Paula, A.P., Machado, C., Barreto, R. and Klechen, C. (2010). A tradição e a autonomia dos estudos organizacionais críticos no Brasil, *Revista de Administração de Empresas*, 50(1): 10–23.

Palacios, A. (1922). *La fatiga y sus proyecciones sociales*. Buenos Aires: Claridad.

Pierbattisti, D. (2008). *La privatización de los cuerpos: la construcción de la proactividad neoliberal en al ámbito de las telecomunicaciones, 1991–2001*. Buenos Aires: Prometeo.

Prestes Motta, F. (1980). *O que é burocracia*. São Paulo: Brasiliense.

Prestes Motta, F. (1981). *Burocracia e autogestão. A proposta de Proudhon*. São Paulo: Brasiliense.

Prestes Motta, F. (1982). *Participação e co-gestão. Novas formas de administração*. São Paulo: Brasiliense.

Prestes Motta, F. (1984). As empresas e a transmissão da ideología, *Revista de Administração de Empresas*, 24(3): 19–24.

Prestes Motta, F. (1986). *Organizacão e poder. Empresa, estado e escola*. São Paulo: Atlas.

Prestes Motta, F. (2001). Mauricio Tragtenberg: desvendando ideologías, *Revista de Administração de Empresas*, 41(3): 64–68.

Prestes Motta, F. and Bresser Pereira, L.C. (1980). *Introdução à organização burocrática*. São Paulo: Brasiliense.

Pulido Martínez, H.C. (2010a). Psychological Knowledge for the Governance of the South. *Critical Perspectives on International Business*, 6(2/3): 177–189.

Pulido Martínez, H.C. (2010b). Autonomía en el trabajo. "El reto por opciones" a la luz de la produccion del sujeto Neo-liberal. *Revista Iberoamericana de Psicología: Ciencia y Tecnología*, 3(1): 7–15.

Rebón, J. (2007). *La empresa de la autonomía: trabajadores recuperando la producción*. Buenos Aires: Picaso.

Rojas, W. (2003). *Modernidad e inhumanidad: Lo inhumano en la organización y en el trabajo*. Cali, Colombia: Editorial Universidad del Valle.

Saavedra Mayorga, J.J. (2006). La administración y el origen de la concepción instrumental del Hombre en la sociedad contemporánea, *Universidad & Empresa*, 5(11): 237–262.

Saavedra Mayorga, J.J. (2009). Descubriendo el lado oscuro de la gestión. Los Critical Management Studies o una nueva forma de abordar los fenómenos organizacionales. *Revista Facultad de Ciencias Económicas—Investigación y Reflexión*, 17(2): 45–60.

Saavedra Mayorga, J.J., Sanabria, J. and Smida, A. (2013). La construcción de sentido de los investigadores en gestión en Colombia acerca de su campo de conocimiento, *Innovar: Revista de Ciencias Administrativas y Sociales*, 23(50): 1–44.

Salazar Borrego, N. and Rivas Torres, F. (2004). La precariedad laboral y su inciencia en las políticas sociales de la V República. Una mirada especial a las misiones. *Visión Gerencial*, 3(1): 62–77.

Schwartzman, S. (1991). *A Space for Science: The Development of the Scientific Community in Brazil*. University Park, PA: Pennsylvania State University Press.

Schwartzman, S. and Balbachevsky, E. (1997). The Academic Profession in Brazil. In P.G. Altbach (Ed.), *The International Academic Profession: Portraits from 14 Countries*, 231–280. Princeton: Carnegie Foundation for the Advancement of Teaching.

174   Ernesto R. Gantman

Tragtenberg, M. (1971). A teoria geral de Administração é uma ideología? *Revista de Administração de Empresas*, 11(4): 7–21.

Tragtenberg, M. (1974). *Burocracia e Ideologia*. São Paulo: Ática.

Tragtenberg, M. (1980). *Administração, Poder e Ideologia*. São Paulo: Moraes.

Vélez, C. and Dasuki, S. (2008). Discurso del capitalismo, consumo y estilo de vida: su incidencia en el trabajo. In R. Carvajal (Ed.) *Gestión crítica alternativa*, 29–52. Calí, Colombia: Editorial Universidad Del Valle.

Ventriss, C. and Candler, G. (2005). Alberto Guerreiro Ramos 20 Years Later: A New Science Still Unrealized in an Age of Public Cynicism and Theoretical Ambivalence. *Public Administration Review*, 65(3): 347–359.

Ventriss, C., Candler, G. and Salm, J. (2010). Alberto Guerreiro Ramos: The "in-betweener" as Intellectual Bridge Builder? *Organizações e Sociedade*, 17(52): 103–114.

Weyland, K. (2013). The Threat from the Populist Left. *Journal of Democracy*, 24(3): 18–32.

Wood, T. and Paes de Paula, A.P. (2003). This is not (quite) an MBA! Paper presented at the Business Education and Emerging Market Economies: Trends and Prospects Conference, Atlanta, GA, 7 November.

Yánez Medina, T., Cuñarro, E. and Guillén de Romero, J. (2012). La episteme popular como elemento dinamizador del quehacer comunitario. Caso: Consejos Comunales en Venezuela, *Revista de Ciencias Sociales*, 18(4): 657–669.

Zangaro, M. (2011). *Subjetividad y trabajo: Una lectura foucaultiana del Management*. Buenos Aires: Herramienta.

12 The Ghost in the System
Critical Management Studies in Turkey

Beyza Oba and Mehmet Gençer

INTRODUCTION

Critical Management Studies (CMS) did not find a place and could not establish itself in Turkish business schools. This is not a new claim; it has been argued by extant research. In an analysis of papers presented in the National Management and Organization Congress (NMOC) and examining curricula of Turkish business schools. Ozcan (2012) claims that in Turkey, management literature and management programmes have not been permeated by Critical Management Studies. Alakavuklar and Parker (2011) make similar claims; in its current forms, critical management would not find a place in Turkey due to the socio-economic realities of the country. Turkey does not have a strong tradition of anti-imperialist, civil society movements or did not experience industrial revolution. That being said, they also propose that in a developing country, local problems can be different than the ones faced by the Global North where the critical theories originated and thus, in the production of critical management, the local priorities should be taken into consideration. In an effort to explore the ideology inherited by the most popular management/organization textbooks written by Turkish academicians, Çoşkun (2009) asserts that all these textbooks strictly utilize a discourse that promotes neo-liberal ideology and neglects alternative arguments.

We focus on a local incident (Soma coal mine accident), a local company (Soma Holding) and problems (increasing productivity, cost cutting and outsourcing) associated with neo-liberal policies in order to understand why CMS did not find its way in Turkey. We examine the incident that caused the deaths of 301 miners in Soma in an effort to explain how the institutionalized management and financialization logic in a late developing country failed to anticipate, recognize and respond. In so doing, we focus on business schools, academicians and try to understand why they have been silent. Although our argument accepts a historical and contextual approach in the establishment of business schools, it takes a further stance that is characterized by recursiveness and transposition of certain practices and ideas in management education in Turkey. More specifically, we study

176 *Beyza Oba and Mehmet Gençer*

the historical background of business schools and academia in an effort to understand how they could not come up with the idea to transpose CMS to Turkish higher education and business practice and how they contributed to the creation of an institutional logic, belief systems and related practices that have shaped individual and organizational action. Focusing only on the historical evolution of business schools and socio-economic conditions in Turkey would provide a base where we can better understand facilitating conditions, but the aim of this study is to scrutinize how individual actions, organizational structures and the higher education environment adapt and maintain the recursiveness of certain ideas and practices and how they all create a taken-for-granted business reality. We claim that mainstream business education persists because it provides an "ontological security" (Giddens, 1984, p. 64) to those involved in the system; the elements of this system are so much embedded within their daily routines that through time they sediment and thus became self-reinforcing (Bourdieu, 1990).

We start by discussing the roots of business schools in Turkey; here our aim is to identify conditions that enabled the institutionalization of a social structure that did not create a motivation for the development of CMS. These conditions are described as Americanization, practice orientation and administrative autonomy. In the second part of this chapter, we focus on academicians, their educational backgrounds, publications and research orientation. In the third part of the paper, we focus on the outcomes of these conditions that characterize the current state of management education in Turkey, values and priorities, performance anxiety and curriculum wars. Before doing so, however, we want to summarize the Soma incident so that it will provide a background for our analysis and highlight the local problems that demand a reconsideration of the existing local practices.

THE SOMA INCIDENT

On May 13, 2014, the coal mine in Soma (Turkey) exploded; the apparent cause of the explosion was an underground mine fire about two kilometres below the ground surface and four kilometres from the mine entrance. With the explosion, the mine elevator stopped, and since refuge chambers were not built, most of the miners were trapped and were poisoned by carbon monoxide; the carbon monoxide levels were about 600–700 ppm. Four rescue teams were deployed and tried to provide fresh air to the trapped miners, but thick smoke and ever-growing fire hindered their efforts. According to a report prepared in 2010 (four years before the accident) by the Chamber of Architects and Engineers (TMMOB), dangers in the mine were clearly stated and authorities were warned against the potential disasters (Çelikkan, 2014). However, these warnings and suggestions were not evaluated by the managerial cadres of the mine in an effort to keep production going.

The Ghost in the System 177

The mine fire started during the shift change with approximately 787 workers in the mines, and as the official statements claim, 301 miners lost their lives. Just after the explosion, miners wanted to continue with their work; as some of them declared they had to work in order to earn their living and pay for their debts (credit card), and they did not have any other alternative than mining in the region (Letsch, 2014).

The mine where the explosion took place is operated by Soma Holding (Soma A.Ş.), which was founded on 1984. In 2005, when the Turkish government in line with their liberalization policies privatized coal mines, the owners (a family) received the mine royalty for Soma from Turkish Coal Authorities (TKİ), a governmental agency. In 2009, Soma A.Ş. had the royalty for the second coal reserve in the same region; in this way, the company became a dominant actor in the region.

Royalty agreements secure government buying of a prespecified yearly amount of coal at a preset price. According to the agreement signed in 2012 between Soma Holding and TKİ, yearly coal production, and thus government purchases, were determined to be 2.6 million tons/year and the purchasing price was determined as 44.34 YTL/ton (Başaran, 2014). This system of royalty promoted eagerness to extract more; for example in 2012 Soma Holding extracted 3,800 million tons of coal (which is 1,200 million tons more than the specified royalty numbers) and all was bought by TKİ.

The royalty agreements in Turkey were initiated in 2004 in line with the liberal economic policies of the majority party. These agreements were a means of privatization; according to Turkish legal system, mines are public goods and are owned by the state. However, for a specific period of time, the state can pass its rights for exploration and extraction to third parties (Topaloğlu, 2001). Furthermore, those corporations that have the agreement and right to extract coal can outsource production. According to the annual report of TKİ, in 2013, 63 per cent of the total coal extracted was realized by royalty agreements, 34.6 per cent by tender bids and only 2.4 per cent was extracted by the state (TKİ Annual Report, 2013, p. 38).

The mine in Soma was appropriated by Soma Holding in 2005. In 2012, the owner of the company, during an interview with Vahap Munyar, a columnist, explained that the results of privatization were very successful.

TKİ [state] was producing coal at a cost of 130–140 dollars/ton, but we made an agreement to produce at a cost of 23.80 dollars/ton including the royalty fee of 15 %. Because of this system government was able to increase its profits from the mines owned by our company without being involved in any production. We have two mines and in one of them we utilize outsourcing model.

(Munyar, 2012)

And Soma Holding did it; in 2014, the cost of coal production was reduced to 23.8 dollars/ton. Furthermore, Soma Holding, according to Istanbul

178   Beyza Oba and Mehmet Gençer

Chamber of Commerce (ISO), composed of 500 of the biggest firm classifications in Turkey, was able to improve its position 34 steps up in the 2014 rankings. The company was able to cut down costs with low wages, not improving the poor working conditions and ignoring the precautions to be taken for workplace safety. According to an engineer who worked in the mines, "productivity has been the main focus. If you make productivity your main focus, the emphasis on the safety regulations decreases relatively. Safety can be prioritized only after a certain performance level has been reached" (Şahnacı and Görgülü, 2014).

BRIEF HISTORICAL BACKGROUND OF BUSINESS SCHOOLS IN TURKEY

In order to provide a better understanding for the silence of business schools, we will give a historical background that explains how prevailing structures, routines and values are established and how they define the potential actions of the actors involved. Regarding the institutionalization of business education in Turkey, we identify three trends: the role of commerce schools that provide more of a vocational training, Americanization (Kipping et al., 2004) and failure in securing administrative autonomy.

THE COMMERCE SCHOOLS: EMPHASIZING PRACTICE

The history of commerce schools dates back to the Ottoman Empire; in 1833, Hamidiye Ticaret Mektebi, a school of commerce for the purpose of educating experts in commerce was founded by state initiative (Güvemli, 2005). The school had a vocational orientation in terms of its curriculum and the academic cadres; main topics included in its curricula were accounting, bookkeeping, commercial geography, commercial correspondence, history of commerce, commercial law, management of commercial organizations, French (Güvemli, 2005) and other courses were taught by part-time practitioners (Üsdiken, 2004). In 1909, 1924, 1936 and 1959, commerce schools were restructured in terms of governance, but their curricula and founding missions remained more or less the same. However, the 1959 restructuring was important in their course of transformation; their names were changed to Academy of Economic and Commercial Sciences (İTİA), their practice orientation was retained and economics was included in their curriculum. In line with the populist policies of the ruling party, the numbers of İTİA increased, especially in cities where there was not a university. During this period, another transformation was related to changes in the staffing policies; emphasis was tilted for full-time academicians and with the resources provided by the Agency for International Development (AID), a medium for faculty exchange was created by establishing ties with

The Ghost in the System 179

the University of Michigan (Kipping et al., 2004; Sargut, 2009). Finally, after 1980 and the structural adjustment measures for homogenization of Turkish higher education, all İTİA's were "converted" to Faculties of Economics and Administrative Sciences (FEAS). In other words, there are some FEASs where business schools or departments are embedded in routines and practices that were instituted in more vocationally oriented schools. One of the consequences of this embeddedness is the development of an academic culture where management studies are taken as an applied science with an emphasis on measurement and decoupling from social sciences.

AMERICANIZATION: NEGLECTING THE LOCAL

Another series of events which heavily affected the present state of business schools in Turkey is the influence of US management education. During late 1940s and early 1950s, with the introduction and implementation of the European Recovery Programme (ERP) or the Marshall Plan, many management techniques and their underlying values, which were the core of liberal capitalism, were instigated, refined and elaborated in European countries (Carew, 1987). The administrative body for the Plan, Economic Cooperation Agency (ECA), through bilateral agreements, was able to promote economic development that aided productivity, financial stability and expansion of foreign trade in the involved countries. In this vein, campaigns for increasing productivity had been the principal issue for assuring economic development and it was also taken as a means for defeating communism and exporting the American way of life (Carew, 1987). The focus of ECA was not only to introduce technological improvements but also to familiarize the recipient countries with the managerial habits, attitudes and practices relevant to improve productivity performance. The institutional background for such a project required two structural adjustments: business schools and national productivity centres.

The second strand of business schools in Turkey is the direct result of this trend; in line with US policies aimed to find political support and develop management education, necessary funding and administrative assistance was provided to establish business schools. Through Marshall aid and later the Ford Foundation, US universities were able to counsel and get actively involved in the transfer of management education, as well as the establishment of organizations to support their management approach (Kipping et al., 2004). In business education, the American tradition initially found its way in the University of Istanbul, which previously established a chair for "business economics". İşletme İktisadı Enstitüsü (İİE), the Business Administration Institute, was established within the Faculty of Economics for delivering the MBA degree. Furthermore, in line with business school tradition in the USA, the institute also had the goal of training practicing managers, especially those who were employed in public organizations. The institute

180   Beyza Oba and Mehmet Gençer

was financially supported by the Ford Foundation and prospective academic staff were sent to Harvard Business School (HBR). With their deliberate effort, the İİE curriculum was designed in line with HBR around functional topics (Üsdiken, 2004), including the adoption of a case study teaching method, and even the seating arrangements in the classrooms were identical to HBR. One of the most notable outcomes of İİE was the establishment of the Faculty of Business Administration in 1968 at İstanbul University. For the first time, business education, at least in terms of governance, was able to separate its domain from economics. However, scientifically and academically, the founding professors of the faculty had a strong background in economics. Besides İİE, two other initiatives were active in importing American-style business education: in 1956, the Middle East Technical University (METU) and, in 1959, Robert College (RC) started to deliver degrees in business administration. One of the parliament members, who had prepared the legislation for METU, stated that "the curriculum should be same as is in American universities and education should be in English" (İlkin, 1972, p. 31), clearly hinting at the direction to be taken. These institutions, (İİE, METU and RC) were instrumental in popularizing management education and providing an exemplar to their followers. Besides providing top- and mid-level managers to public and private sector companies, they had been involved in establishing a management culture and discourse which was shaped by US management education. As these pioneering universities became popular among the potential younger generation, the cultural, structural and processual features associated with their success became over practiced, and the others in the field adopted their curricula and teaching methods with a concern to avoid failure. On the practice side, major companies often partnered and collaborated with US and European firms, and, consequently, there was a rising demand for managerial staff trained in compatible practices. This evidently called for the establishment of management schools (Keskin, 2006) which aimed to train students in "management as conceived in the American way" (Üsdiken and Çetin, 2001, p. 106). Currently, 184 (104 state and 80 private) universities offer degrees in business education, mainly within the umbrella of the Faculty of Economics and Administrative Sciences, and they all follow the same tradition. Amongst this widespread adoption of the American style of management education, there were two exceptions. In 1996, İstanbul Bilgi University was established and had extensive collaboration in the form of offering external degrees or dual diplomas with UK universities. This collaboration enabled the newly founded business department to build a curriculum different from the existing ones and to learn and practice the major methods in critical management education. The second case is the Bilkent University, where, especially in marketing, a different strand in terms of research was initiated in the late 1990s. The case of these two universities as settings where CMS had footage can be explained by the embeddedness of academicians in a totally different institutional setting and having different academic backgrounds.

The Ghost in the System 181

The Americanization trend in Turkey was not limited to business schools; within the framework of the Marshall Plan, the Economic Cooperation Administration (ECA), which was headed by the US ambassador, was held responsible to aid and assess economic development in Turkey (Kılınçkaya, 2013). In line with the recommendations of the ECA and financial resources provided by the Moody Fund for a productivity centre, Vekaletlerarası Prodüktivite Komitesi (VPK) was established with the aim of initiating training courses in public administration. Between 1953 and 1955, 1,141 managers and 7,380 foremen attended courses offered by VKP (Kılınçkaya, 2013). These cadres later became top managers in public organizations, and later in the early 1970s, with the proliferation of private business, they were transferred to private companies as top managers. This group of select managers, or "management intellectuals" (Guillen, 1994), comprised the managerial elites and were influential in establishing pressure groups in later years.

The most important consequence of the Americanization of management education in Turkey has been encouraging the development of a mindset and homogeneous behaviour among practitioners and academicians that neglects the *local* and takes a given set of practices as universal. Such an attitude towards knowledge production and evaluation hinders the enhancement of certain capabilities, such as anticipating, recognizing, interpreting and evaluating issues of different settings. Turkish management education, while accepting universal truth, was not able to apprehend, appreciate and focus on the local.

ADMINISTRATIVE AUTONOMY

The third strand that influenced business schools in Turkey can be explained in relation to administrative autonomy. Initially, management as a field was introduced as business economics; the first business-economics course was offered within the Faculty of Law in İstanbul University and later an institute was established to deliver doctoral degrees in business economics. In 1936, with the establishment of the Faculty of Economics in the same university, a chair was allocated for business economics (Üsdiken, 2004). In 1946, undergraduate degrees in business economics were initiated. Only in 1967 was a separate faculty for delivering undergraduate degrees in business administration established as an offspring of the business economics chair.

Structurally, the first MBA degree in 1954 was offered within the Faculty of Economics. In commerce schools as well, business as a department was associated with economics. Later, in 1980, when higher education was restructured and commerce schools and faculties were aligned, business schools still stayed as a department. This structural tight coupling influenced business schools in terms of resource partitioning but furthermore restricted curricula design choices and recruitment decisions. Structurally and discursively, business departments as compared with economics departments were

182 *Beyza Oba and Mehmet Gençer*

positioned as practice oriented, less theoretical and unsophisticated branches of these faculties. Furthermore, economics departments in Turkey followed the mainstream US model (Görün, 2013), and while shifting towards mathematical formalism, departed from the social sciences (Özdemir and Güler, 2011). Economics education in Turkey is characterized as overquantified, neglectful of historical and political developments and highly based on neoclassical economics (Şenses, 2007).

Being in close proximity to economics departments influenced business schools in two ways: on one hand, a strong power struggle over resources was inevitable and on the other hand, management studies employed more quantitative techniques with little or no emphasis on the social sciences. Furthermore, both departments collectively contributed to the creation of a business mindset which was deeply rooted in the major premises and assumptions of liberal capitalism.

ACADEMIC MILIEU: WHO MAKES BUSINESS SCHOOLS?

In this section, we will focus on academicians who work in business schools and their publications in an attempt to understand how a homogeneous academic culture deeply rooted in mainstream management education is instituted. Since knowledge is culturally mediated and learned through social interaction with more proficient others (Blackler, 1995), focusing on academicians will enable us to explain the recursiveness of mainstream management education in Turkey.

PUBLICATIONS

As can be seen from this brief historical background, business education in Turkey is deeply rooted in the US education model, which was instrumental structurally (undergraduate, MBA) and discursively but furthermore academically. As indicated by Üsdiken and Wasti (2009), publications of Turkish business scholars were mainly involved in an attempt to transfer American theories and practices to domestic audiences. Similarly, Özel (2012), in analyzing the Turkish management literature between 1924 and 2009, found that in domestic publications, management knowledge is transferred in an informative way, rather than processing and applying it to local issues.

The usage and production of textbooks followed a similar trend; in most of the cases, books authored by US academics are adopted. Çoşkun (2009), in a comprehensive study on the most popular Turkish management textbooks, argues that they all had a homogeneous content and discourse in explaining major issues. The dominant discourse in all these books claims that there is an "ideal management" style and it is the one which is promoted

The Ghost in the System 183

by capitalism. They use a particular "language code of business" (Grey, 2002, p. 501) which endorses its agenda; for example instead of "labourer" or "worker", "employee", "organizational member" or "citizen" is used; or "layoff" or "job termination" is replaced by "to leave" (Çoşkun, 2009). "Manager" is defined as someone who completes a task through others and "management" is perceived as a high-level mechanism dedicated to productivity (Çoşkun, 2009, p. 250). This shared, replicated managerial language on one hand provided a gateway to those who would be managers in domestic and global companies, but it also was instrumental in articulating values and priorities to be practiced. Since they were voiced by prominent and well-established members of the academic community, their recognition and diffusion among academia and practitioners was rapid. Furthermore, although all of these textbooks claim that the scientific approach should have a critical stance, none of the authors developed such an approach.

RESEARCH ORIENTATION

Especially from the 1990s on, with an emphasis on research-based academic work as opposed to "conceptual" studies, a "positivist" shift, which can be defined as quantitative, had a vast impact on academic work of Turkish academicians. One of the reasons behind this trend was the emergence and institutionalization of NMOC. The founder academicians of NMOC "shared the logic of scientism" (Özen and Kalemci, 2009, p. 79) and were influential in promoting quantitative techniques in research. Although this was not accomplished directly, the select group of academicians who were responsible from the evaluation, screening and selection of the abstracts were in favour of quantitative academic work. NMCO is one of the most powerful organizations in management studies in Turkey; it is a medium where young academicians are initiated in the community, where reputation for future academic careers is established. Thus its focus on quantitative research techniques has been instrumental in promoting these approaches. In an another study about the bibliometric features of the proceedings of NMCO, Yozgat and Kartaltepe (2009) have found that three international journals (*Academy of Management Journal, Academy of Management Review, Administrative Science Quarterly*) have been frequently cited by the authors. This evidence can be explanative in understanding the limited exposure in terms of ideas and techniques in management and as well provide support for the homogenization of academic culture.

Özen (2002) identifies this problem as "ceremonial empiricism", where the managerialist/universalist tradition perseveres by utilizing quantitative research methods without considering context and theory. This mode of empiricism is employed to verify the absence of and promote the usage of management tools originating in the US among Turkish companies.

184 Beyza Oba and Mehmet Gençer

ACADEMICIANS

In order to provide a better understanding about how this homogeneous academic culture, which favours quantitative research methods, evaluates US management tools as universal and managerialist, we can consider the background of academicians and the recruitment policies employed. The majority of the academicians currently working in business departments have completed their undergraduate degrees in business departments of the universities explained previously as the commerce schools and early adopters of American education (Ardıç and Erdoğmuş, 2009). A similar trend has been seen in graduate degrees. Nearly 45 per cent of the academicians completed their PhDs in the aforementioned universities and 90 per cent of them earned degrees from business departments. More than 70 per cent of the academicians earned their doctorate degrees in Turkey (Ardıç and Erdoğmuş, 2009). One of the justifications for this situation can be given in relation to recruitment policies; traditionally, business schools always preferred to recruit business graduates. However, recently with the new by-laws of the Turkish Higher Education Council (YÖK), recruiting academicians with a PhD from a business department has been a rule.

This closed circle, which is promoted by education, recruitment and acknowledgement by favourable others, has created an assimilative structure which is inwardly focused and an atmosphere where unfamiliar trends and ideas are not accommodated. Consequently, the more we are embedded in this culture, the fewer chances we have to transpose other ideas from other fields. Being involved with other groups, different ideas, values and beliefs can create tensions, since it will require an effort to organize these contradictory values and practices internally.

WHERE ARE WE NOW? BACK TO THE SOMA INCIDENT

Values

While management education was redefined as "mere technical training" (Grey, 2002, p. 498), it was heavily influenced by economic notions of "rationality" and "productivity". Managers had to be rational and thus management knowledge should be shaped around the norms of empirical research and formal rationality. Our discourse analysis of management textbooks written by Turkish academicians reveals that the concept of rationality is explained as "not being emotional, being logical, and being conscious" within the chapter on decision making; emphasis is not on the concept of rationality but on rational decision making. The discourse employed in explaining rational decision making clearly states that if the manager can make rational decisions s(he) would be objective, evaluate all the possible alternatives and, furthermore, the successful decision-making process would

The Ghost in the System 185

be rational. This claim, by suggesting success in better resource allocations, career opportunities and reputation, promotes a universal and timeless discourse and disregards substantive rationality.

Promoting a "value-neutral" (Grey, 2004, p. 182) decision-making process by the majority of academicians becomes an idea and practice that can be accepted without any further enquiry and questioning. However, if management knowledge is to be practice oriented and if management is to be a profession (Trank and Rynes, 2003), values and ethics are to be major components in its articulation. In order to support practice, management rhetoric must stress certain values so that the individual interests of managers, while making decisions, are guided by professional values. Benligiray and Tez's (2011) study on the values promoted in 140 business administration departments in Turkish universities found that risk taking, autonomy, being people oriented, teamwork and communication with internal and external stakeholders were specified as values that underlie educational practices. When we further analysed the data provided by this research, we see that management education with its emphasis on the rational, scientific and pragmatic approach and tools is presented as a remedy to increase productivity, profits and provision of financial resources in a highly competitive and global world. For example, in relation to "people orientation", in the mission statements of some of these departments, it is stated that "it is one of the responsibilities of a managerto find and recruit the right personnel . . . place people in jobs where they will be most productive" (Benligiray and Tez, 2011, p. 60).

So at least some business departments endorse values; but whose values are they? Whose interests are represented and supported by these values? If the priority is the performance of the organization, then for better profitability, productivity and efficiency, values for people are to be less important. Business schools should question and reconsider their priorities in terms of stakeholders and the related values. This reconsideration process recognizes a tension around the interests of various stakeholders. However, currently academicians take for granted that they should equip their graduates with techniques that will improve the organizations they are part of, and only through such techniques can organizations improve their performance. Furthermore, a "good" manager masters these techniques, which guarantees success in all times and places. Under such premises, Soma Holding could have been taken as a case of success, as they have improved their profitability, cut down costs and improved productivity. However, if we accept people-oriented values, we should question the cost-cutting strategies, absence of means for the betterment of working conditions and the implications of outsourcing for employees. Thus we claim that business schools, besides problematizing the extant knowledge and values around which they construct their content, should re-examine their *priorities* in terms of values and the strategies to influence their students and the public.

Performance Anxiety

The owners and top management of Soma Holding were proud, they were taken as a case of success since they were able to cut down costs by nearly five times, and they improved their sales turnover by 20 per cent in one year and, according to the rankings of ISO in 2014, the company increased its position in terms of profits. In the press, they were explaining the managerial know-how beyond their performativity: "we applied management techniques and way of doing business . . . good planning" (Munyar, 2012).

As stated by Fournier and Grey (2000, p. 17), "performativity is taken as an imperative towards which all practice and knowledge is to be geared". This idea is promoted by various agents—business schools, popular media, managers and interest groups—that do not question how it was achieved. If we asked this question and tried to find the real story of Soma Holding's performativity, the answer would be they were able to cut down costs by reducing the number of workers and increasing working hours, cutting costs by not spending on workplace safety and setting salaries at the minimum level. After the incident, some miners claimed that they had been carrying the same emergency mask for eight years and if they operated the mask without any stated cause, 200 TL would be deducted from their salaries (Letsch, 2014). Miners also had to buy their own gloves.

When we analyse the textbooks written on management by Turkish academicians, we see that productivity, profitability and efficiency are taken as the major goals of an organization. In popular media, performance stories of managers and corporations are given prime importance. The Ministry of Science, Industry and Technology, business organizations and chambers publish and announce indices. Indices that rank corporations on various performance measures are one of the instruments that objectify performativity and enhance the power of those agents who evaluate and assess corporations and managers. All of these agents collectively construct a reality where the corporation has the prime importance, and the major responsibility of management is to provide managerial techniques that will provide its productivity. Furthermore, committing to and subscribing to the rules and premises of this constructed world is legitimate; it is rewarding in terms of publicity, visibility and provision of resources. This constructed business reality to perform creates anxiety, especially for those who are supposed to be responsible for the performance of the corporations they manage.

Curriculum Wars

Most of the academicians in business schools in Turkey think that the curriculum should be designed in line with the requirements of business life; however, they feel uneasy that only in some (17 per cent) of the departments is it done (Doğan and Türk, 2005). In more than half of the business departments, decisions about which courses are to be included are made by

The Ghost in the System   187

checking their rivals, and only a very limited number of departments (15 per cent) design their curriculum with the participation and preference of the academic staff (Doğan and Türk, 2005).

What are the requirements of business life in Turkey? Neo-liberal policies. Starting with the extending impact of globalization, Turkey entered a new pathway in 1980 which extends today, leading to the abandonment of protectionist regulations in favour of complete liberalization towards the free-market economy. Articulated through several waves of reforms by both right- and left-wing governments, the role of the state was first minimized then shifted to regulating markets, rather than including provision of certain services. The reforms were pushed by seemingly orchestrated demands of both international bodies and local ones. International bodies were instrumental in the initiation of practices favouring efficiency, profitability and good governance. These measures were welcomed by prominent businessmen, and collectively a reality was constructed. The desired economic growth was epitomized in increasingly praised managerialism, both in the public and private sector. In the Turkish case, a de facto deregulation of the private sector, much like the hidden part of a regulation iceberg, leaves the working class extremely vulnerable, as in the case of the Soma incident. In the process, resorting to technocratic reasoning was the key strategy to counter many objections. The defective habit of explaining decisions at the political level with arguments at the technical level (Ludwig, 2001), has accumulated considerable public discontent, but business schools were silent. And without questioning where they are heading or for whom all these managerialist techniques are for, they willingly became part of this constructed reality. Courses such as unions, employee relations and sociology of work waned from curricula. Business schools in a way naturalized neo-liberal policies and financialization and even assumed a pioneering role in the promotion of their discourse.

Conclusion

Facing a problem—the Soma mine incident—which is deeply rooted in the neo-liberal policies and financialization, business schools in Turkey were silent. Interestingly, engineers and lawyers, individually or collectively, were actively involved in the issue either by taking action or by discussing the possible causes; management scholars were bereft of any response. Although values such as "social responsibility" are embraced by the existing management rhetoric, no academic discussion can proceed without addressing the incompatibility between the talk and the walk.

The historical background of business schools shows how routines in being practice oriented, focusing on the universal rather than the local and decoupling from social sciences have been created. Some of the business schools/departments had roots in commerce schools, and this has instigated a "practice-oriented" approach in terms of curriculum design, delivery and

188 Beyza Oba and Mehmet Gençer

recruiting practitioners without an academic background. Another set of facilitating conditions which deeply affected the current logic among Turkish business schools has been the economic and political enlargement of the US government after World War II in Europe, which mainly focused on the development of an economically strong Europe as to balance the power of the Soviets. In this vein, training of local managers in US management practices and techniques had been the main instrument in transforming an economic logic, which by then had been characterized by statist policies. This era has been characterized by the establishment of business schools structured and designed in line with the American way of managing. At the same time, politically, it has been a period during which liberal economic values were introduced as an alternative to a state protectionist development model. The popularization and establishment of business schools coincides with this construction of the liberal economy, its institutions, practices and dominant values. As a consequence of being active actors in this project, business schools always took liberal economy and US management as a universal given that local management practices and organizations must attune with. Also, importation of the ideas of this universal business reality had been an important factor in the manufacturing of academic and corporate reputations. In this process of establishing the "ideal, universal business reality", business schools and academicians lost their feeling for the local.

Once the routines were instituted, they promoted the establishment of collective repertoires, action guidelines, preferences and also influenced the recognition and solution developing habits of those involved. As academicians become more embedded in this community, taking for granted its established values and practices provided an ontological security leading to the development of a homogeneous culture and mindset. Homogeneous cultures restrict the "accommodative zone of interest" (Jarzabowski, 2005, p. 539), narrow knowledge sources and constrain reflexivity. Within such a community, discussing alternatives and transposing new ideas and practices turns out to be a highly political process.

In the face of such an institutional resistance to any set of practices, values and ideas other than the mainstream, how can CMS find its way in Turkish business schools? Ideas can be transposed between institutional fields with different logics as long as some facilitating conditions exist (Boxenbaum and Battilana, 2005); there has to be a problem which is deemed to question the legitimacy of the established logic, its structural determinants, values and practices. Either business schools or individually some academicians should have a drive to transpose and change, which can be promoted by being exposed to different institutional contexts than their own. This multiple embeddedness provides a different frame to anticipate, evaluate and tackle the problems faced and also improves the knowledge. Since what we study, research and discuss is related to the lives of people, we should assume responsibility towards people but not towards organizations. This requires questioning what and how we study and teach but even more what should be our priorities.

The Ghost in the System 189

REFERENCES

Alakavuklar, O.N. and Parker, M. (2011). Responsibility and the Local: The Prospects for Critical Management in Turkey. *Critical Perspectives on International Business*, 7(4): 326–342.

Ardıç, K. and Erdoğmuş, N. (2009). Öznenin nesneleşmesi:Türkiye'de yönetim ve organizasyon alanında çalışan öğretim elemanlarının akademik özgeçmiş ve eserleri bakımından nicel görünümü. *Eskişehir Osmangazi Üniversitesi İİBF Dergisi*, 4(1): 199–237.

Başaran, E. (2014, Haziran 25). *301 canın üzerinde yükselen servet*. Retrieved from www.radikal.com.tr:http://www.radikal.com.tr/yazarlar/ezgi_basaran/blank-119 8656

Benligiray, S. and Tez, Ö. (2011). Üniversitelerin işletme eğitimi veren bölümleri öğrencilerine genel işletmecilik değerlerini kazandırmayı amaçlıyorlar mı? *Afyon Kocatepe Üniversitesi, İİBF Dergisi*, 13(2): 49–70.

Blackler, F. (1995). Knowledge, Knowledge Work and Organizations: An Overview and Interpretation. *Organization Studies*, 16(6): 1021–1046.

Bourdieu, P. (1990). *The Logic of Practice*. Cambridge, UK: Polity Press.

Boxenbaum, E. and Battillana, J. (2005). Importation as Innovation: Transposing Managerial Practices Across Fields. *Strategic Organization*, 3(4): 355–383.

Carew, A. (1987). *Labour Under the Marshall Plan; The Politics of Productivity and the Marketing of Management Science*. Detroit, MI: Wayne State University Press.

Çelikkan, E. (2014, May 16). *Soma Disaster Blatantly Came, Old Reports Reveal*. Retrieved from http://www.hurriyetdailynews.com: http://www.hurriyetdailynews.com/soma-disaster-blatantly-came-old-report-reveals.aspx?pageID=238&nID=6 6542&NewsCatID=347

Çoşkun, R. (2009). "Yönetim-Organizasyon" Ders Kitaplarında Biçim ve İdeoloji. *Eskişehir Osmangazi Üniversitesi İİBF Dergisi*, 4(1): 239–258.

Doğan, S. and Türk, A. (2005). Üniversitelerde yönetim ve organizasyon anabilim dalı ders ve içeriklerinin verilme düzeyi ve belirlenme şeklinin tespitine ilişkin bir araştırma. *Marmara Üniversitesi Sosyal Bilimler Enstitüsü Dergisi*, 6(24): 61–70.

Giddens, A. (1984). *The Constitution of Society*. Cambridge: Polity Press.

Görün, F. (2013). ODTÜ İktisat Bölümü: Yarım yüzyılı aşan bir süreden bazı gözlemler. *ODTÜ Gelişme Dergisi*, 40: 239–246.

Grey, C. (2002). What are Business Schools for? On Silence and Voice in Management Education. *Journal of Management Education*, 26(5): 496–511.

Grey, C. (2004). Reinventing Business Schools: The Contribution of Critical Management Education. *Academy of Management Learning & Education*, 3(2): 178–186.

Guillen, M. (1994). *Models of Management*. Chicago, IL: University of Chicago Press.

Güvemli, O. (2005). Türkiye'de ticaret liselerinin kuruluş öyküsü. *Muhasebe ve Finansman*, 28(1): 16–23.

İlkin, S. (1972). 1920–1960 Döneminde Türkiye'deki iktisat ve ticaret eğitimi ile ilgili kuruluşların gelişimi tarihi üzerine bir deneme. In F. Gürün (Ed.), *Türkiye'de üniversitelerde okutulan iktisat üzerine*, 3–38. Ankara: Ortadoğu Teknik Üniversitesi Yayınları.

Jarzabowski, P. (2005). Strategy as Practice: Recursiveness, Adaptation, and Practices-in-use. *Organization Studies*, 25(4): 529–560.

Keskin, N. (2006). Türkiye'de kamu yönetimi disiplininin köken sorunu. *Amme İdaresi Dergisi*, 39(2): 1–28.

Kılınçkaya, D. (2013). Marshall Planı ve Milli prodüktivite Merkezi'nin kuruluşu. *Hacettepe Üniversitesi Türkiyat Araştırmaları Dergisi*, 18: 131–146.

190 Beyza Oba and Mehmet Gençer

Kipping, M., Üsdiken, B. and Puig, N. (2004). Imitation, Tension and Hybridization: Multiple "americanizations" of Management Education in Mediterrenean Europe. *Journal of Management Inquiry*, 13(2): 98–108.

Letsch, C. (2014, May 20). *Turkish Miners Reveals Lax Safety Record and Climate of Fear at Soma Mines*. Retrieved from http://www.theguardian.com: http://www.theguardian.com/world/2014/may/20/turkish-miner-lax-safety-record-soma-mines

Ludwig, R. (2001). The Era of Management is Over. *Ecosystems*, 4(8): 758–764.

Munyar, V. (2012, September 30). *TTK 10 milyar alacak*. Retrieved from Hürriyet: http://www.hurriyet.com.tr/yazarlar/21586913.asp

Özcan, K. (2012). From Frankfurt School to Business Schools: Critical Management Studies in Turkey. *International Journal of Organizational Analysis*, 20(1): 107–123.

Özdemir, M. and Güler, E. (2011). Is the Global Financial Crises a Crises of Academic Economics and Economics Education? A Research on the Perceptions of Turkish Economists. *Ankara Üniversitesi SBF Dergisi*, 66(4): 67–100.

Özel, B. (2012). Collaboration Structure and Knowledge Diffusion in Turkish Management Academia. *Scientometrics*, 93: 183–206.

Özen, Ş. (2002). Türkiye'deki Örgütler/Yönetim Araştırmalarında Törensel Görgülcülük Sorunu. *Yönetim Araştırmaları Dergisi*, 2(2): 187–213.

Özen, Ş. and Kalemci, A. (2009). Ulusal yönetim ve organizasyon konresi'nin doğuşu, kurumsallaşması ve alana etkileri. *Eskişehir Osmangazi Üniversitesi İİBF Dergisi*, 4(1): 79–112.

Şahnacı, H. and Görgülü, G. (2014, May 16). *The Pressure More Production Was an Invitation for the Some Disaster*. Retrieved from www.habervesaire.com: http://www.habervesaire.com/news/the-pressure-for-more-production-was-an-invitation-for-the-soma-disaster-2712.html

Sargut, S. (2009). Türkiye'de işletme yönetimi eğitiminin kurumsal çerçevesi:çeşitlilikten eşbiçimliliğe. *Eskişehir Osmangazi Üniversitesi İİBF Dergisi*, 4(1): 51–63.

Şen, B. (2014, May 14). *Soma'da maden faciası: 151 ölü*. Retrieved from Hürriyet: http://www.hurriyet.com.tr/gundem/26411298.asp

Şen, B. (2014, May 14). *www.hurriyet.com.tr/gundem/*. Retrieved from Hürriyet: http://www.hurriyet.com.tr/gundem/26411298.asp

Şenses, F. (2007). *Uluslararası gelişmeler ışığında Türkiye yükseköğretim sistemi: temel eğilimler, sorunlar, çelişkiler ve öneriler*. Ankara: Orta Doğu Teknik Üniversitesi, Ekonomik Araştırmalar Merkezi.

Soma Holding; history/milestones. (2014, August 20). Retrieved from www.tilaga.com.tr: http://www.tilaga.com.tr/tarihce_en.html

Topaloğlu, M. (2001). Rödovans sözleşmesi: hukuksal durum, sonuçlar ve çözüm önerileri. *Türkiye 17 Uluslararası Madencilik Kongresi ve Sergisi*. Ankara: TUMAKS.

Trank, C.Q. and Rynes, S.L. (2003). Who Moved Our Cheese? Reclaiming Professionalism in Business Education. *Academy of Management Learning & Education*, 2(2): 189–205.

Türkiye Kömür İşletmeleri Kurumu (2013). *Yıllık Rapor*. Ankara, Turkey.

Üsdiken, B. (2004). The French, the German and the American: Higher Education for Business in Turkey, 1883–2003. *New Perspectives on Turkey*, 31: 5–38.

Üsdiken, B., & Çetin, D. (2001). From Betriebswirtschaftslehre to human relations: Turkish Management Literature Before and After the Second World War. *Business History*, 43(2): 99–124.

Üsdiken, B. and Wasti, S.A. (2009). Preaching, Teaching and Researching at the Periphery: Academic Management Literature in Turkey, 1970–1999. *Organization Studies*, 30(10): 1063–1082.

Yozgat, U. and Kartaltepe, N. (2009). Ulusal Yönetim ve Organizasyon kongre kitaplarında yer alan bildirilerin bibliyometrik profili: örgüt teorisi ve örgütsel davranış bildirileri üzerine bir araştırma. *Eskişehir Osmangazi Üniversitesi İİBF Dergisi*, 4(1): 149–165.

13 CMS in the United Kingdom

Martin Parker

THE DISUNITED QUEENDOM

As this book makes abundantly clear, CMS doesn't mean one thing.[1] Neither does the UK,[2] for that matter, as residents of its (at least) four constituent parts know very well indeed. So a chapter on the conjunction between two contested terms is unlikely to satisfy all its readers. To make matters worse, since the UK is the country with the largest number of academics who would identify (however hesitantly) with the term that pulls this book together, so does it have the most complex and finely grained history. My job in this chapter is then an impossible one—to try to tell a fractious and complex story in a way that most readers will agree with. I will fail.

So let's just agree that it is my story and that others could be written. This chapter is written by an UK author who identifies as an ex-sociologist who now works in a business school teaching and writing about organizations from a perspective that most people would understand to be located within CMS. That means that I will be telling you about the relationship between critical work in sociology and the social sciences and various 'critical' developments within the business school. This is complicated, because CMS is not the only critical tradition within the UK business school. I argue that different understandings of the role of social science and its relevant theoretical resources provides the deep structure for a tension between CMS on the one hand and industrial relations and the sociology of work and employment on the other. The movement of sociologists and other social scientists to the business school in the UK, combined with the shrinking of sociology, has provided the precondition for two very different understandings of what 'critical' means. Nowadays, this migration of people and knowledge is increasingly forgotten within the business school itself, as new PhDs are socialized within a critical 'tradition' which they experience as substantially indigenous and handed down by professors who might seem to have been doing something called CMS all their lives.

However, it's worth noting that I could be telling this story from a variety of other places—from critical accounting, critical marketing, heterodox economics—or as someone who came to the business school from psychology,

192   *Martin Parker*

history, industrial relations or philosophy. This is to say that my story might be convincing enough for some, but it won't work for many, because CMS in the UK is too big for this chapter, and the list of people and work that I haven't mentioned could fill this entire book. I think that there are too many stories that could be told, and none of which would capture everything. Which is to already say something about my position on some of the debates I will cover in the following section.

'CRITICAL'?

By the 1970s, sociology in the UK had become in part a radical project. Stanislav Andreski, a professor at Reading University, puts this succinctly in a dictionary of modern thought.

> critical sociology. An expression which in principle is a pleonasm, since all good SOCIOLOGY must be critical in the sense of insisting on probing and being ready to challenge current opinions. It is only because the main current of sociology has become apologetic that the justification for 'critical sociology' has arisen.
>
> (in Bullock and Stallybrass, 1977, p. 146)

The 1968 conference of the American Sociological Association saw the publication of *The Insurgent Sociologist*, becoming the journal *Critical Sociology* in 1969 (Fuller, 1996). Reflecting the social and cultural turbulence of the late 1960s, sociology had become a welcoming home for Marxism, critical theory and feminism, as well as forms of thought and method which began with the everyday and celebrated the ordinary, such as ethnomethodology and interactionism. The former trilogy quite explicitly challenged the family, the legal system, education and the work organization, describing them as places in which the powerful produced compliant citizens, always pushing against the resistance of the underdogs. Sociologies of action and language had a less explicit politics, but they were often understood to be suggesting that if the social world was constructed from the ground up, then it could be changed from the ground up too. In theoretical terms, all that was seen to be solid was melting into air.

It seems important to locate these 'radical' critiques in the 1960s, because it is at that point that the university and the knowledge it produces becomes a terrain for explicit dissent from what Andreski had called the 'streamlined sorcerers clad in the latest paraphernalia of science' (1972, p. 238). There were consistent demands to articulate social science as a project which responded to civil rights, anti-war, women's and student's movements in the US (Colfax and Roach, 1971; Fay, 1987; Fuller, 1996, p. 2), to which we might add a politics of class in the UK. Though much British sociology continued in its substantially empirical and theoretically pragmatic manner,

CMS *in the United Kingdom* 193

the tumult of criticism aimed at 'functionalism' effectively meant that by the 1970s most UK sociology textbooks proceeded in a fairly predictable manner. Introduce a topic, and then describe it in terms of the functions it plays in advanced societies. Then describe it from the viewpoint of conflict sociologies, invoking various feminists and Marxists as evidence. Finally, show how everyday interaction reproduces these assumptions about expertise, gender, the role of the media or whatever. The trajectory of the arguments meant that functionalism was being challenged both conceptually and politically with a 'three-little-pigs' style of argument in which the temperature of the functionalist porridge was never right.

This was the setup into which British sociology students of the 1970s and 1980s were being socialized. Not just sociology either, because most of the social sciences and humanities were developing their critical wings around this time too. The journals *Antipode, Critical Sociology* and the *Review of Radical Political Economics* were founded in 1969, *Radical Philosophy* in 1972, *Critique* in 1973, *Critical Enquiry* in 1974, *Critical Social Policy* in 1981, *Critical Studies in Media Communication* in 1984 and *Critical Criminology* in 1989 (see Parker and Thomas, 2011). It was a context in which developments in politics and theory were being seen to overturn the dull conservativism of the founding fathers of many disciplines, a diagnosis that nicely chimed with the noisy countercultural politics of the 1960s and 1970s. For those studying sociology and cognate disciplines in Britain from (say) 1965 to 1985, this was the intellectual milieu into which they were socialized.

In terms of the sociology of organizations in particular, this was a context in which David Silverman's *Theory of Organizations* outlined what a 'social action' model might look like, later describing it as situated against 'functionalism' and 'abstracted empiricism' (1970, 1994). A few years later, Braverman's *Labor and Monopoly Capital* (1974) insisted on the importance of a Marxist account of the labour process, decrying human relations as a form of knowledge that did no more than accommodate the worker to their subordination. So when two big UK books came along within a year of each other—Burrell and Morgan's *Sociological Paradigms and Organizational Analysis* (1979) and Clegg and Dunkerley's *Organization, Class and Control* (1980)—they both reflected this impatience with conventional accounts. Indeed, the former book embeds a story about the dominance of one 'paradigm', and the need for its critique by other 'paradigms'. In other words, structural Marxism, radical humanism and sociologies of action are needed to challenge the dominant but dead versions of structural functionalism. Four little pigs, rather than three, and the functionalist porridge was getting even colder.

These are forms of thought in which opposition is central to identity, and it was a powerful story which those who had studied sociology and cognate areas took with them into the expanding UK business schools of the 1980s. Just as the sociology departments were beginning to shrink slowly, so were

194   *Martin Parker*

other parts of the university beginning to grow rapidly. The labour market for sociologists to teach in their 'home' departments was shrinking, and so they became émigrés with by far the biggest demand from the 'organizational behaviour' parts of business schools, which needed a labour force to teach the 'people and organizations' core courses on undergraduate and postgraduate degrees with very healthy enrolments, including substantial cohorts of non-UK students who were paying higher fees and providing universities with income to offset continual cuts or 'efficiency savings'. The role of the English language here is worth stressing, because it allowed a particular national university system to sell courses globally, using marketing that combined language school, Latin mottos and promises of salary bumps. So the jobs were there for anyone who spoke English (which is to say, spoke 'American'), and, for those who followed the money, my contention is that their commitments were often shaped by the sociology and wider social science that they had left behind.

'MANAGEMENT'?

The oppositional social science that they had learned was likely to be sharpened in the new conditions in which they found themselves. For some, the Marxists who had commitments to developing a labour process critique of capitalism, this opposition was political in the sense that they found themselves working in institutions which tended to orient themselves to management rather than the worker. Not that they were the first to arrive, because industrial relations (IR) academics were earlier inhabitants of the UK business school. As Ian Roberts notes, the development and institutionalization of industrial relations as a discipline really happens in the 1920s and 1930s, whilst sociology only grows from the 1950s onwards (2003, p. 34). There are some clear tensions between IR and industrial sociology from this later period, with the beginnings of an account that sociologists are not interested in structures and institutions, but only in what happens at particular places of work.

> This school applies the techniques of sociology and social psychology direct to 'situations' which it discovers in factories and other places of work . . . (However) much of its published work shows a deplorable lack of historical understanding and, sometimes, a failure to appreciate the nature of the 'situation' studied due to ignorance of the framework of formal institutions which surround it.
>
> (Flanders and Clegg, 1956, in Roberts, 2003, p. 34)

In that sense, the sociologist is being understood as the inheritor of a human relations account of adjustment to the workplace, as opposed to a rigorous understanding of the history and consequences of formal mechanisms for regulating conflict.

CMS in the United Kingdom 195

This initially uneasy relationship seems to have become less problematic as industrial sociologists began to be employed within business schools from the 1970s onwards. One of the key influences on these new recruits had been the 'orientations to work' Weberianism of the affluent worker and occupational community studies (Rose, 1978). This was research which was being carried out at the level of an organization or occupation and which was attempting to develop an empirically driven account of the way that meaning influences action, but it was connecting its concerns to wider issues of class composition. It wasn't that far from a conflict Weberian account to a Marxist (or Marxisant) one and hence unsurprising that industrial sociologists and industrial relations academics influenced by Alan Fox's criticisms of pluralism (1974) should begin to find shared intellectual and empirical ground (see Wood and Kelly, 1978). Questions concerning gender, skill and restructuring came to the forefront, and Braverman's book provided a new intellectual resource with which to rediscover some old problems. The Labour Process conferences, which began in 1983 at business schools in new technology universities in Manchester and Birmingham, began to institutionalize this accommodation, and the UK journal *Work, Employment and Society* began publishing in 1987 to provide a location for the sort of work which brought together three groups—industrial sociologists in declining sociology departments, industrial sociologists who were now working in business schools and industrial relations academics who had been working in business schools for some time.

'CRITICAL STUDIES'?

Of course, this isn't the whole story, because a lot of the sociologists and social scientists who moved were not Marxist or Weberian industrial sociologists, but they were perhaps more influenced by the Frankfurt School, various sociologies of action and the radical philosophies of what came to be called post-structuralism. It was much harder for this group to find much in common with industrial relations or industrial sociology, even though they might have shared an understanding of the importance of the workplace and meaning with the latter. It seems to me that this is why 'organization' and 'management' became such key terms, as opposed to what seem like bigger words such as 'work', 'industry' and 'employment'. It seems to me that this sort of focus had several implications for the beginnings and early development of CMS in the UK. First, to connect to a tradition of largely US interactionist or phenomenological work on organizing from authors such as Garfinkel, Berger, Goffman and Becker. Second, to turn the Weberian and Frankfurt School understandings of bureaucracy and mass society into a diagnosis of the predicament of Marcuse's *One Dimensional Man* (1964), trapped within the iron cage and unable to see the beach because the pavement was in the way. Third, to place language

196   Martin Parker

and culture at the centre of their enquiries and, consequently, to connect to thinkers from 'outside' the English-speaking social sciences, such as Derrida, Foucault and Habermas. Nonetheless, it seems to me that this latter group of émigrés to the business school also preserved a sense of themselves as being 'in opposition' to their employers. That sense of not being endogenous provided a certain sort of distance from the emerging goals and values of the new institution, as well as a developed body of knowledge which was external to the school and which could easily provide the resources for many forms of critique.

The institutionalization of this second sense of 'critical' work happens gradually, but fairly inexorably as conferences, journals and associations are established. The first meeting of the Standing Conference on Organizational Symbolism took place in Exeter in 1982, a breakaway group from the more orthodox European Group for Organization Studies, and was originally jointly organized and attended by people from sociology and the business school. However, by the third conference in 1984, it was clear that SCOS was dominated by attendees from the business school, whilst its concerns continued to reflect the influence of micro-sociologies, as well as structuralism and post-structuralism.[3] Other later conferences originate within the business school itself, such as the biannual 'Discourse' conferences organized from Kings College Business School in London from 1994, the Gender, Work and Organization conference at Manchester and then Keele from 1998, and the CMS Conference itself from Manchester in 1999.[4] The UK journals that were established in this period also tended to be dominated by academics from business schools—such as *Organization* (1994), *Gender, Work and Organization* (1994) and *Culture and Organization* (1995). Each were justified in terms of their difference from the mainstream, whether that was a neglect of certain sorts of themes or an active contestation of dominant approaches.

The unfolding of something called Critical Management Studies in the mid-1990s was hence never going to be a big enough umbrella. It needed to cover these interactionists, Frankfurt School Marxists and post-structuralists, as well as industrial sociologists and industrial relations academics if it was going to include everyone within the UK business school who was, in some way, thinking against it. Despite a shared hostility to the business school, they shared little else. In the event, the edited volume that named CMS claimed to be inaugurating a subdisciplinary field (Alvesson and Willmott, 1992), not merely collecting together leftists with common gripes. All but one of the contributors to the book worked in management schools, and 6 of the 14 worked in the UK. The explicit claim made in the introduction to the volume concerned the application of critical theory to management, and the avoidance of a 'sociologism' which would dissolve the specificity of CMS into a more general understanding of 'ideological and cultural phenomena' (*op cit*: 18). Like other critical projects in the social sciences (Parker and Thomas, 2011), the prefix was vital here, but so

CMS in the United Kingdom   197

too was the idea that this could be a generic area of study. There is an interesting balancing act being engaged in, with an attempt to claim that CMS is not the same as sociology, its most obvious parent, but neither is it part of the business school. Just like Durkheim's attempt to claim that the new discipline of sociology was not psychology, history, philosophy, anthropology or political economy (1895/1982), so do Alvesson et al. have to claim that the domain of CMS is not just a version of sociology or management but something new.

Over the past 25 years, I would argue that the 'not-management' part of this description has become the constitutive one and any need to distance CMS from sociology or other social sciences has become irrelevant. This is in part because the labour market for staff to teach the 'people and organizations' topics is gradually becoming internal to the business school, consisting of PhD students who have been trained within it. This doesn't mean that those interested in CMS see its contents and purposes as settled, rather that their identity work remains constituted oppositionally. The nature of the opposition varies—whether managerialism, contemporary forms of organizing, the deans of business schools, capitalism, patriarchy, imperialism and so on—but the narrative of struggle is common. Indeed, the amount of writing which has mediated upon the possibilities and co-optations of CMS is now vast, constituting a kind of running commentary on the practice of CMS which sometimes threatens to obscure any actual content at all. The very existence of all this literature speaks of the instability and insecurity of the field, of its need to establish an intellectual and political credibility within what is perceived to be hostile terrain.

Nevertheless, the remarkable institutionalization of CMS in the UK compared with some other places had clear implications for other 'critical' constituencies within the business school. First, the 1950s diagnosis of sociology by industrial relations academics could now be rerun but this time aimed at CMS for being too focused on action at the neglect of structure, politically pluralist or unitarist and largely doing work at the level of meaning and organization. Indeed, the interminable reflexivity and theoretical innovation which is characteristic of CMS could easily be understood as a recipe for political quietism which masquerades as intellectual radicalism (Parker, 1999; Thompson et al., 2000; Rowlinson and Hassard, 2011). Not so much champagne socialism as a form of posturing without action or consequences. The IR diagnosis was also echoed by industrial sociologists within the business school, even though they were using different terms in order to locate themselves—critical realism, institutional theory, labour process theory and so on (Thompson, 2004). If we compare UK-based journals such as *Work, Employment and Society* and *Organization*, we can see the consequences of this divide. Two largely different groups, who tend to go to different conferences and use different founding texts. Yet, and this is the biggest irony of all, both would largely claim to be 'critical' and pretty much all of them work in the business school.

198   *Martin Parker*

'CRITICAL MANAGEMENT STUDIES'?

The migration of sociologists into the business school has nowadays become a trickle, but this also reflects some changes in sociology itself. From the 1980s onwards, there is a decline of interest in work and organizations within sociology. This tendency seems to be made more visible by the relative decline in the number of people working in sociology departments, and the closure of lots of departments too, set against a huge growth in the organizational behaviour parts of business schools. So when the British Sociological Association started publishing *Work, Employment and Society*, it was largely the growing number of sociologists and IR academics in business schools who provided the authors and readers, not the sociologists themselves. Indeed, as Thompson and Smith suggest, it was the Labour Process Theorists who 'played to and built on the strengths of British industrial sociology' (2009, p. 924). For *WES* authors, increasingly based within business schools but having intellectual roots in industrial relations and labour process theory, the task was to empirically document questions of power and control. Development of new theory or methods was certainly not at the forefront of concern per se, and the concept of *the* organization was assumed, rather than problematized. The critical edge is almost always provided by the empirical materials with a broadly 'social scientific' justification for their selection, analysis and presentation.

Compare this with what was coming to be CMS, in which a fetish of theory development and the use of novel methodologies was becoming characteristic of journals such as *Organization* and *Culture and Organization*. Almost exclusively based in business schools, the development of interactionist, phenomenological and philosophically inclined work took 'the organization' as both a site for micro-social analysis of questions of identity, narrative and culture, but it also problematized the idea of 'organizing' and 'managing' itself. Resistance to the very notion of there being rigid structures at all provides a metaphorical expansion of many arguments. We see ideas about language, method, thought, autonomy, authority and so on being rethought in terms of the overarching idea of organization and management as verbs, or even disorganization as a tactic and/or virtue itself. This did not exclude the possibility of empirical evidence, but instead privileged the theoretical as the site for critical work. It is not necessarily the structures of the world which should be the springboard for concern, but structures of thought—the habitual, common sense, the taken for granted. Rather like the cultural studies which grew from sociology in the 1970s, the impetus for a piece of work was to discover resistance and power, often using qualitative accounts and lashings of theoretical decoration.

There is, of course, no one meaning of the word 'critical'. It depends entirely on context, because what might be critical in a business school might not be critical in a sociology department, and what might be critical in France might not be critical in the UK. That being said, the business school,

CMS in the United Kingdom 199

as a context for dissent, has one key feature. This is a general tendency to be doing research *for* management rather than *on* management, usually because its students have aspirations to become managers, and the funders of management research tend to expect 'useful' knowledge. It seems to me that in the UK, its critical inhabitants have understood this setup in two quite different ways. One is to say that there is nothing wrong with a social science of business and management as such, but that it needs to be aimed at the problems of the majority, not the minority who hold power. The second is to suggest that the problem is the very idea of teaching a science of control and hence to question foundational assumptions about knowledge and representation. Both of these can reasonably be called critical. The first begins with evidence, by documenting the actually existing cruelties and inequalities of capitalism, patriarchy and imperialism. This is a politics of truth in which the froth of ideology is contrasted with an account of what the world is 'really' like. The second begins with epistemology, insisting that the prison begins in the mind and that there is a politics to the act of representation. The critical edge here then comes with an attempt to think and write differently, to open new possibilities for action and organizing which are constrained by a lack of imagination.

This, it seems to me, is the divide which structures critical work in UK business schools at the present time. The former, with its roots in IR and industrial sociology, demands a balanced social science from the business school and insistently reminds us that knowledge might set us free. The latter, the CMS that in part developed from sociology's immersion in the counter culture of the late 1960s, requires a rethinking of the very idea of the university itself and claims that knowledge is always power. Both are marginal to the business school, but apart from a shared sense of distaste for the dean, they share little else.

'MANAGEMENT STUDIES'?

The story I have told about UK CMS is one that has relied on a line up which pitches 'macro' against 'micro', 'structure' against 'agency', a 50-year 'turf war' (Roberts, 2003, p. 36) between industrial relations and sociology and a migration from sociology to the business schools. It is also one which has involved the definition of terms as belonging to one side rather than another—'work', 'employment', 'industry' versus 'organization' and 'management'. It would be easy enough to play up the differences here, but what I want to do in this last section is to say something about similarities and hence try to comment on the future prospects for critical work on organizations, work and employment in the UK. It seems to me that there are threats to this sort of work as a whole which should far outweigh factional differences.

One of the features of the arrangement which has provided both 'sides' with their intellectual energy over the past 30 years has been that industrial

200 Martin Parker

relations, industrial sociology and critical social science are not indigenous to the business school. In fact, very little is, simply because this is such a recent settlement in intellectual and institutional terms in the UK. It is only over the last four decades that the business school has emerged in its modern mass form, well within the span of a single academic career. No wonder then that there are many inhabitants who don't feel quite at home—whether they be from economics, mathematics, psychology or wherever. This sense of estrangement was intensified for those who moved from sociology—or even philosophy, history and cultural studies—simply because these were domains which had been hugely influenced by the counterculture of the '60s and '70s. It was unsurprising that they then built their own colony on new shores.

Nowadays, UK business schools have become substantial institutions in their own right and located in a global labour market for English-speaking students and staff. For those who can teach the 'people and organizations' modules, this makes for a very comfortable situation, because in most institutions there are more jobs in this area of the business school than in the whole of the sociology department. In terms of CMS, certain schools, superstar professors, journals, conferences, textbooks and so on have made what once seemed 'outsider' into something rather insider. The inaugural 1992 volume has a second companion, there is a reader, a handbook, a key concepts book, a four-volume set of readings and even a 'classics' collection (Alvesson and Willmott, 2003; Grey and Willmott, 2005; Alvesson et al., 2009; Tadajewski et al., 2011; Alvesson and Willmott, 2011; Alvesson, 2011), and this is not to mention books on 'critical' research methods and so on. Importantly for this chapter, these books are overwhelmingly UK centred. For example, 34 of the 44 contributors to the Oxford handbook are either working in the UK, from the UK or did their PhDs in the UK. Yet, as is obvious, there are risks in such 'success', in CMS reaching for its pipe and slippers, and it seems very necessary to think hard about the conditions for critical work, whether that be IR, industrial sociology or CMS itself. This is particularly important at the time of this writing, when it seems that the effective privatization of UK universities is making them even more attentive to the markets that they sell into and hence even less enthusiastic about alienating possible sources of revenue and managing research to targets established by lists which are based on measures of central tendency (Parker, 2014).

Given these contexts, can CMS survive in the UK? Or rather, can a critical CMS survive, since the label now appears to mean increasingly little in substantive terms as it gets attached to more and more product? It seems to me that criticism, in the most general sense of a questioning of the value of a particular practice seems most likely to come from outside the institution that houses that practice. When words such as 'co-optation' or 'recuperation' are being used, they reflect that sense of a losing of a dissenting status and the taking on of the values associated with the centres of power. This doesn't mean that criticism can't come from within an institution, merely

CMS in the United Kingdom 201

that it is less likely to do so. One of the further implications here is that it is in the early years of institutional formation that we might expect to find more heterodoxy, as a diverse range of interests and forms of understanding are being brought together. This is a general description of the early years of the business school in the UK, as it pulled a diverse range of disciplines together in order to produce a new settlement. Intellectual baggage from elsewhere was being unpacked in a new place, and for some this was a matter of an orientation to social scientific knowledge in general. If you had been trained in a form of industrial relations which predated the business school by half a century, and which had been reshaped by Marxism since the 1970s, then the business school presented itself as predictably managerial. If you had been trained in a countercultural sociology or social science which pitched action against structure, and critique against orthodoxy, then the business school looked very much like an example of the ideological state apparatus or working for the man. No doubt the historical accounts that might be produced by someone who works in critical accounting, or critical marketing, will be different here, even within the UK, but I suspect that they will share that sense of being, at least initially, a stranger in a strange land.

The threats to critical understandings are rarely direct in the sense of a silver-haired patriarchal dean telling someone what they should do, though they can be like this (Parker, 2014). It's more a matter of a gradual redescription of aims and a solidification of assumptions. This might involve a tendency to neglect the importance of a broad understanding of the politics and experience of working life, for students, teachers and researchers. Categories such as class, ethnicity, sexuality and gender are likely to get subsumed within ideas about diversity and effective management. Questions about the state, its relationship to corporate capitalism, inequality, the relentless drive to growth, alternative organization and so on are likely to disappear from view. For those interested in organizations and management, the slippage is one which often moves towards the unitarist social psychology which reproduces the complaint made by Flanders and Clegg concerning the human relations school in the 1950s. Under the rather US label of organizational *behaviour*, questions of leadership, change, culture and structure are approached as if there were no politics to knowledge about who controls resources and gets rewards. Even when pluralist in its assumptions, and now described as organization *studies*, a great deal of work on identity, narrative, discourse and so on can be understood in this way and certainly is by many industrial sociologists and IR academics. It does seem to me that much of what is now described as CMS ends up as a reinvention of 1960s interactionism but rarely with the same methodological rigour or conceptual innovation. For IR itself, the slide into the business school has very often meant that studies of trade unions and collective bargaining have gradually become redescribed as personnel and HRM. Departments have changed their names, and a hand wringing humanist 'critical' HRM has emerged which intellectually and politically converges with the discursive version of CMS.

202 Martin Parker

Now as I have already acknowledged, there is no transcendental critical position, which is perhaps just why the disputes over who can own and use such a label and what it might mean are so bitter. So when Rowlinson and Hassard (both professors in UK business schools) ruminate on the problems with the 'critters' (a US term for CMS academics) and characterize them as 'disaffected academic drifters' (2011), it is hard not to imagine that they are describing themselves too. Since this chapter is concerned with CMS in the UK, then it must also articulate their and my critical positions as having some relation to local history, institutions and language. The latter needs to be stressed here, since one of the key reasons for the expansion of the UK business school was that we happen to speak the same language as the US. A useful coincidence, in terms of persuading students and staff to come to this small wet island. That being said, and as I hope this chapter has shown, the rapid and recent congealing of the UK business school has also involved bringing intellectual assumptions from other places, and I think it is precisely this partial sense of 'self-estrangement' which has provided the impetus for so much work within it (Fay, 1987, p. 10). Whether industrial relations, industrial sociology or the post 1970s sociologies of action and language, the key issue is that something was imported which didn't fit with the increasingly imperial and strident rhetoric which surrounded the rise of managerialism. This is in part because these aliens use forms of legitimacy which were developed in other places and can hence recall a different way of thinking. But if we were to look at the next 50 years of the business school, can we imagine such a vibrant range of 'not-management' thought? Can the business school develop its own immanent critique?

After noting that not all academic work in business schools is necessarily managerial, Halford and Strangleman, two British sociologists who are interested in organizations, suggest:

> Nonetheless, sociologists should ask what knowledge is produced under these conditions and what type of sociologist is produced in such circumstances. (. . .) The danger here is that the sociological imagination that exists in business schools is almost bound to be diluted through generational shifts, organizational structural development, and recognition and reward strategies. If we look to the business schools to produce future generations of sociologists of work then we would be complacent to expect a set of people interested in, and with a commitment to, a wider sociology'.
>
> (2009, p. 819)

Halford and Strangleman know that we can't go back to a golden age and must acknowledge fragmentation and the necessity of interdisciplinarity, but at the same time, insist that we mustn't allow 'the collapse of disciplines into indistinctiveness' (*op cit*: 821). They celebrate 'a strong sense of discipline'

CMS in the United Kingdom 203

and insist that 'real interdisciplinary research and writing comes best from those secure in their own field' (*op cit*: 822).

There is a really important insight here, but I don't agree with Halford and Strangleman that there is something particularly special about sociology as such. There isn't, and we should assume that any imperialistic or nostalgic claim about any form of disciplinarity should be treated with suspicion. But what Halford and Strangleman have also implicitly suggested here is that critical work comes from an awareness of not being at home, not being settled into particular intellectual assumptions and that suggests that any institution that becomes sclerotic, and which begins to produce inhabitants who have never been anywhere else, is in danger of losing the possibility of critical reflection. For myself, I doubt whether CMS can stay very critical, in part because it has institutionalized so effectively in the last quarter of a century. It runs the danger, in the UK, of becoming mere Management Studies, indistinguishable from the orthodoxy of Andreski's 'streamlined sorcerers' in anything other than rhetorical terms. In the places I have worked, and I remind you again that this is my story, there is nothing inherently critical in writing about language, process, narrative, identity, discourse, subjectivity and associated terms. This is particularly true in a context where an academic career can be made rapidly by publishing work which just reminds us that meaning is complicated and identity is fragmented. As Olivia says in Shakespeare's *Twelfth Night*, 'There is no slander in an allowed fool'. If criticism is not a little bit dangerous to the people who voice it, if it does not bring the sweaty-palmed fear of consequences (Foucault, 2001), then it is unclear just who might be offended by it. In that sense, CMS might now be rather common in the UK, but that doesn't mean that it is always very critical.

NOTES

1. Parts of this chapter are shamelessly ripped off from my 'Between Sociology and the B School: Critical Studies of Organization, Work and Employment in the UK' in the *Sociological Review* (2015) with no apologies to the author. Thanks to the editors of this volume for their comments on an earlier draft of the chapter. Thanks to the Sex Pistols for the title.
2. A term, which includes Northern Ireland, unlike Britain, which doesn't.
3. Thanks to Pippa Carter, Norman Jackson and Deborah Kerfoot for information on SCOS and GWO.
4. A conference that, at the time of this writing, has only been held outside England once since then.

REFERENCES

Alvesson, M. (Ed.) (2011). *Classics in Critical Management Studies*. Cheltenham, UK: Edward Elgar.

204 Martin Parker

Alvesson, M., Bridgman, T. and Willmott, H. (Eds.) (2009). *The Oxford Handbook of Critical Management Studies*. Oxford: Oxford University Press.

Alvesson, M. and Willmott, H. (Eds.) (1992). *Critical Management Studies*. London: Sage.

Alvesson, M, and Willmott, H. (Eds.) (2003). *Studying Management Critically*. London: Sage.

Alvesson, M. and Willmott, H. (Eds.) (2011). *Critical Management Studies. Four Volume Set*. London: Sage.

Andreski, S. (1972). *Social Sciences as Sorcery*. London: André Deutsch.

Braverman, H. (1974). *Labor and Monopoly Capital*. New York: Monthly Review Press.

Bullock, A. and Stallybrass, O. (1977). *The Fontana Dictionary of Modern Thought*. London: Fontana.

Burrell, G. and Morgan, G. (1979). *Sociological Paradigms and Organisational Analysis*. London: Heinemann.

Clegg, S. and Dunkerley, D. (1980). *Organisation, Class and Control*. London: Routledge and Kegan Paul.

Colfax, J. and Roach, J. (Eds.) (1971). *Radical Sociology*. New York: Basic Books.

Durkheim, E. (1895/1982). *The Rules of Sociological Method*. Basingstoke: Macmillan.

Fay, B. (1987). *Critical Social Science*. Ithaca, NY: Cornell University Press.

Foucault, M. (2001). *Fearless Speech*. Los Angeles: Semiotext(e).

Fox, A. (1974). *Beyond Contract: Work, Power and Trust Relations*. London: Faber and Faber.

Fuller, A. (1996). Producing Radical Scholarship: The Radical Sociology Movement, 1967–1975, *Sociological Imagination*, 33(1). Retrieved from http://comm-org. wisc.edu/si/fuller.htm, accessed 17/1/12

Grey, C. and Willmott, H. (Eds.) (2005). *Critical Management Studies: A Reader*. Oxford: Oxford University Press.

Halford, S. and Strangleman, T. (2009). In Search of the Sociology of Work: Past, Present and Future. *Sociology*, 43(5): 811–828.

Marcuse, H. (1964). *One Dimensional Man*. London: Routledge and Kegan Paul.

Parker, M. (1999). Capitalism, Subjectivity and Ethics: Debating Labour Process Analysis. *Organization Studies*, 20(1): 25–45.

Parker, M. (2014). University, Ltd: Changing a Business School. *Organization*, 21(2): 281–292.

Parker, M. (2015). Between Sociology and the B School: Critical Studies of Organization, Work and Employment in the UK. *Sociological Review*, 63/1: 162–180.

Parker, M. and Thomas, R. (2011). What Is a Critical Journal? *Organization* [1350–5084], 18(4): 419–427.

Roberts, I. (2003). Sociology and Industrial Relations. In P. Ackers and A. Wilkinson (Eds.), *Understanding Work and Employment: Industrial Relations in Transition*, 32–42. Oxford: Oxford University Press.

Rose, M. (1978). *Industrial Behaviour*. Harmondsworth: Penguin.

Rowlinson, M. and Hassard, J. (2011). How Come the Critters Came to be Teaching in Business Schools? Contradictions in the Institutionalisation of Critical Management Studies. *Organization*, 18(5): 673–689.

Silverman, D. (1970). *The Theory of Organizations*. London: Heinemann.

Silverman, D. (1994). On Throwing Away Ladders: Re-Writing the Theory of. In J. Hassard and M. Parker (Eds.), *Towards a New Theory of Organizations*, 1–23. London: Routledge.

Tadajewski, M., Maclaren, P., Parsons, L. and Parker, M. (Eds.) (2011). *Key Concepts in Critical Management Studies*. London: Sage.

Thompson, P. (2004). A critical reflection on Critical Management. In S. Fleetwood and S. Ackroyd (Eds.), *Critical Realist Applications in Organization and Management Studies*, 54–70. London: Routledge.

Thompson, P. and Smith, C. (2009). Labour Power and Labour Process: Contesting the Marginality of the Sociology of Work. *Sociology*, 43(5): 913–930.

Thompson, P., Smith, C. and Ackroyd, S. (2000). If Ethics is the Answer, You Are Asking the Wrong Questions: A Reply to Martin Parker. *Organisation Studies*, 21(6): 1149–1158.

Wood, S. and Kelly, J. (1978). Towards a Critical Management Science. *Journal of Management Studies*, 15(1): 1–24.

14 Galumphing and Critical Management Studies
Perspective and Paradox from the United States

Gordon E. Dehler and M. Ann Welsh

> The study of complex organizations has been guided by a succession of rational and functional theories and by positivist methodology. . . . the sociology of organizations has failed to develop a critical posture.
>
> —J Kenneth Benson (1977)

> Yet, because it takes work to create order within play, play always (subliminally) reminds us that the world is fundamentally chaotic and that my meaning within this chaos is always provisional and artificial.
>
> —Donncha Kavanagh (2009)

BY WAY OF INTRODUCTION

In the midst of writing this chapter, during dinner with a colleague (and occasional co-author) who is an active and prolific researcher, the "what are you working on now?" conversation arose. When we mentioned writing a chapter on the state of Critical Management Studies in the US, the response was wry, terse and on point, "Well, that will be a short chapter"! Developing an account of Critical Management Studies (CMS) from a US-based perspective presents a daunting, yet intriguing challenge. It would be so much simpler and more straightforward to provide insights through European eyes, especially British (but see Parker, this volume)! And at this early point, we pause to submit an emphatic caveat: while we are US scholars in origin and training, our intent is absolutely *not to represent* the many excellent critical North American scholars within the ideas, interpretations and conclusions we present in this chapter. In true critical fashion, we seek to be transparent from the outset in suggesting that our insights are heavily biased by context: our own doctoral training, the evolution of our careers, our involvement in the CMS project over more than 15 years and, more crucially, our own interpretations of the emerging domain as it unfolds. That is, we intend the comments that follow to serve not as a definitive summary, but as an attempt to advance dialogue among the many knowledgeable and insightful scholars who have been working in this area—American and international.

EARLY ROOTS

It may seem odd to begin a discussion of Critical Management Studies with the late American icon Chris Argyris. Yet in acknowledging his significant contribution to the realm of management and organization studies, we take special note of his critical perspective. His early work (1957) represents a first textbook on the specific topic of organizational behavior: "A new behavioral science 'field' is developing which focuses on understanding human behavior in ongoing organizations. We may call it *'organizational behavior'*" (p. 229). He contends that the

> increasing acceptance and use of the behavioral sciences as integral parts of the teaching and research curricula (in schools of engineering, business, and public administration) and the realization of the importance of understanding the *why* of human behavior in organizations represent a significant trend in the field of organization and administration. (p. *ix*)

But in the nucleus of this groundbreaking treatise, Argyris adopts a distinctly critical stance. His explicit argument is built around the fundamental disconnect between the way organizations are managed and how workers interpret their experience in those organizations. In essence, his central thesis is to expose organizations as sites of worker alienation. Chris Argyris and "critical" in the same spotlight—imagine that!

The comments that follow are organized in this way. After an overview of our definition of CMS, the beginning of the CMS movement in the US is briefly summarized. This humble start is thin, albeit meaningful. The context within which CMS operates is then explored, drawing comparisons largely with the UK, which we see as the birthplace of CMS. In particular, we strive to capture how differences between the nature of academic work in the US and the UK impacts the evolution of CMS in each context. We invoke the anthropological notion of *galumphing* (Miller, 1973) as a mechanism for assessing the distinctly different patterns of research, writing and publishing within the CMS domain characterizing the two scholarly communities. Finally, to promote dialogue on the future of CMS in a US academic context, we examine what we describe as the critical management paradox.

CRITICAL MANAGEMENT STUDIES: A FOUNDATION

As with most concepts in management studies, definitions and interpretations typically are contested, subject to debate and more accurately characterized as problematic. Thus in the spirit of clarification, the understanding of CMS adopted here is guided by Fournier and Grey's (2000) notion that critique follows practice. So first we see CMS as a *form of analysis* that "questions the authority and relevance of mainstream thinking and practice" (Alvesson

208 Gordon E. Dehler and M. Ann Welsh

et al., 2009, p. 1). That is to say, CMS as a movement is not intended as a prescriptive recipe to inform management technique, but rather to promote processes that remedy inequality, authoritarianism and systemic exploitation in organizations, i.e., responsive. Second, we see CMS's role as a *catalyst for debate* on issues central to understanding management and organizations. Here the "focus is 'management' not as a group or as a function, but as a pervasive institution that is entrenched within capitalist economic formations. Its concern is with the study *of*, and sometimes *against*, management rather than with the development of techniques or legitimations *for* management" (Alvesson et al., 2009, p. 1).

The third role of CMS is to *foster social change and emancipation*. Parallel with the foundations of critical theory (see Brookfield, 2005), a key purpose of critique in the CMS movement is to challenge an inherently unequal status quo with the intent of radical (or discontinuous) transformation. Again, turning to the CMS Division's own words, the movement is "driven by a shared desire to change this situation, we aim in our research, teaching, and practice to develop critical interpretations of management and society and to generate radical alternatives". Finally, the CMS movement adopts an expressly *anti-positivist bias*. An important tenet of CMS is that knowledge is contextual and transient, in essence, problematic. Although positivism "is not a systematically elaborated doctrine", it is typically referred to as "a style of thought that is informed by certain assumptions about the nature of knowledge"—primarily "the claim that *valid knowledge can only be established by reference to that which is manifested in experience*" (Carr and Kemmis, 1986, p. 61). By implication, this implies that value judgments that cannot be founded on empirical knowledge, cannot meet the standard of "valid knowledge" (p. 62). From the standpoint of CMS, *no* knowledge is value neutral; in other words, *all* knowledge is embedded in values.

Even a quarter century ago, Carr and Kemmis (1986, pp. 71–79) claimed that the appeal of positivism has subsided and provide a substantive argument to support their stance. Most would argue, however, that while there have been inroads by nonpositivist approaches, the Academy of Management journals remain an unabashedly stalwart proponent of positivism in spirit if not substance. One of the latest initiatives in the US, toward evidence-based management (e.g., Rousseau, 2006), represents a further attempt to embed positivism as the dominant (exclusive?) approach to management studies. It is noteworthy that the most strident criticisms of evidence-based management emanate from the UK (e.g., Learmonth, 2006, 2008; Learmonth and Harding, 2006; Morrell, 2008). CMS, then, simply does not fit within the dominant paradigm of Kuhn's view of "normal science". Instead, "knowledge is not, as positivism suggests, the objective, universal and value-neutral product of the 'disinterested' researcher. Rather, it is subjective, context bound, normative, and in an important sense, always political" (Carr and Kemmis, 1986, p. 73).

Creating such definitions is always fraught with angst—and no claim is made that the aforementioned represents *the* definition of CMS (other

Galumphing and Critical Management 209

chapters in this volume make this clear.) But these components seem consistent with the CMS literature and meet the needs of the ideas being discussed in this chapter. Next, we turn to the evolution of the critical movement in the US. A diagram is employed to locate some American scholars recognized for their contributions to the critical management domain as an attempt to capture the CMS presence in the US.

ON BEING CRITICAL: CRITICAL BEINGS IN AMERICA

Our aim in the following observations is to provide an abbreviated account of the evolution of CMS in the US. To state the obvious, CMS as an academic domain is not as developed in the US as internationally, particularly in the UK. For example, of the Academy of Management CMS Division's 719 members, only one-third (238) are from the US (Mir, 2015). Of the contributors to the *Oxford Handbook of Critical Management Studies* (Alvesson, et al., 2009), only three are US-based (or 15per cent of 44 authors and editors). And in Alvesson's (2011) *Classics in Critical Management Studies*, a similar one-third (13 of 37) of the authors are from the US. Yet, despite the relative dearth of CMS work conducted by US scholars, it is imperative to point out that CMS does have origins as well as a presence in American scholarship—but in a way that locates those scholars among a more global than domestic set of collaborators. In other words, those we consider our "closest CMS colleagues" are more likely to conduct their scholarship in British, Australian, New Zealand, European or other global institutions rather than the US.

As noted in the earlier discussion, the history of US-based critical scholarship within business schools is thin, at best. It may be that the nature of critique itself poses the most serious dilemma, "being oppositional, inherently involves antagonism and therefore threat, danger and risk. For critique to act as critique, it must have the force to 'go against', shock, shake, provoke" (Fournier and Smith, 2012, p. 467). Further,

> critique cannot be conveyed by speech that is 'free' or gratuitous, that carries no consequences for the speaker. Rather it requires some personal engagement and sacrifice. In other words, critique has to come at a cost to those who make it. It cannot be free.
>
> (p. 268)

Citing Jack (2004), Fournier and Smith (2012, p. 468) contend that "CMS academics are probably not prepared to engage in fearless speech because of the potentially adverse material consequences that would follow".

Research on the impact of publications in *Organization Studies* by Battilana et al. (2010) offers insight on this point. (*OS*, published by EGOS/ the European Group for Organization Studies, has editors-in-chief from the Netherlands and UK, 29 senior editors [one from the US], and its editorial

210　*Gordon E. Dehler and M. Ann Welsh*

office in Greece [in 2015].) As might be expected, they found American scholars tend to publish in US outlets and British scholars in UK outlets, substantially reducing the potential for adverse consequences. Further, Battilana et al. note that US scholars publishing in OS are likely to be tenured and well known within their research stream (2010, p. 708). Their examination of citation patterns showed that US researchers were likely to cite US scholars publishing in OS. Similarly, UK scholars cite UK scholars publishing in Academy journals. This leads to an interesting and troubling result—the creation of an academic divide as the work of US scholars published in UK outlets was imported back into the US and the work of UK scholars publishing in US outlets was imported into the UK. What appears as boundary spanning is more accurately characterized as a self-referential reinforcement of critical ideas. Also troubling was the "Americanization" of international business school research—as reflected in the increasing emphasis on academic publication being grounded in the US. (The top 33 journals in the ABS [Association of Business Schools] *Academic Journal Guide 2015* are US based.) There are no American "critical" journals; the journals that publish the majority of critical work are European (see Parker and Thomas, 2011; Cunliffe and Sadler-Smith, 2015). While we know "where" critical scholarship tends to be published, we now address the question of *who* among American scholars engages in critical research.

Since it would involve a Herculean task to acknowledge every US academic active in the critical movement, we attempt to position the work of some exemplary scholars known for their contributions to the CMS literature to provide readers with context (and grist for debate). We begin, however, with a few pre-1992 contributors to the CMS movement (including Chris Argyris at the outset of this chapter). Ken Benson (1977, 1983a, 1983b) is frequently identified as an early exemplar of a critical viewpoint, employing "dialectical analysis" to contest the dominance of established positivist perspectives. (Professor Benson was an early mentor and dissertation committee member for one of this chapter's co-authors.) These groundbreaking ideas evolved from psychology and sociology, as this time frame precedes, the fully fledged emergence of the field of management studies. The first curricula in organizational behavior emerged in the early to mid-1970s, as it relocated theories from psychology, social psychology, sociology, industrial/organizational psychology and early management writings into the context of organizations. Benson's (1977) groundbreaking work in *ASQ*, which advanced his early-1970s conference presentations, took aim at the already prevalent hegemony of rationalist perspectives and the accompanying positivist methodologies. He highlighted the "uncritical acceptance of the conceptions of organizational structure" based on "a succession of rational and functional theories" (p. 1). Thus "the sociology of organizations has failed to develop a critical posture" (p. 1). He later (1983a, p. 346) concluded, "I found the prevailing functional and rational approaches to the field unsatisfactory . . ."

Galumphing and Critical Management 211

In the same vein, Steffy and Grimes (1986) articulated a critical approach to organization science, which at its core entailed a discussion of ontology, epistemology and methodology from the perspective of critical theory. While they described the elements of a critical theoretic approach to analyzing organizations, the tone was highly deferential to the Academy; the treatment was sanitized and did not represent a challenge to the legitimation of management practice. While both of these articles were visible and significant (in *ASQ* and *AMR* respectively), we note that Benson is a sociologist, *ASQ* is a true interdisciplinary journal and the latter piece addresses little beyond philosophies of organization science that would now relate to central elements of CMS—albeit in a manner designed to be palatable to Academy readership. Finally, a brief *AMR* article by the late Peter Frost (1980) raised the topics of alienation and justice, bringing us full circle to Argyris.

Thematic elements of criticality converged when the *Academy of Management Review* published the special theory forum "New Intellectual Currents" (Smircich et al., 1992). In the initial call for papers, the editors' aspirations were to initiate conversation between new approaches and conventional ones. At the end of the project (which was subject to the traditional review process of *AMR*), they freely acknowledged how thoroughly modern the endeavor turned out to be. Yet they retained the hope that papers in the forum, representing a variety of approaches including neo-Marxism, critical theory, post-structuralism, feminism, Foucauldian, British Cultural Studies and postmodern aesthetic analysis would stimulate dialogue and encourage greater reflexivity by management researchers. Alas, the most tangible source of influence appears on the CMS Division's website where the question "Where can Critical Management Studies be published?" is answered by a journal list headed by the *Academy of Management Review*! From a CMS perspective, however, the most influential work to appear in that special issue turned out to be by Alvesson and Willmott, which is now considered the origin of the CMS domain.

Following Alvesson and Willmott's (1992) article, the 1990s saw the gradual emergence of contributions by American scholars, such as Jermier and Nord (e.g., Jermier et al., 1994; Jermier, 1998). But, while these could be considered "critical" in substance, in practice their work mostly revolves around the British notion of labour process theory, especially the concepts of control and resistance—topics of greater salience in the UK than the US (hence the noteworthy inclusion of a British co-editor in the 1994 volume). Our point in this brief account is to argue that, while these contributions serve as a meaningful foundation to what was to become critical approaches to organizations, they are not representative of what ultimately emerged as *Critical Management Studies*.

In order to render a picture of critical work in the US since 1992, we adapt a research categorization schema from Alvesson and Deetz (2000), which aids in making sense of US critical theorists' contributions. Simply, their schema involves two dimensions: the extent of consensual discourse (consensus vs. dissensus) and the locating source of research focus (local/ emergent vs. elite/a priori). When combined, these two dimensions provide descriptions of four distinct research types: normative, interpretive, critical and dialogic. Both normative and interpretive research streams are conceived within a consensus discourse, share an instrumental goal of improving performance and are thoroughly non-critical. Figure 14.1 illustrates the Alvesson and Deetz (2000) framework.

As Fournier and Grey noted, "there is no single way of demarcating the unitary 'critical' position from the non-critical" (2000, p. 16). Instead, the

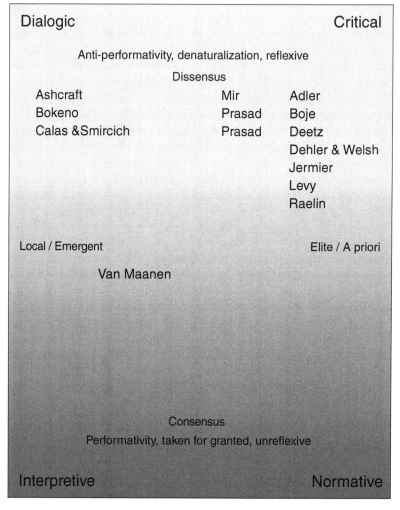

Figure 14.1 A Mapping of Exemplar Critical Scholars onto the Alvesson and Deetz (2000) Framework

Galumphing and Critical Management 213

boundaries are framed by "the kinds of work referenced by authors"; "there is no ultimate way of tracing boundaries between critical and non-critical work" (p. 17). Both critical and dialogic research operate from a dissensus discourse, viewing the organization as a political site full of suppressed conflict. The goal of critical research is to both demonstrate and critique "forms of domination, asymmetry, and distorted communication" (Alvesson and Deetz, 2000, p. 35). The underlying assumption is that through such critique, the conflicts between different interests can be "resolved with fairness and justice" (p. 35) through an active political agenda. Dialogic studies focus on the fragmentation and potential disunity in discourse and, in common with critical theorists, are concerned with issues of domination and asymmetry. In dialogic studies, language is a system of distinctions central to the social construction process, reality is understood to be partial and one-sided and the source of domination and asymmetry is situational and mobile. The intention of dialogic research is to uncover suppressed conflicts and enhance local forms of resistance. While the early work by Benson, Jermier and Steffy and Grimes falls within the critical category, the work of critical theorists such as Cunliffe and Smircich and Calas fall in the dialogic quadrant. Other exemplary scholars work in a variety of areas, among them labour process theory, anti-colonialism, post-structuralism and critical management education, and are positioned as well to convey their place in the CMS movement. Yet this work has yet to acquire sufficient critical mass within business schools to form a network of scholars or stand on its own as a legitimate scholarly domain in the US.

GALUMPHING: CRITICAL MANAGEMENT IN PLAY

While the US and UK shared some important sociopolitical features growing out of the 1990s' embrace of neo-liberalism, CMS advanced faster within the UK (Fournier and Grey, 2000). The slower progress in the US reflects contextual differences arising from the different patterns of the birth and growth of business schools in the US and the UK. In the US, business schools were established in the early twentieth century by proponents of scientific management (often trained as industrial engineers and/or mathematicians) and later were thoroughly embedded in the post-WWII positivist orthodoxy around the nature and value of scientific approaches. In contrast, many UK management scholars were less wedded to positivist approaches as a consequence of its social science roots. These roots supported a "ready-made critical tradition", albeit from diverse perspectives (Fournier and Grey, 2000, p. 14). Not so in the US, where management was considered a science, a "real" discipline, i.e., one whose theories/models/prescriptions would be worthy of *application*. (This trend continues today, as noted, in the emerging popularity of evidence-based management.) The designation as an applied science reinforces the purpose and the status of management studies within US universities (discussed further later in the chapter).

214   *Gordon E. Dehler and M. Ann Welsh*

Congruent with Fournier and Grey's account of the origins of management studies in each country, and building on their argument, we would suggest that it is the values about the purpose and conduct of research that emerged within the two work contexts that accounts for the more rapid advance of CMS in the UK. The work of scholarship occurs in both contexts, but the work proceeds differentially as its means and ends are connected differently. These differences are particularly relevant to explaining discrepancies in the development of CMS between the two countries.

In searching for an organizing framework for our discussion of these differences in work contexts, we were drawn to anthropologist Stephen Miller's (1973) notion of *galumphing*. Miller sought to explain the concept of play and used the term galumphing to describe the behavior of gorillas at play (primate play was a hot topic for anthropologists in the 1960s–1970s). The difference between play and not-play, according to Miller, could be observed by examining the form and pattern of the gorillas' movements. In "not-play" situations, ones where survival is the focus, the gorillas moved in ways that were efficient and purposive. In "play" situations, their movements were exaggerated, uneconomic and cumbersome—galumphing.

Galumphing behavior was both adaptive and flexible, including lots of repetition and reordering. Play was organic, exhibiting a great range of behaviors (means), the play process interesting in itself. Participation in play was a-hierarchical. While ends exist in play, they don't determine means. This autonomy in means enables new or novel behavior. In contrast, non-play gorilla behaviors were structured, with a clear social hierarchy, exhibited agreed upon rules and sanctions for rule violation. Participants in not-play are in a learning or task mode where activities are clearly linked to and controlled by goals. Activities are programmed and agreed upon by participants, thus the ends determine means.

To summarize, we are suggesting that the differences in origin between the UK and US academies impacted and shaped the work contexts that emerged, creating different signaling about the form and patterns of scholarship. Following Miller's scheme, we would argue that CMS advanced more quickly and broadly in the UK because messages about scholarship were akin to the messages about play, and because UK management scholars represent a greater breadth of intellectual traditions, their treatments of CMS similarly demonstrate greater breadth in ontology and methodology. In the US, scholarship was not-play, influenced by strict rules, clear means-ends relationships and limited variation—the positivist orthodoxy.

What is it about play that stimulated work in Critical Management Studies? To be critical requires questioning assumptions: efficiency as the "end" (anti-performativity), explicit analysis of power relations (denaturalization) and concern with emancipation (reflexivity) (Reynolds, 1997; Fournier and Grey, 2000). Each of these attributes is easier when galumphing because of the loose connection between means and ends when "in play". The diverse social science foundations of critical management in the UK are mirrored by

Galumphing and Critical Management 215

diverse approaches in how to be critical. This promotes a more a-hierarchical nature within the UK community of critical scholars whose embrace of a variety of approaches indicates greater scholarly autonomy, a key element necessary to the diffusion of CMS. Critical Management Studies in the UK makes no claims regarding actual change in practice—the means are largely disconnected from the ends. The process of critique is of interest by itself, "primarily, an academic phenomenon"—not because it is tightly coupled to organizational practice (Fournier and Grey, 2000, p. 12).

Just like Miller's gorillas focused on survival, research in the US is "not-play". As noted earlier, management studies is considered an applied (as opposed to basic) research field. The "applied" designation is significant as it amplifies the need to be "scientific" in approach. The underlying assumption is that following best methodological practice will cause our insights to be perceived as objective and useful (both inside the domain of management and the hierarchy of the American university). Yet, as Alvesson and Deetz observed, the abundance of normative research around issues such as structure, culture, motivation or leadership has not yielded empirically well-supported theories with expanded explanatory and predictive capacity (2000, p. 50; Petriglieri, 2015). But instead of adopting a different (e.g., critical) approach to research, management "scientists" continue to produce more similarly designed research. The consequence of this rule-bound, problem-solving, sanction-laden culture of scholarship is a reduction in the adaptive capacity to experiment with variation.

Scholarship in the US displays a tight connection between means (positivist orthodoxy) and ends (efficiency, maximizing shareholder wealth, i.e., performativity). Even as a broader set of methodologies (neo-positivist or neo-empiricist) are employed, the ontology of management studies in the US remains largely unchallenged and, consequently, unchanged. Socialization around the importance of ends and the primacy of positivist approaches begins with doctoral training (a telling terminology). A UK scholar we know characterizes doctoral education in the UK as the "learned" PhD in contrast to the US version characterized as a "taught" PhD. (Conditions in the current political-economic environment may be causing this to change.) Presumably, when guiding one's own course of study, it is easier to question assumptions and engage reflexively and critically with concepts and contexts. In our "taught" PhD, communications about the purposeful (instrumental) nature of scholarship to improve practice are unambiguous.

Further, the job market for career academics is increasingly precarious in the US. Over the past three decades, the preponderance of tenure-track academic positions has dissipated. Bradley (2004) reported that in 1969 only 3.3 per cent of faculty appointments were off the tenure track. By the 1990s, this had increased to over half, and recent data indicate only 25 per cent of faculty appointments are full-time, tenure-track positions. She raises more serious concerns surrounding traditional issues such as academic freedom and governance in a "sweatshop university". Under more dire conditions

216   *Gordon E. Dehler and M. Ann Welsh*

of declining public funding for post-secondary education in the US, university budgetary pressures have squeezed permanent faculty lines severely with provosts and deans replacing them with low-pay contingent faculty (adjuncts, teaching-only faculty). (This trend is spreading to the UK as well.)

Reinforcing orthodoxy is the need to place publications within a restricted set of "A" journals for a chance at career success. Part of the AACSB International accreditation process requires faculties to agree to a ranking of publications that will be used to assess faculty and programmatic quality. Like the gorilla that can only engage in play in the absence of conflicting motivations (i.e., no threats to survival), a US scholar interested in CMS is almost necessarily conflicted. Two examples are suggestive of this point.

When the fledgling OMT LISTSERV published the call for papers on the run-up to the First International Critical Management Studies Conference in 1999, one American academic's memorable response proposed that anyone who developed a submission would, in essence, be writing their last paper as an academic! Indeed, his submission title included "How *Not* to Get Tenure in One Easy Publication" and went on to express the pessimistic prediction that it is "unlikely" that CMS would gain traction in US business schools (Ehrensal, 1999). The explicit message to US-based scholars was clear: adopting a critical stance toward the sacred, accepted beliefs of the management studies domain, or even worse of the emerging corporate-managerialist university, was tantamount to career self-destruction. The timeworn sentiment that "one does not bite the hand that feeds it" appeared paramount. (Yet this academic remains an active, contributing critical scholar, albeit on the faculty of anthropology and sociology in his institution.)

Moreover, a full decade after Alvesson and Willmott's (1992) "breakthrough" *AMR* treatise grounded in critical theory, a US-trained journal editor reported that he had "stumbled" into an Academy of Management annual meeting session and "discovered a group of highly dedicated [CMS] members" (Eden, 2003, p. *xx*). His observations that (1) "'Here I am, Mr. Mainstream, an associate editor of *Academy of Management Journal*, in a hotbed of dissent, sedition, and insurrection. What am I doing here?'" (p. 390) and (2) that the CMS agenda is more "politically driven than scientifically motivated" (p. 391) exemplify CMS's standing in the US, even to the present day. Reflecting on his so-called discovery, he confessed to the hegemony of his socialization:

> (u]nintentionally, imperceptively, and ever so gradually, I internalized the profession's dominant norms as formulated by those faceless 'powers that be.' Only recently have I been coming around more and more to the realization that we editors and associate editors are those 'powers'. (p. 391)

It is also interesting to note that Eden did not ask, "How did they (critters) get here?" Because allowing CMS's identity and visibility within the

Galumphing and Critical Management 217

Academy was a classic example of co-optation: "inassimilable persons are processed through the Academy as a special interest group" (Boje, 1996, p. 191). Finally, we should note that the designation as a "breakthrough" CMS publication is more reflective of UK perceptions than those of US academics. The much recognized Alvesson and Willmott (1992) *AMR* article is cited mostly in UK/EU journals. (Tellingly, only 9 of 144 citations between 1992 and 2014 [Social Science Citation Index] are in the leading US journals, *AMR*, *AMJ*, *ASQ*; three of those are by American authors.) This is consistent with the findings of Battilana et al. (2010) noted earlier.

This view that "critical" is both tantamount to sedition and poorly understood persists today in US universities and is made more problematic by the principle of academic freedom. A long-held precept of American academia, this central value is based on the AAUP's 1915 *Declaration of Principles on Academic Freedom and Academic Tenure*. Kurland (2015) succinctly recounts a half-century of challenges and administrative interference in this academic autonomy. He summarizes key cases revolving around denial of reappointment or tenure, or outright dismissal without due process. Dissenting voices are subjected to disciplinary actions. For example, critiquing sacred values associated with economic efficiency, e.g., capitalism, could put a career in jeopardy. (See Pearson's [2009] account of the Friedmanite legacy of the Reagan and Thatcher administrations of the 1980s and its place in business schools.) These challenges to academic freedom persist today, with university administrators, trustees and even elected officials sometimes deciding what is "appropriate" to teach in classrooms. The bottom line is that while education is portrayed to be value neutral, the existing positivist orthodoxy is reinforced by the political bias now endemic in state legislatures.

Further, there are key differences between the UK and the US in the formal and social contracts between academic and institution. Academic job security in the UK is commonly accepted, absent egregious misconduct. UK employment laws tend to favor faculty in universities. It is not easy and quite unusual for academic staff to be sacked (Vince, 2015). This suggests, then, that UK academics who engage in critical commentary of the creeping managerialism of their institutions and the profession (e.g., Parker, 2002, 2014) are tolerated if not accepted. Thus, broadly speaking, criticality on the part of scholars' published work carries less risk or threat to career and livelihood. In the US, employment, tenure and promotion decisions are based on a scholar's ability to conduct research and place publications in journals that endorse and reinforce a positivist approach. The result is a chilling effect for any scholars drawn (or daring) to embrace a critical approach.

To revisit our argument, differences in the origins and development of business schools in the US and UK led to metacommunications regarding the means and ends of management research. These metacommunications begin in doctoral programs and are reinforced by journal editors, institutional hiring, promotion and tenure policies, accreditors and even state

218 *Gordon E. Dehler and M. Ann Welsh*

legislatures. In the US, coupling the positivist emphasis on leading and/or improving practice as the purpose of scholarship, with a publish-or-perish performance model in a shrinking labor market, makes the clear pattern of ends driving means endemic in US business schools apparent. Undertaking CMS work involves repudiation of the mainstream orthodoxy about the ends and means of research. Further, critical methodologies tend to be perceived as failing to meet the relevance or rigorous standards (or both) of highly ranked journals (e.g., those published by the Academy of Management or ranked by the ABS), thereby threatening employment security and/or career progress through the ranks. Indeed, manuscripts embodying a critical approach are more likely to be published in edited anthologies (like this one!) or lower-ranked outlets, rather than in Academy or other "A" journals. Unlike the UK, where CMS "has been quite successful at establishing a respectable place for itself within the academic community" (Fournier and Smith, 2012), the climate for critical management in the US is indeed chilly—the approach is outside the mainstream, the methods challenge the prevailing "rules" and the sanctions come when critically oriented publications are discounted in deliberations for awarding promotion and tenure or merit (salary) increases. The resulting academic culture is non-critical—the performativity bias is reinforced by power in organizational relationships.

CRITICAL MANAGEMENT PARADOX

Fournier and Smith (2012) note that despite a clear identity forming around Critical Management Studies and the existence of an established network of CMS scholars within the UK, managerial practice remains largely unchanged. The underlying premises of CMS, questioning and/or opposing the authority and relevance of management thinking and practice, identifying the generative mechanisms holding current practice in place, challenging the inherently value-laden legitimating logics and unequal power relationships with an eye towards meaningful transformation have failed to occur. Indeed, please forgive us for thinking that neither the positivist orthodoxy nor CMS has resulted in disruption, challenge or even substantive alterations in managerial practice.

This implies the existence of a critical management paradox in that (1) there is a lag between the adoption of a critical stance and the realization of critical ends (emancipation) and (2) that unleashing critical management depends on two things: changes in the workforce and changes in academic culture to embrace anti-performativity, denaturalization and reflexivity. In this final section, we address how this paradox plays out in the US.

As noted earlier, American universities are essentially under siege as a consequence of neoconservative politics, global financial conditions and a change in the social contract around education itself (Welsh and Dehler, 2007). In the 1990s, a research stream called "critical university studies"

Galumphing and Critical Management 219

emerged in the US (Williams, 2012). The foci of interest for these scholars included academic capitalism, corporatization of the university and the conditions of academic labor. Despite the clear relevance and overlap of these issues with CMS, this work was produced by scholars in various domains, including literary and cultural criticism, higher education, sociology, history and labor studies—not by academics within business schools and curiously absent any consideration of research emerging from CMS (see Prichard, 2000).

What accounts for the absence of a management and business school presence within this critical university studies project? We would argue that the overt "oppositional" stance and the sharp focus upon power relationships within both academia and its engagement with the broader society provide potential explanations. Kavanagh (2009, p. 576) points to the "coercive and normative pressures" that external agents impose on universities, while at the same time the advent of managerialism led to administrators replacing faculty as the central agents (p. 583). Within the university hierarchy, the rise to prominence of business schools was highly correlated with the need to grow enrollments and demonstrate value with essential constituencies (relevance, career preparation focus), including fundraising in the corporate community. Power shifted away from "autonomous scholars, whose requirements—freedom, community and intimacy—are precisely the opposite of the University managers" (Kavanagh, 2009, p. 583).

This disruption of the power status quo within universities resulted in business schools being variously viewed with condescension (as an applied field providing job training, not real education), suspicion (the tendency for faculty to identify themselves as "management" but not labor meant an absence of solidarity on issues such as faculty or graduate student unionization) and envy (increasing enrollments, yet lower teaching loads, higher salaries in an era of declining resources) by faculty in the humanities, social sciences and, to a lesser extent, natural sciences. This situation has two significant results: to reinforce the performativity bias within business schools in their continuing effort to develop networks that validate their relevance and extend their influence, and to discourage business school faculty from engaging in critique of a system from which they have so clearly benefited. After decades of marginalization by university administrators and an environment of declining public resources, the increasing centrality of business schools to university fortunes makes critique of the very institution that provides them with standing risky—both in career terms and in terms of being taken seriously (Fournier and Smith, 2012).

But what about critical scholars within business schools? Tatli (2012) suggests that although critical scholars in the UK may have built an identity around the potential for being marginalized, this has not come to pass. (It would be interesting to poll UK scholars for their agreement—marginalization can be as much perceptual as real). In the US, however, while the general fortunes of business schools were on the rise, critical scholars found themselves

220   *Gordon E. Dehler and M. Ann Welsh*

increasingly marginalized. Absent either publications in Academy journals or engaging in fundable research, managerialist administrators from department chairs to provosts invoke their biases by negatively impacting academic work life and careers through subtle punishments, such as adverse course scheduling and increased student loads, stalled progress through the ranks and capricious denial of deserved merit increases, even as minimal inflation outpaces salary gains. These tactics compromise a scholar's ability to devote the time required to either learning-centered, scholarly instruction (see Dehler, Beatty and Leigh, 2010) or crafting submissions for quality journals. A vicious circle unfolds, of course, as performance is adversely impacted in both teaching and research.

The nature of resistance in the US tends to be covert. Disengagement is a common reaction, staying off the radar screen and laying low to avoid punishment. Collinson (1994) describes this as resistance through distance—a response to practices of managerial control. The plight of American academics presciently fits this tactic articulated by Jermier et al. (1994, p. 12) as a response to being

> treated like commodities, the workers distanced themselves mentally from their work and from management's efforts to make them part of the "team". But, as commodities, they completely refused to take any responsibility for production other than complying minimally with the demands made of them by a management to whom they conceded a full prerogative but for whom they had no respect".

Thus as the academic role in the US becomes increasingly commodified and administrators cope with declining resources by slashing full-time academic positions, remaining faculty are subject to increasingly autocratic decisions.

Of course, this is not happening just in the US. Willmott highlights similar changes in the UK: "the commodification of academic labor and managerial control of academic work results from politico-economic pressures to demonstrate that [public] funds are being directed in ways that are ostensibly congruent with the commodifying logic and priorities of capitalism" (1993, p. 993). Anderson's (2008) research in Australian universities provides other responses to managerialism, which she defines simply as the "introduction of private sector management practices to public sector institutions" and a "more muscular management style" (p. 251). Drawing on Scott's (1985, 1986) notion of "everyday forms of resistance", Anderson identifies several strategies that appear likely practices by academics everywhere in response to this creeping managerialism, including overt defiance via refusal and more passive actions such as avoidance and qualified reluctant minimal compliance.

The end point here is that critique can only have impact, be meaningful, if it starts from the personal. Denouncing certain practices seems insufficient if we are not prepared to look at our own position in relation to these

Galumphing and Critical Management 221

practices, and this means both considering the choices we adopt, can or fail to exercise in relation to these practices and the way these choices may make us complicit (Fournier and Smith, 2012, p. 465).

WHERE DO WE GO FROM HERE? MAKING THE MOST OF THE PARADOXICAL

Paradoxical thinking (Lewis, 2000) is a constructive tool in both analyzing and addressing the progression of Critical Management Studies. First, it helps to identify sources of tension that create paradoxes (or in our lexicon, generative mechanisms); so, for example, the discussion of a failure of business schools to be actively engaged in critical university studies is an example of what Smith and Berg (1987) call a paradox of belonging. Second, accepting the existence of paradox is liberating. If critical scholars are marginalized in the US, then celebrate that marginalization. Rather than search for an elusive (and artificial) consensus, explore dissensus with appreciation, humor and respect—be playful and galumph away.

We see (at least) two roads to follow. The first involves critical management education. Welsh and Dehler (2007) used the lens of critical realism to assess the state of management education and concluded by suggesting that one way to deal with the generative mechanisms preventing transformation of management education was to focus on how the dominant logic was placing many universities in a position of permanent failure. (Few of the universities with the *US News & World Report* top-100 business schools ranking possess an endowment sufficient to buffer them completely from the winds of competition, discord and globalization.) Conforming to the performativity bias has had the (un)expected result of making efficiency more difficult to achieve. Similarly, invoking the taken-for-granted goal of shareholder value in the face of rampant inequality undercuts arguments about legitimation. Finally, the egregious behavior of so many firms leading up to the 2008 recession has led to legislation directed toward preserving the potential to behave egregiously in the future instead of leading to a reflexive consideration of what matters most. (We might call this "too big to have a moral compass".)

A pedagogy of praxis (Welsh and Dehler, 2004, 2007; Dehler, 2009) would not only explicate the paradox more broadly but also would expand it to include what management education could be within the logic of Critical Management Studies. As Brookfield (2005, p. 31) suggests, praxis in this instance would liberate students from the beliefs and structures that serve the few against the well-being of the many. Critical management education, by bringing the generative mechanisms and reinforcing institutional logics into the debate, would enable us to problematize management in ways that "confront the political, ethical and philosophical nature of its practice" (Welsh and Dehler, 2007, p. 417). (The same may be said regarding its potential

222　*Gordon E. Dehler and M. Ann Welsh*

to inform the debates within critical university studies.) A recent anthology (Holtom and Dierdorff, 2013) on the condition of graduate management education also recognizes the existence of the generative mechanisms and suggests that disruption of the status quo is necessary to prevent management education from becoming irrelevant. But the disruption they envision fits squarely within the existing performativity bias—to survive, business schools must differentiate themselves from each other, using evidence-based techniques to select their niche, abandon their "overt reluctance to be normative" and transmit a "prosocial set of values" (Petriglieri, 2015, p. 134). Indeed, most of the authors argue for reframing, but not in ways that would seriously challenge the taken-for-granted purpose of management education. Their discussion appears far closer to rebranding rather than to disruption.

We have argued that doctoral training is a key source of socialization around management education orthodoxy. A chapter in the aforementioned anthology specifically targets such training and concludes, "instead of pursuing bold intellectual ends" it leads to PhD students being taught to be "risk-averse journeymen" (Spender and Khurana, 2013, p. 155). Their recommendation is for the rise and cultivation of dissent. For CMS, there is not likely to be a more clear invitation for dialogue that starts from an anti-performativity stance. We have argued that an important difference between the US and UK is the existence of a strong connection between the means and ends of research. While greater diversity in means has characterized the last 25 years, a failure to legitimate greater diversity in the ends (of both education and organizations) persists. This leads to the second opportunity highlighted by examining the critical management paradox—linking up with proponents of critical university studies.

Existing at the margins of management studies makes this linkage relatively risk free. Engaging with critical university theorists not only offers the potential for the identification of a larger network of critical scholars, it also provides a platform for dialogue around those taken-for-granted metacommunications. Welsh and Dehler (2004) argue that such dialogue is organized reflection. This broader dialogue shapes attention to alternative positions by raising or spreading questions of justification and can draw attention to what actions are necessary, thereby loosening the positivist stranglehold on both means and ends. Collaboration with others is necessary as a "check on self-deception" whereby "the collaborating group becomes an enclave from which distortions in social life in general can be identified" (Kemmis, 1985, p. 153). At the collective level, Raelin (2001, p. 16) argues that such dialogue works to "develop shared values, and subject their actions and values to *deep scrutiny*" (emphasis added). In this way, reflection addresses the "common good". This is a starting point for critique. Critical reflections, organized through ongoing social interactions, hold greater potential to transform organizations by institutionalizing democratic practices. "Being on the margins may actually be a good place to be" (Fournier and Smith, 2012, p. 472).

THE PATH TO CMS

We began this discussion invoking the words of Chris Argyris, whose contention that behavioral approaches to management were needed to focus on the sources of worker alienation made him, arguably, a CMS pioneer. Our assessment of the US perspective on CMS parallels his argument, noting that the way management is studied remains disconnected from the lived experience of workers, while directed toward their continued subjugation. Further, scholars who pursue Critical Management Studies in the US continue to find themselves marginalized and alienated from their colleagues. While we have argued that the galumphing character of UK scholarship has allowed them to advance the CMS agenda more strongly and in a more focused manner, we acknowledge that the adoption of a challenging stance is always fraught with the potential for marginalization. At the end of the day, whether in the US or in the UK, a positivist orthodoxy remains firmly in place. But then, without this, where would we be? What happens to a critical scholar when there is no longer something to be in opposition to? Our concluding sentiment is this: CMS will continue to progress *as a result of* the collaborative efforts of a smart, committed cast of *international contributors*. The overwhelming message derived from this account of US academics' contribution to the CMS movement is that, ultimately, national origin doesn't matter. One of the most rewarding aspects of working on the CMS project is the variety of interpretations and understandings of such a wide range of scholars around the world—a true collaborative undertaking. Will the CMS movement continue to evolve? Of course, but with the confidence that it is the journey rather than the destination that matters the most—we will continue to galumph our way on the path to CMS!

REFERENCES

Alvesson, M. (Ed.) (2011). *Classics in Critical Management Studies*. Cheltenham, UK: Edward Elgar.
Alvesson, M., Bridgman, T. and Willmott, H. (2009). Introduction. In M. Alvesson, T. Bridgman, and H. Willmott (Eds.) *The Oxford Handbook of Critical Management Studies*, 1–26. Oxford: Oxford University Press.
Alvesson, M. and Deetz, S. (2000). *Doing Critical Management Research*. Thousand Oaks, CA: Sage.
Alvesson, M. and Willmott, H. (1992). On the Idea of Emancipation in Management and Organization Studies. *Academy of Management Review*, 17: 432–464.
Anderson, G. (2008). Mapping Academic Resistance in the Managerial University. *Organization*, 15: 251–270.
Argyris, C. (1957). *Personality and Organization: The Conflict Between System and the Individual*. New York: Harper and Row.
Association of Business Schools (2015). *Academic Journal Guide 2015*.
Battilana, J., Anteby, M. and Sengul, M. (2010). The Circulation of Ideas Across Academic Communities: When Locals Re-import Exported Ideas. *Organization Studies*, 31: 695–713.

224 Gordon E. Dehler and M. Ann Welsh

Benson, J.K. (1977). Organizations: A Dialectical View, *Administrative Science Quarterly*, 22: 1–21.

Benson, J.K. (1983a). A Dialectical Method for the Study of Organizations. In G. Morgan (Ed.), *Beyond Method: Strategies for Social Research*, 331–346. Beverly Hills: Sage.

Benson, J.K. (1983b). Paradigm and Praxis in Organizational Analysis. In L.L. Cummings and B.M. Staw (Eds.), *Research in Organizational Behavior*, 5: 33–56. Greenwich, CT: JAI Press.

Boje, D. (1996). Management Education as a Panoptic Cage. In R. French and C. Grey (Eds.), *Rethinking Management Education*, 172–195. London: Sage.

Bradley, G. (2004). Contingent Faculty and the New Academic Labor System, *Academe*, January–February: 28–31.

Brookfield, S. (2005). *Becoming a Critically Reflective Teacher*. San Francisco: Jossey-Bass.

Carr, W. and Kemmis, S. (1986). *Becoming Critical: Education, Knowledge and Action Research*. London: Falmer Press.

Collinson, (1994) Strategies of Resistance: Power, Knowledge and Subjectivity in the Workplace. In J. Jermier, D. Knights and W.R. Nord (Eds.), *Resistance and Power in Organizations*, 25–68. London: Routledge.

Cunliffe, A.L. and Sadler-Smith, E. (2015). *Management Learning*: The Journal for Critical, Reflexive Scholarship on Organization and Learning. *Management Learning*, 46: 3–5.

Dehler, G.E. (2009). Prospects and Possibilities of Critical Management Education: Critical Beings and a Pedagogy of Critical Action. *Management Learning*, 40: 31–49.

Dehler, G.E., Beatty, J.E. and Leigh, J. (2010). From 'good teaching' to 'scholarly teaching': Legitimating Management Education and Learning Scholarship. In C. Wankel and R. DeFillippi (Eds.), *Being and Becoming a Management Education Scholar*, 93–116. New York: Information Age Publishing.

Eden, D. (2003). From the Editors: Critical Management Studies and the *Academy of Management Journal*: Challenge and Counterchallenge. *Academy of Management Journal*, 46: 390–394.

Ehrensal, K.N. (1999). Critical Management Studies and American Business School Culture: Or, How NOT to Get Tenure in One Easy Publication. First International Critical Management Studies Conference, Manchester, UK.

Fournier, V. and Grey, C. (2000). At the Critical Moment: Conditions and Prospects for Critical Management Studies. *Human Relations*, 53: 7–32.

Fournier, V. and Smith, W. (2012). Making Choice, Taking Risk: On the Coming Out of Critical Management Studies. *ephemera*, 12: 463–474.

Holtom, and Dierdorff (2013) *Disrupt or Be Disrupted: A Blueprint for Change in Management Education*, B. Holtom and E. Dierdorff (Eds.). San Francisco: Jossey-Bass.

Jack, G. (2004). On Speech, Critique and Protection. *ephemera*, 4: 121–134.

Jermier, J. (1998). Introduction to Critical Perspectives on Organizational Control. *Administrative Science Quarterly*, 43: 235–256.

Jermier, J., Knights, D. and Nord, W.R. (1994). Introduction: Resistance and Power in Organizations: Agency, Subjectivity and the Labour Process. In J. Jermier, D. Knights and W.R. Nord (Eds.), *Resistance and Power in Organizations*, 1–24. London: Routledge.

Kavanagh, D. (2009). Institutional Heterogeneity and Change: The University as Fool. *Organization*, 16: 575–595.

Kemmis, S. (1985). Action Research and the Politics of Reflection. In D. Boud, R. Keogh and D. Walker (Eds.), *Reflection: Turning Experience into Learning*, 139–163. London: Kogan Page.

Galumphing and Critical Management 225

Kurland, J.E. (2015). Ten Decades of AAUP Investigations. *Academe*, January–February: 21–24.

Learmonth, M. (2006). Is There Such a Thing as 'evidence-based management?': A Commentary on Rousseau's 2005 Presidential Address. *Academy of Management Review*, 31: 1089–1093.

Learmonth, M. (2008). Evidence-Based Management: A Backlash Against Pluralism in Organization Studies? *Organization*, 15: 283–291.

Learmonth, M. and Harding, N. (2006). Evidence-Based Management: The Very Idea. *Public Administration*, 84: 245–266.

Lewis, M.W. (2000). Exploring Paradox: Toward a More Comprehensive Guide. *Academy of Management Review*, 25: 760–776.

Miller, S. (1973). Ends, Means, and Galumphing: Some Leitmotifs of Play. *American Anthropologist*, 75: 87–98.

Mir, R. (2015). CMS Division Chair. Personal Communication. March 31.

Morrell, K. (2008). The Narrative of 'evidence-based' Management: A Polemic. *Journal of Management Studies*, 45: 613–635.

Parker, M. (2002). *Against Management: Organization in the Age of Managerialism*. Cambridge, UK: Polity Press.

Parker, M. (2014). University, Ltd: Changing a Business School. *Organization*, 21: 281–292.

Parker, M. and Thomas, R. (2011). What is a Critical Journal? *Organization*, 18: 419–427.

Pearson, G. (2009). *The Rise and Fall of Management: A Brief History of Practice, Theory and Content*. Aldershot, UK: Gower.

Petriglieri, G. (2015). Book and Resource Reviews: *Disrupt or Be Disrupted: A Blueprint for Change in Management Education*, B. Holtom and E. Dierdorff (Eds.), 2013. San Francisco: Jossey-Bass, *Academy of Management Learning and Education*, 14: 133–149.

Prichard, C. (2000). *Making Managers in Universities and Colleges*. Maidenhead, UK : McGraw-Hill Education.

Raelin, J. (2001). Public Reflection as the Basis of Learning. *Management Learning*, 32: 11–30.

Reynolds, M. (1997). Towards a Critical Management Pedagogy. In J. Burgoyne and M. Reynolds (Eds.), *Management Learning: Integrating Perspectives in Theory and Practice*, 312–328. London: Sage.

Rousseau, D.M. (2006). Is There Such a Thing as 'evidence-based management?'. *Academy of Management Review*, 31: 256–269.

Scott, J. (1985). *Weapons of the Weak—Everyday Forms of Peasant Resistance*. New Haven, CT: Yale University Press.

Scott, J. (1986). Everyday Forms of Peasant Resistance. In J.C. Scott and B.J.T. Kerkvliet (Eds.), *Everyday Forms of Peasant Resistance in South-East Asia*, 5–35. Abingdon, UK: Frank Cass.

Smircich, L, Calas, M.B. and Morgan, G. (1992). Afterward/After Words: Open(ing?) Spaces. *Academy of Management Review*, 17: 607–611.

Smith, K.K. and Berg, D.N. (1987). *Paradoxes of Group Life*. San Francisco: Jossey-Bass.

Spender, J.C. and Khurana, R. (2013). Intellectual Signatures: Impact on Relevance and Doctoral Programs. In B. Holtom and E. Dierdorff (Eds.), *Disrupt or Be Disrupted: A Blueprint for Change in Management Education*. San Francisco: Jossey-Bass.

Steffy, B.D. and Grimes, A.J. (1986). A Critical Theory of Organization Science. *Academy of Management Review*, 11: 322–336.

Tatli, A. (2012). On the Power and Poverty of Critical (Self) Reflection in Critical Management Studies: A Comment on Ford, Harding and Learmonth. *British Journal of Management*, 21: 22–30.

226   *Gordon E. Dehler and M. Ann Welsh*

Vince, R. (2015). Personal Communication. February 4.

Welsh, M.A. and Dehler, G.E. (2004). P(l)aying Attention: Communities of Practice and Organized Reflection. In M. Reynolds and R. Vince (Eds.), *Organizing Reflection*, 15–29. Aldershot, UK: Ashgate.

Welsh, M.A. and Dehler, G.E. (2007). Whither the MBA? Or the withering of MBAs? *Management Learning*, 38: 407–425.

Williams, J.J. (2012). Deconstructing Academe: The Birth of Critical University Studies. *Chronicle of Higher Education*, February 19.

Willmott, H. (1993). Managing the Academics: Commodification and Control in the Development of University Education in the UK. *Human Relations*, 48: 993–1027.

Conclusion
Diverse Accents, Common Voice?

Laurent Taskin, Véronique Perret, Isabelle Huault and Christopher Grey

> The emancipatory transformations in the world may follow grammars and scripts other than those developed by Western-centric critical theory, and such diversity should be valorized.
>
> (de Souza Santos, 2014, p. viii)

At the end of this attempt to give voice to the many critical perspectives that are expressed in the world of CMS, we must admit that our initial idea was an ambitious one. This book has been for us, as it is intended to be for its readers, a voyage of exploration. The diversity of CMS is not reducible to questions of language and national (or regional) culture: yet exploring those questions turns out to give a better insight into what its diversity consists of. In this concluding section, we propose, first, to account for some of the observed diversities in the way critical thinking on management is expressed, trying to identify some commonalities that should help to consider the nature of the relationships between the so-called cores and peripheries, as presented in the introductory chapter. Second, we argue that beyond diversities (of languages, regions, institutions, contexts, topics studied, methodologies and epistemologies) that this book has, in several ways, contributed to highlighting, there is, after all, a common voice that expresses itself, asking for an adequate recognition of injustice and for the overcoming of oppression in organizations.

DIVERSITIES AT WORK: THE MANY VOICES OF CMS

CMS has attracted under its umbrella a lot of researchers, in many different contexts. This is a major event that needs to be emphasized given the increasing sub-sub-(and micro-) division of disciplines, methodologies, fields of research and publication. For against that background, it is surely noteworthy to see in CMS a bringing together rather than a fragmentation of intellectual effort. Perhaps it is all the more noteworthy given the very great diversity of political situations within which, as the chapters of this book show, CMS operates. For the time being, at least, CMS is able to operate as a meaningful and, for those who use it, useful term.

228   *Taskin et al.*

VARIETIES OF OBJECTS, PURPOSES AND WAYS OF STUDYING MANAGEMENT CRITICALLY

However, under this common umbrella there are many realities for and versions of CMS. This book has attempted to make them somewhat more visible. At a first sight, two groups of regions may be identified. In both groups, CMS seems to contribute to the legitimization of critical research. In a first group, the commonly accepted CMS background is not so much questioned, and the contribution to critical research lies primarily in its empirical nature. In a second group, the shared ambition is to contribute to the *apparatus* (i.e. theoretical, epistemological and methodological corpus) of the critical research tradition itself, by expanding the existing set of commonly accepted critical theories. To put this another way, we can see the localization of CMS as taking at least two forms: one form is the expansion of CMS to address new empirical locations, the other to expand the range and nature of the theorization of critique. In both cases, something is happening which cannot be captured by a model of diffusion from a core to a periphery. Rather, it is an ongoing process through which CMS itself is rearticulated.

A Pragmatic Engagement in CMS

In most of the localities covered in this book, CMS appears to be associated with specific research areas and constitutes a powerful vehicle for doing critical research on specific managerial objects or issues. This pragmatic nature is sometimes asserted by the authors themselves, as in the chapter on Canada. So a common way of describing CMS has been to identify the topics that are studied critically and to associate 'critters' to them. Of course all the usual caveats apply in such an endeavour: all the authors shared their feeling of discomfort when attempting to label the work of colleagues as critical studies of management (or not). That being said, specific topics studied critically were identified.

Thus power relationships emerged as a very popular topic in the CMS community, since it is shared by critters in the USA, UK, Australia/New Zealand and Benelux. Gender issues also appear as a common ground for critical studies in management, especially in Scandinavia, Benelux and German-speaking countries. Other topics are specific to some locales, for example workplace transformations, entrepreneurship and ethics in the Benelux; project management, narratives and language issues in Scandinavia; self-management and communal organization in Argentina and Venezuela.

This pragmatic deployment of CMS can be seen as constituting critique in and of itself. Mainstream research in management, modelling production or decision-making processes or accounting and quantitative data analysis is seen as failing to capture the *real* workplace context and actors (Palpacuer

Conclusion 229

et al., 2015). Of course, among the regions mentioned earlier, we also find theoretical discussions (e.g. Canada) and other epistemological reflections (e.g. Benelux). However, when theoretical debates take place, the ambition is to understand observed phenomenon differently, to apprehend other facets of the same reality.

Finally, another face of this critical pragmatism lies in the central role given to management education. Though management education may constitute an object of critical enquiry (as in the USA, where managerialism is studied in the context of business schools, or in Canada, where the Sobey PhD programme in management is analysed through an actor-network perspective), it is most often presented as a means to transform management practices (e.g. China). In some contexts, management education is under pressure. A major pressure comes from the lack of resources dedicated to the support of critical management education and the difficulties encountered for investing in that kind of project and the associated academic recruitment (for example in Turkey, UK, Italy and Israel). Another pressure comes from the reinforcement of boundaries between disciplines, making management disappearing from the map of disciplines in social sciences or appearing as an extension of economics or, less often, sociology or industrial relations. Anyway, the willingness to engage in management education, and the identification of the necessity to be able to influence management education programmes, is a common feature of the chapters presented here, which entails both the rejection—or, at least, the questioning—of the explicit anti-performativity intent of the harder version of CMS and the articulation of CMS as a social movement.

A Fundamental Contribution to Critical Research

The early Anglo-Scandinavian articulation of CMS drew primarily upon Frankfurt School critical theory and, to a lesser extent, versions of post-structuralism. Moreover, it owed something, at least, to Anglo-American labour process theory. CMS continues to bear that imprimatur, but in several locales it is possible to see substantive developments in CMS theory. This is the case in France, with an interesting paradox: the institutionalization of CMS led French critters to rediscover their own critical authors (among which number Foucault, Derrida, Lyotard, Deleuze) that many Anglo-Saxon researchers mobilize in their work. Simultaneously, and this is part of the paradox, French critters importantly contributed to the global institutionalization process of CMS through publishing articles in . . . English. As a result, nowadays, a clearly identified French (-speaking) community of critical thinkers of management can be identified. And they do share a common purpose: by reappropriating the rich French critical tradition of social sciences, they intend to enlarge the critical theory, namely by considering two other issues: suffering at work, and the research tradition that studies it for

230   *Taskin et al.*

a while (Dejours, Enriquez, De Gaulejac, Pagès), and the instrumentation of management (Chiapello, Gilbert, Callon, Latour).

Something similar could be said about South America, and especially Brazil. There are parallels to the case of France, if we consider the foundational influence that Paulo Freire's work had on the development of, especially, critical management education. At the same time, Prestes Motta and Guerreiro Ramos amongst others have undertaken fundamental theoretical work germane to CMS, a tradition continued by Faria and Mandiola, amongst many others. Another variant of this can be found in the case of China, where both traditional and contemporary understandings of the deeply rooted concept of 'harmony' may be deployed to both enable and to challenge CMS theory. Relatedly, in Japan, Buddhist and Confucian traditions offer promising possibilities for the reworking of CMS away from forms of critical theory which are, somehow, rooted in Judeo-Christian traditions. Moreover, it is from countries such as Brazil and Israel that postcolonial theorizations of management are most forcefully emerging. We might tentatively conclude that even if it is true that CMS theory is most commonly associated with certain Anglo-Scandinavian authors, both its roots and much of its current vibrancy lie elsewhere.

We do not, of course, seek to imply that in some countries CMS is simply an empirical project, bereft of theorizing, and in others the opposite. Rather, that we can see the complex interweaving and transmission of ideas that, as we suggested in the introduction, transcends the apparent core and periphery that might otherwise be thought to exist.

LOCAL ACCENTS AND LINGUA FRANCA

A major impetus for this book was to offer the opportunity to make more visible, discover and appreciate the richness of local critical thinking. We assumed such knowledge would be written in the local language and disseminated in local journals. And so we hoped to bring to the reach of the majority these local theories and practices of critical research on management. This was especially the case for German-speaking countries (discovering specific research traditions, such as AOEWL, and authors, such as Türk and Krell), Turkey and South America (helping to understand the specificities of the context on which CMS development rely) and in France (with the evocation of the renewal perspective for the critical research agenda). It is noteworthy that more than a half of the references mentioned in these chapters are not texts published in English but in the local language (the 'prize' goes to Germany-speaking countries where 90 per cent of the references come from books and articles published in German). This would perhaps attest to a local dynamism of critical research.

By contrast, some regions only present a limited proportion of non-English written references: one-quarter approximately for China, Benelux and Italy.

Conclusion 231

There are no references at all to the non-English critical literature in the chapters on the UK and the USA (perhaps unsurprisingly), Canada (more surprisingly since there is also a significant proportion of French-speaking critters there) and Scandinavia. This count has no real value since the CMS activism presented in these chapters are limited to their authors' representation, as pointed out by most of them. Still, although this is a biased view, it underlines the role lingua franca English plays in the CMS theatre. And to which, of course, this book contributes.

This seems unlikely to change any time soon, and it seems unlikely that CMS in and of itself has much capacity to influence that change. It remains important continually to draw attention to the hegemonic and disempowering consequences of Anglophone dominance (Pennycook, 1998). One important aspect of that is the way the translation of English texts into other languages entails multiple complexities of meaning and, ineluctably, power. As the chapter in Japan, for example, illustrates, not only do words such as 'enlightenment' or 'empowerment' carry different connotations in different languages, but they are heavily freighted with cultural meanings that go well beyond 'technical' issues of translation. Above and beyond this, of course, lies the increasingly hegemonic demand that researchers must publish in English in order to be accepted as working at 'international' levels of scholarly excellence.

Yet CMS is hardly unique in facing this and, in one way at least, has a particular opportunity as a result of it. For the business schools in which much CMS occurs (Israel being a notable exception) are a prime example of, and vehicle for, the global hegemony of English. They are thus also a site within which a 'Globish' CMS may relatively easily get a hearing, as well as being a site where it most obviously must get a hearing. For that matter, the globalized nature of business schools seems to be an important reason for the development of CMS in that, as many of the chapters attest, scholars, including doctoral students, moving between countries or undertaking visiting posts or engaging in transnational research projects, often prove to be catalysts for CMS as they travel. Indeed our editorship of this volume is one example.

FROM A CORE-PERIPHERY CONSIDERATION TO THE ASSERTION OF A SOCIAL MOVEMENT: CHALLENGES FOR CONSIDERING THE VARIETIES OF CRITICAL MANAGEMENT STUDIES AND SCHOOLS

Although it is hardly a revelation, this book reveals that there are many ways of studying management critically and, in some ways, there is a pluralism of CMS. Whilst as just noted there was perhaps less diversity in the language of sources and references than might have been anticipated, in other ways we have found this diversity expressed more strongly than we imagined at the

232 Taskin et al.

outset. We did not expect to find five different schools and clusters in Scandinavia, for example. And this is due to the ways in which the field of CMS is defined. Hartmann et al. (this volume) identify two forms of CMS, regarding its critical intensity: there would be a hard version and a lighter or softer one. This would be another way of considering the core and the periphery of CMS, but it would not be helpful in understanding what has clearly now become a social movement (Willmott, 2013). Better to regard 'hard' and 'soft' as being themselves different accents of CMS, in a different sense to the national/regional meaning of accent that structures this volume. In this diversity—at least assuming mutual tolerance, and acceptance, of it—lies a potential major strength of CMS which, as an institutionalized label, offers a comfortable and increasingly recognized umbrella for many critters. From the inside, this diversity is a guarantee for intellectual freedom, recognition and societal involvement. These are some of the 'universal' values of higher education that animated the foundation of many universities, something that presents CMS with a fertile ground for legitimation.

So whilst most of the chapters collected here—although notably not all, e.g. China, Israel, Japan—started with the description of what CMS is expected to be (typically drawing on widely referenced sources such as Fournier and Grey, 2000, and Alvesson and Willmott, 1992), trying to present some unity of thought, they also immediately pointed to the specificities of the critical perspectives in the geographical area considered. Indeed, that is so even within the chapters on the UK and Scandinavia. In some regions, pre-existing research streams now find themselves under the umbrella of CMS. This is well illustrated by the case in German-speaking countries where three different traditions cohabit (labour-oriented business administration, a critique of the political economy of organizations and a deconstructing tradition of gender issues). In other cases, the US and Japan for example, the emergence of CMS has itself provoked the development of new streams of research. The most literal example of this seems to be Italy, where, as the chapter explains, the hosting of the CMS Conference was a pivotal moment for the development of CMS in that country.

The issue of the boundaries of CMS is also understandable in the terms of disciplines. Martin Parker clearly explains how CMS in the UK constitutes a label that refers to the tensions between industrial sociology and industrial relations in the context of their migration to business schools. There the CMS banner is "an umbrella for those working in business schools but thinking against it". In Turkey, by contrast, CMS can be understood at least to some degree as an oppositional banner for those working outside the discipline of (neoclassical) economics that dominates management research and teaching. The latter case, in particular, can also be understood in terms of a boundary between an imported US model of business schools and management research and various forms of alternative to this. Indeed the significance of this is apparent in many of the chapters, especially South America and Israel, and with echoes in all the chapters, albeit for obvious reasons differently inflected in the case of the US itself.

Conclusion 233

However, this consideration of CMS diversity should lead us to make at least two pessimistic observations. First, in comparison to the (perceived) unity of mainstream approaches, CMS appears like patchwork. As some authors mention, alarmingly, in 'times of war', this is a necessity in order to gain influence on the resource-allocation processes and decisions that are shaping tomorrow's business schools. This seems especially to be the case in Italy, Turkey and the UK. Second, and in relation to the previous point, in some regions that have been investigated here, it appears that the multidisciplinary nature of CMS is threatened by the reinforcement of boundaries between disciplines and the need for researchers and professors to identify with these. The institutional context of higher education appears determinant in this trend, as for US, UK, Italy and Turkey, but also in a more optimistic perspective, in Scandinavian countries where business schools are not so constrained by "authoritarian and mechanistic forms of managerialism exercised at some metric-driven UK business schools".

These considerations become important if CMS is to be thought of as a global movement. As perhaps is inevitable amongst intellectuals and academics, much energy can be expended on trying to define, refine and argue over the theoretical, epistemological and methodological tenets of what CMS consists of. One aspect of this book has been to show how those kinds of debates play out in different locales and how they relate to and draw upon local intellectual traditions. But the institutional conditions within which CMS operates are no less worthy of attention from a social movement perspective. As a movement, CMS won't get very far if it fails to appreciate the institutional possibilities and constraints faced by its constituent parts. On the one hand, that means recognizing the very different but still very challenging difficulties of doing CMS in, say, China and the US. It also means recognizing that there may be more constraints on doing CMS in, say, the UK or Sweden than might be imagined from the outside. On the other hand, it is necessary to appreciate the very different possibilities that different locales hold for CMS, possibilities that go a long way beyond those envisaged in its Anglo-Scandinavian variant. For example, the strongly postcolonial accent of Brazilian CMS or the Confucian and Buddhist approaches to Japanese CMS offer real and invigorating alternatives to a CMS rooted in the Frankfurt School. CMS may be, or aspire to be, a global movement, but it occurs within localities with specific institutional, cultural and political circumstances in ways that this volume begins to disclose and from which CMS in other localities may draw inspiration.

Is There a Core and a Periphery to CMS (Anymore)?

On one reading, the core of CMS remains associated with UK and Scandinavia. It suffices to note the references that are mobilized by authors to characterize the field of CMS. Yet this reading may be questioned by looking in more detail. In some cases (e.g. in the chapters on China, Japan, Israel and South America these references are marginal or non-existent). Moreover,

234 *Taskin et al.*

this book offers the opportunity to look more precisely to what happens in those CMS core regions, from the inside. Martin Parker describes a quite pessimistic situation for CMS in the UK, arguing that its relatively successful establishment means that it has become somewhat institutionalized, to the point where it may not be so very different from the mainstream, nor especially critical. Hartmann et al. reveal to what extent the identification of Scandinavian countries as being part of the CMS core could on one reading be said to lie in the activism of one single person, in an isolated school of critical thinking in Scandinavia (namely, Lund). In light of these local analyses, the core of the global CMS movement seems very fragile. So would this core not draw strength from its periphery, so as to be merged with it, in a global—but diverse—movement? If so, this would call into question the categories of core and periphery, with each operating to mutually legitimate the other and each therefore being dependent upon the other in advancing the, necessarily pluralized, global projects of CMS.

In conclusion, while this book allows us to consider and identify the specificities of Critical Management Studies (their objects, the theoretical, methodological and epistemological options) in different locations, and according to specific institutional contexts, it also raises the main issue of CMS *borders*. One version of that might be thought of in terms of 'internal borders', perhaps those between different disciplinary allegiances but more especially that between 'hard' and 'soft' versions of CMS: how extensive or inclusive is, or should be, the CMS umbrella? Such distinctions probably only matter for those engaged with CMS. Indeed, in this volume, we considered CMS from the inside by inviting colleagues known for their involvement in critical studies to portray CMS realities in their regions. One interesting—and additional—alternative would have been to invite other colleagues (labelled as mainstream or not) to characterize CMS as it seems from outside. If, indeed, it registers at all.

If we focused on that border, it might make for some uncomfortable reading. In particular where CMS has been institutionalized as one component of business schools, it may be less of an oppositional project than might be hoped. After all, even the heterodox publish in good journals and bring research contracts—and perhaps legitimate business schools— by giving them a patina of intellectual and moral respectability to business schools. On that reading, the border around CMS may be rather a porous one with 'hard' critters working in benign environments rather peripheral to the struggles of their ostensibly 'softer' counterparts to gain a foothold in less propitious environments. Certainly one of the lessons of this volume is quite how varied, and in some cases difficult, the contexts are within which CMS-oriented academics must operate. For example, the stable and relatively peaceful social democracies of Scandinavia are greatly in contrast to the often more turbulent political circumstances described in the chapter on South America or the more repressive political situation in China.

We began this volume by referring to a conversation between us about what it meant to 'do' CMS outside of Anglo-Scandinavian contexts, given

Conclusion 235

that it seemed to be Anglo-Scandinavian writings that dominated the meaning of CMS. We now have a much clearer sense of the ways that CMS is being done in a wider (although, as noted in the introduction, still limited) range of settings. In the process, it has become abundantly clear how reductive it is to see CMS solely, or even primarily, in Anglo-Scandinavian terms (and even how reductive it is to speak of 'Anglo-Scandinavian terms'). Still less does it make sense to speak of a proper 'hard' version of CMS and a somehow deficient, inferior or even bogus 'soft' CMS.

Elsewhere (Grey, 2005) it had been argued that a 'mature politics' for CMS entails that it not fall into internal bickering about theoretical purity. That argument applies equally to divisions based upon geographical or cultural location, and for the same reasons, the overwhelming priority for CMS must be to fight corporate injustice and managerialism in general and to articulate and incorporate that fight into management education and research in particular. If we take that seriously, then the political consequences should be clear. Strength in unity is a maxim which has been used in various versions in many different countries, and in support of many different political projects, throughout history. For CMS at least, unity does not need to mean homogeneity, and the primary contribution of this volume has, we hope, been to show and celebrate diversity. Yet that need not mean that CMS cannot articulate itself as a common project with a common voice. One of the most difficult things when learning a language is to understand, and even more difficult to be able to place, the local accents of different users. Eventually, even this is possible with sufficient exposure to those accents. Such has been the purpose of this volume; but the end game is to use the fluency gained in order to refine and make heard more widely the voice of critique in all of its accents.

REFERENCES

Alvesson, M. and Willmott, H. (1992). *Critical Management Studies*. London: Sage.
De Souza Santos, B. (2014). *Epistemologies of the South: Justice Against epistemicide*. London: Paradigm Publishers.
Fournier, V. and Grey, C. (2000). At the Critical Moment: Conditions and Prospects for Critical Management Studies. *Human Relations*, 53: 7–32.
Grey, C. (2005). Critical Management Studies: Towards a More Mature Politics. In D. Howcroft and E. Trauth (Eds.), *Handbook of Critical Information Systems Research. Theory and Applications*, 174–194. Cheltenham, UK: Edward Elgar.
Palpacuer, F., Taskin, L. and Balas, N. (2015). Quelle est la place du terrain dans les recherches critiques en management ? *Economies et sociétés. Série K, Economie de l'Entreprise*, 4(2): 251–269.
Pennycook, A. (1998). *English and the Discourses of Colonialism*. London: Routledge.
Willmott, H. (2013). Changing Institutions: Critical Management Studies as a Social Movement. In V. Malin, J. Murphy and M. Siltaoja (Eds.), *Getting Things Done, Dialogues in Critical Management Studies*, Vol. 2, 123–164. Bingley: Emerald Press.

Index

AACSB International accreditation process 216

Abilitazione Scientifica Nazionale 121–2

Academy of Economic and Commercial Sciences (ITIA) 178

Academy of Management (AoM): Australia 3, 6–7, 10; Benelux 22; Brazil 163; Canada 41; Italy 117; New Zealand 16; Turkey 183; United Kingdom 208; United States 209, 211, 216–17

Academy of Management Review (AMR) 211

Accademia Italiana di Economia Aziendale (AIDEA) 116, 122

Actor Network Theory (ANT): Brazil 164; Canada 36–40, 48–50; France 79; Scandinavia 153, 154

Adler, Paul 6–7

administrative autonomy 181–2

Agency for International Development (AID) 178

Aharoni, Yair 106

Aktouf, Omar 166

Alcadipani, Rafael 164

Americanization 70, 176, 178–81, 210

American Sociological Association 192

American War of Independence 1

Andreski, Stanislav 192

Anglophone dominance of management studies xvii, xix, 58, 231

anti-positivist bias 208

anti-Vietnam War movement 6

Aotearoa New Zealand, critical management studies 13–16

Argentina, critical management theory 160–1

Argyris, Chris 207

Association to Advance Collegiate Schools of Business (AACSB) 42

Atlantic Schools of Business (ASB) 44

Australia, critical management studies: critical management émigrés 3–7; émigrés 3–7; immigrants 7–10; overview 1; southern theory 1–3

Australian National University (ANU) 5

authoritarian form of managerialism 144

Bamford, Kenneth 4

Barnes, John Arundel. 4–5

Ben-David, Joseph 107

Benelux Region, critical management studies: entrepreneurship 27; gender, diversity, and identity 23–5; global *vs.* local dynamics 28–30; management, ethics and sustainability 28; overview 21–2; pragmatic perspective 22–3; qualitative research, epistemology and reflexivity 28; workplace transformations 25–7

Benschop, Yvonne 23

Benson, J. Kenneth 206, 210–11

Bergische Universität Wuppertal 89

Berry, Michel 79

Bettin, Caterina 41

bildung in management education 150

Bion, Wilfred 4

Bocconi School of Management 121

Bolivarian Revolution 166

Boltanski, Luc 80

Brazil, critical management theory 161–4

Brazilian Academy of Management (ANPAD) 163

238 Index

Brazilian Solidarity Economy 164
Briggs, Asa 1–2
British Mandatory rule 105
British Sociological Association 198
Bruch, Michael 89
Buddhism 59, 131–3
Bureaucracy and Self-Management
(Prestes Motta) 162
Burrell, Gibson 42, 45
business schools in China 55–6

Canada, critical management studies:
Actor Network Theory and
36–40, 48–50; enrolment
process 48–9; "Halifax School"
37–8, 47; intellectual spaces
of possibilities 46–7; othering
process 37, 44–6; politics of
knowledge 36–8; Sobey PhD
Programme 38, 40–7
capitalism and critical management 21,
126–7, 149
capital-oriented rationality 88
Carnegie Tech 70
centre for scientific management (CGS)
70
Centre for the Sociology of
Organizations (CSO) 71
ceremonial empiricism 183
CESAN school 124
Chamber of Architects and Engineers
(TMMOB) 176
Chanlat, Jean-Francois 166
Chavez, Hugo 166–7
Chiapello, Eve 80
Chile, critical management theory
164–5
China, critical management studies:
absence of 58–60; business
schools 55–6; Chinese Wisdom
60; Confucianism xx, 56–7,
59–61; critical thinking in
56–8; harmony-with-difference
approach 65; overview 54–5;
possible approaches, overview
63; Taoism 62–3; unlearning
approach 64–5
Christianity *vs.* Marxism 131
Clarke, Marcus 7–10
Classics in Critical Management Studies
(Alvesson) 209
Clegg, Stewart 3, 8, 9–10
Cohen, Bernard 110
Cold War dynamic 104

Colombia, critical management theory
166
commerce schools in Turkey 178–9
communicative interaction 151
Confucianism: Chinese critical
management studies xx,
56–7, 59–61; Japanese critical
management studies 131, 133–6,
134, **135**
Connell, Raewyn 2
consensus and marginalization 70–2
Constantinidis, Christina 24, 27
construction/institutionalization of
discipline 68–9
contextual study of Israeli society
107–8
Copenhagen School 145, 149–50
Costas, Jana 86
critical management studies (CMS):
centres, margins and beyond
xix–xxi; challenges of studies
and schools 231–5; context of
xxi–xxiii; core and periphery
of 233–5; diversities and 227;
fundamental contribution to
229–30; local accents and
lingua franca 230–1; overview
xxiv–xxvi, 227; pragmatic
engagement in 228–9; variety in
studying of 228; *see also* specific
countries
critical sociology 192–3
critical theoretical perspective xxv
Critical Theory 153
critical thinking in China 56–8
critical university studies 218–19
Crozier, Michel 71–2
Czarniawska, Barbara 153

Dan, Hillel 105
*Declaration of Principles on Academic
Freedom and Academic Tenure*
(1915) 217
Dejours, Christophe 78
dependency theory 159
Derrida, Jacques 37–8, 86
dialogic studies 213
dimension of collectivity 91
dimension of order 91
dimension of structured entity 91
disengagement reaction 220
diversities and critical management
studies 227
Dupont, Claire 26

Index 239

Durepos, Gabrielle 41
Dussel, Enrique 165

Economic Cooperation Agency (ECA) 179, 181
Economies et Sociétés journal 74
Edo Period 140
emancipation methodologies 87–9, 136–42
Emery, Fred 5
The Engineering Foundations of the Managerial Revolution (Shenhav) 111
Enlightenment concept 58, 63, 132–3
Enriquez, Eugène 164
entrepreneurship: Benelux 23, 27; Israel 101; Scandinavia 149, 228
Environmentalism 153
Essers, Caroline 27
Etkin, Jorge 165
Eurocentric traditions of thought 165
European Group for Organization Studies 196, 209
European Recovery Programme (ERP) 179
European School of Entrepreneurship 149, 150
"everyday forms of resistance" notion 220
evidence-based management 208
existentialism 37, 48

Faculties of Economics and Administrative Sciences (FEAS) 179
fair distribution 89
Faria, Alex 164
Faria, José Henrique de 164
Fatigue and Its Social Projections (Palacios) 160
feminism 43, 122, 153, 192, 211
Ferreras, Isabelle 25
financialization 73
First International Critical Management Studies Conference (1999) 216
Fletcher, Colin 9
Flores, Fernando 165
Fondation Nationale pour l'Enseignement de la Gestion des Enterprises (FNEGE) 69
Foucault, Michel 86, 94, 111
Fox, Alan 195
France, critical management studies: consensus and marginalization

70–2; construction/ institutionalization of discipline 68–9; identity assertion 74–80; institutionalization of management 69–70; instrumentation *vs.* tools of management 78–80; legitimization of 72–4; reappropriating social sciences tradition 75–6; renewal of agenda 77–80; research landscape 72; suffering *vs.* stress in workplace 77–8
Frankfurt School xxiv–xxv, 2, 145, 155, 164, 195, 229
Free University of Amsterdam 23
Freie Universität Berlin 93
Freire, Paulo 165, 230
Friedman, Milton 110

Gallego, López 166
galumphing notion 207, 213–18
gedatsu as self-problematization 137–8, 140–1
gender (de-)construction 85, 87, 93–5
General Federation of Jewish Workers 105
German critical management studies: concluding remarks 95–6; emancipatory rationality 87–9; gender (de-)construction 85, 87, 93–5; overview 85–7; political economy of organization 85, 87, 89–92, 92
Gilli, Jose Angel 160
global power relations xxiii
global *vs.* local dynamics 28–30
glocalization theory 100, 102–4
Gothenburg Cluster 145, 153–4
"Great Harmony" concept 59–61
Griffith University 9
Grosz, Elizabeth 2
Guerreiro Ramos, Alberto 161, 162–3, 168, 230

Halford, Susan 202–3
"Halifax School" 37–8, 47
Hall, Mike 9
Hamidiye Ticaret Mektebi 178
Hans Böckler Foundation 87
Hardy, Cynthia 3, 8, 10
harmony concept 57, 59–61, 65
Harvard Business School (HBR) 180
Harvard University 2–3

240 Index

Hasselt University 24
Hax, Karl 95
Hebrew University of Jerusalem 106
Helsinki Cluster 145, 152–3
Hickson, David 9
Hiromatsu, Wataru 128
Histadrut (General Federation of Jewish Workers) 105–6
Hobsbawm, Eric 7
homogenous globalization 102
Hooper, Keith 11–12
Howard, John 8
humanist theorists 155–6
Human Relations School of Elton Mayo 2–4

imperialism 2, 4, 159, 197, 199
Inamori, Kazuo 131–2
industrial relations (IR) 194, 197
Institute of Economic and Social Research (WSI) 87–8
intellectual spaces of possibilities 46–7
intentionality, defined 48
interactive *vs.* institutional phenomenon 90
Israel, critical management studies: contextual study of Israeli society 107–8; emergence of 104–6; glocalization theory 100, 102–4; international quality control *vs.* local politics 108–9; professional boundary work 106–7; sociology, organization, and labor studies 110–13
Israel Management Center 106
Italy, critical management studies: context for 120–2; contributions to 123–4; overview 117–20, *118–19, 120*

Jacques, Elliott 4
Janssens, Maddy 24, 25
Japan, critical management studies: alternate emancipation methodologies 136–42; Buddhism methodology 131–3; Confucianism methodology 131, 133–6, *134, 135*; critical negative *vs.* constructive 130–2; critical perspectives in 127–9; future studies 140–2; *gedatsu* as self-problematization 137–8; historical context 126–30; modernization,

Westernization, and capitalism 126–7; popularity of 129–30; self-cultivation and problematization 136
Jin, defined 133

kaizen, defined 141
Kappler, Ekkehard 86
Kavanaugh, Donncha 206
Kings College Business School 196
Kliksberg, Bernardo 160
Krell, Gertraude 85, 87, 93–5
Krysa, Isabella 41
KU Leuven 24
Kunda, Gideon 110, 111–12
Kungliga Tekniska Hogskolan 145

Labor and Monopoly Capital (Braverman) 21, 193, 195
labour movement/unions 105, 148
labour-oriented business administration (AOEWL) 87–8, 95–6
Labour Process Theory 153
Lacan, Jacques 77
Laer, Koen Van 24
legitimate authorship 96
Lemke, Thomas 89
Léonard, Evelyne 25
liberal democracies 147
Littler, Craig 8
local accents and lingua franca 230–1
"locale-based" critical studies 12
London School of Economics 5, 8
Luiss Business School 121
Lund School 145, 150–2
Lund University Management and Organizations Studies (LUMOS) 150
Luxemburg, critical management studies *see* Benelux Region

Mackellor, Dorothy 3
Management and Development Strategy (Guerreiro Ramos) 162
Management and Organization Studies (MOS) 36, 159, 162–4
Management Thought and the Management Environment (MGMT) 43
Managerial Ideologies in the Age of Rationality (Shenhav) 111
Mandiola, Marcela 165
Maanen, John Van 111
Maori peoples 11–14

Index 241

marginal development (marginalization) xxvi
Mariña, Díaz de 167
Maori people 15–16
Marshall Plan 179, 181
Martinez, Pulido 166
Marxism and critical management: Christianity *vs.* 131; France 71, 79; Germany 86, 90; Israel 111; Italy 122; South America 162; UK 193, 195
Massachusetts Institute of Technology 111
master of business administration (MBA) 100
Matsushita, Konosuke 131–2
Maturana, Humberto 165
Maxism framework 9–10, 56
Mayo, Elton 2–4
Mayorga, Saavedra 166
mechanistic form of managerialism 144
Meerstemmigheid:Organiseren met verschil/Multi-Vocality: Organising with Difference (Steyaert) 24
Meiji Period 132, 140
metacommunications 222
Middle East Technical University (METU) 180
migration issues xx, 2, 191
Miller, Stephen 214
Mills, Albert J. 41, 43–4
Mills, Jean Helms 41, 43–4
Misoczky, Maria Ceci 164
modernization 126–7
Morgan, Gareth 42, 45
multiparadigmatic approach 42–3

Nanteuil, Matthieu de 25, 26
National Management and Organization Congress (NMOC) 175, 183
nation-state xxi, 103
neoclassical economic ideology 110
neo-liberal ideology 175, 213
Netherlands, critical management studies *see* Benelux Region
New Zealand, critical management studies: developments in 3–4; flows to and from 10–11; local and global voices 15–16; Maori peoples 11–14; overview 1
Nienhüser, Werner 86
nirvana, defined 132–3

Nogueira, Martinez 160
non-Critical Management Studies 46
non-essentialist perspective 37
non-governmental organizations (NGOs) 58

object of study 95–6
One Dimensional Man (Marcuse) 195
Organization, Class & Control (Clegg, Dunkerley) 9, 193
Organization, Identity and Locality (OIL) 14
Organization and Management Theory (OMT) 111
The Organization Machine: A Critical Inquiry into the Foundations of Management Theory (Shenhav) 109, 111
Organization Studies (Battilana) 209
organization theory (OT) 100
Ortlieb, Renate 93
Osterloh, Margit 94
othering process 37, 44–6
Oumi-shonin merchants 139
Oxford Handbook of Critical Management Studies (Alvesson) 209

Pakeha peoples 11–15
Palacios, Alfredo 160
Paludi, Mariana 41
Paris-Dauphine centre 70
Parker, Martin 232
Pérez, Barboza 167
Pichault, François 25–7
political economy of organization 85, 87, 89–92, 92
Political Economy of Power (Faria) 164
politics of knowledge 36–8
post-Marxist intellectual discourse 100
The Postmodern Condition: A Report on Knowledge (Lyotard) 48
postmodernism 152, 153
post-positivist perspective 37
pragmatic engagement 228–9
Prestes Motto, Fernando 161, 162, 230
private *vs.* public goods 88–9
problematization: *gedatsu* as self-problematization 137–8, 140–1; overview 136; *toku* as relational problematization 138–9, 140–1
production control 88
professional boundary work 106–7
"prosocial set of values" 222

242 Index

Radboud Universiteit Nijmegen 23, 24
Raffée, Hans 86
Rangatiratanga, Tino 15
Rastetter, Daniela 93
rational-legal authority 58
relational problematization 138–9
representative committee xxii
Riveline, Claude 70
Robert College (RC) 180
Rodríguez, Carlos Fernández 166

Sabelis, Ida 23, 25
Salaman, Graeme 8
samurai period 131
sanpo-yoshi discourse 139
Scandinavia, critical management
  studies: Copenhagen School
  145, 149–50; discussion
  154–5; Gothenburg Cluster
  145, 153–4; Helsinki Cluster
  145, 152–3; Lund School 145,
  150–2; research context of
  147–9; schools and clusters 149;
  Stockholm Cluster/s 153
Scandocrits 146
Scienze Economiche (SECS-P) 121
Scott, Richard 110
self-cultivation methodologies 136
Seventh International Critical
  Management Studies Conference
  xxv, 116, 117–20
Shenhav, Yehouda 109, 110–12
Shibusawa, Eiichi 132
Sieben, Barbara 93
Siebers, Hans 23, 25
Sievers, Burkard 86–7
Silverman, David 193
Small and Medium-sized Enterprise
  (SME) companies 124
Sobey PhD Programme (Canada) 38,
  40–7
social change and emancipation 208
social democracies 147
social movements in Taiwan 54–5
Social Sciences and Humanities
  Research Council (SSHRC) 43–4
social sciences tradition in France 75–6
*Sociological Paradigms and
  Organizational Analysis* (Burrell,
  Morgan) 45, 193
The Sociological Reduction (Guerreiro
  Ramos) 162
Soma Incident (Turkey) 176–8, 185

South America, critical management
  theory: Argentina 160–1; Brazil
  161–4; Chile 164–5; Colombia
  166; comparative remarks
  167–9; nature and extent of
  160–70; prospects for 169–70;
  Venezuela 166–7
Southern Theory 2
Soviet invasion of Hungary 5
Spaghetti Organization 148
Staehle, Wolfgang 86
Standing Conference on Organizational
  Symbolism (SCOS) 196
Steyaert, Chris 24–25
Stockholm Cluster/s 153
Stolz, Hans-Jürgen 89
Strangleman, Tim 202–3
subjectivism 48
sweatshop university 215

Tabatoni, Pierre 70
Taiwanese social movements 54–5
Taoism xx, 62–3
Taskin, Laurent 25
Tavistock Institute 3–6
Tel Aviv University 106, 110
Terra Nullius (empty land) policy 1
Theory and Criticism journal 112
Theory of Organizations (Silverman)
  193
Thoelen, Annelies 27
Thoenig, Jean-Claude 71–2
Tienari, Janne 152
toku: defined *132*, 132–3, *133*; as
  relational problematization
  138–9, 140–1
Tragtenberg, Mauricio 161–2
Treaty of Waitangi (1840) 15
Trist, Eric 4
Türk, Klaus 85, 87, 89–92, *92*, 95
Turkey, critical management
  theory: academicians 184;
  academic milieu 182;
  administrative autonomy
  181–2; Americanization
  179–81; commerce schools in
  178–9; curriculum wars 186–7;
  performance anxiety 186;
  publications 182–3; research
  orientation 183; Soma Incident
  176–8, 185; values 184–5
Turkish Coal Authorities (TKI) 176
Turner, Bryan S. 2

Index 243

uchi community 129
United Kingdom, critical management theory: brief history 192–4; critical studies 195–7; management and 194–5; management studies and 199–203; questions and changes over 198–9
United States, critical management theory: early roots 207; evolution of 209–13, 212; foundation of 207–9; future of 221–2; *galumphing* notion 207, 213–18; paradox of 218–21; path to 223
United States Operations Mission to Israel (USOM) 105–7
Université catholique de Louvain 25, 27
Université de Liège 26
Universiteit van Tilburg 23
University of Luxembourg 24
University of Mons 26
unlearning approach 64–5

Vaara, Eero 152
vacancy specific concorsi 121
van den Brink, Marieke 23, 24

Varela, Francisco 165
Vekaletlerarasi Prodüktivite Komitesi (VPK) 181
Venezuela, critical management theory 166–7
Victorian Cities (Briggs) 1–2
Vida objective 16
Vikings and paganism 147
Volvo cars 148

Wächter, Hartmut 86
Warwick Business School 10
Weatherbee, Terrance 41
Weberianism 195
Weinstall, Teddy 106
Weiskopf, Richard 86, 93
Westernization 126–7
Workplace Research Centre at the University of Sydney 8
workplace transformations 25–7

Ybema, Sierk 23, 25

Zanoni, Patrizia 24
Zionist-Socialist elite 105
Zune, Marc 25, 26